The World Bank Legal Review

Volume 4

Legal Innovation and Empowerment for Development

The World Bank Legal Review

Volume 4

Legal Innovation and Empowerment for Development

The World Bank Legal Review is a publication for policy makers and their advisers, judges, attorneys, and other professionals engaged in the field of international development with a particular focus on law, justice, and development. It offers a combination of legal scholarship, lessons from experience, legal developments, and recent research on the many ways in which the application of the law and the improvement of justice systems promote poverty reduction, economic development, and the rule of law.

The World Bank Legal Review is part of the World Bank Law, Justice and Development Series managed by the Research and Editorial Board of the Bank's Legal Vice Presidency.

The World Bank Legal Review

Volume 4

Legal Innovation and Empowerment for Development

Hassane Cissé

Sam Muller

Chantal Thomas

Chenguang Wang

Editors

THE WORLD BANK
Washington, D.C.

The World Bank

1818 H Street NW

Washington, DC 20433

Telephone: 202-473-1000

Internet: www.worldbank.org

1 2 3 4 15 14 13 12

ISBN (paper): 978-0-8213-9506-6

eISBN (electronic): 978-0-8213-9507-3

DOI: 10.1596/978-0-8213-9506-6

Cover photo: ©iStockphoto.com/Mark Wragg; *Cover design*: Nigel Quinney

Library of Congress Cataloging-in-Publication data has been requested.

The World Bank Legal Review

Volume 4

Legal Innovation and Empowerment for Development

Editors

Hassane Cissé
Deputy General Counsel, Knowledge and Research, World Bank

Sam Muller
Director, HiiL

Chantal Thomas
Professor, Cornell University Law School

Chenguang Wang
Professor of Law, Tsinghua University

Production Editor

Matthew Moorhead
Legal Associate, World Bank

Contents

Foreword

Jim Yong Kim

In this time of extreme fragility in the world economy, when the needs of the world's poor are as pressing as ever, all who work or study in the field of economic development must constantly reconsider what's working, what's not working, and what can work better. Economists, scientists, activists, politicians, investors, workers: all have a responsibility to carefully consider how best to contribute to the development agenda. Lawyers are no exception. Lawyers and legal specialists who work in the development sphere must engage in unending self-examination if they are to continue to make a useful, indeed essential, contribution to fighting poverty.

The role of law, or rather the role of the "rule of law," in achieving development outcomes has been acknowledged and studied extensively in recent decades. More analysis and debate are required, however, to understand the complicated and multifaceted nature of this role. That is a task that requires the input of practitioners, legal experts, and many others who encounter or work with legal systems. *The World Bank Legal Review* gathers this input from around the world and compiles it into a useful resource for all development practitioners and scholars. The subtitle of this volume, *Legal Innovation and Empowerment for Development*, highlights how the law can respond to the challenges posed to development objectives in a world slowly emerging from an economic crisis. The focus on *innovation* is a call for new, imaginative strategies and ways of thinking about what the law can do in the development realm. The focus on *empowerment* is a deliberate attempt to place the law into the hands of the poor; to give them another tool with which to resist poverty. The two themes are linked by their shared importance in the face of economic uncertainty. There is an urgent need for new, innovative thinking, and a great need to empower the poor to defend themselves.

This volume shows some of the ways that the law can make an innovative and empowering difference in development scenarios. Development problems are complex and varied, and the theme of innovation and empowerment naturally has a broad scope. Consequently, this volume reaches far and wide. It considers the nature, promise, and limitations of legal innovation and legal empowerment. It looks at concrete examples in places such as Africa, the Asia-Pacific region, and Latin America. It considers developments in issues with universal application, such as the rights of the disabled and the effectiveness of asset recovery measures.

The World Bank Legal Review contains many valuable lessons and creative responses. I hope that the exciting ideas in this volume will inspire lawyers and non-lawyers alike to consider what new contribution they can make to our shared poverty-fighting mission

Preface

Anne-Marie Leroy

The effects of the global financial crisis and the ensuing Great Recession are still being felt throughout the world and continue to be a preoccupation of the World Bank and other development institutions. Meanwhile, the Bank's member countries face a range of other economic challenges and crises. As a result, demand for the Bank's assistance remains elevated. In addition to responding to debilitating crises, both real and potential, the Bank ensures that its resources are focused on the long, hard road to economic development.

The Bank's team of lawyers and legal specialists has a crucial role to play in proactively supporting the Bank in the achievement of its development objectives. It is our responsibility to provide a sound legal response to these many challenges. It is also our responsibility to ensure that that response represents world's best practice and is at the cutting edge of contemporary thinking about what the law can and should do to support development goals. With these responsibilities in mind, we have compiled the fourth volume of *The World Bank Legal Review*, subtitled *Legal Innovation and Empowerment for Development*. In a time of difficulty and change, innovative ideas and strategies to empower the poor are more important than ever.

Many (although not all) of the contributions to this volume of *The World Bank Legal Review* emerged from the second annual World Bank Law, Justice and Development Week, held in Washington, D.C., in November 2011. Jointly hosted by the General Counsels of all the World Bank Group organizations, the Law, Justice and Development Week brought together leading scholars, legal practitioners, development experts, policy institutes, universities, and other concerned parties to share lessons and inspiration. A sense of the great range of legal innovations and empowerment strategies that were discussed and debated is captured in this book. All of the diverse issues under discussion were linked by the understanding that the law must respond with solutions that are innovative and empowering. New problems call for new answers.

I thank the contributors to this volume. The diverse topics they discuss and the varied perspectives they represent have been organized by four distinguished editors: Chenguang Wang of Tsinghua University, Sam Muller of the Hague Institute for the Internationalization of Law (HiiL), Chantal Thomas of Cornell University, and our Deputy General Counsel for Knowledge and

Research, Hassane Cissé. Dr. Nigel Quinney provided invaluable editorial assistance. This volume deals with important and intriguing topics in law and development, and the contributors' analyses will assist anyone who is interested, the place of law on today's development agenda.

Contributors

Rita Adam is Vice-Director of the Directorate of Public International Law (DPIL) at the Swiss Federal Department of Foreign Affairs (FDFA). At the DPIL, she leads the Division of International Law, International Treaties and the Law of Neighbouring States. Ms. Adam also serves as the Ambassador of Switzerland to the Principality of Liechtenstein (based in Bern). Before joining the FDFA in 1999, she worked as a legal advisor in civil and criminal matters at the District Court of Thun, Switzerland. After assignments at the Swiss Mission to the United Nations in Geneva and the Embassy of Switzerland in Pretoria, South Africa, she returned to Bern in 2001 to join the Political Affairs Division, where she was appointed Deputy Head of the International Organizations and Host-Country Policy Section in 2004. In 2005, Ms. Adam became Head of the Legal Affairs and Press Service of the Swiss Embassy in Paris, France. From 2008 until July 2010, she was in charge of the Multilateral Peace Policy Section of the Political Affairs Division before being appointed Vice-Director of the DPIL. Ambassador Adam graduated from the University of Bern Law Faculty in 1996 as an attorney at law.

Luciano Alvarenga is a professor and associate researcher at the Brazilian Society for Scientific Progress. His research focuses on the interrelationship between law and a variety of other subject areas, such as art and science, the maintenance of the Cerrado biome, environmental and forestry legislation directed at biodiversity, otherness and environmental justice, responsibility for risk and environmental damage, ethics, and new theoretical and methodological approaches in the environmental sciences. Professor Alvarenga graduated from the Federal University of Minas Gerais with a law degree, having been awarded a scholarship from the National Council for Scientific and Technological Development. He also holds an M.S. in Natural Sciences from the Federal University of Ouro Preto, Brazil, and a Specialist's Degree in Environment, Education and Sustainability from the University of Evora, Portugal.

Luciano Badini has been a prosecutor at the Public Ministry of Minas Gerais (PMMG) since 1993. He has also served as Coordinator of the Operational Support Center for District Attorneys Working on Environmental Protection, Coordinator of Interstate Justice Prosecutors for the Protection of the São Francisco River, and Executive Coordinator of the agreement between the PMMG and the World Bank that aims at technical and technological improvements of the PMMG for the protection of the environment. He was the recipient of the 2010 Innovare Award for his work in implementing the project that organized the Public Ministry's actions for the protection of natural resources of all river basins in the state of Minas Gerais.

Stéphanie Balme is a research fellow at Sciences Po Paris and professor at the Centre for International Studies and Research (CERI) and the Paris School of International Affairs (PSIA), and the head of the "Law, Justice, and Society in China" program. Her research and teaching focuses include comparative constitutional law and rule of law developments. Her research applies to "emerging countries," in particular China and post-socialist countries. She lived in mainland China and Hong Kong SAR, China for many years, working at Tsinghua University Law School as a delegate for the Civil Law Initiative and the Chinese University of Hong Kong. She has authored six books and a number of other academic publications and public policy papers in English, Chinese, and French. She also is a consultant on China for European and international organizations.

Maurits Barendrecht is Academic Director at HiiL and has been a professor of private law at Tilburg University since 1992. He practiced law at a major Dutch law firm from 1982 to 1997. He studies dispute systems (e.g., legal procedures and informal dispute mechanisms) from an interdisciplinary perspective, and systematically looks for knowledge from other disciplines (e.g., economics and organization theory) that can be integrated with best practices in order to improve dispute systems for the people who rely on them. His research is conducted through the Tilburg Institute for Interdisciplinary Studies of Civil Law and Conflict Resolution Systems. Professor Barendrecht has led several large-scale innovation projects in the area of justice and governance that directly addressed urgent needs not being met through existing legal arrangements. These interactive research and development projects usually take place in cooperation with stakeholders such as client groups, ministries of justice, the judiciary, and the legal-services community.

Renaud Beauchard, a French national and U.S. resident, is an attorney and legal consultant specializing in rule of law, justice reforms, and anti-corruption. A fellow of the Institut des Hautes Études sur la Justice in Paris and counsel for the law offices of Peter C. Hansen in Washington, D.C., Mr. Beauchard practiced law in France for six years as a litigator in a maritime and transportation law. More recently, he has worked as a consultant for the World Bank's Office of Evaluation and Suspension and for the U.S. Millennium Challenge Corporation on its Access to Justice program in Benin. Mr. Beauchard has written several publications on topics as diverse as international assets recovery, corporate social responsibility, anti-corruption, and the evaluation of legal systems. He holds law degrees from Poitiers University (LL.M.), Cambridge University (LL.M.), and Tulane University Law School (J.D.), and has both practiced and taught law.

Peter Blanck is University Professor at Syracuse University, Chairman of the Burton Blatt Institute, also at Syracuse University, and Honorary Professor, Centre for Disability Law and Policy, National University of Ireland, Galway. He has published widely on the Americans with Disabilities Act and related laws, serves as Chairman of the Global Universal Design Commission (GUDC), and has practiced law at Covington & Burling, where he served as law clerk to the late Honorable Carl McGowan of the United States Court of Appeals for the D.C. Circuit. Professor Blanck's recent books include *Disability Civil Rights Law and Policy* (with Hill, Siegal & Waterstone) (2009), *Race, Ethnicity, and Disability: Veterans and Benefits in Post-Civil War America* (with Logue) (2010); and *eQuality 3.0: Towards a Right to the Web for People with Cognitive Disabilities* (forthcoming). He received a J.D. from Stanford University, where he was President of the *Stanford Law Review*, and a Ph.D. in Psychology from Harvard University.

Hassane Cissé, a national of Senegal, joined the World Bank in 1997 after serving for several years as Counsel at the International Monetary Fund. He has been Deputy General Counsel, Knowledge and Research, of the Bank since 2009. In this capacity he advises on strategic legal issues facing the Bank and leads the Bank's work on law, justice, and development. Previously, Mr. Cissé served as Chief Counsel for Operations Policy of the World Bank. He is the editor-in-chief of the World Bank's Law, Justice and Development Series and has published papers on rule of law and development and on international economic law matters. Mr. Cissé obtained his LL.B from Dakar University in Senegal. He also holds an LL.M degree from Harvard Law School, graduate law degrees from the universities of Paris I Panthéon-Sorbonne and Paris II Panthéon-Assas, as well as a graduate degree in history from Paris I Panthéon-Sorbonne University. He is a member of the World Economic Forum's Global Agenda Council on the Rule of Law.

Diogo R. Coutinho is an Associate Professor of Law at the University of São Paulo, where his courses include economic law, political economy, and law and development, and a research fellow at the Brazilian Center of Analysis and Planning (CEBRAP). Currently, he serves as investigator of LANDS, the project on Law and the New Developmental State. He was a researcher at FGV São Paulo Law School and at the Brazilian Society of Public Law. Also, he was a visiting professor at the London-based Center for Transnational Legal Studies (2009). Professor Coutinho has written on law and development; administrative, economic, and social law; and regulatory and antitrust policies in Brazil. He holds an M.Sc. from the London School of Economics and Political Science (2002) and a doctorate from the University of São Paulo Faculty of Law (2003).

Conrad C. Daly is a Legal Consultant for the Operations Policy practice group of the World Bank's Legal Vice Presidency, where he has been engaged principally in the Bank's work in governance and anti-corruption. Mr. Daly graduated from a dual-degree program between Cornell Law School and the Ecole de droit de la Sorbonne (Université Paris I Panthéon-Sorbonne). He is also a graduate of Heythrop College, University of London, where he read for a Master in systematic theology, and of Boston College, where he double-majored in biochemistry and history. While in Paris as a visiting fellow at the Université Panthéon-Assas (Paris 2), he researched issues in competition law and taught classes in U.S. and British constitutional and administrative law. His work experience also includes work with GRC Counsel, as well as legal internships at the German gas and engineering company, Linde AG, and at the U.S. Court of International Trade. Prior to making law his chosen profession, Mr. Daly worked at the *Southern Medical Journal* as the special projects editor.

Frank Fariello, a graduate of Brown University and New York University School of Law, is currently Lead Counsel, Operations Policy, in the World Bank's Legal Vice Presidency (LEG). He is LEG's primary focal point for the Bank's sanctions regime and governance and anticorruption policies. In that capacity, he coordinated the recent comprehensive reforms of the Bank's sanctions process and advised Integrity Vice Presidency in connection with the Agreement on Mutual Enforcement of Debarment Decisions among Multilateral Development Banks. Before joining the Bank in 2005, Mr. Fariello worked for nine years at the International Fund for Agricultural Development (IFAD) as Senior Counsel and subsequently as Special Advisor to the Vice President. For the first ten years of his career, prior to his service at IFAD, he practiced corporate law, with an emphasis on international financial transactions, at a number of New York firms, including Skadden Arps Slate Meagher and Flom.

Marc Frilet is the managing partner of the Paris law firm Frilet Société d'Avocats, which specializes in construction, infrastructure, and mining projects, in France and internationally, with a particular focus on developing nations, mostly in Africa. The firm is also active in general corporate and privatization law. He teaches international investment law at the University of Paris V: Descartes and mining law at l'Ecole de Mines. He is a frequent lecturer and author, and the former co-chair of Committee T, an international construction project of the International Bar Association (IBA), and a former Council member of the IBA. Mr. Frilet is Secretary General of the French Institute of International Legal Experts, sponsored by the Paris Bar.

Stephen Golub is an adjunct professor, attorney, and consultant, who teaches courses on International Development and Legal Empowerment at the University of California at Berkeley Law School and at the Central European University Public Policy Department in Budapest. He has edited volumes on legal empowerment and related topics for the Ford Foundation, the Open Society Foundations, the International Development Law Organization, the *Hague Journal on the Rule of Law,* and the Asian Development Bank. He has more than 25 years of experience in 40 countries, consulting and conducting research on legal empowerment, traditional justice systems, the rule of law, and governance for the World Bank, the Carnegie Endowment for International Peace, Amnesty International, development institutions, foundations, policy institutes, and nongovernmental groups. Professor Golub has written over 30 published pieces for law journals, aid agencies, and other policy and scholarly outlets.

Georgia Harley is an Executive Legal Adviser with the Australian Department of Foreign Affairs and Trade and a Legal Consultant for the Justice Reform Unit of the Legal Vice Presidency at the World Bank. At the Bank, Ms. Harley works for the Justice for the Poor program, and is engaged principally on natural resource governance in fragile states. Previously, she served in the

Office of International Law at the Australian Attorney-General's Department, the Regional Assistance Mission to Solomon Islands, and on various rule of law projects in Southeast Asia and the Pacific. Ms. Harley earned a Bachelor of Arts and Bachelor of Laws (Hons.) from the University of Queensland, an LL.M. in International Law from the Australian National University and a Masters in International Development Policy (Applied Economics and Peace and Conflict Resolution) from Duke University.

Karyn Kenny is an International Attorney Advisor for the U.S. Department of Justice, responsible for negotiating asset sharing agreements and building global capacity in anti-money laundering sectors. A former justice expert consultant for the World Bank, she served as a U.S. Supreme Court Fellow in 2007, one of four Fellows selected from an international pool by a commission appointed by Chief Justice John G. Roberts. In 2006, she served as a U.S. Fulbright Scholar in Lithuania, teaching comparative constitutional and criminal law. She has served as an Assistant United States Attorney prosecuting federal economic crimes and as an Assistant District Attorney in the Manhattan District Attorney's Office prosecuting violent street crime. Ms. Kenny teaches law internationally and has received an award for outstanding teaching. A published author on international legal issues, she frequently serves as an expert speaker, including presentations for the Brookings Institution and the World Bank.

Jeni Klugman is the Director of Gender and Development at the World Bank Group. Prior to taking up this position, Ms. Klugman was the director and lead author of three global *Human Development Reports* (2010, 2011, and 2012) published by the United Nations Development Programme. From 1992 to 2008, she held various positions at the World Bank, focusing on poverty, inequality, and human development in low-income countries in Africa, Europe, and Asia. She currently serves on the World Economic Forum's Advisory Board on Sustainability and Competitiveness and is a fellow of the Human Development and Capabilities Association. Ms. Klugman has published books, papers, and reports on topics ranging from poverty reduction strategies and labor markets to conflict, health reform, education, and decentralization. She holds a Ph.D. in Economics from the Australian National University, as well as postgraduate degrees in Law and in Development Economics from Oxford University, where she was a Rhodes Scholar.

Janet Lord is an international lawyer and development practitioner with more than 20 years of professional experience. Ms. Lord directs the human rights and disability inclusive development practice at BlueLaw International LLP and provides subject matter expertise in human rights law and policy reform, advocacy, monitoring and complaints mechanisms, election access for marginalized populations, building and strengthening national human rights institutions, and international disability rights. She also serves as Senior Research Associate at the Harvard Law School Project on Disability and is Adjunct Professor of Law at the University of Maryland Francis King Carey School of Law. She is internationally recognized for subject-matter expertise in the area of human rights for marginalized populations, inclusive development, and disability and has authored a wide array of scholarly, as well as practitioner-oriented international law, development, and human rights publications. She holds an LL.B. and an LL.M. in law from the University of Edinburgh, and an LL.M. in international and comparative law from the George Washington University Law School.

Siobhán McInerney-Lankford is Senior Counsel in the World Bank Legal Vice Presidency and former Senior Policy Officer, Institutions, Law and Partnerships for Human Rights, Nordic Trust Fund, Operations Policy and Country Services. She has been advising the World Bank on human rights law issues since 2002 and regularly represents the World Bank in international human rights fora, including at the United Nations (UN), European Union (EU), and Organisation for Economic Co-operation and Development (OECD). From 2006 to 2008, she served as chair of the OECD DAC Human Rights Task Team and was World Bank representative to the UN High-Level Task Force on the Right to Development from 2007 to 2009. Before joining the World Bank, she worked in private practice in Washington, D.C. She has published widely on human rights law and teaches occasionally. Dr. McInerney-Lankford holds an LL.B. from Trinity College, Dublin, an LL.M. from Harvard Law School, and a B.C.L and D.Phil. in EU human rights law from Oxford University.

Nicholas Menzies is a Justice Reform Specialist in the Legal Vice Presidency of the World Bank. He works on institutional reform of the formal justice sector and on mainstreaming justice into development programming with the Justice for the Poor program, with particular interests in impact evaluation, indicators, and gender. Prior to the World Bank, he worked at the intersections of plural legal systems as a land and natural resources lawyer for indigenous communities in Australia, on legal empowerment and access to justice issues in Cambodia, and in providing policy advice to the Papua New Guinean cabinet. Mr. Menzies has an LL.B. and a B.A. from the University of Sydney and a Master of Public Policy degree from the Hertie School of Governance, Berlin.

Sam Muller is the founding Director of HiiL. He has also served as Special Adviser to the Registrar on External Relations at the International Criminal Court (ICC), interim Deputy Director of the Common Services Division, and Acting Director of the Public Information and Documentation Section of the Registry. Before heading up the Advance Team to set up the ICC, he worked as Senior Legal Adviser and head of the Legal Department of the Registry of the International Criminal Tribunal for the former Yugoslavia and as a legal officer at the headquarters of the UN Relief and Works Agency in Gaza. In the mid-1990s he was Associate Professor and Programme Coordinator of the Public International Law LL.M. programme of Leiden University. Mr. Muller holds a law degree and a doctorate from Leiden University. He has published and spoken extensively on various topics, focusing on the law of international organizations, international justice issues, and, over the past two years, global legal trends and justice innovation. He serves on various boards, including The Hague Prize Foundation, and is chairman of the Board of the Hague Academic

Coalition and of the Rule of Law Action Council of the World Economic Forum.

Deepti Samant Raja is the Director of International Programs at the Burton Blatt Institute, Syracuse University. Samant Raja has over seven years of work experience in promoting the social inclusion and economic empowerment of people with disabilities. She has worked on mainstreaming disability in poverty reduction and development programs, developing programs to promote access to low-cost assistive devices for people with disabilities in resource-limited environments, ICT accessibility, and full participation in the labor market. She worked for the Secretariat of the Global Partnership for Disability and Development, managing research and knowledge translation activities. Ms. Samant Raja has published and presented on ICT accessibility in development and the implications of the Convention on the Rights of Persons with Disabilities on employment outcomes. She holds an M.S. in Rehabilitation Counseling (University of Illinois at Urbana-Champaign), an M.S. in Electrical Engineering (University of California–Irvine), and a B.A. in Telecommunication Engineering (University of Mumbai).

Mario Schapiro is a full-time professor of law at Getulio Vargas Foundation School of Law (FGV Law School), where his courses include law and development, administrative law, competition law, and law and finance. Currently, he serves as investigator of LANDS, the project on Law and the New Developmental State, and also as investigator of the Brazilian Institute of Applied Research (IPEA), a project on legal capacity for development. He was a visiting researcher at the Columbia Law School (2008) and visiting scholar at King's College London (2012). Professor Schapiro has written on law and development, administrative law, economic law, and, his main area of interest, the governance of industrial policy and development policies as a whole. He holds a master's from the University of São Paulo Faculty of Law (2005) and a doctorate from the University of São Paulo Faculty of Law (2009).

Yuan Tao is Counsel at the Environmental and International Law practice group of the Legal Vice Presidency of the World Bank, where he works on sustainable development, climate change, environmental and social safeguard policies of the World Bank, and Global Environmental Facility operations. Before joining the World Bank, Mr. Tao served as an Editor of the *Harvard Environmental Law Review*, and practiced law with the international law firm Allen & Overy LLP in Beijing, China, and London, where he advised on various international and environmental law issues. His experience also includes advising on legal aspects in relation to China's business environment, foreign direct investment, financial regulations, and anti-corruption. He obtained his LL.M. degree from Harvard Law School. Previously, he graduated with an LL.B. and an LL.M. from Tsinghua University, China, and an LL.M. from University College London, England.

Chantal Thomas is Professor of Law at Cornell University Law School, where her courses include International Trade and Development Law and International Labor Law. She also directs the Clarke Initiative for Law and Development in the Middle East and North Africa. Prior to joining Cornell, Professor

Thomas chaired the Law Department of the American University in Cairo. Professor Thomas serves on the U.S. State Department's Advisory Council on International Law, and is a Counsellor of the American Society of International Law. She has consulted for the USAID Bureau for Democracy, Conflict, and Humanitarian Affairs, and before entering the legal academy practiced international financial law at Shearman & Sterling's New York offices. She has published widely on the relationship between international law, political economy, and global social justice in a variety of contexts. Professor Thomas earned her law degree from Harvard University and her bachelor's degree from McGill University.

David M. Trubek is Voss-Bascom Professor of Law and Dean of International Studies Emeritus at the University of Wisconsin–Madison and Senior Research Fellow at the Harvard Law School. He served as director of the UW's Institute for Legal Studies from 1985 to 1990 and was appointed as University Dean of International Studies in 1990. In 1995 he became the founding director of the UW-Madison International Institute. A pioneer in the field of law and development, his work includes *Law and the New Developmental State: The Brazilian Experience in Latin American Perspective* (forthcoming, 2013), *Direito, Planejamento e Desenvolvimento do Mercado de Capitais Brasileiro 1965-70* (2nd edition 2011), and *The New Law and Economic Development: A Critical Appraisal* (2006). Currently, he serves as Principal Investigator of LANDS, the project on Law and the New Developmental State and Co-Director of GLEE, the Project on Globalization, Lawyers, and Emerging Economies.

Sarah Twigg is a consultant in the World Bank Gender and Development Unit. In her current role she conducts research on areas related to gender equality issues in laws and policy, and supports communications, outreach, and advocacy efforts in support of the World Bank's gender and development priorities. Prior to joining the World Bank she worked as a researcher for two global *Human Development Reports* (2010 and 2011) published by the United Nations Development Programme, and as a gender and climate finance consultant for UN Women. Ms. Twigg also has experience practicing as a commercial lawyer in New Zealand and New York. Ms. Twigg holds a master's degree in International Politics and Business from New York University and bachelor's degrees in Law and Political Science from the University of Otago, New Zealand.

Roy F. Waldron is Senior Vice President, Associate General Counsel, and Chief Intellectual Property Counsel at Pfizer Inc., where he leads the team of attorneys and professionals who procure patents; works closely with R&D, Business Development, and the Pfizer Business Units; and ensures enforcement of trademarks. He represents Pfizer on the committees of various industry organizations, including the International Federation of Pharmaceutical Manufacturers and Associations, where he is chair of the International IP and Trade Committee; the Pharmaceutical Research and Manufacturers of America, IPO, where he represents Pfizer on the Board of Directors; and INTERPAT. Mr. Waldron joined Pfizer in 1999 from White & Case's IP practice group, and was previously an associate at Fish & Neave. He has a J.D. from

New York University School of Law, a Ph.D. from Yale University (physical-organic chemistry), and a B.A. from Dartmouth College (chemistry). He was a DAAD Scholar at the Albrecht-Ludwigs-Universität in Freiburg, Germany, and a JSPS Post-Doctoral Fellow at Kyoto University in Japan.

Chenguang Wang is Professor of Law and Director of the Health Law Research Center at Tsinghua University. He taught at Peking University Law School and Hong Kong City University Law School before joining Tsinghua in 2000. He has also taught as a visiting professor at the law schools of New York University, Cornell University, the University of Toronto, and the University of Pennsylvania. He has been a Special Adviser to the Supreme People's Court since 2003, an arbitrator at the China International Economic and Trade Arbitration Commission since 1993, and a Deputy Chair of the China Association of Legal Theory (since 2003), the China Association of Legal Education (since 2007), and the China Health Law Association (since 2007). His teaching focuses on legal theory, comparative law, and health law. He is the Co-Editor of *China's Journey toward the Rule of Law: Legal Reform, 1978–2008*, and has published more than 40 scholarly articles on topics such as judicial system, legal education, comparative law and heath law. He received a B.A. (1980), M.A. (1983), and Ph.D. in Law (1999) from Peking University, and an LL.M. (1996) from Harvard University Law School.

Zhenmin Wang is Professor of Law and Dean at the Tsinghua University School of Law and Vice President of the China Association of Constitutional Law. He is a member of the Committee for the Macao Basic Law and the Committee for the Hong Kong Basic Law under the Standing Committee of the Chinese National People's Congress. In 2007, he was elected Deputy to the 13th Beijing City People's Congress. He is the author of *The Central-Special Administrative Region Relationship in China: From a Legal Perspective* (2002) and *Constitutional Review in China* (2004). Professor Wang has published over 60 articles and presented papers at many regional and international conferences on Chinese constitutional law and legal reform. He is a Member of the Forum of Young Global Leaders of the World Economic Forum. Dean Wang received an LL.B. from Zhengzhou University (1989) and an LL.M. and Ph.D. in Law from People's University of China (1992 and 1995, respectively). He also studied in the Law Faculty of Hong Kong University from 1993 to 1995. He was a Fulbright Visiting Scholar at Harvard Law School in 2000–2001.

The World Bank Legal Review

Volume 4

Legal Innovation and Empowerment for Development

Empowerment and Innovation Strategies for Law, Justice, and Development

CHANTAL THOMAS

The concept of the rule of law has now garnered near-universal recognition both as a means and as an end of socioeconomic improvement in poor countries. Yet, the very universality of the concept has generated next-level problems. The rule of law as an abstract goal offers little guidance about the practical aspects of such a goal in specific contexts. As Hassane Cissé notes in this volume, "[d]evelopment policymakers have learnt through bitter experience that a uniform, one-size-fits-all approach to policy interventions in poor countries can have unfortunate, indeed disastrous, consequences."[1] The challenge for rule of law reformers, then, is to overcome the pitfalls of a one-size-fits-all approach and instead to devise regulatory strategies suitable and responsive to the local environment.

An additional challenge for rule of law and related "good governance" reforms is that the economic liberalization programs accompanying such policies often have failed to address social inequities and hierarchies. Some contemporary development policy analysts have focused on how to incorporate these social goals. For example, Amartya Sen's *Development as Freedom* provides a template for understanding how the fulfillment of civil, political, and social rights could be factored into development policy.[2] The challenge is to ensure that opportunities for, and benefits of, prosperity are equitably enjoyed, and that the least advantaged are able to share them.

Both of these challenges—transposing policies to particular contexts and ensuring more equitable processes and outcomes of policy reform—inspire the theme of this volume: *Legal Innovation and Empowerment for Development*. The fourth installment of a research effort under way at the World Bank, this volume highlights both the necessity of innovating law and policy to address specific development contexts and the importance of doing so in a way that will contribute to socioeconomic empowerment. In this way, the volume makes the case that legal innovation can drive, rather than simply reflect, empowerment and development.

The theme of legal innovation and empowerment for development complements substantive and institutional sensibilities in current development policy. Substantively, development policy discourse seems to have moved away from tacking hard toward statist policy or neoliberal policy. Rather,

1 *See*, in this volume, Hassane Cissé, *Legal Empowerment of the Poor: Past, Present, Future*.

2 Amartya Sen, *Development as Freedom* (Oxford U. Press 1999).

something of a more self-consciously moderate approach is emerging in which the basic commitment to market-oriented regulation is affirmed, but the importance of meeting social needs as a concurrent rather than a long-term goal is simultaneously recognized.[3]

Institutionally, this self-styled pragmatism is reflected through the endorsement of "new governance" techniques that blend public sector and private sector approaches. Public-private partnerships constitute one important example, but there are many variations, such as a bottom-line approach to measuring policy effects that resembles market metrics.

There is cause for hope that these new approaches may help balance out some of the excesses of prior eras. They may be reflected in a greater focus on locality, as well as a greater focus on inclusiveness in processes of governance. Equally welcome is the greater awareness of the importance of self-assessment by the range of actors who participate in the development policy cosmos: developed-country governments, international organizations, and nongovernmental organizations (NGOs).

Still, one might ask how much of this apparent change remains only surface deep. Can these reforms transform deeply entrenched policy orientations on the ground? Is the turn to social innovation and empowerment merely cosmetic, leaving underlying structural dynamics and biases intact? How possible is genuine interdisciplinary exchange among the various categories of experts in law, economics, and public policy? There is much evidence that deep institutional "inefficiencies" remain. Key among these are imperfect information, powerful interests, and subjective models.[4]

Despite these persistent questions, many new developments in the field are promising and interesting, and some of these are presented in this volume. In exploring contemporary examples of legal innovation and empowerment, the volume offers a variety of focal points. Some chapters focus on elaborating the broad concepts of innovation and empowerment. Others focus on governmental innovations in particular country contexts. Still others discuss the role of NGOs and civil society. Finally, some chapters describe emerging trends in international laws and organizations. Although this brief introduction cannot do justice to the richness and complexity of these contributions, it does consider each focal point in turn.

The Conceptual State of Play

What precisely is meant by "legal innovation" and "legal empowerment"? The general issue of legal, judicial, and constitutional innovation is addressed

3 *See*, in this volume, David M. Trubek, Diogo R. Coutinho, & Mario G. Schapiro, *Toward a New Law and Development: New State Activism in Brazil and the Challenge for Legal Institutions*.

4 Chantal Thomas, *Law and Neoclassical Economic Development: Toward an Institutionalist Critique of Institutionalism*, 96 Cornell L. Rev. 968, 1018–1023 (2011).

by Sam Muller and Maurits Barendrecht in "The Justice Innovation Approach: How Justice Sector Leaders in Development Contexts Can Promote Innovation." The authors stress competition among potential providers (alternative dispute resolution is envisioned as a potential competitor to traditional judicial processes) as well as a redefinition of members of society as stakeholders.

Within this framework, Muller and Barendrecht emphasize a few key aspects of desirable "justice innovation." First, it is low cost and bottom up. Second, it emphasizes that even though policy goals should be clear, the factors leading to their realization will inevitably be complex, reflecting the environment on the ground. Third, this version of justice innovation favors public-private partnerships in the delivery of access to justice, including something like a "Build-Operate-Transfer" model (in which investors are permitted to build and operate a firm for a period of time in exchange for, among other things, an agreement to transfer possession eventually to the owner). Finally, this version emphasizes the importance of protecting and rewarding innovation and experimentation.

The authors offer a pragmatic approach to the question of how to deliver a public good, such as justice, through a model based on the ideal of private sector competition. Such an approach may have the virtue of encouraging clearer quantification and greater accountability through a "marketized" focus on systemic "profits," in the form of increased satisfaction with access to justice, which might permit more precise measurement of the "deliverables" of reform. At the same time, some implications of competition in the justice sector remain unclear. For example, if competition leads to the proliferation of dispute resolution fora, will the "forum shopping" that likely ensues improve the justice sector through regulatory competition, or encourage negative externalities (i.e., gaming the system)? More profoundly, what danger might privatizing justice pose to public policy goals?

As for legal empowerment, this concept is taken up in Hassane Cissé in "Legal Empowerment of the Poor: Past, Present, Future." Now that the "idea that law has an important role to play in promoting economic development has become well established," Cissé notes that the "traditional focus on institutions and government machinery has been widened to bring the people themselves into view."

Legal empowerment of the poor (LEP) is in part a reaction to classical rule of law approaches, which focus too much on "institutions and state structures," perhaps with the unstated premise that these automatically benefit the poor, rather than on whether such benefits are quantifiably delivered. Cissé emphasizes the point made by Muller and Barendrecht that earlier approaches have been overly top down and therefore likely to misapprehend the context of those on the lower rungs of society.

Despite these improvements, Cissé notes some difficulties with LEP. First, there is the problem of "causality versus correlation" that characterizes the entire field of good governance policy—does economic empowerment result from, or lead to, better institutions? Second, there is the delicate matter of compliance of LEP reforms with the World Bank Articles of Agreement, which prohibit interference in political matters. Third, in the form it has taken up to now, most visibly in the Commission on Legal Empowerment of the Poor (CLEP), LEP has come under criticism for overestimating the impact of legal exclusion as opposed to other factors on poverty and adopting neoliberal economic assumptions. Among the latter, property rights enforcement is "possibly the most contested" on the CLEP agenda.

Beyond these conceptual difficulties, there are some applied challenges in implementing LEP policy. Cissé writes of the need to see LEP as not merely a technocratic strategy, but also as one that entails confronting the reality of entrenched power elites and interests. Additionally, vigilance against one-size-fits-all policies must continue. Examples of local LEP solutions include greater incorporation of informal justice systems.

If the perils of one-size-fits-all are to be taken seriously, then general ideas about legal empowerment and innovation must take into context more specific social hierarchies. A useful intervention in thinking through one kind of particularity—gender equality—is offered by Jeni Klugman and Sarah Twigg in "The Role of Laws and Institutions in Expanding Women's Voice, Agency, and Empowerment." As these authors point out, gender equality has now been mainstreamed as a focus of development policy, one example of which is the 2012 World Development Report, whose title is *Gender Equality and Development*.

A focus on gender equality encourages analytically productive attention to the effects of law. The authors focus in part on formally unequal rules, pointing out that although more and more countries have incorporated nondiscrimination principles into their basic laws, many "still have legal provisions that overtly discriminate against women in both formal statutory and customary law." These formal inequalities affect, among other things, access by women to entrepreneurial opportunity through restriction of their ability to sign contracts, open bank accounts, and undertake other business activities.

A gender equality analysis requires looking at whether the laws apply formally unequal rules as well as at whether they enforce a regulatory structure that is conducive to the kind of economic growth that would increase the well-being of women (and, by extension, children and households more generally). For example, family law can enforce differential treatment, as in the case of many inheritance laws. It can also enforce seemingly neutral provisions that nevertheless generate a disparate adverse impact on women. The authors give an example of the latter when discussing the failure of some legal systems to provide for joint ownership in marriage.

The potentially disparate effects of titling practices point to the importance of understanding context before adopting prescribed LEP reforms such as property registration. Without understanding the existing legal and economic distribution of resources, such registration might have the effect of disowning less powerful members of a community. The authors describe one project, the Reconstruction of Aceh Land Administration System, which addressed this issue by introducing land registration and creating joint titling at the same time—a significant social intervention. Such examples suggest the importance of context within the more specific category of gender.

Country Contexts

Further to the centrality of context in shaping development policy, the volume considers a variety of country studies. Among the most innovative in the field have been the emerging developing country economies. Brazil and China are leaders within these ranks, and this volume offers multiple perspectives on each country.

China

In "Legal Transplantation and Legal Development in Transitional China," Chenguang Wang takes on the debate about the benefits of legal transplants in the specific context of China. Wang notes that transplantation should not be viewed as exceptional: every legal system has evolved through reference to others. Yet, transplants are vulnerable to several critiques. Synthesizing these two sides of the debate, he offers a view of transplants that seeks to capture their benefits while minimizing their potential harms.

As Wang demonstrates, China in the past several years has boldly adopted numerous legal transplants, but with two innovative characteristics that have increased the chances for success. First, policy makers have integrated transplanted laws with "aboriginal" laws. Second, transplants have involved selective, as opposed to wholesale, adoption.

In "Achieving Development through Innovative Constitutionalism: A China Story," Zhenmin Wang and Yuan Tao tell a story that bears out Chenguang Wang's narrative of incremental transplantation. Wang and Tao describe the gradual and piecemeal reform of China's constitution from socialist legal and political commitments to the constitutionalism of liberal capitalist economies. They argue that this style of reform has contributed significantly to China's economic rise. Regardless of actual causality, these reforms form an important part of the larger legal picture.

In "Rule of Law as a Watermark: China's Legal and Judicial Challenges," Stéphanie Balme, looks beyond China's constitution to its massive adoption, from the late 1970s onward, of new legislation and administrative regulations—an exertion she dubs "quantitative legislative reforms."

These reforms coincided with the adoption of the 1982 constitution, and, in many cases, provided processes for redressing grievances that were administrative rather than judicial, such as the proliferation of *xinfang* offices. Balme suggests that China's process of legalization is incomplete and ongoing. This process is evidenced by, among other things, a gradual increase in both formal legal and nonlegal mediation disputes over *xinfang* complaints; improvement of the legal system's "hardware" through better education and regulation of the legal profession and judicial system; and increased incorporation of human rights discourse.

Among the remaining challenges are the legal guarantee of ownership rights, which suffers because the current system is complex and the judicial system does not have clear authority to regulate. Underlying all this is the fact that, even though the adoption of the new constitution precipitated much of this reform, there continues to be a

> lack of respect for the constitution . . . explained by the de facto absence of a hierarchy of norms (despite a clear definition of the "sources of the law," [*fa yuan*]), resulting in confusion both in the organization and in the legal texts, administrative regulations, and decrees. It can also be explained by the lack of a clear conception of the position of the constitution in the hierarchy of the normative system.

The chapters by Balme and Wang and Tao support Chenguang Wang's general analysis of the piecemeal and partial nature of legal transplantation and reform in China. This process leaves much to be desired. At the same time, one might see the disorganized quality of legal reform in China as an acceptable price for a greater legitimacy borne of incremental change as opposed to radical transplantation.

Brazil

As with China and its adoption of a new constitution in 1982, the adoption of a new constitution in 1988 marked a watershed moment in the transformation of the structure of economic law and regulation for Brazil. In "Toward a New Law and Development: New State Activism in Brazil and the Challenge for Legal Institutions," David M. Trubek, Diogo R. Coutinho, and Mario G. Schapiro identify a resulting new wave of governance that seeks to avoid perceived extremes of prior eras in development policy in Brazil—both the unrelenting statism of the early decolonization period and the adamantly deregulatory orientation of the Washington Consensus.

Although Brazil's government adopted characteristic policies in both eras, by the late 1980s, the country was beginning to move toward the approach that Trubek et al. deem "new state activism." Beginning with the 1988 constitution, building through the Cardoso administration of the mid-1990s, and maturing after the 2002 election of Lula da Silva, new state activism embraces innovation in governance in two respects. First, innovation as an end is encouraged, particularly in industrial policy. Specialized measures designed to boost select market sectors have been adopted successfully over objections that "governments were not able to strategically identify targets." Second, innovation characterizes the means by which policies are implemented. In particular, new state activism features partnerships between the government and the private sector that improve capacity on both sides.

The authors describe a series of structural conditioning factors that have driven innovation in these various manifestations. Legal protections for property rights and against expropriation, arising from domestic constitutional law and from international treaty commitments, arguably forced the Lula administration to pursue social policy goals through new techniques that ultimately were friendlier to both domestic and foreign investors.

The innovative approach to governance that Trubek et al. describe is further detailed in the context of environmental and water law by Luciano Badini and Luciano Alvarenga in "The Role of the Public Ministry in the Defense of the Environment: Hydrogeographical Regions and Attitudes for Coping with Socioenvironmental Conflicts." Badini and Alvarenga focus on the techniques that the Brazilian Public Ministry has used to achieve environmental protection and conservation objectives related to freshwater.

The authors begin by noting that the Public Ministry is a product of the 1988 constitution, and as such exemplifies that document's combination of ambitious social goals and institutional prudentialism, as described in Trubek et al. Badini and Alvarenga then discuss the particular strategies adopted in relation to freshwater regulation: first, the reorganization of the territorial objects of regulation from a fragmented scheme to one based on the drainage basin as the basic unit of analysis; and second, the pursuit of nonjudicial and therefore presumably less costly approaches to conflict resolution.

In the cases of both Brazil and China, we see the operation of the pragmatic and synthetic approaches that are also invoked in more general form in the discussions of Muller and Barendrecht and of Cissé. In both countries, successful reform policies arose out of careful attention to context and a comparatively gradual pace. Concessions were made to external and internal constraints of legal and economic liberalism, but socially transformative goals were no less vigorously pursued. A comparative reading of these chapters highlights a notable difference between the two countries: whereas in Brazil the overarching focus of socially transformative policies appears to have been direct poverty-reduction measures, in the Chinese context, more traditional economic growth has remained a priority; and although these measures are also achieving poverty reduction, they may do so at the immediate (though increasingly contested) expense of the environment and the displacement of socially marginal populations.

The Global North

Within good governance policy, anticorruption efforts play a major role in supporting rule of law reform. The legal innovations discussed by Rita Adam in "Innovation in Asset Recovery: The Swiss Perspective" and Karyn Kenny in "International Asset Sharing: A Multipurpose Tool for Development" point to the beginnings of an important trend in anticorruption policy—one in which developed countries interrogate their own legal systems to identify and correct connections to theft of public assets in poor countries. The complicity of financial institutions and legal systems in the global north contributes to these broader enabling conditions. The temptation of financial corruption in poor countries is magnified by the ability to secure ill-gotten gains in legal jurisdictions out of the reach of local actors.

Adam describes legal reforms in Switzerland that allow the Swiss Federal Council to freeze assets reasonably suspected to be the product of public theft and to repatriate those assets to the home country without the cooperation of either the home country government (which, Adam argues, may be too weak and ineffective to mount an effective request) or local prosecutorial authorities. Kenny describes multilateral, bilateral, and unilateral arrangements to share assets among countries when those assets constitute the proceeds of crime that implicates multiple jurisdictions, such as drug trafficking or money laundering.

Much of the contemporary global anticorruption campaign has been hampered by a failure to realize that corruption in poor countries arises not only from local malfeasance, but also from enabling conditions across borders and within a globalized political economy. Both Adam and Kenny describe innovations that have disrupted and minimized the perverse incentives that foreign jurisdictions offer to commit corruption.

NGOs and Civil Society

Whereas the chapters described above focus on governmental reforms, others in this volume take on the role of NGOs and civil society in pursuing legal innovation and legal empowerment.

In "The Political Economy of Improving Traditional Justice Systems: A Case Study of NGO Engagement with Shalish in Bangladesh," Stephen Golub examines the advantages and disadvantages of employing traditional and customary forms of dispute resolution such as *shalish*. The advantages, according to Golub, include increased effectiveness due to greater legitimacy and lower user and operational costs. The disadvantages include unwieldiness and unpredictability, as well as reinforcement of traditional hierarchies such as gender inequality.

Golub describes how NGOs have worked to modify traditional shalish so as to address some of the disadvantages. In so doing, these NGOs are taking an innovative approach to the goal of increasing access to justice. Rather than replacing traditional justice with a legal transplant, they are seeking to adapt tradition to contemporary concerns while retaining institutional advantages. At the same time, extensive NGO involvement can raise questions of accountability or neutrality in influencing the outcomes of disputes. Moreover, efforts to correct ingrained social prejudices may fail, resulting in their inadvertent retrenchment. Golub concludes by recommending a cautious optimism with respect to shalish but also emphasizes the need for further study, not only of shalish, but also of other fora for alternative dispute resolution.

In "'We Want What the OK Tedi Women Have!' Guidance from Papua New Guinea on Women's Engagement in Mining Deals," Nicholas Menzies and Georgia Harley tell the story of a mining agreement negotiation in Papua New Guinea in which some participants in the negotiations represented women as a community group. These interests were not represented by a formally constituted NGO, but rather more informally in the sense of women representing a significant group in civil society.

The participation of women in the OK Tedi negotiations is a promising example of bringing civil society to the table and more generally of recognizing the interests of noncorporate stakeholders in investment. Menzies and Harley identify specific characteristics that allowed the women representatives to negotiate successfully—most important, the experience and skills of the negotiators themselves.

Yet, the various benefits that were negotiated have suffered from spotty implementation. Once the agreement was concluded, the national government of Papua New Guinea failed to take an interest in implementing the measures it called for, and the negotiators left the scene, leaving the community ill-equipped to attend to implementation. This points to some of the structural disadvantages of bringing civil society or the community in as a separate group in the formation of large foreign investment agreements. Although the "community development" aspects of the agreement represented a laudable innovation on the standard foreign direct investment model inspired by the goal of empowerment, further innovation in implementation will be required to realize this goal more fully.

Multilateral Contexts

Particularly in this age of globalization, the regulatory environment in most countries is significantly shaped by the values and practices of international legal regimes and organizations. These domains of international law extend across a range of subject matters, from human rights to finance.

Innovations in this area involve creating stronger connections between the goals of particular specialized regimes. In "Human Rights and Development: Regime Interaction and the Fragmentation of International Law," Siobhán McInerney-Lankford speaks to this question. Her chapter begins with a general observation of the phenomenon of fragmentation in international law and a demonstration of fragmentation in regards to human rights law and development law. Institutionally, these fields remain largely separate.

McInerney-Lankford argues, however, that there is also an increasing convergence between human rights and development. Substantively, this convergence arises in "shared principles such as equality, participation, accountability, transparency, and voice, as well as in attention to vulnerable groups." These policies are acknowledged by international organizations from the United Nations to the International Finance Corporation.

However, "not all such provisions translate into a reliance on human rights in a direct operational sense." McInerney-Lankford points to regional systems, particularly those in Europe, that intertwine human rights and development more extensively. For example, the European Union formally incorporates human rights principles in its economic partnerships with non-European countries.

Such integration, McInerney-Lankford believes, should be more broadly adopted. In this way, she calls for regime interaction as both an innovation and an empowerment strategy. Ideally, international law will eventually consist of "human rights as a shared legal framework, highlighting both partner and donor obligations under international human rights law and offering concrete operational entry points for their application in development activities."

In "Beyond the Orthodoxy of Rule of Law and Justice Sector Reform: A Framework for Legal Empowerment and Innovation through the Convention on the Rights of Persons with Disabilities," Janet E. Lord, Deepti Samant Raja, and Peter Blanck show how this convention—one of the newer additions to the United Nations' "core" human rights treaties—innovates by establishing extensive guidelines for domestic implementation of the treaty's principles.

In "Transforming through Transparency: Opening Up the World Bank's Sanctions Regime," Conrad C. Daly and Frank A. Fariello, Jr., describe the Bank's sanctions regime, which was established in 1996 to combat corruption and fraud in the disbursement of funds. The regime forms part of a greater effort by the Bank to increase accountability and transparency in its operations, and stands alongside better-known innovations of the Bank such as its Inspection Panel, which examines compliance with Bank protocols more broadly.

Such reforms represent commendable efforts to bring good governance policy home; that is, to prioritize good governance principles not only in borrower countries but also in the Bank's own institutional practices. One question that emerges in considering these reforms is why the Inspection Panel and the sanctions regime are separate institutions. It seems debatable whether the reasons for such separation extend beyond mere historical contingency. As these kinds of internal reforms develop, perhaps the Bank will integrate and consolidate its various monitoring functions.

In "Intellectual Property: Facilitating Technology Transfer for Development," Roy F. Waldron discusses the innovative arrangements that pharmaceutical companies are entering into with public sector actors in order to increase access to medicines, framed by the author as the transfer and application of medical technology to national public health.

Such innovations are directly linked to empowerment in that they may allow developing countries to increase levels of public health in vulnerable populations and in society more generally. Although many of the specific details of these agreements are not discussed for reasons of confidentiality, they appear to be highly promising responses to the problem of access to medicines, in which the research and development prowess of pharmaceutical companies can be harnessed by nonprofit organizations with public health as their main priority.

These arrangements involve a number of different types of international organizations, including the World Intellectual Property Organization (WIPO), the Joint United Nations Programme on HIV/AIDS (UNAIDS), and the World Health Organization (WHO). These organizations often take leading roles in these arrangements, as do other nonprofit and research organizations such as the Oswaldo Cruz Foundation in Brazil and the Geneva-based Drugs for Neglected Diseases Initiative.

Furthermore, these initiatives take place against the backdrop of international economic law established by the World Trade Organization (WTO) Agreement on Trade-Related Intellectual Property Rights (TRIPS). Since the adoption of TRIPS, the WTO membership has taken several strides to clarify that the more stringent patent-protection rules in TRIPS should not apply to many developing country access-to-medicine issues.[5]

These developments in international intellectual property rules have rearranged the leverage of the parties Waldron describes in his chapter. These parties are "bargaining in the shadow of the law"[6]—in this case, TRIPS law. Thus, although it is true that, as Waldron points out, pharmaceutical companies are willing to engage in these technology transfer agreements only because patent-protection rules are in place, willingness is likely enhanced by the emergence of legally valid exceptions to those rules. In other words, these companies have an incentive to reach voluntary agreements rather than be subjected to the compulsory licensing permitted by the TRIPS exceptions.

In "OHADA Nears the Twenty-Year Mark: An Assessment," Renaud Beauchard looks at the regional context of the Organization for the Harmonization of Business Law in Africa (OHADA). An ambitious integration scheme, OHADA represents a step forward for the region in terms of the recognition of the benefits of intraregional trade. At the same time, OHADA bears signs of adverse side effects of legal transplantation. Considering the chapters on China presented in this volume, a comparison between modes of transplantation is perhaps instructive. Whereas China's transplants were relatively piecemeal, OHADA constituted a major and sudden overhaul involving some elements that were not particularly useful in the local context, such as a bankruptcy act. Whereas China's reforms integrated aboriginal practices, OHADA's seemed to ignore local practices and instead emphasized uniformity and conformity with national and international standards.

---

5 WTO Declaration on TRIPS and Public Health, WT/MIN(01)/DEC/2 (Nov. 20, 2001), which was followed by the Decision on the Implementation of Paragraph 6 of the Doha Declaration on the TRIPS Agreement and Public Health, WT/L/540 (Sep. 2, 2003).

6 Robert H. Mnookin & Lewis Kornhauser, *Bargaining in the Shadow of the Law*, 88 Yale L. J. 950 (1979).

For example, the author discusses the difficulty in convincing local actors to settle transactional matters according to OHADA law: they observe that the complex structure of local markets in the central location of Cotonou "operates almost entirely outside the realm of formal law and ignores OHADA." Although some efficiencies are probably be gained by coming into compliance with OHADA, the possibility of competing efficiencies of local practices and "private ordering"[7] appear to have been wholly dismissed, creating the danger that OHADA will cause greater disruption than improvement of regional markets.

Given these difficulties, the history recounted in Marc Frilet's "Legal Innovation for Development: The OHADA Experience" is instructive. Frilet explains that OHADA drafters sought to correct deficiencies in business law practices in the newly independent francophone African countries. Because of difficulty in ascertaining applicable principles of local law, and other information and capacity asymmetries, Frilet states, French law firms servicing local clients tended to provide "authoritative interpretations" based on the company law of their home country. Although this practice may have served as a useful stopgap measure in the early days of independence, the need for a clearer and more locally accessible legal framework inspired the efforts that culminated in OHADA.

Thus, the reasoning behind OHADA was largely sound. The member countries stood to capture efficiency gains through legal harmonization that could spur much-needed regional growth. Moreover, the initiative and participation of distinguished experts and regional authorities to achieve this objective was commendable. As Frilet notes, however, both the substantive and the institutional realization of OHADA's objectives remain incomplete. Substantively, the framework does not address topics that Frilet asserts are crucially important to current development strategies, such as public contract law. Institutionally, OHADA continues to struggle with implementation, both for reasons of capacity and because the framework is not yet widely understood by or familiar to local actors.

Consequently, the "OHADA experience" offers insights into what kinds of innovative approaches are likely to be successful. Perhaps a more widely consultative and participatory process could have yielded a more readily adaptive legal framework. In addition, OHADA reinforces the critical need for institutional and administrative capacity to implement legal innovations once adopted. At the same time, such recommendations come with a number of challenges. OHADA drafters may have avoided wider consultation for fear that it would slow or stop momentum. And the devotion of scarce institutional resources to the ambitious goals of OHADA requires costly choices both economically and politically. OHADA exemplifies both the appeal and the pitfalls of legal innovation strategies.

---

7 Melvin A. Eisenberg, *Private Ordering through Negotiation: Dispute-Settlement and Rulemaking*, 89 Harv. L. Rev. 637 (1976).

Conclusion

This volume reflects the interconnected roles that actors in development policy—governments, donors, lenders, investors, and civil society—play in shaping the substance and the effect of legal reforms. Legal innovation and empowerment for development recognizes and responds to this interdependence. The analytics of attentiveness to context, participatory decision making, and systemic institutional assessment that emerge from these studies offer valuable contributions to the ongoing effort to revitalize contemporary approaches to law, equity, and global justice.

The Justice Innovation Approach

How Justice Sector Leaders in Development Contexts Can Promote Innovation

SAM MULLER AND MAURITS BARENDRECHT

In September 2012, the UN General Assembly devoted its opening debate to the rule of law.[1] A clearer signal that the community of states attaches great importance to the development of the rule of law is hardly imaginable. In *Delivering Justice: Programme of Action to Strengthen the Rule of Law at the National and International Levels,* the secretary-general of the United Nations proposed a program called "delivering justice." According to this report, the rule of law involves more than the state and its institutions: it "is at the heart of the social contract between *the State and individuals* under its jurisdiction, and ensures that justice permeates at *every level.*" The report continues: "responsibility for ensuring rule of law . . . lies with *member States and their citizens.*"[2] Clearly, the rule of law is about more than simply setting rules; it also involves mechanisms to ensure that rules and dispute-resolution processes actually work. *Delivering Justice* contains sections about budgeting and planning, accountable and transparent delivery at the national level, monitoring, the role of civil society, and informal and traditional justice systems. Rather than encouraging states to enact more laws or ensuring that new rights are protected, the secretary-general proposes that states set goals for ensuring the rule of law, assume a monitoring role, measure effectiveness, perform benchmarking exercises, and report progress against indicators. In sum, the report encourages state actors to rethink their role in delivering justice.

This chapter develops this idea further. It shows how justice sector leaders—ministers of justice, secretaries-general of ministries, strategy departments of ministries, chief justices, and directors of public prosecution agencies—can help society deliver justice rather than simply providing justice themselves. The chapter assumes that the process of delivering justice can be improved in a way similar to the delivery of health care, education, or electricity: through continuous innovation. It addresses the issue of how justice sector leaders can enable effective justice innovation.

1 *See* UN General Assembly Resolution A/Res/66/102 (Jan. 13, 2012), available at http://www.unrol.org/files/GA%20Resolution%202012.pdf, paragraph 15 et seq.

2 *See Delivering Justice: Programme of Action to Strengthen the Rule of Law at the National and International Levels*, Report of the Secretary-General 2, 6–8 (Mar. 16, 2012).

The analysis is written with the development context in mind. However, the suggested approach is relevant for all countries, albeit with different priorities and areas of emphasis.

This chapter first explains the meaning of justice innovation. Then it sets out what a strategic justice leader can do to stimulate and consolidate rule of law. The chapter ends by explaining exactly why the justice innovation approach is worth pursuing and how it can help deal with a number of challenges.

What Is Justice Innovation?

Building on the *Wikipedia* definition, we say that justice innovation is the effort to create better or more effective justice products, processes, services, technologies, or ideas that are accepted by markets, governments, and society. Two concepts stand out in this definition: the emphasis on better or more effective justice products and the need to ensure that these products are actually used and liked by all stakeholders.

Rule of law assistance and justice sector budgets tend to fund the building or strengthening of existing state institutions. The image of basic rule of law institutions has not changed much in the past 200 years. Courts, bar associations, law-making procedures, and parliaments are all founded on ideas developed during a period in Western history when empires and kings were being replaced by states and democracies. Until recently, justice sector leaders and the organizations that supply development funds felt responsible for training and resourcing judges, prosecutors, and police officers; building bar associations and national councils for the judiciary; developing constitutions and other laws modeled on Western standards; and setting up national gazettes in which to publish the laws.

However, most rule of law mechanisms emerged independent of state institutions. Informal justice systems—with communication, negotiation, mediation, and adjudication—tend to develop whenever groups of people live or work together and conflicts must be managed.[3] Protection of property rights is triggered by demand when people start investing in assets of a certain value that become scarce.[4] Often, the state incorporates successful innovations that were developed privately.

In line with this reality, and taking criminal justice as an example, the question at the core of the justice innovation approach should be not "how do

---

3 Deborah Isser ed., *Customary Justice and Rule of Law in War Torn Societies* (United States Institute of Peace Press 2011).

4 *See* Francis Fukuyama, *The Origins of Political Order, from Prehuman Times to the French Revolution* 247 (Farrar, Straus and Giroux 2011) ("Of all the components of contemporary states, effective legal institutions are perhaps the most difficult to construct"); Lee J. Alston & Bernardo Mueller, *Property Rights and the State*, in Claude Ménard & Mary M. Shirley, *Handbook of New Institutional Economics* 573 (Springer Verlag 2008).

we build a good prosecution service?" but rather "how do we empower and stimulate the stakeholders in the criminal justice system—judges, prosecutors, police officers, victim support services, civil servants, legal aid lawyers, psychologists working with drug offenders, academics, correction services, and social entrepreneurs—to continuously improve criminal justice mechanisms?" In other words, how can strategic justice leaders contribute to the innovation process so that more justice is delivered?

What Can Justice Sector Leaders Do to Foster Innovation?

The literature on innovation shows that successful innovation processes cannot be forced by following a simple set of prescriptions. Innovation is a matter of doing many things well and involves many factors.[5] One survey found no less than 40 factors associated with successful innovation.[6] Many are related to what happens on the ground, as justice sector professionals improve their processes step by step and through trial and error. But there are quite a few things that justice sector leaders can do to help justice innovation thrive.[7]

Generate Possibilities

In the innovation initiation phase, the literature lists nine factors associated with innovation. Innovation is stimulated by creating a setting with diverse views, people, and backgrounds. Practitioners should focus on users of rule of law mechanisms and the people directly serving them. They know best what is needed and what might work. Time and space are required for innovation, as are clear goals for the innovation process. A justice sector leader can take several actions in this phase.

Articulate a Clear Vision

Innovation can be inspired by a clear vision that shows political commitment and a desire to redirect resources in a particular area. This is a critical factor because innovation—for instance, when dealing with employment conflicts—will require efforts from a wide variety of actors—for instance, employers, lawyers, trade unions, lawmakers, and courts. Typically, the organizations in the justice supply chain are independent and cannot be managed in one common direction. They must be inspired, and they must see that others in the supply chain are adapting to change.

---

5 *See The Best Story in Development*, The Economist (May 19, 2012), available at http://www.economist.com/node/21555571, which cites a study of the many things that contribute to a significant drop in child mortality.

6 Nizar Becheikh, Réjéan Landry & Nabil Amara, *Lessons from Innovation Empirical Studies in the Manufacturing Sector: A Systematic Review of the Literature from 1993–2003*, 26 *Technovation* 644–64 (2006).

7 *See* the Innovation Model, available at http://www.innovatingjustice.com/innovationlab/innovation-assistance/innovation-model/?subcategoryID=15535, developed on the basis of factors that have been found to support innovation in the public sector.

Politicians are subject to many pressures and can unknowingly sow confusion. A minister may make a speech one day in which he (or she) states that access to justice should be improved. The next day he might argue before a different audience that courts are overburdened and that people should do more to resolve their own conflicts. The visions of justice sector leaders should be realistic: in many postconflict contexts, donors demand the articulation of a national rule of law plan. (Interestingly, the donor states that demand such national rule of law plans rarely have one themselves.) Those plans are often very wide in scope (they are, after all, "national"), they rarely clearly prioritize, and they often contain unrealistic timelines,[8] making it hard for potential innovators to coalesce around a common agenda.

To be realized, a vision must be as specific as possible, couched in plain language, ambitious but doable, and consistent, not changing with every new administration. The Millennium Development Goals are an excellent example of a clear, concrete, ambitious, doable, and consistent vision. Other examples of justice innovation visions are "to increase the number of people living on land and in houses with tenure security by 20 percent in the next year," "to make a judge available to every village of more than 500 people within the next two years," and "to ensure that employers and employees get a solution within two months after filing a claim." It would not be difficult to list a number of priorities for justice sector innovation based on an assessment of the most frequent and urgent justiciable problems the population experiences; such surveys have been done before.[9]

Break the Rules

Innovation means doing things in new ways. The innovation literature urges innovators to challenge every rule of the game. For justice sector professionals, this directive creates a dilemma, because their legitimacy is built on following the rules, not breaking them. Changing procedures in a relevant way almost always requires a change in the rules or at least in the way rules are applied. So everywhere in the world, professional judges, lawyers, and others are more likely waiting for the rules to change than taking initiatives to improve procedures.

Justice sector leaders can address this dilemma by allowing experiments, provided that the experiments are clearly motivated by goals such as decreasing costs, preventing error, increasing procedural justice, or speeding up

---

8 One of the more extreme examples is the Afghanistan Compact, agreed to between Afghanistan and the international community, in London in 2006, which provides as benchmarks: "By end-2010, the legal framework required under the constitution, including civil, criminal and commercial law, will be put in place, distributed to all judicial and legislative institutions and made available to the public" and "By end-2010, functioning institutions of justice will be fully operational in each province of Afghanistan, and the average time to resolve contract disputes will be reduced as much as possible."

9 *See* Basic Justice Care, available at http://www.hiil.org/publication/strategies-towards-basic-justice-care, which lists some basic justice needs.

trials. Instead of stressing formal barriers to new solutions, justice sector leaders can urge stakeholders to develop, try, and test new procedures and to ask for changes in the rules if necessary. Procedures for experimental treatments in the health care sector may be a source of inspiration.

Foster Competition

Innovation is hardly conceivable without competition. Innovation in an environment like Silicon Valley is not based on monopolies and rigid agreements between players as to who will deliver what to the exclusion of others. Such incubators are messy, chaotic places where smart ideas compete with other smart ideas for funding, duplication is not frowned upon, and the shared assumption is that the best idea will win out in the end. What is "best" is measured by sales figures, demand by clients, and the willingness of venture capitalists to invest. Organization is limited: it is aimed at creating a place where innovators can meet other innovators and where people who are interested in funding start-ups can find the best ones. What happens next is thanks to the magic of the marketplace and innovation.

Can this concept be transposed to the world of order, norms, and justice? Not if one perceives the delivery of justice as the application of a master program emanating from a state's constitution. In the real world, delivering justice is a messy process, as every practicing lawyer will testify. There are many ways to solve conflicts, and many rule makers (national, international, local, formal, informal, public, private) work on the same problems. Justice sector innovators should be able to develop the best approaches in an attractive, competitive environment in which there are a few generally accepted ways to measure potential success of innovations (such as satisfaction of all types of users).[10]

Fostering competition in the justice sector can be part of a ministerial innovation policy. This policy would put the minister less in the position of the holder of power who acts, and more in the role of creating a level playing field to make sure that the fairest, most effective, fastest, and lowest-cost solutions survive.

For example, take the provision of fair and efficient dispute settlement processes for employment conflicts or coping with the aftermath of large-scale violence. Various civil and criminal public courts might offer different procedures (national, international), industry tribunals, truth and reconciliation commissions (local or national), commissions establishing adequate compensation, semibinding mediation services based on existing informal justice mechanisms, or online dispute-resolution platforms.[11]

---

10 See *Non State Security and Justice in Fragile States*, Overseas Development Institute Briefing Paper 73 (Apr. 2012), which also lists some useful rules of engagement in respect to nonstate actors, available at http://www.odi.org.uk/resources/docs/7640.pdf.

11 *See*, for example, David Pimentel, *Rule of Law Reform without Cultural Imperialism? Reinforcing Customary Justice through Collateral Review in Southern Sudan*, 2 Hague J. on the Rule of L. 1–28 (2010).

In the Netherlands, E-Court promises its clients quick and cheap awards by arbitrators for money claims. Its initiators tell a story of many obstacles based on resistance from bailiffs, state courts, and the ministry of justice, who all saw the existing way of doing things threatened by the concept of E-Court rather than welcoming a new supplier of fair and speedy solutions.[12] Yet, this innovation forced the courts to rethink their ways of dealing with similar claims, seeing that the income for the state justice sector from money claims was no longer guaranteed. Did fostering competition enhance the performance and effectiveness of state courts and private sector dispute resolution?

Competition requires a level playing field based on transparency of quality and costs so that clients seeking access to justice can make informed choices and defendants are protected against unfair procedures. In theory, it should be possible, for example, to send all users of a justice process a brief e-mail or text message on their mobile phones asking them to assess a court process they have just gone through based on a number of criteria.[13] Their responses could be aggregated and fed into a website for all to see. And based on that, justice clients, justice providers, and ministry officials could see what works best.

Justice sector leaders can foster competition by making the performance of justice services more measurable and transparent, by avoiding general monopolies, and by allowing differentiation and specialization.

Develop Innovations

Once the innovators are at work, the most fruitful ideas must be selected for the actual innovation process. This requires a situation where people with a positive attitude and sufficient resources can nurture the innovative concept. Partnerships between public services providers and private sector organizations can be very fruitful: legal expenses insurance companies can help ensure access to legal aid; online dispute-resolution platforms can be integrated into court procedures. In today's world, these are no longer rich-country options. Building a prototype early on is recommended, as well as involving end users in the development process. Again, a justice sector leader can take specific actions.

Manage Risk

Once the developing process starts, a safe environment in which to develop a new concept, allowing for trial and error, is important. In an environment that is not "safe," where failure is immediately linked to blame and consequences, innovation tends to be difficult. The appetite of the public for trial and error in the justice sector may not be big, however. A minister of justice may be genuinely committed to creating more room for such an approach, but he too is subject to cabinet, parliamentary, and media scrutiny. So creating safe

12 *See* http://www.innovatingjustice.com/innovations/e-court-the-first-online-private-court.

13 *See*, for example, the measuring access to justice tool at http://www.innovatingjustice.com/innovations/measuring-the-costs-and-quality-of-access-to-justice.

spaces for experiments requires risk management. The minister must build it upward within the cabinet, vis-à-vis the prime minister or president and with respect for parliament. The minister of justice must also have a smart media strategy. The minister of justice must project a strong commitment to gradual innovation processes, allowing for trial and error at the ground level, where the innovations need to come from. Quick wins are likely to be important here—specific improvements that show that the innovation climate is producing results, such as savings in the budget, a higher level of satisfaction from victims, more efficient court hearings, less recidivism, or decreasing juvenile delinquency.

Reward Innovation Champions

People are important. Almost all successful innovations are linked to a key person who devoted years of hard work to making a dream come true. The justice sector is not very good at rewarding such innovation champions. Making substantial money from innovation is hard, and one of the strengths (and weaknesses) of the justice sector is stressing the professional roles of judges and civil servants rather than personal qualities and strong personalities. A minister of justice is in a unique position to reward people who have worked for many years on improving procedures or systems of rules. Attaching people's names to innovations can be done easily; one should never underestimate the effect of simple and consistent praise for good achievements.[14]

Fund Early Development

Many innovations in the justice sector—good as they are—trip over two wires: funding for early development and funding for a sustained period of time.

The justice sector tends to be funded in a rigid way. The budget and planning cycle is generally quite short. Budgets are structured around fixed deliverables, which rarely if ever include money for systematic research and development. Courts cannot invest money now that they can recoup in the next years by cost savings or by an increase in court fees for better services or more plaintiffs bringing cases. Justice sector donors may be interested in trying new procedures, but they tend to want specific deliverables: so many judges trained, so many courts and prisons built, a bar association set up. The situation is slightly different in the legal services industry, where research and development budgets from suppliers to law firms have created innovations in specific areas, such as software to help with e-discovery.

A minister of justice can make sure that research and development budgets exist and that there are ways to recoup initial investments. He can do that within his own ministry, and he can initiate public-private partnerships with

---

14 An excellent example is the relationship between the International Criminal Court and the partners of the Legal Tools database and Case Matrix Network. The partners carry the costs of their contribution to the network but are also part of the innovation team. Signs of appreciation and commitment by the court stimulate the partners in this innovative network. *See* http://www.legal-tools.org/en/what-are-the-icc-legal-tools/.

donors that provide investments in justice innovation with a commitment, for example, that the ministry will take over responsibility for funding the services once an innovation has been successfully developed. Developing states can lead the way here.

Replicate and Scale Up

Once an innovation is up and running, its potential for replication and scaling up should be exploited. Models for interactive court hearings developed for civil justice courts can be adapted to administrative law or criminal justice. What has been developed in one court may be useful for similar courts in other countries, but standardizing new practices too early may stifle innovation. Change management is necessary as well.

Create Incentives

A minister of justice can create incentives for justice leaders to try out well-tested innovations that have been developed elsewhere. Allocating extra budgets to those who are willing to adopt an innovation is one method. One factor inhibiting justice sector innovation is that each court in each country tends to develop its own working methods, without relying on external suppliers of procedures, supporting software, or protocols for dealing with certain types of crime. A minister of justice can urge justice sector organizations to consider buying tools that are readily available, either those developed by specialized private sector companies or those developed by colleagues in the public sector. If a worldwide market for justice sector technologies were to evolve, the rule of law could be enhanced substantially and many cost savings would be possible. Ministers of justice from developing countries have more choice than ever. Tanzania need not look only at things that worked in Germany, the United Kingdom, or France; it can also look at innovations from, for example, Brazil, India, South Africa, Ethiopia, and Rwanda.

Be Aware of Disruptive Innovations

Justice sector leaders should be aware of the possibilities of disruptive innovations. Online services, such as those offered by Legal Zoom,[15] disrupt the market for lawyers and notaries in civil law countries, who are likely to protect their markets by favoring legislation that has been designed without new possibilities in mind, such as the prohibition of legal advice by nonlawyers or the monopolies of notaries public. Because innovations can make basic justice care available to groups that were unable to get any legal assistance in the past, there is every reason to create a level playing field for such new technologies. The paralegal program Timap for Justice has had a disruptive effect on the legal services market in Sierra Leone.[16]

---

15 *See* http://www.legalzoom.com/.

16 *See* http://www.timapforjustice.org/.

Consider Long-Term Business Models

Assuring longer-term funding for successful justice innovations after the research and development phase is often challenging. One of the reasons for this is that consideration of such funding tends to start only once an innovation has been developed. Justice sector leaders should be thinking about the management and budgeting of research and development processes right from the start of any justice innovation initiative.[17]

Analyze and Learn

Innovation cannot exist without critical reflection. Justice sector leaders should ensure that monitoring mechanisms are in place and that new insights can be implemented in improved versions immediately (real-time learning).

One reason why the health care sector is so innovative is that benchmarks for new treatments are easy to establish: symptoms disappear and the patient feels better and does not return with the same complaints. Similar metrics for the justice sector would greatly enhance innovation processes, for example, through lower costs, timelier decisions, and higher satisfaction of users (procedural justice, outcome justice).

A minister of justice can ensure that a segment of the core budget is reserved for developing such measurement tools and for applying them to the processes and procedures of the system. This is an area par excellence where the minister can enlist civil society organizations, academic networks, and external donors. Civil society organizations can be stimulated to play a role in assessing elements of the justice system and showing where improvements are needed. Outcomes measurement could interest donors; and more and more academic institutions are developing rule of law measuring tools.[18] What the minister cannot outsource is working with senior civil servants to build a culture in which the challenges that measuring makes visible are harnessed toward justice innovation.

Challenges and Benefits of a Justice Innovation Approach

The best way to make the case for a new role for justice sector leaders is to provide an example. Tunisia will go down in history as the spark that set off a forest fire in the Arab world. After President Ben Ali fled, a transitional government organized rather effective and open elections, on the basis of which a constitutional assembly worked on a new constitution; as of July 2012, a provisional government was running the country. Ambitions and expectations are high, also relating to the rule of law. There is a general yearning for a better justice system. However, the challenges are tremendous, and there are

---

17 A very useful tool for this is http://www.businessmodelgeneration.com.

18 For a good overview, *see* Special Issue on Measuring Rule of Law, 3(2) Hague J. on the Rule of L. (Sep. 2011).

no easy answers.[19] Stimulating gradual innovation processes around practical problems and showing quick wins may be the most promising way forward.

However, justice sectors leaders in Tunisia and other countries in transition face the following challenges.

Lack of Trust

In Tunisia, a new social contract is being put in place in the midst of a difficult economic and social context. Trust in the state is low.[20] For many citizens, state institutions are linked to capricious behavior by people in positions with authority. So most people avoid getting in touch with the state institutions; the idea that law protects and can work for people needs to be sold. State institutions are not automatically viewed as legitimate.

Trust must be regained. The *World Development Report 2011* (WDR) convincingly argues that legitimate institutions are the best immunizer against internal and external stresses such as the ones Tunisia faces.[21] The WDR shows that legitimacy comes with the responsiveness of institutions and that "capacity, inclusion, and accountability" are needed.[22] In many developing countries, state institutions have limited capacity, are not seen as fully inclusive, and face little accountability. To build legitimate institutions, the WDR argues, justice sector leaders must work from the bottom up, with "good enough coalitions" to create quick and visible wins that show that rule of law is essential.

Any minister of justice can build on processes that work in a country. By examining at informal justice systems for medium-level crime, rule-making processes in specific industries, or court procedures giving effective protection against eviction, the minister of justice can stimulate the people involved to innovate and extend these services to the more urgent justice problems the state faces. Coalitions can be built to nurture these processes and to shield them against attempts to corrupt them.

Lack of Funds

Unemployment, especially in youth, is very high in Tunisia, making investments in labor-intensive industries a priority among the many other economic

---

19 To name a few: budgets are limited, ideas of justice differ, trust in public officials in the justice sector is limited, and expectations are high. In May 2012, a dispute arose between the government and the association of judges after eighty-one judges were fired for alleged corruption; *see* http://www.tunisia-live.net/2012/05/31/judges-strike-lifted-following-agreement-with-ministry-of-justice/.

20 *See*, for example, a survey by the World Justice Project according to which 51 percent of Tunisians believe that the police forces are the most corrupt institution in Tunisian society, available at http://www.tunisia-live.net/2012/05/29/according-to-poll-80-of-tunisians-feel-free-to-express-themselves/. *See* also remarks by the head of the national anticorruption agency during a HiiL seminar held in Tunis (Apr. 2011), on record with the authors.

21 *World Development Report 2011: Conflict, Security and Development* 74 et seq. (World Bank 2011).

22 *Id.*, at 84.

challenges. In 2009, the Tunisian GDP stood at around US$40 billion, or US$8 per person.[23] This is three to five times less than the GDP in Euro Area countries, making it inconceivable that Tunisia will be able to invest heavily in court infrastructure and expensive professionals to deliver justice sector services. But Tunisian citizens do not want less "justice" than European ones, nor should they be asked to accept less. So a country like Tunisia has every interest in stimulating innovation in the justice sector so that it can deliver better justice for its money.

Innovative ways to deliver justice at low cost can be found throughout the world; a transitioning country such as Tunisia presents a window of opportunity to adopt and adapt these innovations to a local setting. Can court processes be organized in such a way that more solutions are delivered per judge? In Nicaragua, the Facilitadores Judiciales program equipped a judge with a team of *facilitadores*, who live in villages far away from the courthouse. They mediate under the judge's supervision and assist with bringing the cases that do not settle to court. Sierra Leone and South Africa pioneered the use of paralegals at a fraction of the cost of training judges and lawyers. In large-scale litigation, which will also occur in Tunisia, expert evidence is often key. Increasing the reliability of the fact-finding process and decreasing the costs of dealing with expertise were the goal of a procedure for a dialogue between experts at a court hearing developed in Australia.[24] Online dispute resolution now resolves 60 million disputes between buyers and sellers on eBay, holding promise for dealing with large numbers of disputes anywhere in the world.[25]

Power Relations

Influence on justice sector institutions is always part of a broader struggle for power, especially in situations of transition. Military versus civilian power brokers. Landowners versus landless. Employers versus employees. Dominant ethnic groups versus groups that feel oppressed. Secular versus religious norms. Rule of law gets politicized quickly.

The stimulation of justice innovation can be a road to reform without political turmoil. It is less about big principles (which is not to say they do not count) and more about little steps that deal with specific problems. Gradual but deliberate improvement of employment complaint procedures can be organized from the bottom up: targets can include more voice for parties at hearings, speedier resolution, more settlement, lower costs, clearer criteria for remedies, and clearer reasons in judgments. This approach is likely to be more effective than a heated discussion about the independence of courts or whether employees should have protection against dismissal. Innovation includes developing transparent monitoring mechanisms that show the extent

---

23 The Economist, *World in Figures*, 2012, at *The Economist* website.

24 *See* http://www.innovatingjustice.com/innovations/concurrent-expert-evidence.

25 *See* http://pages.ebay.com/coverage/index.html.

to which the clients of the courts experienced a neutral procedure with equal opportunities for both parties.

Indonesia has found interesting ways to cope with the sharia versus secular dilemma. The area of family relationships is perhaps the foremost area where sharia law has impact (corporal punishment in criminal law is seldom applied in practice in most countries that have sharia law). Facing a choice between formal courts and religious courts, Indonesian couples wanting a divorce overwhelmingly choose religious ones. Religious courts are more open to innovation, working in close cooperation with Australian courts to improve their services.

Transitional Justice

Tunisia is a place where the concept of transition permeates. The judicial organization needs fundamental reorganizing: some judges too closely linked to the former regime may have to go, a role for council for the judiciary must be found, performance mechanisms to hold judges accountable and effective ways to distribute budgets must be developed, and the question of specialization versus generalization is on the table, as is the question of how it can support courts. Law making represents a huge challenge. The country is embarking on a fundamental redesign, facing the task of ensuring the quality and coherence of laws. Both the judges and the clients of the justice system need better access to legal information. Key elements of the "hard" justice infrastructure—courthouses and published and available laws—are in bad shape. For a minister of justice, these issues are fraught with choices for which it will be difficult to build support within the courts and the institutions involved in law making.

A strategy based on creating a level playing field for justice innovation assumes that justice sector innovators take initiatives to start improving services. And those improved services should be the point of departure, not the organization itself: ways to create needs for higher quality, more trustworthy services, and lower-cost delivery. For example, if a group of judges decides that disputes over land is an urgent priority and they propose terms of reference for a new procedure, such as transparency of criteria for allocating land and compensation, the more organizational problems of specialization and court independence may be solved on the way. The goal is for the government to be less the structure that is supposed to solve a problem and more a place where leaders work to empower those closest to the problem to creatively resolve concrete, close-to-the-ground issues.

Conclusion

Justice sector leaders can improve the rule of law by incorporating the justice innovation approach. Because this approach enlists the whole of society (justice users and providers), benefits from best practices and technologies developed in other countries, and harnesses the knowledge of those working on problems already, it can deliver more value and justice with less money than other approaches. However, organizing the necessary space for justice innovation is not easy in any context, and is even more challenging in the context of a developing state.

Good justice sector leadership is a key component of the effort. Legal systems have their own dynamics and tend to move slowly. The WDR estimates that it takes 17 to 41 years to establish basic trust in the rule of law.[26] The attitude of expecting central, top-down coordination is very strong in the justice sector, and many very good ideas now wait until a new constitution is enacted, the law of procedure is changed, or a budget is cleared. However, there are many opportunities for a justice sector leader to create and manage justice innovation in the meantime. There is certainly risk involved in doing so, but the potential benefits are huge.

26 *World Development Report, supra* note 21, at 11.

Legal Empowerment of the Poor: Past, Present, Future

HASSANE CISSÉ

The concept that law plays a significant role in promoting economic development is well established. The nature of that significance, in the context of development narratives, traditionally has been rooted in law's connection to strong institutions and good governance: the presence of law can be considered a prerequisite for effective government. Effective government has come to be treated as an essential ingredient in the development recipe, and law or, more specifically, the "rule of law," is the condition for that ingredient.

In an effort to reimagine how law can fit into development strategies, scholars and practitioners have widened the traditional focus on institutions and government machinery to bring the people themselves into view: the poor have become a subject in law and development discourse, rather than simply the indirect, long-term beneficiaries of institutional reform. Many scholars and practitioners now argue that law can be used as a tool in the hands of the poor, a tool that they can use to improve their own lives. This process has become known as *legal empowerment*.

This chapter maps the emergence and progress of the legal empowerment movement, if it can be called that. This field is still young, and disagreements over its direction are unresolved. Basic questions of priorities and strategies remain contested; assumptions must be tested further; more data need to be collected. Nevertheless, the movement has much promise and is gaining acceptance. It should be taken seriously by everyone concerned with using the law to end poverty.

The Emergence of Legal Empowerment and Its Place in the Rule of Law Agenda

Legal empowerment of the poor (LEP) is a relatively new frontier in thinking about how the law can affect the lives of the poor and what can and should be done to empower the poor to use the law for their betterment. By evoking law and power together, LEP directly challenges traditional ideas about the role of law in the lives of the poor. At the same time, the LEP paradigm is not a complete rejection of other ways of theorizing about the purpose of rule of law in development. LEP both reaffirms and reacts against the older development agenda of advancing the rule of law, and remains closely connected to

The author thanks Matthew Moorhead for his invaluable assistance in the preparation of this article. Stephen Golub and Sam Muller also provided constructive comments. Responsibility for errors or omissions remains with the author.

it. To understand the origins and evolution of LEP, and possibly its future, one must also understand the nature of this connection with traditional rule of law approaches.

The importance of the rule of law in human development is generally acknowledged, despite enduring disagreements about the degree of that importance. Lawyers, economists, and development specialists must continue to explore new ways in which the law can alleviate poverty. As practitioners endeavor to improve the imperfect understanding of the role of law in human welfare, advances continue to be made in rule of law scholarship.[1] As new insights are uncovered, many traditional ways of thinking about how law can lift people out of poverty become ripe for reevaluation. As the scholarship grows and this process of reevaluation unfolds, elements of what might be termed the "classical rule of law approach" receive more critical attention. In particular, an excessive focus on institutions and state structures, a supposed hallmark of the classic rule of law approach, has been criticized for overlooking the needs of the poor. A growing awareness of this risk has caused scholars and development practitioners to conceive of a new way of thinking about how the law can contribute to development: LEP. A central claim of the LEP approach is that poverty endures because, in part, people are forced to live their lives without legal protection.

The focus on legal empowerment is intended to strengthen existing and ongoing efforts to further the rule of law agenda. It is also, to some extent, a reprimand of those efforts. Legal empowerment as a strategy for development has gained prominence, in part, on the back of criticism of, or frustration with, the outcomes of the more established rule of law agenda. That agenda can mean many things to different people, and some sense of its meaning is set out here.

"Rule of law" is a concept with a broad scope that was established as a development objective and method decades before LEP emerged. Generally, the rule of law is defined in one of two ways. The first emphasizes elements of substantive justice; the second emphasizes the procedural aspects of a system in which the rule of law prevails.[2] The conditions of both definitions must be met if the rule of law can be said to exist in any given system. A functional rule of law system that provides both procedural effectiveness and substantive justice is obviously important to human welfare and the satisfaction of justice claims. What is less clear is exactly how much the rule of law matters, and how effective rule of law interventions have been in improving development outcomes for the poor.

---

1 *See*, for example, Thomas Carothers ed., *Promoting the Rule of Law Abroad: In Search of Knowledge* (Carnegie Endowment for International Peace 2006); James J. Heckman, Robert L. Nelson, & Lee Cabatingan ed., *Global Perspectives on the Rule of Law* (Routledge 2010); and Michael J. Trebilcock & Ronald J. Daniels ed., *Rule of Law Reform and Development: Charting the Fragile Path of Progress* (Edward Elgar 2008).

2 Paul P. Craig, *Formal and Substantive Conceptions of the Rule of Law: An Analytical Framework*, 467 Public Law (1997).

The impact of improvements in the rule of law environment on development outcomes is notoriously hard to quantify. A number of attempts have been made. Daniel Kaufmann and his colleagues measured several aspects of governance, including the rule of law, over time and across more than two hundred countries.[3] They suggest that a nation's GDP increases noticeably by moving ahead when improvements are made in an index of rule of law indicators. Despite efforts such as these, however, it may never be possible to measure the impact of the rule of law in neat percentages. Kaufmann's study acknowledges that the difficulties inherent in proving a link between the rule of law and economic growth may preclude such measurement. Nevertheless, the study supports a general consensus that there is a positive correlation between economic development and strong legal systems.

The way in which the rule of law has evolved en route to becoming part of mainstream development orthodoxy is perhaps best exemplified by the approach of the World Bank, one of the world's foremost development institutions, to the issue. When the Bank realized that the rule of law and judicial reform were related to economic development, the Bank became involved in LEP efforts. The connection to economic development is a critical factor that enables the Bank to engage in legal reform, because its Articles of Agreement prohibit it from taking into account anything other than "economic considerations" in its lending operations.[4] Before the Bank could be comfortable involving itself in LEP work, it needed to accept that the quality of governance affects economic development. This was a delicate task for an institution that is prohibited from "interfering in the political affairs" of its members, yet as evidence of the importance of governance and the rule of law in economic performance grew, the Bank responded. In 1990, the general counsel of the Bank issued a legal opinion concluding that the Bank "may favorably respond to a country's request for assistance in the field of legal reform, if it finds it relevant to the country's economic development and to the success of the Bank's lending strategy for the country."[5]

Although hard to quantify, the correlation between rule of law indicators and economic development is real. Beyond this assumption, what matters to people is identifying precisely what kind of rule of law initiatives serve them best. As the field matures and the evidence of what works and what does not starts to mount, the "second generation" of rule of law scholarship is challenging many assumptions about how to conduct legal reform and what to expect from the results. In the past decade, some scholars and commentators have

---

3 Daniel Kaufmann, Aart Kraay, & Massimo Mastruzzi, *Governance Matters VI: Governance Indicators for 1996–2006*, World Bank Policy Research Working Paper No. 4280 (2007). *See* also, for example, Juan Carlos Botero, Robert L. Nelson, & Christine Pratt, *Indices and Indicators of Justice, Governance and the Rule of Law: An Overview*, 3 Hague J. on the Rule of L. 153 (2011).

4 International Bank for Reconstruction and Development, article IV, section 10.

5 Ibrahim Shihata, *Issues of "Governance" in the Borrowing Members—The Extent of Their Relevance under the Bank's Articles of Agreement* 25 (Dec. 21, 1990).

come to question the dominant ways of thinking about the rule of law. LEP has emerged from this persistent questioning.

As Stephen Golub posits, LEP is partly an alternative to the perceived failings of rule of law orthodoxy.[6] Golub classifies many of the law-reform efforts of the major international development actors as top-down efforts that pay insufficient attention to the actual needs of the poor. According to Golub, rule of law orthodoxy has been said to focus "too much on law, lawyers, and state institutions, and too little on development, the poor, and civil society."[7]

LEP is intended to address these particular deficiencies. In the words of critics such as Thomas Carothers, typical efforts to promote the rule of law cannot convincingly demonstrate "how the rule of law develops in societies and how such development can be stimulated beyond simplistic efforts to copy institutional forms."[8] LEP, however, is more focused on the real needs of the poor. As a development strategy, it has been said to both advance and transcend the rule of law. LEP advances the rule of law in the sense that empowered people will be in a position to demand good governance, and it transcends the rule of law by lifting the focus from governance to more general poverty alleviation.[9]

A number of definitions of LEP are used in the literature. The UN Commission on Legal Empowerment of the Poor (CLEP) defines LEP as "a process of systemic change through which the poor and excluded become able to use the law, the legal system, and legal services to protect and advance their rights and interests as citizens and economic actors."[10] Golub expands on the basic definition of LEP by differentiating it from rule of law orthodoxy on four issues. First, LEP requires lawyers to view the poor as partners instead of simply providing advice. Second, the poor should aspire to influence public policy directly in order to avoid falling into a top-down approach. Third, LEP should employ nonjudicial strategies alongside strictly legal ones. Fourth, law should be integrated into a broader range of development-related activities.[11] These features enable LEP to serve as a "useful organizing framework to navigate through the complex landscape which has resulted from the fusion of

---

6 The term "rule of law orthodoxy" is used by Frank Upham in *Mythmaking in the Rule of Law Orthodoxy*, Carnegie Endowment Working Paper No. 30, Rule of Law Series, Democracy and Rule of Law Project (Carnegie Endowment for International Peace 2002).

7 Stephen Golub, *Beyond Rule of Law Orthodoxy: The Legal Empowerment Alternative*, Carnegie Endowment Working Paper No. 41, Rule of Law Series, Democracy and Rule of Law Project 3 (Carnegie Endowment for International Peace 2003).

8 Thomas Carothers, *Promoting the Rule of Law Abroad: The Problem of Knowledge*, Carnegie Endowment Working Paper No. 34, Rule of Law Series, Democracy and Rule of Law Project 3 (Carnegie Endowment for International Peace 2003).

9 Golub, *supra* note 7, at 7.

10 Commission on Legal Empowerment of the Poor, *Making the Law Work for Everyone: Volume One, Report of the Commission on Legal Empowerment of the Poor* 3 (2008).

11 Golub, *supra* note 7, at 4.

the two tectonic plates driving development today: governance and poverty reduction."[12]

Cementing the Place of Legal Empowerment: The Commission on Legal Empowerment of the Poor

Scholars such as Banik[13] and Golub have been working in the area of LEP for years, but the idea that LEP can be a force for development gained international recognition when it became the subject of a landmark UN commission in 2008. The CLEP report brought international attention and credibility to LEP and provides a road map for mainstreaming LEP into development work.[14] The report does not understate the view of the commissioners that legal empowerment is of the utmost importance. Central to the report is the bold claim that "four billion people around the world are robbed of the chance to better their lives and climb out of poverty, because they are excluded from the rule of law."[15] Influential names lend their authority to this statement. The commission was cochaired by former US secretary of state Madeline Albright and renowned Peruvian economist Hernando de Soto, and comprised 23 members, of whom 19 were current or former presidents, prime ministers, senior jurists, or other government officials of the highest rank.

For the commissioners, poverty partly stems from "legal exclusion," or exclusion from the protections of the rule of law. The report concluded that "by expanding and deepening legal protection, poor people will be better able to free themselves from poverty."[16] Four areas, or "pillars," are critical to the task of extending legal protection to the 4 billion excluded people, according to the CLEP report. The first pillar, access to justice and the rule of law, is essential to the others. Legal empowerment is impossible if poor people do not have access to a functional judicial system of some kind. Efforts in this regard include a range of measures to make judicial systems more accessible to the poor and oriented to their needs. The three other pillars are legal rights: property rights, labor rights, and so-called business rights. The CLEP report emphasizes the foundation of LEP in international human rights law, particularly in Article 1 of the Universal Declaration of Human Rights, but it does not elaborate on the nature of this connection to human rights discourse.[17]

The CLEP report is a welcome contribution to the broader international development agenda. It moves from the traditional focus on strengthening laws and institutions to a focus on the needs of the poor. The prestige and

12 Ana Palacio, *Legal Empowerment of the Poor: An Action Agenda for the World Bank* 14 (2006).

13 Dan Banik ed., *Rights and Legal Empowerment in Eradicating Poverty* (Ashgate 2008).

14 Commission on Legal Empowerment of the Poor, *supra* note 10.

15 *Id.*, at 1.

16 Gordon Brown, Foreword to Commission on Legal Empowerment of the Poor, *supra* note 10.

17 Commission on Legal Empowerment of the Poor, *supra* note 10, at 29.

scale of the commission have permanently elevated the status of LEP as a development strategy and have similarly increased the general awareness of its purpose and benefits. The response to the CLEP report has included a UN General Assembly resolution endorsing the findings, as well as discussions about possible funding initiatives among key donors.

Rather than assuming that the poor will automatically benefit by increasing the resources available to courts, the report argues that poverty is best addressed by moving resources and power directly into the hands of the poor. It provides a map to redirect the poverty-fighting rule of law agenda toward a more constructive path.

Nonetheless, the report has been the subject of criticism. Golub, for example, criticizes it for unquestioningly adopting certain neoliberal economic assumptions, for attaching excessive importance to the role of legal exclusion in perpetuating poverty, for taking insufficient notice of preexisting research on LEP, for proposing a top-down approach to what is claimed to be a bottom-up development strategy, and for assuming that rational persuasion will suffice to convince elites to surrender political power to the poor.[18]

The CLEP report arguably overreaches in claiming that 4 billion people are impoverished as a result of their exclusion from the protection of the law. Many scholars, such as Banik, have noted that this claim is not properly substantiated.[19] In addition to legal exclusion, many important factors interact in complex and opaque ways to produce poverty, including cultural exclusion, economic failure, high population growth, and political instability. To overemphasize the poverty-fighting effect of LEP is to risk undermining the entire LEP project.

If the CLEP report risks overreaching in its 4-billion-people claim, the focus on four pillars is equally limiting. Property, labor, and business rights are not the only areas in which empowerment can make a difference in poor people's lives. The poor must be empowered to gain access to education, to benefit from criminal justice, and to combat violence against women, for example.[20]

Certain policy prescriptions proposed by the CLEP report are vulnerable to the charge that they are unworkable in practice and do not acknowledge the entrenched political obstacles that stand in the way of LEP.[21] The CLEP report says that political leadership is necessary for change and assumes that elites can be persuaded by rational arguments to empower the poor. In the words of

---

18 Stephen Golub, *The Commission on Legal Empowerment of the Poor: One Big Step Forward and a Few Steps Back for Development Policy and Practice,* 1 Hague J. on the Rule of L. 101, 105 (2009).

19 Dan Banik, *Legal Empowerment as a Conceptual and Operational Tool in Poverty Eradication,* 1 Hague J. on the Rule of L. 117, 118 (2009).

20 Banik, *supra* note 19, at 125.

21 Sam Muller & Maurits Barendrecht consider how justice sector leadership can overcome these obstacles in their chapter in this volume.

CLEP, LEP "does not require its political champions to be saints (although that could be useful) but only to recognize an enlightened self-interest . . . what better political legacy than to have made a lasting contribution to the development of one's country."[22]

The unavoidable truth is that power is a relative concept. When one person is empowered, the power that another person has over him or her is diminished. In the relationships between people, power is both won and lost. In other words, the process of empowering people creates winners and losers. It is not realistic to assume that elites, when confronted by rational economic arguments, will surrender their relative advantage over the poor to further a greater good. Shifting power to the poor is a difficult and highly political task that requires a political strategy to accompany economic theorizing. A technocratic approach that fails to directly address local political exigencies will not succeed. In many developing countries, networks of elites connecting the government and private sector will staunchly resist LEP because LEP presents a direct challenge to the existing power structure. As Matthew Stephens notes, the CLEP report does not adequately address this formidable challenge. The report contains "no strategy for political change, little evidence produced to justify the suggested reforms and an absence of implementable responses to turn theory into practice. These deficiencies diminish [the CLEP report's] value to practitioners and will curtail its policy impact."[23]

No commission, no matter how distinguished or experienced its membership, can reveal a magic recipe to make political obstacles to good development policy disappear. It would be unfair and unrealistic to demand such a recipe from CLEP. However, CLEP does not offer much guidance on this issue beyond stating that "politics cannot be wished away. Powerful actors must be co-opted, won over."[24] Many entrenched elites will not be amenable to cooption under any circumstances and will never be partners in LEP. If elites are uncooperative, the only approach that remains is a bottom-up strategy that empowers the poor and the disenfranchised to protect their own interests. This is, fundamentally, what LEP is about: empowering the poor to improve their own situation.

Contemporary Issues in Legal Empowerment of the Poor

As the responses to the CLEP report make clear, there are limits to what LEP can achieve and substantial barriers in the way of success. Although law has a significant role to play in defeating poverty, the poor themselves often see the law as a barrier to prosperity and security, rather than as a tool for overcoming

---

22 Commission on Legal Empowerment of the Poor, *supra* note 10, at 45–46.

23 Matthew Stephens, *The Commission on Legal Empowerment of the Poor: An Opportunity Missed*, 1 Hague J. on the Rule of L. 132, 147 (2009).

24 Commission on Legal Empowerment of the Poor, *supra* note 10, at 43.

poverty.[25] LEP is about transforming the way the poor experience the law, shifting from a constraining to an empowering experience. Efforts to move in this direction can be grouped by themes, or perhaps by challenges. This section explores a few of the more prominent issues faced by the LEP movement.

Access to Justice

The CLEP report's focus on access to justice is appropriate. LEP has significant potential as a development strategy, particularly through the promotion of access to justice for the poor. Making justice available to the poor can unlock the greatest development benefits of LEP. Accessing justice means seeing wrongs righted and having the confidence that remedies are available to correct such wrongs that may occur. These are important outcomes to people everywhere. Confidence in the capacity to access justice gives the poor the green light to invest in their own future and that of their families, secure in the knowledge that their entitlements will be protected. More formally, "access to justice" means "the ability of people to seek and obtain a remedy through formal or informal institutions of justice, and in conformity with human rights standards."[26]

This definition acknowledges that access to justice is about more than simply the formal, or official, justice system of courts and judges. Informal justice systems, often in the form of precolonial conflict resolution systems, have an essential role to play. Poor people in developing countries tend to seek justice from informal systems rather than from the formal court system.[27] There is a long list of well-known obstacles between the poor and a just outcome in the formal justice system: procedural deficiencies, prohibitive costs, mistrust of the law, fear of the authorities, corruption, language barriers, excessive delays in decision making, and perceived institutional illegitimacy.[28] These are just a few examples of the many reasons that formal justice systems are usually out of reach of the poor and why the poor turn to informal systems. Of course, formal systems are extremely important and must be strengthened. Informal justice systems alone are not a long-term solution to the problem of providing justice to the general population. Informal justice systems can perpetuate discrimination against women or be problematic from other human rights perspectives. Nevertheless, allowing for these limitations, the role of informal systems in delivering justice to poor people must be acknowledged and supported as part of any comprehensive LEP strategy.

It must be noted that access to justice has been a concern of legal practitioners and legal policymakers for centuries and was a central objective of legal reform long before the emergence of LEP. The World Bank, for example, targeted access to justice in several of its earliest legal reform projects. Ac-

---

25 Commission on Legal Empowerment of the Poor, *supra* note 10, at 3.

26 UNDP, *Access to Justice Is the Ability of People to Seek and Obtain a Remedy through Formal or Informal Institutions of Justice, and in Conformity with Human Rights Standards* (2005).

27 Banik, *supra* note 13, at 14.

28 Banik, *supra* note 13, at 15.

cess to justice first appeared as a World Bank objective in 1996 in the Ecuador Judicial Reform Project.[29] Since then, access to justice has been an objective in legal reform projects in countries such as Armenia, Bangladesh, El Salvador, Guatemala, Honduras, Kazakhstan, Mexico, Mongolia, Morocco, Peru, and the Philippines.[30] Thus, although much that LEP offers is new, its concern with access to justice is not. What the proponents of LEP promise, however, is that LEP, with its focus on empowering those most in need of improved access to justice, can provide better ways of doing just that.

A recent World Bank project in Sierra Leone is an example of a project designed to empower the poor to access justice. The World Bank's Justice for the Poor program worked with Namati, an organization devoted to legal empowerment, to train community-based paralegals to overcome obstacles in the delivery of health services.[31] Inadequate or nonexistent health care is one of the gravest disadvantages endured by Sierra Leone's poor. The delivery of health care services is impeded by corruption, mismanagement, and a lack of resources. The failure to provide health care on such a scale is a grave injustice, and the paralegal program is an attempt to use the law to empower Sierra Leoneans to demand justice from health care providers.

Health care is a good candidate for a LEP strategy because the delivery of health services encompasses much more than medical staff and medicines. To be effective, the delivery of any public service must be accountable. Much of Sierra Leone's underperformance in health care can be attributed to the failures of the state institutions that are nominally responsible for health care delivery. The paralegal program grew from the view that addressing these failures requires an understanding of the policy and regulations governing health care, which in turn means an understanding of what the state is supposed to provide and to whom, and where pressure should be applied when the state fails to deliver.

Sierra Leone does not have enough lawyers for this task. In many of Sierra Leone's districts, community paralegals—that is, nonlawyers with some training in law and government administration—help citizens navigate government services. Until now, however, paralegals have not been used to improve accountability in the delivery of health services. The Justice for the Poor program assesses whether paralegals help improve service outcomes by, for example, making regular, unannounced visits to the health clinic to help ensure that maternal and child health services are truly provided free of charge.

Ultimately, the goal is for paralegals to help empower their communities. A general increase in the level of "social accountability" in Sierra Leonean villages will help people access the services to which they are entitled. Once

---

29 Roberto Laver, *The World Bank and Judicial Reform: Overcoming "Blind Spots" in the Approach to Judicial Independence*, 22 Duke J. Comp. & Intl. L. 183, 196 (2012).

30 *Id.*

31 Justice for the Poor.

taught how to pursue redress in the health system, people will gain experience and confidence in engaging with state institutions and will learn how to hold them accountable.

Gender Inequality

In practice, empowering the poor largely means empowering women. The *World Development Report 2012: Gender Equality and Development* examines and details the many ways poor women are disempowered.[32] Despite progress in recent decades, the likelihood of women dying in childbirth in Sub-Saharan Africa and parts of South Asia remains comparable to that in Northern Europe in the nineteenth century.[33] In many countries, women enjoy fewer legal protections and property rights than do men. Women are far more likely than men to work in low-paying, low-status "pink collar" occupations, to face life-threatening violence in the home, and to be unrepresented in senior levels of politics and management.[34] In its extent, severity, and ubiquity, gender inequality is perhaps the most pressing area calling for LEP strategies. As the *World Development Report* concludes, gender inequality matters for two reasons:

> First, gender equality matters intrinsically, because the ability to live the life of one's own choosing and be spared from absolute privation is a basic human right and should be equal for everyone, independent of whether one is male or female. Second, gender equality matters instrumentally, because greater gender equality contributes to economic efficiency and the achievement of other key development outcomes.[35]

An example of the way in which targeting women can empower large numbers of the poor and how grassroots legal empowerment can instigate change at a national level is a project conducted by the World Bank and its partners in Indonesia. The Bank's Justice for the Poor program, together with the Australian Agency for International Development (AusAID), the Family Court of Australia, and PEKKA (an Indonesian civil society organization supporting women-headed households), developed a number of innovative programs to empower women to use their legal identity to exercise their rights and access benefits.

A few statistics demonstrate the importance to poor people of establishing legal identity in Indonesia. According to the Indonesian Bureau of Statistics, women head almost 10 million Indonesian households.[36] In order to access

32 World Bank, *World Development Report 2012: Gender Equality and Development* (World Bank 2011).

33 *Id.*, at 2.

34 *Id.*

35 *Id.*, at 3.

36 Indonesian Bureau of Statistics (Badan Pusat Statistik), *Statistik Gender 2009* 18 (Bureau of Statistics 2010).

government services such as health insurance, rice subsidies, and cash transfer payments, female heads of household must prove to local government authorities that they are, in fact, the head of the household. To obtain an identity card giving her head-of-household status, a woman must prove that, if she has been married or divorced, her marriage or divorce was legally registered. This presents a serious obstacle for many women. Research by PEKKA shows that more than 50 percent of the marriages and 86 percent of the divorces of its members are not legally registered because they were not brought before a court.[37] In Indonesia, the relevant court is usually a religious court. The religious courts handle 98 percent of divorce cases, which themselves account for 50 percent of all court cases in Indonesia.[38]

To access poverty alleviation programs, health services, and education programs for herself and her family, a woman must have a legal identity and a status as the head of her household. Legal marriage and divorce also matter to her children. Unregistered or illegal marriages and divorces, and the resulting lack of birth certificates for the children of such unions, feed an intergenerational cycle of poverty and social exclusion. When women are disempowered, their children and other family members often join them in poverty.

The Women's Legal Empowerment (WLE) program was designed to help women in West Java formalize their legal identity by building on PEKKA's existing empowerment programs. The WLE program had both demand- and supply-side empowerment objectives. On the demand side, the program aimed to inform communities of their rights and encourage them to insist that those rights be respected; on the supply side, it aimed to improve the capacity of the government administration and legal system to recognize and protect the rights of poor women. The WLE program used various tools to work toward these objectives. In the villages, trained paralegals disseminated legal information about family law and domestic violence, provided assistance to local women, and supported grassroots advocacy efforts. A forum, comprising judges, public prosecutors, police, local government officials, NGO representatives, and academics, was established at the district level to conduct legal awareness and outreach activities. Women used the services of the paralegals and the forum members to obtain hundreds of birth certificates for their children and to organize circuit courts to visit villages to formalize marriages and divorces.

The outcome was the empowerment to a transformative degree of the individual women concerned. On a larger scale, the research and results generated by the WLE and its associated projects contributed to policy developments across Indonesia. After becoming aware of the problems of accessing justice in the religious courts, the government increased the religious courts'

---

37 Justice for the Poor, *Increasing Access to Justice for Women, the Poor, and Those Living in Remote Areas: An Indonesian Case Study*, Briefing Note 6, No. 2 (Mar. 2011).

38 *Id.* Data taken from Supreme Court annual report for 2009.

budget 18-fold in two years.[39] New laws have been passed requiring Indonesian courts to provide legal aid services to the poor, an encouraging example of the impact that LEP can have on policy making by elites.

Property Rights

LEP is a work in progress. Even as the concept has gained currency as a development strategy in government and international institutions, the contours and nuances of what LEP means in practice, or what a good LEP policy looks like, remain unresolved. To a frustrated observer, LEP may appear to suffer "from a lack of clarity at many levels of definition, operation, and evaluation."[40] The connection between theory and public policy has not been clearly identified, despite the work of CLEP. Much research remains to be done about what policies and interventions are the most effective at empowering the poor. In the meantime, certain theories about the best kind of LEP policies remain hotly debated. The most important, and possibly the most contested, issue in the brief history of LEP concerns the protection of property rights.

Hernando de Soto, the cochair of the CLEP report, has long argued that developing countries are constrained by the dominance of informal economies.[41] According to this view, without an effective legal system that recognizes and enforces property rights, a country cannot develop a functioning market and consequently cannot produce or allocate capital. If poor people in developing countries are to escape poverty, their property rights must be formalized and protected so that they can exploit the capital value of that property.

This view forms a central pillar of the CLEP report, which urges developing countries to extend property rights to more people by accommodating access to housing, protecting the supply of credit, enacting land reform, and standardizing and uniformly applying property law in the court system.

This focus on the importance of formal property rights is influential, and variations of it are widely shared,[42] but it has been criticized by some scholars. Alan Gilbert has said that de Soto is guilty of "fanning the delusion that anyone, anywhere, can become a fully fledged capitalist," whereas in fact focusing on securing property rights tends to "persuade policy makers that they need do little more than offer title deeds and then leave the market to do everything else."[43] Others have argued that a Western-inspired vision of individual property rights is ill suited to economies that have long operated under a system of collective or community ownership of land.

---

39 Justice for the Poor, *supra* note 37.

40 Palacio, *supra* note 12, at 6.

41 Hernando de Soto, *The Mystery of Capital: Why Capitalism Triumphs in the West and Fails Everywhere Else* (Random House 2000).

42 *See*, for example, Robert D. Cooter & Hans-Bernd Schäfer, *Solomon's Knot: How Law Can End the Poverty of Nations* (Princeton U. Press 2012).

43 Alan Gilbert, *On the Mystery of Capital and the Myths of Hernando de Soto: What Difference Does Legal Title Make? International Development Planning Review* 15 (Liverpool U. Press 2002).

Development policy makers have learned through bitter experience that a uniform, one-size-fits-all approach to policy interventions in poor countries can have unfortunate, and sometimes disastrous, consequences. The same principle certainly applies to legal reform and to property law reform. If a legal reform is to take hold and be effective, it must be perceived as legitimate, not as an alien custom imposed by external forces. Property law reform will have a better chance of taking root if it strengthens rights that individuals already believe they possess or should possess. The reforms must support existing aspirations, not completely reorder society. That is, reforms to systems of property law must incorporate local understandings of the relationship between people and the land they inhabit. This is particularly important where a collective or spiritual attachment to land prevails: land is not always conceptualized as "property," something that can be bought and sold.[44] If policy makers bear these sensitivities in mind, much can be done to empower the poor in the area of property rights.

Networks

LEP is not solely, or perhaps even primarily, a "legal" strategy to reduce poverty. As Golub notes, "legal empowerment is about power more than about law."[45] An aim of LEP is to avoid the fixation on formal legal institutions (and lawyers) that some say is a mark of the traditional rule of law agenda and to focus on more community-based methods. Supporting strong and effective judicial institutions is an important part of strengthening the rule of law in a country, but without complementary efforts to empower poor people to use the law, this cannot be considered a LEP strategy. LEP activities can be categorized in a number of different ways. Golub's list is a good example: investing in civil society, engaging NGOs at a country-specific level, integrating with socioeconomic development projects, taking a long-term approach, supporting impact-oriented research, incentivizing government personnel to support legal empowerment, and making LEP a policy priority for donor countries as well as for developing countries.[46]

The emergence of organizations that are dedicated to these community-based activities is an indication of the status of LEP within the broader development agenda. Consider Namati, with which, as noted above, the World Bank is working on a project in Sierra Leone. Namati describes itself as an organization that is focused on "innovations in legal empowerment" and that supports grassroots programs that move away from the familiar model that involves many lawyers.[47] Typically, according to Namati, a legal empowerment program will contain a small group of lawyers and a larger front-line

---

44 For an interesting discussion of this issue, *see* Edward Robbins, *Formalisation of Land and Housing Tenure to Empower the Poor: Simple Nostrum or Complex Challenge?* in *Rights and Legal Empowerment in Eradicating Poverty* 175 (Dan Banik ed., Ashgate 2008).

45 Golub, *supra* note 18, at 108.

46 Golub, *supra* note 18, at 113–16.

47 *See* http://www.namati.org.

group of community paralegals. Paralegals work closely with communities, deploy a flexible range of tools, and connect to lawyers for high-level advocacy if their front-line efforts prove to be insufficient or inappropriate. In addition to these community-level programs, Namati believes that LEP requires reforms to state institutions to encourage the participation and ownership of individuals and communities. Examples of such institutional reforms include simplifying land registration procedures, strengthening grievance mechanisms to respond to failures in public service delivery, and improving access to government information.

As more organizations and development agencies adopt LEP approaches, evidence of a global LEP discourse is emerging. The Global Legal Empowerment Network is an interesting example. The network, the result of a collaboration between the World Bank and the Open Society Justice Initiative and hosted by Namati, provides a forum for those involved in LEP, including development agencies, community paralegals, concerned citizens, NGOs, public interest lawyers, journalists, and government officials, to share knowledge and experience. The network aims to connect practitioners to each other and to build a strong foundation and momentum for LEP. As of this writing, the network consists of an online database for exchanging practical resources, such as a paralegal training manual. Practitioners are invited to form subgroups based on geographical regions or themes and to participate in face-to-face regional meetings.

The future of the LEP movement lies in networks that connect development practitioners with the poor, development practitioners with development practitioners, and the poor with the poor. If poor people are to realize the benefits of empowerment, such connections must be made. Solidarity and the strengthening of community ties are essential if the power of the poor is to be expressed; that is, if it is to be any kind of power worth having.

Conclusion

LEP is a new movement in a much older tradition, and it shares with that tradition a commitment to bring the law to bear on development challenges. By focusing on those who are directly affected by a lack of economic opportunity and by prioritizing their needs, LEP has the potential to make the development agenda work better for the poor. That is, after all, the purpose of development efforts. Prominently inscribed in the foyer of the World Bank headquarters in Washington, DC, are the words "Our dream is a world free of poverty."

LEP can contribute to turning that dream into a reality, but substantial challenges exist. The priorities for LEP should be to launch pilot projects based on solid LEP principles, to examine the results of those projects for insights, and, above all, to collect more data: data about what the poor want, what the poor think the law can do for them, and how the poor want to empower themselves. As the data grow and the principles and basic strategies of LEP are refined, LEP will assume an important place in the antipoverty agenda.

Beyond the Orthodoxy of Rule of Law and Justice Sector Reform

A Framework for Legal Empowerment and Innovation through the Convention on the Rights of Persons with Disabilities

JANET E. LORD, DEEPTI SAMANT RAJA, AND PETER BLANCK

The Convention on the Rights of Persons with Disabilities (CRPD),[1] the first legally binding international human rights treaty to address the rights and fundamental freedoms of one billion persons, provides a framework for legal empowerment and innovation that challenges traditional conceptualizations of justice-oriented development intervention. The CRPD implicitly renounces the orthodox view that top-down justice sector and rule of law initiatives should be the primary target of law and development efforts. Although the CRPD does not discount—in fact, it explicitly requires—the reform of legal systems, justice sectors, and institutions in meeting its obligations, it goes well beyond the traditional focus on development donors to embrace an empowerment model that implicates nonformal and decentralized justice and administrative systems and processes, local communities in development, and the duties of private as well as public actors in fostering inclusion. The legal empowerment framework set forth in the CRPD has significant implications not only for bridging rights and development in the context of disability but also more broadly for other marginalized groups living in poverty.

The UN General Assembly adopted the CRPD, along with its Optional Protocol,[2] by general consensus and the instruments were opened for signature by states parties on March 30, 2007.[3] It attained the requisite 20

This research was funded in part by grants to Blanck from the U.S. Department of Education, the National Institute on Disability and Rehabilitation Research (NIDRR), and Syracuse University; for details *see* http://bbi.syr.edu. This chapter is adapted from presentations made at the session "Persons with Disabilities: Innovation and Empowerment through the Convention on the Rights of Persons with Disabilities," World Bank Law, Justice and Development Week, Washington, D.C., 2011. The authors wish to thank participants in the panel session for their inputs. The authors wish to acknowledge and thank Jesse Feitel, Max Smith, and Josh Tumen for assisting with background research for this chapter.

1 Convention on the Rights of Persons with Disabilities, GA Res. 61/106, UN Doc. A/RES/61/106 (Dec. 13, 2006) (hereinafter, CRPD).

2 Optional Protocol to the Convention on the Rights of Persons with Disabilities, GA Res. 61/106, Annex II, UN Doc. A/RES/61/106 (Jan. 24, 2007) (hereinafter, Optional Protocol).

3 Updated information on signatures and ratifications is available at http://www.un.org/esa/socdev/enable/rights/humanrights.htm (accessed Jul. 25, 2012).

ratifications in short order, triggering its entry into force on May 3, 2008.[4] The impetus for drafting the treaty was the exclusion of an estimated 1 billion persons with disabilities from their communities, where they are routinely denied access to education, employment, health care services, and basic needs.[5] More often than not, persons with disabilities live in poverty and experience lower levels of education and income compared to the general population.[6] Research indicates that in all countries, disability prevalence rates are significantly higher among groups with lower economic status, underscoring the reinforcing relationship between poverty and disability.[7]

Prior to the adoption of the CRPD, no international instrument comprehensively addressed the multitude of barriers experienced by persons with disabilities, and only a handful of states had well-developed disability rights law and policy frameworks.[8] Where states did have disability-related legislation, often such laws explicitly introduced disability discrimination, for example, denying persons with disabilities the right to vote, to obtain an education, to serve as a juror, to open a bank account, to own property, or to work in certain sectors. In other instances, provisions relating to disability evoked welfare-oriented as opposed to comprehensive human rights protection. Although the human rights of persons with disabilities were implicitly addressed within the framework of general human rights law, and were to some extent reflected in several disability-specific nonbinding initiatives, this framework was insufficient to advance disability human rights and provide an impetus for change at the state level.[9]

---

4 For more on the rights of persons with disabilities generally, *see Human Rights and Persons with Disabilities*, www.un.org/esa/socdev/enable/rights/humanrights.htm (accessed Jul. 24, 2012). For a comprehensive overview of the CRPD, *see* Rosemary Kayess & Phillip French, *Out of Darkness into Light? Introducing the Convention on the Rights of Persons with Disabilities*, 8(1) Human Rights L. Rev. 1–34 (2008); M. A. Stein & J. E. Lord, *Future Prospects for the United Nations Convention on the Rights of Persons with Disabilities*, in *The UN Convention on the Rights of Person with Disabilities: European and Scandinavian Perspectives* (O. M. Arnardóttir & G. Quinn ed., Martinus Nijhoff 2008).

5 *See* World Health Organization and World Bank, *World Report on Disability* 29 (2011), available at http://www.who.int/disabilities/world_report/2011/report/en/ (accessed Jul. 25, 2012).

6 *Id.*, at 39.

7 Daniel Mont, *Measuring Disability Prevalence*, SP Discussion Paper No. 0706 (Disability & Development Team, HDNSP, World Bank, Mar. 2007), available at http://siteresources.worldbank.org/DISABILITY/Resources/Data/MontPrevalence.pdf. *See* also Sophie Mitra, Aleksandra Posarac, Brandon Vick, *Disability and Poverty in Developing Countries: A Multidimensional Study* World Development (Jul. 27, 2012).

8 *See* Gerard Quinn, *Resisting the "Temptation of Elegance": Can the Convention on the Rights of Persons with Disabilities Socialise States in Rights Behaviour?* in *The UN Convention on the Rights of Persons with Disabilities: European and Scandinavian Perspectives* 215, 224–29 (1st ed., O. M. Arnardóttir & G. Quinn ed., Martinus Nijhoff 2009).

9 For a review of the need for further development of domestic disability law frameworks, *see* Theresia Degener & Gerard Quinn, *A Survey of International, Comparative and Regional Disability Law Reform, Disability Rights Law and Policy: International and National Perspectives* 3, 25-45 (Mary Lou Breslin & Sylvia Yee ed., Disability Rights Education and Defense Fund 2002), available at http://www.dredf.org/international/degener_quinn.html (accessed Jul. 24, 2012).

The CRPD fills this gap insofar as it provides a road map for the development and reform of domestic disability law and policy in alignment with international human rights principles, but also in its creation of mechanisms and duties to foster the empowerment of disability advocates and their representative organizations. In obligating states parties to pursue specific national-level implementation measures to give full effect to its provisions, the CRPD advances the kind of broad-based approach to human rights advocacy contemplated in the legal empowerment literature.[10] Moreover, recognition of the link between poverty and disability in the CRPD provides added support for legal empowerment approaches in the context of disability.[11] In sum, the CRPD calls for innovation to advance domestic disability advocacy to support the human rights and fundamental freedoms of the globe's "largest minority."[12]

CRPD: Structure and Overall Content

The CRPD comprises 25 preambular paragraphs and 50 operative articles that set out the historical progression of international disability rights and highlight issues of particular import.[13] It has an introductory set of provisions outlining its purpose (Article 1), key definitions (Article 2), and several general (cross-cutting) articles that are to be interpreted and applied across all articles of the treaty text (Articles 3–9).[14] The CRPD is the first international human rights treaty to prohibit discrimination on the basis of disability and, significantly, to require the provision of reasonable accommodation in order to meet its nondiscrimination and equality requirement. It has a novel provision (Article 9, Accessibility) detailing state obligations in the area of accessibility that is broadly defined and is driving innovation in numerous spheres and affects not only states but private actors as well. The CRPD enumerates specific substantive civil, political, economic, social, and cultural rights (Articles 10–30). It establishes a system of monitoring and implementation (Articles 31–40), and it includes provisions that govern the operation of the CRPD (Articles 41–50).

The general requirements set forth in Article 4 make clear the need to ground CRPD obligations in national law, policy, and programming in consultation with persons with disabilities. Thus, Article 4 requires states parties to consult with and involve persons with disabilities in developing and implementing legislation and policies and in decision-making processes, including development planning. In this sense, the CRPD underscores the need to engage with stakeholders and their representative organizations, reflecting a

---

10 *See* Stephen Golub & Kim McQuay, *Legal Empowerment: Advancing Good Governance and Poverty Reduction*, in *Law and Policy Reform at the Asian Development Bank* (ADB 2001); Anna Palacio, *Legal Empowerment of the Poor: An Action Agenda for the World Bank* (ARD 2006).

11 *World Report on Disability*, *supra* note 5, at 39.

12 *Id.*, at 29.

13 CRPD, *supra* note 1.

14 The CRPD articles are available at http://www.un.org/disabilities/default.asp?id=259 (accessed Jul. 25, 2012).

shift toward legal empowerment approaches, as opposed to only stand-alone, top-down rule of law interventions. Top-down initiatives are needed and are required by the CRPD—including training of lawyers and judiciaries—but these interventions rest within the context of a legal empowerment, access to justice approach.

The CRPD lays out a framework for national-level monitoring that includes cross-governmental coordination, independent monitoring (inferred to be performed by a national human rights institution, or NHRI), and stakeholder participation (Article 33). A Committee on the Rights of Persons with Disabilities—the CRPD's treaty-monitoring body—is tasked with monitoring implementation by states parties through its oversight of the mandatory reporting requirement and the issuance of general recommendations for the state party concerned.[15] The Optional Protocol to the CRPD,[16] consisting of 18 articles, gives the committee competence to examine individual complaints with regard to alleged CRPD violations by parties to the protocol. It allows states parties to opt into participation in individual and group communications procedures, as well as an inquiry procedure, all of which are overseen by the committee.[17] These mechanisms are important vehicles for empowering local disabled people's organizations (DPOs) to bring individual violations and systemic abuses to the attention of the committee for its review.

An innovative mechanism that can facilitate disability advocacy is the establishment of a periodic meeting of a Conference of States Parties (COSP), as set forth under Article 40 of the CRPD. Disability advocates and their representative organizations are using the COSP in ways that reflect creative approaches to legal empowerment.[18]

The CRPD stands out among the core human rights conventions in affirming the role and impact of international cooperation in promoting the implementation of progressive disability reforms and in establishing a framework to foster international cooperation and inclusive development programming. Through Article 32, the CRPD is the first human rights convention to detail the kinds of measures states parties can take to facilitate the implementation of the convention.[19] Article 32 promotes the need to ensure that international

---

15 For an overview of the development, mandate, and future potential of the CRPD committee, see M. A. Stein & J. E. Lord, *Monitoring the Committee on the Rights of Persons with Disabilities: Innovations, Lost Opportunities, and Future Potential*, 31 Hum. Rights Q. 689 (2010).

16 Convention on the Rights of Persons with Disabilities, Optional Protocol, United Nations, available at http://www.un.org/disabilities/default.asp?id=311 (accessed Jul. 25, 2012).

17 The committee undertook consideration of an individual communication in which it found a violation of CRPD rights. See Committee on the Rights of Persons with Disabilities, *HM v. Sweden, Communication No. 3/2011*, Views adopted by the committee at its seventh session (Apr. 16–27, 2012), available at http://www.ohchr.org/EN/HRBodies/CRPD/Pages/Jurisprudence.aspx.

18 *See* UN Enable, *Conference of States Parties*, available at http://www.un.org/disabilities/default.asp?id=1535 (accessed Jul. 25, 2012).

19 Katherine Guernsey, Marco Nicoli, & Alberto Ninio, *Convention on the Rights of Persons with*

cooperation initiatives, including development programs, are accessible and inclusive of people with disabilities.[20] Thus, it gives credence to the importance of mainstreaming disability in development to achieve not only the goals and objectives of this convention but also goals for poverty reduction and empowerment within the development community as a whole.[21] States are encouraged to support capacity building and the exchange of knowledge and best practices, strengthen research collaborations and access to scientific knowledge, and offer technical and economic assistance to help meet a state's obligations under the convention.[22] This provision may extend CRPD standards, via development programming, to effect change in discrete contexts such as electoral law reform and practice, community-based rehabilitation, and DPO capacity building.

The convention sets forth general obligations familiar to human rights treaties—prompting national law reform and domestic incorporation of its provisions. It provides a framework for national-level disability rights advocacy and action. Significantly, the convention draws together a diverse set of obligations that, when surveyed, constitute a map of advocacy and empowerment opportunities at the local, national, and international level. In so doing, the CRPD plots a course for a human rights practice that goes beyond traditional justice sector and rule of law interventions and includes legal empowerment and innovation that is locally driven, community focused, and civil society oriented.[23]

The CRPD as a Framework for Empowerment and Innovation: Beyond Rule of Law and Justice Sector Orthodoxy

The CRPD evokes a model of disability rights realization reflective of the literature on legal empowerment. This is specifically reflected in the following articles:

- Articles 4 and 8 specify that raising disability rights awareness is a general obligation requiring strategies aimed at dismantling barriers posed by stigma and discrimination, making the justice system more accessible.
- Article 4 proposes that law is a tool for strengthening legal rights through disability legal reform and legal framework development in terms of both substance and process.

Disabilities: Its Implementation and Relevance for the World Bank, SP Discussion Paper No. 0712 (World Bank 2007).

20 CRPD, *supra* note 1.

21 UN Enable, *The Millennium Development Goals (MDGs) and Disability*, available at http://www.un.org/disabilities/default.asp?id=1470 (accessed Jul. 25, 2012).

22 CRPD, *supra* note 1.

23 For a discussion of the limitations of orthodox justice sector and rule of law interventions, *see* Golub & McQuay, *supra* note 10.

- Articles 13, 28, and 32 facilitate disability rights implementation through strategies of inclusion, including in justice sector institutional capacity building.
- Articles 16, 33, and 34–40 provide strategies for strengthening the monitoring and enforcement of disability rights.

Although countries have enthusiastically supported, ratified, and signed the CRPD,[24] many face challenges in implementing the convention due to disempowering social contexts for persons with disabilities and underdeveloped legal systems. This reality raises a variety of issues, among them the differentiation between developed and developing countries in capacities for implementation and the varied perspectives on the nature and definition of disability.

The CRPD does not provide a concrete definition of disability but states that "persons with disabilities include those who have long-term physical, mental, intellectual or sensory impairments which in interaction with various barriers may hinder their full and effective participation in society on an equal basis with others."[25] This conceptualization demands a shift in how policymakers think about disability. For example, disability laws in some countries define disability with a finite list of observable impairments, ignoring hidden disabilities that arise from chronic or mental illness, learning and cognitive difficulty, and accident, and disregarding environmental and interactional issues completely.[26]

Prior to the adoption of the CRPD, many disability laws and policies operated mainly from the perspective of medical and welfare perspectives on disability, in which a person with a disability is presumed to be incapable of equal participation in society.[27] This conception leads to a dependence on welfare policies and charity programs to address the "needs" of persons with disabilities and their families.[28] Many of the concepts set forth in the CRPD may seem foreign to policymakers and at times may be at odds with the legislative approaches used in some countries. Thus, states parties need to bring about significant law and policy reform and development to align with the shift required by the CRPD[29]—presenting challenges, but also creating opportunities for significant innovation.

---

24 For an updated list of ratifications and signatories, see http://www.un.org/disabilities/countries.asp?id=166 (accessed Jul. 25, 2012).

25 CRDP, Article 1, *supra* note 1.

26 *See*, for example, the case of India in Andrew Byrnes, *Disability Discrimination Law and the Asian and Pacific Region* (Paper 3), in *Resources on Harmonization of National Legislation with the Convention on the Rights of Persons with Disabilities in Asia and the Pacific*, available at http://www.unescap.org/sdd/issues/disability/crpd/files/Paper-III-Andrew-20110121.pdf.

27 Kayess & French, *supra* note 4.

28 *Id.*

29 Arlene Kanter, *The Promise and Challenge of the United Nations Convention on the Rights of Persons with Disabilities*, 34 Syracuse J. Intl. L. & Com. 287 (2007).

The provisions and motivations under Article 32, which covers international cooperation, offer the potential to assist states parties struggling with challenges in crafting required innovations and facilitating access to resources to aid in implementation. Promoting the exchange of technical knowledge and best practices while providing resources for capacity building will aid government workers and practitioners at all levels to usher in improvements and reforms to policies, programs, and practices. Addressing disability in international aid and development funding and support will help low- and middle-income states parties to provide far-reaching and inclusive programs that meet their goals and obligations under the CRPD.

The following sections discuss the general schema of legal empowerment and innovation set forth in the CRPD and provide illustrations of how CRPD obligations are pursued in different ways to effect change. These include raising awareness of disability rights; strengthening disability rights; facilitating disability rights; and improving monitoring and enforcement of disability rights.

Raising Awareness of Disability Rights

The various barriers faced by persons with disabilities in developing countries combine to restrict their access to information and awareness of their rights, a situation also faced by persons living in poverty and other disadvantaged groups. As emphasized in the *World Report on Disability*, persons with disabilities are likely to live in poverty and are very often restricted in their access to education, employment, transportation, and health care and often live in isolation from the wider community.[30] The social determinants of legal empowerment, therefore, are severely restricted for persons with disabilities. The need for awareness-building initiatives, including legal literacy programs, participatory human rights education tied to action at the local level, legal aid bureaus, and inclusive development programming aiming to integrate persons with disabilities into mainstream programming (such as health, economic development, democracy and governance, and education), are important and implicit in the CRPD framework.

The CRPD recognizes in Article 8 (awareness raising) that a precondition to legal empowerment is combating the stigma that seeds discrimination. In so doing, the CRPD signals the central role that legal empowerment plays in addressing the situation of persons with disabilities (and indeed any historically marginalized group). Consistent with legal empowerment models, awareness raising is a fundamental precondition of disability rights realization and comprises both understanding of legal rights and an appreciation of how to claim those rights through action.[31] CRPD provisions that require public consultation as well as accessibility measures in the contexts of law and policy making,

30 *World Report on Disability*, *supra* note 5, at 39.

31 Golub & McQuay, *supra* note 10, at 7.

training health professionals in disability rights awareness, and the general obligation to promote the training of professionals and staff working with persons with disabilities in the CRPD rights framework are important facilitators of rights awareness and are central to legal empowerment.[32]

There are numerous examples of innovative disability rights awareness-raising initiatives, many of which are integrated into development programming, as opposed to implementation limited to one-off training events. In Liberia, during the historic 2004 elections in which the first woman African head of state was elected, DPOs used the electoral process to raise the voice and visibility of Liberians with disabilities. At the time, Liberian DPOs were aware of the CRPD drafting process and requested, as part of their election work, information about international standards on disability to help them draft a national disability law. Facilitated through the international election administration organization, the International Foundation for Electoral Systems and BlueLaw International LLP, the project's goal was to foster DPO cooperation through the creation of a coalition that affected all phases of the electoral process—voter education and registration, polling, electoral observation and monitoring, and postelection assessment.[33]

The methodology was to position members of the Liberian disability community as leaders and experts and to conduct participatory human rights education in raising awareness and understanding about election access on the part of election commissioners.[34] A poignant illustration of successful advocacy occurred during a training of 50 election officials from the Liberian National Election Commission. During the workshop, disability advocates, including persons with various types of disabilities, simulated vote casting at a polling station to illustrate the numerous barriers that they had experienced in previous elections.[35] This method used humor that was effective, and it imparted serious messages of discrimination and exclusion based on stereotyping and generalized lack of knowledge. Drawing on their individual experiences, members of the group demonstrated the barriers that can stand in the way of access and participation for a voter with disabilities, ranging from physical and communication barriers experienced by persons with physical and sensory disabilities to barriers rooted in ignorance and stigma.

---

32 CRPD, *supra* note 1, at Article 4.

33 Janet E. Lord & Michael A. Stein, *Participation in International Agreements as Transformative Social Change: The UN Convention on the Rights of Persons with Disabilities*, in *Making Rights Real* (Jody Heymann ed., Cambridge U. Press 2012).

34 *Id.*

35 For more on using participatory human rights education to forward disability rights, *see* Janet E. Lord and Nancy Flowers, *Human Rights Education and Grassroots Peace Building*, in *Human Rights and Conflict: New Actors, Strategies and Ethical Dilemmas* (Julie A. Mertus & Jeff Helsing ed., United States Institute of Peace 2006).

Strengthening Disability Rights

To strengthen disability law frameworks so they are more in line with international standards on disability rights, the substance as well as the process of the law must be reformed. Substantive and procedural reforms can create accessible and consumer-oriented dispute-settlement procedures. These range from legal claims brought before courts and human rights tribunals to electoral complaints mechanisms to complaints procedures of national human rights institutions. Procedural reforms are a core part of enhancing access to justice for marginalized groups, including enhancing the accessibility of notice requirements, the right to be heard, access to information rights, and the provision of reasonable accommodations.

Legislative Reform to Modify Legal Frameworks and Stimulate Legal Empowerment

Although legislation and policies by themselves do not assure full implementation of the CRPD, they are a necessary pillar of the effort to facilitate change. Similar to states parties to other core human rights conventions, states parties to the CRPD are required to adopt specific legislation that prohibits discrimination in all spheres.[36] Such laws should aim at eliminating barriers to access that constitute both formal and substantive discrimination, attribute obligations to public and private actors, and introduce measures to bring about equitable access to all rights. Although the CRPD is relatively new, it has already promoted significant law and policy shifts. This work is being undertaken at various levels, including in constitutional development and reform, national-level law reform and development, and targeted law reforms in discrete contexts.

For some countries, antidiscrimination legislation will require a change in the overall approach toward tackling inequities. For example, Japan does not have comprehensive antidiscrimination laws and policies, and the concept of nondiscrimination in regard to disability is not considered a part of the broader civil and human rights initiative.[37] With its ratification of the CRPD, Japan is developing disability discrimination law and policy for the first time.[38] States parties should consider using incentives to encourage public and private actors to change their attitudes and behavior in relation to individuals and groups facing systemic discrimination, or penalize them in case of noncompliance. The identification and elimination of barriers will frequently require devoting greater resources to issues of access. Particular attention must be given to ensuring that laws and policies are implemented in practice.

In Nepal, DPOs worked to ensure that the voices of persons with disabilities were heard during the drafting of a new constitution. The Kathmandu

---

36 CRPD, *supra* note 1, at Article 4.

37 J. Nakagawa & P. Blanck, *Future of Disability Law in Japan: Employment and Accommodation*, 33(1) Loy. L.A. Intl. & Comp. L. Rev. 173 (2010).

38 *Id.*

Center for Independent Living in Nepal held workshops that were strategically designed by the organizers to build linkages among DPOs, civil society organizations, and international actors—such as the United Nations—in the constitution-drafting process. Although few DPOs in the country had previously focused on law and policy advocacy, one objective of the constitution-drafting participation was to help build the capacity of DPOs to engage actively in law and policy reform and development and to engage with international civil society partners to increase understanding of international standards on disability.[39]

In other countries, notably South Africa, Uganda, Zambia, and Thailand,[40] DPOs have likewise used constitution-building processes to leverage disability rights. Ecuador issued a presidential executive decree in 2007 to promote the development of disability programs across all sectors and introduced a chapter on disability in its 2008 constitution.[41] Article 54 of Kenya's 2010 constitution "seeks to minimize barriers to equalization of opportunities in all aspects of social-cultural, economic and political life" for persons with disabilities.[42] In Egypt, efforts are under way to adopt a national disability law, situate disability within the new constitutional framework, and revise the election law in conformity with the CRPD. Enhancing political participation is critical in postconflict and transitioning countries.

Legal Empowerment to Support the Reform of Policies, Plans, and Strategies

Since the adoption of the CRPD, countries have started developing disability action plans where none existed previously, as well as incorporating disability into their broader national action plans. Thailand developed the National Plan for Persons with Disabilities' Quality of Life Development Plan 2007–11 to issue guidelines for an integrated approach to disability and development programs in the country.[43] States parties should ensure that strategies, policies, and plans of action are in place and implemented in order to address barriers to access. Economic policies, such as budgetary allocations and measures to stimulate economic growth, should take into account the need to guarantee the effective enjoyment of all CRPD rights. Public and private institutions should be required to develop plans of action to address nondiscrimination,

---

39 Lord & Stein, *supra* note 33.

40 The Thai constitution of 2007 includes "anti-discrimination provisions and guarantees accessibility to social welfare and services for persons with disabilities." For legislative developments as reported to the CRPD committee, *see* United Nations, *Compilation of Legislative Measures Undertaken in the Implementation of the Convention on the Rights of Persons with Disabilities: 2011 Update* (CRPD/CSP/2011/CRP.5), available at http://www.un.org/disabilities/documents/COP/crpd_csp_2011_crp.5.doc (accessed May 24, 2012).

41 *Id.*

42 *Id.*

43 *Id.* For a more extensive discussion of law and policy within the context of HIV and disability, see Janet E. Lord, *HIV/AIDS, Disability and Discrimination: A Thematic Guide on Inclusive Law, Policy and Programming* (One Billion Strong, Washington, D.C. 2012).

and states should conduct human rights education and training programs for public officials and make such training available to judges and candidates for judicial appointments.

Projects aimed at building human rights knowledge and advocacy techniques are often pursued in a vacuum, effectively disconnected from follow-up action plans. For instance, some efforts to train local DPOs regarding the CRPD have been provided without enabling those groups to exercise their newly acquired capabilities. Consequently, although DPOs have gained knowledge, they remain unsure how to appropriately utilize it. The Harvard Law School Project on Disability, in cooperation with BlueLaw International and American Institutes for Research, worked with a coalition of DPOs in Zambia. The objectives were to learn more about the CRPD with a specific aim to make public health services, including HIV/AIDS education, be disability inclusive.[44] One of the strategies was the placement of a disability advocate on the team implementing a large-scale HIV program involving a large international organization and a number of local organizations. The provision of disability expertise in the form of a dedicated staff member and the provision of training to a network of disability advocates engaged in both disability policy and HIV education at the community level increased the capacity of DPOs and enabled them to achieve better access to health care, the CRPD goal they identified as a priority.

Facilitating Disability Rights

Measures in the CRPD aim to ensure the facilitation of the rights set forth in the treaty. The CRPD is a framework in which disability rights may be exercised through a variety of measures that identify and then dismantle the barriers that stand in the way of the legal empowerment of persons with disabilities. Such facilitation efforts include the accessibility measures identified in Article 9, the measures of reasonable accommodation and positive measures in Article 5, institutional and individual capacity building, and means to facilitate access to the mechanisms of justice.

Accessibility in Virtual Spaces

The CRPD has helped to bridge another major frontier in disability empowerment and inclusion in the mainstream—ensuring that accessibility is not limited to the physical realm alone but extends to virtual spaces as well. Information and communication technologies (ICTs) are a major driver in social and professional interchange in today's world and permeate almost all transactions and interactions in society. Today, ICT-enabled services and resources are central features of many socioeconomic development initiatives, including promoting access to banking, health care, education, income

---

44 For a brief discussion of this project, *see* http://www.bluelawinternational.com (accessed Jul. 24, 2012).

generation, disaster response and management, and social networking and civic participation.[45] This raises the stakes in ensuring that ICTs are accessible to people with disabilities for two reasons: one, ICT-enabled development can significantly help to level the playing field for people with disabilities;[46] and two, the lack of accessibility will add to their exclusion from major development programs, leading to further marginalization.[47]

The CRPD addresses accessible ICTs and assistive technologies (AT) throughout, most specifically in Articles 9, 21, and 26, emphasizing the critical role these technologies play in realizing all rights, such as access to justice, freedom of expression, and rights to political participation, education, health rehabilitation, and employment.[48] However, Web accessibility and the availability of accessible ICTs remain low despite the wide ratification of the CRPD. The Global Initiative for Inclusive ICTs (G3ict) issued the CRPD Progress Report on ICT Accessibility 2010 based on a survey of 33 countries. This report found that

- Only 58 percent of the countries studied included ICT in accessibility definitions in laws or regulations.
- Only 36 percent had laws, policies, or programs to define public procurement rules for accessible ICTs.
- Sixty one percent enabled persons with disabilities to input information in accessible and usable formats to access services offered online.
- Sixty seven percent had laws, policies, or programs that ensure that government communications using ICTs are provided in accessible and alternative formats (for example, sign language or Braille).

The pervasiveness of ICTs in most socioeconomic domains requires states parties to develop laws and policies to support a comprehensive, coordinated, and successful approach to promoting ICT accessibility for all. Peter Blanck and colleagues at the Burton Blatt Institute at Syracuse University have worked closely with the European Union (EU) to assess the adequacy of laws and policies to ensure broad ICT accessibility. The lessons learned through this work resonate across countries.

---

45 Deepti Samant, Rebecca Matter, & Mark Harniss, *Realizing the Potential of Accessible ICTs in Developing Countries*, in *Disability & Rehabilitation: Assistive Technology* (Informa Healthcare 2012, doi:10.3109/17483107.2012.669022, available at http://informahealthcare.com/doi/pdfplus/10.3109/17483107.2012.669022) also forthcoming in print.

46 *Id.*

47 Peter Blanck, *Towards a Right under the ADA to Web Access for People with Cognitive Disabilities* (Coleman Institute for Cognitive Disabilities 2012), available at http://www.colemaninstitute.org/images/documents/research_development/2012CTowardsARightUnderTheADA.pdf; M. V. Vicente & A. J. Lopez, *A Multidimensional Analysis of the Disability Digital Divide: Some Evidence for Internet Use*, 26(1) The Information Society 48–64 (2010).

48 CRPD (2006), available at http://www.un.org/disabilities/default.asp?navid=13&pid=150 (accessed Jul. 24, 2012).

Laws, policies, and regulations must address accessibility in the entire accessibility supply chain, including "content production, content transmission, and content rendering."[49] Thus, policies must cover the producers and developers as well as the deployers of technology (that is, service providers such as banks).[50] Different countries have different approaches for such an undertaking. For example, in the United States different pieces of legislation covering different products, agencies, and sectors that utilize ICT-based services—a piecemeal approach—coexist with broad-sweeping legislation such as the Americans with Disabilities Act.[51] Depending on the political climate and national interest, both approaches may need to be used. Additionally, states parties should promote collaboration and agreement among the different stakeholders such as consumers, service providers, manufacturers, and law enforcement to create broad support for institutional drive due to the differing interests of and impacts on each stakeholder group.[52] Issues such as ICT accessibility encompass the need for top-down (impose direct obligations on the supply side) as well as bottom-up (rights for users/consumers) types of legislation.[53] Some states will need to support public and private mechanisms for harmonization toward uniformity of law.

Another issue that is increasingly a challenge for law and policymakers is that of convergence—the "erosion of boundaries" between different types of previously separate ICT products and services such as the transmission of television content delivered over the Internet.[54] The expansion of such services may fall in the gray areas not clearly covered by accessibility legislation or regulation. As discussed by Cullen et al.:

> Telephony over the Internet often falls outside the scope of legislation dealing with accessibility of voice telephony and there is a lack of clarity as to whether interactive TV is a broadcast or a telecommunications service, or neither of these but a new class of service from an e-Accessibility regulatory point of view.[55]

Finally, it is important to address the issue of the existence and transferability of standards and regulations for ICT products and services across

---

49 Kevin Cullen et al., *Accessibility of ICT Products and Services to Disabled and Older People: Towards a Framework for Further Development of EU Legislation or Other Co-ordination Measures on eAccessibility* (European Commission 2008).

50 *Id.*

51 William N. Myhill, *Law & Policy Challenges for Achieving an Accessible eSociety: Lessons from the United States*, in *European Yearbook on Disability Law* vol. 2 (L. Waddington & G. Quinn ed., Intersentia 2010).

52 Samant, Matter, & Harniss *supra* note 45.

53 Cullen et al., *supra* note 49.

54 Rajendra Singh & Siddhartha Raja, *Convergence in Information and Communication Technology: Strategic and Regulatory Considerations* (World Bank 2010), available at http://publications.worldbank.org/index.php?main_page=product_info&cPath=0&products_id=23785 (accessed Jul. 25, 2012).

55 Cullen et al., *supra* note 49, at 65.

national boundaries. The lack of accessibility standards and policies across regions can create significant challenges for individuals with disabilities in an increasingly global society and impede progress toward the fulfillment of the CRPD. The challenge of CRPD implementation in the context of virtual spaces raises numerous issues pertaining to developing-country needs and underdeveloped capacity.

Common but Differentiated Obligations between Developed and Developing States?

The notion that international obligations may introduce flexibility and differential treatment for rich and poor countries is a pragmatic response to real disparities in technical and economic capacities to comply fully with treaty standards. Bodansky's typology of treaty design features that affect obligatory stringency in the international environmental realm is instructive in this regard; it includes flexible or contextual commitments; differential standards; and reservations.[56] Although it may be anathema to suggest that human rights obligations are somehow contingent or differential on the basis of resources, there are indeed concepts that do, in essence, render obligations either less stringent in the sense of temporality (that is, progressive realization in relation to economic, social, and cultural rights)[57] or more flexible in the sense of providing states with a margin of appreciation for the operationalization of a requirement to suit country contexts or in allowing reservations, declarations, and understandings.[58]

Thus, it is possible to speak in terms of "common but differentiated responsibilities" in the CRPD.[59] However, legal, institutional, and economic underdevelopment is not an escape hatch for avoiding compliance. The CRPD goes further than any other human rights convention in establishing a framework for international cooperation that accommodates divergent levels of economic development and unequal capacities to address disability rights in a comprehensive manner.[60] Article 32 represents one model for making international human rights law responsive to such challenges and to foster substantive disability rights equality among states.[61]

---

56 D. Bodansky, *The Art and Craft of International Environmental Law* (President and Fellows of Harvard College 2010).

57 CRPD, *supra* note 1, at Article 4(2).

58 *Id.*, at Article 46.

59 C. Stone, *Common but Differentiated Responsibilities in International Law*, 98 Am. J. Intl. L. 276–301 (2004).

60 Philippe Cullet, *Differential Treatment in International Law: Towards a New Paradigm of Interstate Relations*, 10 European J. Intl. L. 549–82 (1999). For a helpful discussion of implementation challenges in another context, *see* G. Shaffer, *The Challenges of WTO Law: Strategies for Developing Country Adaptation*, 5(2) World Trade Rev. 177–98 (2006).

61 CRPD, *supra* note 1, at Article 32.

Reasonable Accommodation as a Primary Means of Rights Facilitation

One of the most important facilitators of the rights recognized in the CRPD is the concept of required reasonable accommodation. The failure to provide reasonable accommodation to an individual with a disability, whether to facilitate access to education, work, health care, cultural activities, or other spheres of life, constitutes discrimination.

Reasonable accommodation is being implemented at the domestic level in numerous ways. One example of using the tools of legal empowerment to equip persons with disabilities and employers to better understand how to operationalize reasonable accommodation is the Job Accommodation Network, an initiative of the Office of Disability Employment Policy in the US Department of Labor. The Job Accommodation Network is a model for the provision of free, expert, and confidential guidance on workplace accommodations and disability employment issues.[62] The service helps to identify practical solutions that benefit employers in meeting their reasonable accommodations duties and employees in negotiating job accommodations. The initiative focuses on workable solutions according to which legal requirements are satisfied within a framework that assists the employer and the employee in understanding legal requirements and measures that may be undertaken to meet them. This approach and similar initiatives are being operationalized as countries implement the obligations set forth in the CRPD. Other applications of reasonable accommodation under development pertain to the obligations set forth in Article 12 to facilitate empowered decision making. Law reform initiatives in Ireland and South Africa, for example, are putting into place models that will reasonably accommodate individuals with disabilities in decision making about all aspects of life, including medical and rehabilitation issues, financial and property matters, and political participation.[63]

Improving Monitoring and Enforcement of Disability Rights

National legislation, strategies, policies, and plans should provide for mechanisms and institutions that effectively address the individual and the structural nature of the harm caused by disability discrimination and inequality of access to rights in all fields covered by the CRPD. Institutions dealing with allegations of disability discrimination customarily include courts and tribunals, administrative authorities, national human rights institutions, and ombudspersons. These institutions should be accessible to all persons with disabilities without discrimination and consistent with principles of accessibility.

---

62 *See* Job Accommodation Network, http://askjan.org/ (accessed Jul. 24, 2012).

63 For a discussion of the Irish initiative, *see Amnesty International Ireland, Mental Health Act 2001: A Review, Summary Paper* (undated). For a review of the South African effort to draft legislation on supported decision making, *see* South African Law Reform Commission, *Current Investigations, Progress Report,* available at http://www.justice.gov.za/salrc/progress.htm.

Institutions should be empowered to provide effective remedies, such as compensation, reparation, restitution, rehabilitation, guarantees of nonrepetition, and public apologies, and states parties should ensure that these measures are effectively implemented.

Improving Access to Dispute-Settlement Mechanisms

The drafters of the CRPD understood the barriers that exist for persons with disabilities in seeking access to justice for the vindication of their rights. Some of these barriers parallel those that all marginalized groups experience and that contribute toward disempowerment, while others are more specific to disability. There is an overall lack of awareness or unintended insensitivity to disability-related concerns and needs among court personnel, including inflexible court policies, practices, and procedures and inaccessible public information about courts and court services.

Given recognition that access to justice programs for marginalized groups is essential and must be pursued in conjunction with top-down justice sector reform strategies, there are numerous possibilities for the use of existing platforms to enhance disability inclusion. In Afghanistan, Global Rights partnered with local women's organizations and several universities to establish legal assistance bureaus in order to enhance women's access to family courts and justice.[64] Improving the accessibility of these courts to women, persons with disabilities, and other marginalized groups is essential to create well-trodden pathways for the enforcement of legal rights. DPOs are working to ensure that such community-based legal services are accessible to persons with disabilities. This is consistent with measures set forth in Article 13 of the CRPD.

Eliminating Barriers through Litigation

Legal empowerment approaches stress not only top-down training of judges and lawyers but also how to work within civil society to build capacity to engage in a range of activities that enhance and facilitate access to justice. Strategic litigation at the local level and through regional as well as international human rights mechanisms is an effective tool for change provided it is designed and implemented by local organizations and not driven by ill-informed outsiders. Experience with existing domestic disability laws and existing regional systems discloses the possibilities for change.

Antidiscrimination legislation with remedial measures is a tool that can help ensure equality and fair treatment in the face of continuing stigma and negative attitudes toward people with disabilities. In the United States, the Americans with Disabilities Act (ADA)[65] has significantly affected the ability of persons with disabilities to combat stigma and discrimination in the work-

---

64 *See* Global Rights, Afghanistan, http://www.globalrights.org/site/PageServer?pagename=www_asia_afghanistan (accessed Jul. 25, 2012).

65 *See,* generally, P. Blanck et al., *Disability Rights Law and Policy: Casebook* (Thomson/West 2009).

place. Consider the case of Don Perkl, an individual with intellectual disability, who was fired from Chuck E. Cheese, a pizza restaurant, because of his disability.[66] Despite support from his supervisor and his coworkers, he was fired by a regional manager who believed that Perkl was threatening to the restaurant patrons due to his disability and unfit for the job. A jury disagreed, awarding Perkl back pay, legal fees, and compensatory damages under the ADA, as well as US$13 million in punitive damages, to deliver a strong message.[67] Without the ADA for recourse, Perkl would have faced severe difficulty in challenging the regional manager for blatant disability-based discrimination.

Across the globe, lawyers are undertaking similar cases in areas of disability rights. This work, including development projects that aim to strengthen the ability of civil society and legal aid clinics to undertake legal empowerment work, must target the elimination of systemic disability discrimination and segregation that inhibit equitable access to all rights for persons with disabilities. The Harvard Law School Project on Disability, for example, has served as amici in a number of cases before the European Court of Human Rights, as well as the European Committee of Social Rights.[68]

Innovations in Monitoring: Disability Rights Budget Analysis

Standard rule of law approaches overemphasize legal interventions that not only are top-down and disconnected from the marginalized groups that legal frameworks are intended to serve but also privilege practices that emphasize court-focused action over other equally valid and in some instances more effective forms of interventions for marginalized groups. Legal empowerment approaches increasingly point to the efficacy of budgetary analysis as an important tool in bringing legal obligations to bear on government action.[69] In this regard, the CRPD sets up a framework that brings such approaches within its aperture.

The CRPD conceptualizes nondiscrimination and equality and encompasses a cross-cutting obligation that may be realized only through its application to specific substantive human rights, whether civil, political, economic, social, or cultural. It asserts a substantive equality approach that goes beyond formal equality and advances socially, economically, and historically marginalized groups.[70] Moreover, the CRPD is an affront to the discredited notion

---

66 *See* P. Blanck, *Americans with Disabilities and Their Civil Rights: Past, Present, and Future*, 66 U. Pitt. L. Rev. 687–719 (2006), for a discussion of this and other ADA cases in which Blanck was involved as an expert witness and legal counsel.

67 *Id.*

68 *See Alajos Kiss v. Hungary, App. No. 38832/06* (Eur. Ct. of Human Rights, May 20, 2010), paragraph 4.

69 *See* Gillian MacNaughton & Paul Hunt, *A Human Rights–Based Approach to Social Impact Assessment*, in *New Directions in Social Impact Assessment: Conceptual and Methodological Advances* 355, 360 (Frank Vanclay & Ana Maria Esteves ed., Edward Elgar 2012) (Budget analysis "reveals human rights problems and affords means to tackle them").

70 Janet E. Lord & Rebecca Brown, *The Role of Reasonable Accommodation in Securing Substantive*

that civil and political rights require little in the way of positive action and investment of resources by states in order to effect implementation.[71] The CRPD brings the human rights framework together in requiring reasonable accommodation through positive measures in all areas of life.[72]

The implications of this model for legal empowerment underscore the sophistication of the CRPD framework. In projecting the need for a multifaceted approach to implementation, the CRPD embraces the need for budget analysis to track the extent to which states parties undertake the measures required to realize all rights under the CRPD, even those subject to progressive realization. Disability rights budget analysis encompasses an approach according to which a state party's allocation of resources in a given area (for example, education, employment, or community living) is scrutinized and assessed.[73] Budget analysis can be used to identify the sufficiency of resource allocation in an attempt to secure the rights of a particularly disadvantaged group.[74] In this regard, the Limberg Principles on the Implementation of Economic, Social, and Cultural Rights[75] stress that statistical information and information on budgetary allocations and expenditures should be presented in such a way as to facilitate the assessment of compliance with economic, social, and cultural rights obligations.[76]

Equality for Persons with Disabilities: The UN Convention on the Rights of Persons with Disabilities, in *Critical Perspectives on Human Rights and Disability Law* 273 (Marcia Rioux, Lee Ann Basser, & Melinda Jones ed., Martinus Nijhoff 2011).

71 *See* Anna Lawson, *Disability and Equality Law in Britain: The Role of Reasonable Adjustment* (Hart 2008).

72 *See* Lord & Brown, *supra* note 70.

73 *See* Gillian MacNaughton, *Human Rights Frameworks, Strategies, and Tools for the Poverty Lawyer's Toolbox*, J. Hum. Rights Prac. 83, 95. *See* also Janet E. Lord & Michael Ashley Stein, *The Domestic Incorporation of Human Rights Law and the United Nations Convention on the Rights of Persons with Disabilities*, 83 Wash. L. Rev. 449, 459 (2008) (asserting that budget analysis in the disability rights context is an "essential component" of disability rights advocacy work).

74 S. Farrior, *Human Rights Advocacy on Gender Issues: Challenges and Opportunities*, 1 J. Hum. Rights Prac. 83–100 (2009). *See* I. Diokno and M. Socorro, *A Rights-Based Approach towards Budget Analysis* 8 (International Human Rights Internship Program 1999), available at http://www.crin.org/docs/resources/publications/hrbap/RBABudgetAnalysis.pdf (accessed Feb. 22, 2012); Helena Hofbauer et al., *Dignity Counts: A Guide to Using Budget Analysis to Advance Human Rights* (International Budget Partnership 2004), available at http://www.iie.org/en/Programs/IHRIP/~/media/Files/Programs/IHRIP/Dignity_Counts.ashx (accessed Feb. 22, 2012). Budget analysis can also serve an important role in the realm of women's rights. *See*, for example, Debbie Budlender & Rhonda Sharp, *How to Do a Gender-Sensitive Budget Analysis: Contemporary Research and Practice* (Commonwealth Secretariat 1998), available at http://www.thecommonwealth.org/shared_asp_files/uploadedfiles/%7B1171EF87-2C5C-4624-9D76-B03CF35F4E65%7D_AusAIDTr.pdf (accessed Feb. 22, 2012).

75 United Nations, Economic & Social Council, Limburg Principles on the Implementation of Economic, Social, and Cultural Rights, paragraph 79, UN Doc. E/CN.4/1987/17 (Jan. 8, 1987).

76 *Id.*

Inclusive Development Monitoring, Indicators, and Benchmarks

States parties are obliged to monitor the implementation of measures to comply with CRPD obligations. Monitoring should assess both the steps taken and the results achieved in the elimination of barriers to effective access. National strategies, policies, and plans should use appropriate indicators and benchmarks in operationalizing the CRPD. Monitoring and evaluation practitioners have made significant advances in developing performance indicators to simplify the task of monitoring and evaluating human rights implementation and development interventions. Although most countries have a long way to go before they have effective monitoring and evaluation in the realm of disability and other areas, many are establishing monitoring and evaluation working groups comprising representatives from government, donor agencies, civil society, the UN system, and academic institutions. These groups seek to identify and adapt the indicators appropriate for their countries and to harmonize the collection, analysis, and reporting of data.

As the first human rights convention to explicitly call upon states parties to reform their development assistance programs to include people with disabilities, the CRPD provides an important impetus for international cooperation and assistance. Considerable effort must be taken to ensure that donor governments and recipient developing countries adhere to the inclusive development mandate. This is unlikely to be achieved through the vehicle of national disability legislative reform, but instead must be implemented through the adoption and monitoring of development policies. Participation in development decision making is a major focus of many DPO capacity-building endeavors, and is reflected in the Australian Agency for International Development Disability Strategy, along with other donor initiatives. Groups such as Handicap International have worked to ensure that development tools, such as the processes to develop poverty reduction strategy papers in developing countries, are inclusive and conducted in collaboration and consultation with local DPOs.

Looking Forward

The CRPD provides a conceptual model for the legal empowerment of persons with disabilities through innovative and broad-based interventions. Its obligations are to be implemented through actions required by the mechanisms familiar to the rule of law orthodoxy. Moreover, beyond law and policy change, CRPD obligations are to be applied through culture building, participatory and empowering engagement in decision making, inclusive development practices, disability rights education, rights-based budget analysis, and other activities. The CRPD calls upon states, as well as development actors and DPOs, to engage in a variety of human rights actions in order to realize its implementation—from scoping exercises that examine accessibility obligations in law and policy to law reform, law development, and human rights education that raises awareness among a wide array of stakeholders.

The CRPD embodies the potential for a significant transformation in disability legislation, policies, and programs around the world to empower persons with disabilities through full and equal enjoyment of all human rights and fundamental freedoms. Many governments and development practitioners realize this necessity, but do not have adequate knowledge of effective practices and solutions. The CRPD addresses this concern prominently through Article 32, which highlights the role that capacity building, technical assistance, and the exchange of evidence-based knowledge and best practices can play in facilitating the changes that may be required after ratification. Intellectual assistance plays a role, as does monetary assistance to support actions by low- and middle-income countries to put the convention into practice.

Article 32 encourages financial assistance to aid in CRPD implementation through inclusive and accessible aid programming. When international development addresses disability only as a separate issue distinct from mainstream programs, the result is a vicious circle where individuals with disabilities are further excluded and marginalized from the benefits of most economic and social development reforms and actions.[77] Hence, Article 32 is critical to assist states parties in meeting their obligations under the CRPD and requires strong international cooperation. The international development community, together with the international disability rights community, can play a significant role in assisting states parties to reform their laws, policies, and programs to implement the CRPD by strengthening technical assistance, providing financial support to implement the articles of the convention, and exchanging knowledge on best practices. Article 32 requires states parties to work with each other and with relevant organizations to support capacity building "through the exchange and sharing of information, experiences, training programmes and best practices" and to "facilitate cooperation in research and access to scientific and technical knowledge."

Knowledge and practices can be exchanged via networks that encourage dialogue and collaboration through multiple communication strategies among researchers in academic institutions, think tanks, and governments across geographic regions. Participants in such networks can share findings from their activities that increase awareness and understanding about people with disabilities in areas such as deinstitutionalization and community living, employment and economic empowerment, legal capacity, human rights, and access to health care, education, and technology.

One example of such a network is the Global Forum on Law, Justice and Development (GFLJD), initiated by the World Bank's Legal Vice Presidency together with a number of academic and institutional partners from around the world. The GFLJD aims to bring together stakeholders in the fields of law, justice, and development, combining the economic, legal, and technical aspects of a range of targeted issues beyond disability. By introducing disability into this network, practitioners can work toward mainstreaming the needs of

77 Samant, Matter, & Harniss, *supra* note 45.

persons with disabilities across the spectrum of law, justice, and development programs around the world.

The approaches to legal empowerment and innovation called for in the implementation of the CRPD can be built upon to advance an emerging disability rights narrative with roots at the community as well as national level. Empowerment and innovation will be achieved in these reform efforts only with the full participation of and meaningful consultation with persons with disabilities and their representative organizations.

The Political Economy of Improving Traditional Justice Systems

A Case Study of NGO Engagement with Shalish in Bangladesh

STEPHEN GOLUB

In the past decade, the role that traditional justice systems (TJSs) play in the lives of the rural poor has received increasing attention.[1] Sometimes referred to as customary justice systems, nonstate justice systems (because they have not originated as legal systems devised and administered by the state), or alternative dispute resolution (when viewed as alternatives to the courts), TJSs handle most disputes and other justice processes in many societies, particularly in rural areas.

Across the globe, institutions such as development agencies, national governments, and civil society groups are exploring whether and how to work with TJSs. TJSs merit this focus because they are so central to the lives of so many. Yet, they often are blatantly unfair to women and other populations who suffer from power imbalances in their disputes and in their lives. The powerful can use TJSs as a mechanism to control the relatively powerless. They are often instruments, then, for the administration not just of justice but also, informally, of local governance. With these considerations in mind, what can and should development, government, and civil society institutions do to help make TJSs more equitable in their operations?

This chapter aims to address this question by examining how NGOs in Bangladesh attempt to employ, modify, or monitor the country's main TJS, known as *shalish*, so as to retain its meritorious features and ameliorate its drawbacks.[2] Most Bangladeshi NGOs seek to make shalish less gender biased, corrupt, and punitive, as well as fairer and more accountable. As with any customary system, the way shalish functions varies among communities

1 The World Bank, the UK Department for International Development (DfID), the United Nations Development Programme (UNDP), and the International Development Law Organization are but a few of the major international agencies conducting relevant research, programs, or other initiatives.

2 This chapter draws on the author's numerous visits to Bangladesh between 1993 and 2012 in the course of consulting for DfID, the Asia Foundation, the Asian Development Bank, the Ford Foundation, and other internationally oriented organizations, as well as additional research conducted by the author.

and regions. However, the picture painted with broad strokes in this chapter applies to much of the country.

The TJS operations of Bangladeshi NGOs take on additional salience for the international community in view of the recently launched the Community Legal Services Programme, which will support such work (as well as related, justice-oriented activities). Funded by the United Kingdom Department for International Development (DfID), this five-year (2012–17), 17 million GBP initiative will provide a substantial base of experience and research that other development institutions and countries can draw on.[3]

This chapter first delves into the importance of TJSs. It then discusses the nature of shalish in its conventional, unmodified form, unaffected by NGO influence. It moves on to address NGO efforts to improve shalish operations or to act as substitutes for the process. Finally, the chapter offers some reflections on the implications of this analysis for international development, including for NGOs and governments concerned with customary justice.

The political economy approach taken in this discussion mirrors the strategies of many NGOs seeking to improve shalish. Traditional justice is not just about dispute resolution. It is also about power, politics, governance, gender, community dynamics, and resource allocation.

Any approach to justice and development that relies mainly on technical analyses and solutions is bound to fall far short of the mark in its attempts to formulate, promote, and implement reforms. This kind of approach is especially misguided in the case of customary justice. For instance, an NGO or government program that trains traditional leaders how to mediate intracommunity conflicts addresses a minor or nonexistent need. That organization or program should instead focus on the economic, political, and cultural influences and incentives that shape the behaviors of community leaders and members alike. To their considerable credit, many Bangladeshi NGOs do exactly that in grappling with the considerable challenge of improving shalish.

In taking this tack, these NGOs take a legal empowerment approach to working with traditional justice. That is, the NGOs use the law (in this case, customary law) and rights (involving gender equity, for example) specifically to help the disadvantaged gain greater control over their lives.

The Global Context: The Main Way the Poor Seek Justice

DfID has estimated that "in many developing countries, traditional or customary legal systems account for 80 percent of total cases."[4] The Development Assistance Committee of the Organisation for Economic Co-operation and

---

3 *See* http://www.communitylegalservice.org/index.php (accessed Sep. 28, 2012).

4 DfID, *Safety, Security and Accessible Justice: Putting Policy into Practice* 58 (undated).

Development (OECD) similarly points to research suggesting that "non-state systems are the main providers of justice and security for up to 80–90 percent of the population" in fragile states.[5] These calculations reflect the fact that, by virtue of choice or necessity, the poor in many societies use customary forums to seek justice more than they do formal governmental institutions, especially in rural areas.

Why is this the case? Due to cost, inconvenience, incomprehensibility, or corruption, justice through judiciaries (and other state institutions) can be difficult or impossible for poor people to access. Even where access to justice through state institutions is feasible, it is not necessarily the preferred option.

In the relatively rare instances where free legal aid is available and effective, the act of going to court can be an expensive one. It can involve court fees and other expenses, and repeated court visits can drain a great deal of time away from earning a living. Going to court also can be inconvenient, due to those repeated visits and the great distances that the rural poor must travel for trials and other legal proceedings. Once a plaintiff is in court, the proceedings may be incomprehensible, often conducted in languages (such as those of the nations' former colonial rulers) that may be foreign to him or her. In addition, legal discourse is highly technical and beyond the grasp of even educated nonlawyers, not to mention the illiterate or impoverished. Finally, there is no guarantee that judicial proceedings are free from corruption, political control, gender biases, or other undue influences that undercut their fairness, particularly for the poor.

None of this is to deny the value of well-functioning courts for many purposes, not least addressing serious crimes, human rights abuses, and public policy issues. Nor is it to claim that TJSs always operate fairly; as already emphasized here, that is far from the case. But the fact that a well-functioning judiciary is desirable does not mean it is achievable. Efforts to address judicial inadequacies have proven problematic in many nations, including Bangladesh. Notwithstanding the presence of some fine Bangladeshi jurists, the country's court system has been resistant to change. A 2011 World Bank report, *Disputes, Crimes and Pathways of Redress: A Household Survey on Citizens' Perceptions and Experiences of the Justice System in Bangladesh,* indicates widespread lack of public confidence in the courts, police, and other formal justice sector institutions.[6]

In terms of cost, convenience, and comprehensibility, TJSs do have distinct advantages over the courts. The poor do not have to pay to use them. TJSs usually take far less time than court cases do, even if they do not always offer instant justice. Their dispute-resolution sessions typically take place much closer

---

5 OECD/DAC Network on Conflict, Peace and Development Co-operation, *Enhancing the Delivery of Justice and Security in Fragile States* 4 (Aug. 2006).

6 Saku Akmeemana, *Disputes, Crimes and Pathways of Redress: A Household Survey on Citizens' Perceptions and Experiences of the Justice System in Bangladesh* (World Bank 2011).

to where the poor reside. TJS proceedings are conducted in languages that the poor understand and are often conducted by fellow community members.

Being more comprehensible and rooted in their communities can make some TJSs more transparent and accountable to the poor—at least compared with incomprehensible judicial systems that leave the poor open to manipulation by judges, court personnel, or even their own attorneys. Nevertheless, although TJSs may be preferable to the courts for many purposes, that fact constitutes faint praise.

Conventional Shalish: An Overview

The term *shalish* (or *salish*) refers to a traditional, community-based, largely informal Bangladeshi process through which small, loosely constituted panels of influential local figures help resolve community members' disputes and/or impose sanctions on them. The term is applied in at least four ways: to the process in general, to an individual hearing, to a series of hearings about a specific dispute, and to the panel conducting a hearing. The panel members are called *shalishdars*.

Although practiced across most of the country, shalish is not the only local, informal method of dispute resolution in Bangladesh. Cultural minorities employ their own, varied methods. As in many societies, Bangladeshi disputants may seek out influential individuals for advice or decisions without turning to a panel of such persons. But the widespread use and diverse forms of shalish make it potentially fertile ground for international efforts to understand analogous processes and external efforts to improve them.

Shalish may involve voluntary submission to arbitration (which, in this context, involves the parties agreeing to submit to the judgment of the shalish panel) or mediation (in which the panel helps the disputants devise a settlement themselves). Frequently, shalish blends the two, such that the two parties are nominally free to accept or reject shalishdars' recommendations, but pressure from the shalishdars or other community members may undermine the voluntariness of such decisions.

A harsh (though relatively rare) version of shalish can take a punitive form. In such instances, the forum constitutes a de facto criminal court that inflicts trial and punishment on individuals who have not consented to its jurisdiction.

With the exception of the summary judgment imposed under that harsh version, a shalish can result in a quick resolution or may extend over numerous sessions and months. Negotiations between disputants, often including or represented by family members, sometimes also take place outside these sessions, complementing the discussions that take place within them.

The term "dispute-resolution process" suggests calm deliberation, with the parties patiently putting forth their perspectives and impartial facilitators soberly sorting through the issues. Although not the product of a scientific survey, this author's impressions of more than a dozen (NGO-organized) shalish sessions during the 1990s were rather different:

> The actual shalish is often a loud and passionate event in which disputants, relatives, [shalish panel] members and even uninvited community members congregate to express their thoughts and feelings. Additional observers—adults and children alike—gather in the room's doorway and outside. More than one exchange of opinions may occur simultaneously. Calm discussions explode into bursts of shouting and even laughter or tears. All of this typically takes place in a crowded school room or other public space, sweltering most of the year, often with the noise of other community activities filtering in from outside. The number of participants and observers may range from a few dozen to well over one hundred.[7]

Even more significant, it can be misleading to characterize shalish as constituting alternative dispute resolution. As Siddiqi explains:

> The shalish should not be thought of as an *alternative* [emphasis in original] dispute resolution mechanism in Bangladesh. The concept of Alternative Dispute Resolution (ADR) was developed in relation to a specific set of needs within various "western" legal systems. While many features of ADR are similar to those that characterize the shalish, the latter does not by any means constitute an alternative for the vast majority of the rural population. Indeed, despite its visibility and prominence, available statistics would argue for viewing the formal justice system as the "alternative" form of dispute resolution.[8]

Siddiqi's insight applies to most disputes involving most rural Bangladeshis and many urban ones. Even if the country's problematic courts operated more efficiently and equitably, they still would represent an alternative to shalish, rather than vice versa.

The Main Types of Disputes Addressed via Shalish

Shalish most commonly addresses two types of disputes: one category involves family and gender issues; the other involves property, including land and petty theft.

Gender/family disputes can pertain to *dowry* (the price, in cash or kind, that the bride's family typically pays that of the groom), *dower/denmohor* (a payment that the groom may promise the bride but that she usually forgoes

---

7 Stephen Golub, *From the Village to the University: Legal Activism in Bangladesh*, in *Many Roads to Justice: The Law-Related Work of Ford Foundation Grantees around the World* 137–38 (Mary McClymont & Stephen Golub ed., Ford Foundation 2000).

8 D. M. Siddiqi, *Shalish and the Quest for Gender Justice: An Assessment of Strategic Interventions in Bangladesh*, report prepared for Research Initiatives, Bangladesh, 11 (Mar. 17, 2004).

unless he divorces her), maintenance payments (for a wife's and children's expenses in the event of separation or divorce), polygamy, "torture" (a term that usually refers to physical or psychological abuse, such as by the husband's family against the wife, rather than to protracted infliction of pain for purposes of sadism or interrogation), and divorce.

Given the nature of Bangladeshi households and family structures, many such disputes are not confined to two individuals. Entire families often become involved and may even instigate conflict. In such instances, not all mistreatment is by men against women. A husband's mother may be the lead actor in abuses against his wife. And gender-related power imbalances notwithstanding, there certainly are instances in which women treat men unfairly.

That being said, abusive treatment of women cuts across many gender-related disputes. This can involve both physical and psychological mistreatment (the latter sometimes called "mental torture"). Young women who are taken into the homes of in-laws after marriage may be especially victimized in this way. The new wives are often just girls.[9] Such abuse often is linked to ongoing dowry demands by the husband's family.

Dowry does not appear deeply rooted in the history of the lands that became Bangladesh. White[10] and Rozario[11] both suggest that dowry dates back only several decades at most, and that previously it was common for the husband's family to pay that of the wife in connection with a wedding. Why dowry has become dominant is a matter of conjecture. Geirbo and Imam discuss an array of possible economic, social, and historical causes—including supply and demand for husbands versus wives—but do not draw firm conclusions.[12]

In any case, dowry triggers or is otherwise related to gender disputes because it involves demands by the husband or his parents for payments by the wife's parents. The convention must be seen in the context of a society in which poorly educated girls are viewed as economic liabilities; families may be anxious to see daughters wed because (if the families are impoverished) they represent extra mouths to feed and/or marriages may represent a road to the families' social advancement; and girls and their families may be socially ostracized if they remain single.

As with gender-related disputes, land conflicts blend with other societal issues. They are embedded in the nature of the society's poverty, structure,

---

9 In one area studied by the Bangladeshi Rural Advancement Committee (BRAC) and the Population Council, 80 percent of brides were under 18 years old. BRAC and Population Council, *Bangladesh Adolescent Survey 2004* (Dhaka 2004).

10 S. White, *Arguing with the Crocodile: Class and Gender Hierarchies in a Bangladeshi Village* 102 (U. Press Limited 1992).

11 S. Rozario, *Purity and Communal Boundaries: Women and Social Change in a Bangladeshi Village* 131–35 (U. Press Limited 2001).

12 H. C. Geirbo & N. Imam, *The Motivations behind Giving and Taking Dowry*, Research Monograph Series No. 28, 2–3 (BRAC Research and Evaluation Division Jul. 2006).

and agrarian constraints.[13] Problems involving land are not always distinct from gender matters, and they may be intrafamily in nature.

Conventional Shalish as Both Dispute Resolution and Social Control

Before considering efforts to modify shalish, it is important to consider what shalish constitutes in its conventional, traditional form. As summarized by Khair, traditional shalish

> is basically a practice of gathering village elders and concerned parties, exclusively male, for the resolution of local disputes. Sometimes Chairmen and elite members of the *Union Parishad* [a local government unit] are invited to sit through the proceedings. Shalish has no fixed dimension and its size and structure depend entirely on the nature and gravity of the problem at hand.[14]

A shalish may be completed in one day, but it may extend over a number of sessions and involve private negotiations between disputants, often encompassing their families. Traditional shalish may inappropriately and illegally handle even the most serious criminal actions, including rape.

Whether a specific shalish constitutes mediation or arbitration, or a blend of the two, hinges on the dynamics at play. Community mores and the opinions of powerful leaders often exert such strong influences that outcomes are imposed on a disputant contrary to his or her wishes. In the alternative, the disputant may have a nominal choice, but pressure to act in accord with mores and opinions effectively forces acquiescence. Thus, a woman victimized by domestic violence may be forced to return to her husband because the shalishdars tolerate such treatment and because they chastise the husband only in a pro forma manner.

Khair and her colleagues highlight some of the problems afflicting conventional shalish:

> Sometimes solutions are arbitrary and imposed on reluctant disputants by powerful village or community members. Such "solutions" are based less on civil or other law than on subjective judgments designed to ensure the continuity of their leadership, to strengthen their relational alliances, or to uphold the perceived cultural norms and biases. The shalish also is susceptible to manipulation by corrupt touts [persons who exploit some nominal knowledge of the law] and local musclemen who may be hired to guide the pace and direction of the process by intimidation. Furthermore, because the traditional

---

13 *See*, for example, E. G. Jansen, *Rural Bangladesh: Competition for Scarce Resources* (Norwegian U. Press 1987).

14 S. Khair, *Alternative Approaches to Justice: A Review of ADR Initiatives under the Democracy Partnership*, report prepared for the Asia Foundation, 5 (May 2001).

> shalish is composed exclusively of male members, women are particularly vulnerable to extreme judgments and harsh penalties.[15]

One additional, crucial dimension of traditional shalish that must be emphasized is its role as an institution for perpetuating the social control of women and the poor. Hashmi explicates this point when describing the "member-matbar-mulla" triumvirate that controls village affairs, including shalish:

> The *members* of the Union Parishad (the lowest electoral unit) are elected officials, in charge of the disbursement of public goods and relief materials among the poor villagers, and are the most powerful in the triumvirate. They are often connected with the ruling political party of other influential power-brokers in the neighboring towns or groups of villages. The *matbars* (*matabbars*) or village elders, who also sit on the *salish* (village court), are next in the hierarchy, having vested interests in the village economy as rentiers and moneylenders. They often get shares in misappropriated relief goods along with government officials and *members-chairmen* of the Union Parishads. The *mulla*, associated with the local mosques and *maktabs* (elementary religious schools), are sometimes quite influential as they endorse the activities of village elders albeit in the name of Islamic or *Sharia* law. They often sit on the *salish* and issue *fatwas* in support of their patrons, the village elders. The rural poor, often women, are victims of these *fatwas*.[16]

The increasing involvement of women and younger political figures in village affairs may run counter to the bleak picture painted here. However, with the increased politicization of society involving armed thugs, these influences are further tainting traditional shalish, according to a number of sources.[17]

Why, then, do Bangladeshis still turn to traditional shalish to address their disputes? The reasons echo the reality that customary justice systems are often favored by the poor across the globe. Thus, although otherwise highly critical of the institution, Siddiqi notes:

> For poor villagers, especially women, the shalish offers many advantages. First, a shalish hearing does not require any serious expenditure. Second, it takes place locally, at a time that is convenient for all of the parties involved. Proceedings occur in a language and frame-

---

15 S. Khair et al., *Access to Justice: Best Practices under the Democracy Partnership* 8–9 (Asia Foundation, Apr. 2002).

16 T. Hashmi, *Women and Islam in Bangladesh: Beyond Subjection and Tyranny* 137 (Macmillan 2000).

17 For a summary of recent scholarship concerning these trends, *see* Harry Blair, *Civil Society, Dispute Resolution and Local Governance in Bangladesh: Ideas for Pro-Poor Programme Support*, report prepared for the Department for International Development, UK High Commission (May 2003).

> work of justice that is comprehensible to the litigants. Third, disputes are resolved relatively quickly, usually in one to three sittings.[18]

The bottom line is that shalish is often the first and only choice available to impoverished Bangladeshis. It is affordable, comprehensible, convenient, and efficient, even in contrast with a well-functioning judicial system—not to mention the country's courts.

Efforts to modify conventional shalish, then, should not be seen simply in terms of improving dispute resolution or access to justice. To the considerable degree that traditional shalish perpetuates poverty and the poor's lack of control over their lives, efforts to reform it can contribute to the fundamental development goals of poverty alleviation and good governance.

The Punitive Approach: Shalish as Trial

From time to time, harshly punitive versions of traditional shalish have been reported. These reports describe incidents of people being lashed or even stoned to death for violation of local norms. The reports, which received attention from Amnesty International in the 1990s,[19] have attracted significant attention in the Bangladeshi press over the years.

The kind of shalish documented in these reports goes far beyond mediation or even arbitration and amounts to de facto trials. These trials result in fatwas decreed by mullas who belong to the shalish panels or otherwise influence them. The mullas interpret or misinterpret sharia to subject the "defendants" to horrible punishment that exceeds the more mundane (though still unfair) edicts described by Hashmi.

While egregious, these punitive shalish processes appear to be relatively rare. According to a 2006–07 study conducted by the Asia Foundation for DfID:

> Only a few NGOs consulted in the study had even heard of such abuses taking place anywhere close to their areas of operation. Even then, their responses to questions about the practice suggest that the few dozen newspaper reports of the abuses may represent the sum total of the problem rather than a window on a problem that is more prevalent than reports would suggest. This is also the opinion of ASK [Ain O Salish Kendra, a women's rights NGO discussed in further detail below], which tracks violations of this kind. Local and national NGOs are sometimes able to mobilize police to prevent such actions before they occur.[20]

---

18 D. M. Siddiqi, *Paving the Way to Justice: The Experience of Nagorik Uddyog, Bangladesh* 10 (One World Action 2005).

19 *See*, for example, Amnesty International, *Bangladesh: Taking the Law in Their Own Hands: The Village Salish* (ASA Dec. 13, 1993).

20 Asia Foundation, *Promoting Improved Access to Justice: Community Legal Service Delivery in Bangladesh* 22 (Asia Foundation, Mar. 2007).

This is not to minimize the threat that punitive shalish could become if it were to grow in rural areas, particularly given the increasing influence of ultraconservative religious elements in some parts of the country in recent years. At this point, however, the problem seems to be severe in nature but limited in scope.

Four Prominent Approaches to Modifying Shalish

There appear to be four main approaches that NGOs take to modify shalish.[21]

NGOs Organize Shalish

Possibly the most common form of NGO interaction with shalish occurs when an NGO organizes shalish panels and sessions, sometimes building on other rights-oriented or development-oriented activities it has undertaken in the community. NGOs are able to take such initiatives for varying reasons, including their long-standing presence and credibility in a community, the influence they derive from their other operations, and in some cases their success at co-opting traditional shalishdars.

Much of this approach is derived from the pioneering efforts of the Madaripur Legal Aid Association (MLAA, named for the district in which it mainly works). MLAA's work reaches back nearly 30 years. In addition to its own direct engagement with shalish, MLAA provides lawyers to assist clients when necessary (such as when they are victims of violent crimes) and trains NGOs from across the country in its approach.

The nature and degree of NGO engagement with shalish varies considerably. NGOs such as MLAA and Nagorik Uddyog (NU) may include traditional shalishdars in the new panels in order to maintain the presence of influential persons. But they supplement them with educated persons (such as teachers) who may have broader and less-traditional perspectives, women from various backgrounds, and men who may be relatively uneducated or impoverished. Once the NGO convenes a shalish, its own personnel may play passive roles at the session, with the shalishdars managing the mediation.

There are distinct differences among organizations taking this approach. MLAA is distinguished by a fairly extensive network of personnel covering a district (and nearby areas) of more than 1 million people and close, longstanding connections with the local bar associations. The community-based organizations it forms are mainly shalish panels.

In contrast, the Bangladesh National Women Lawyers Association (BNWLA) works with partner NGOs that in turn train community members

---

21 Although the author has been able to update the information upon which he bases this section via correspondence and three 2012 visits to Bangladesh, much of the analysis in this section draws on research conducted five or more years ago. It is possible that the nature of the engagement of certain NGOs with shalish changed during the intervening period.

to conduct shalish. Unlike with MLAA, BNWLA personnel do not attend shalish sessions, but representatives from partner NGOs do.

NU organizes and trains shalish panels on a local (ward) level, requiring that at least one-third of the shalishdars be women. NU then draws on these panels to form higher-level (Union Parishad) legal aid committees that both review shalish outcomes and monitor the more general human rights situation in their areas. Unlike BNWLA and MLAA, NU does not include attorneys on its staff.

Like NU, the women's development NGO Banchte Shekha, which in many respects is also a membership organization, often plays active and diverse roles with respect to its partner populations. It is active, for instance, in the areas of livelihood, credit, health, education, and other gender-oriented work. Many years of efforts to improve women's perspectives, knowledge, financial well-being, and status bolster the NGO's local credibility and influence in its approach to shalish. Its shalish panels are accordingly more heavily weighted with untraditional shalishdars, especially women, drawn from its partner populations. Its personnel play active roles in suggesting and even directing shalish deliberations.

Although there is no typical model for NGO-organized shalish, Hasle provides a useful summary of a process employed by NU. She bears quoting at some length, for she illustrates the many stages of the organization's engagement with the process:

> NU seeks out members of the traditional shalish that are open to a more democratic and just form of dispute resolution—as identified through participatory local level workshops—and invites them to become members of a local NU shalish committee, along with other individuals representing a cross-section of the community. One third of the members are women, and a particular effort is made to include women Union members [i.e., women who have been elected to the local Union Parishad, or governing council].
>
> As a matter of strategy, NU seek[s] to *transform* rather than *replace* the existing power structure through a method of cooptation, and in particular by bringing together "influential" and ordinary ("non-influential") members of the community in training and mediation, thereby fostering new allegiances. . . .
>
> Once established, NU aims to provide the committee members with necessary tools for promoting greater justice in the shalish process. Emphasis is given to education and training, combining human rights education with information about the law, including civil and criminal laws, as well as religious and customary laws. Committee members are also introduced to local lawyers who stand ready to assist them on a case-by-case basis. Role-plays and other forms of participatory exercises are used to enhance the members' sensitivity to prevailing attitudes and norms that discriminate against women, and develop legal and moral arguments for how these can be coun-

> teracted through the shalish. Members of the shalish committee are not, however, on NU's payroll, and are free to take part in the traditional shalish in their own capacity.
>
> One of NU's main activities is to organise shalish hearings (NU-shalish hereafter). These are convened on the basis of an application from an aggrieved member of the community, which is filed with one of NU's Community Organisers (CO). COs are volunteers from the respective communities where NU operates, and each CO cover[s] one Union. All COs have received human rights and legal training from NU, and have access to local lawyers.
>
> When NU has accepted an application . . . the CO undertakes a fact-finding exercise, to verify the applicant's claims and to collect other relevant information. Provided the application is considered valid (i.e. that the fact-finding confirms that there is a grievance), a formal notice inviting the respondent to a NU-shalish is sent. . . . It should be noted that NU would not convene a shalish in criminal cases, as a part of their strategy to promote greater respect for the rule of law; and would take action to ensure that these cases are adjudicated by formal courts, with assistance from NU as relevant.
>
> Assuming the respondent is willing to meet in a NU-shalish, a mediation session is convened. While NU facilitates the mediation by organising the venue, NU staff plays a passive role in the discussion, which is led by members of the NU-shalish committee, representatives from NU's women leadership programme and representatives from each of the parties (which may include non-NU shalishdars and other influential people). According to NU policy, a resolution should be reached through mediation and not arbitration. As discussed with project staff, this is understood to imply willingness to compromise on both sides, and while law is a relevant factor in the negotiation, it is not the only—or even the dominant—consideration. . . .
>
> Provided an agreement is reached, which is overwhelmingly the case, this is recorded in the minutes of the hearing, which is signed by both parties. . . . If the opposing party is unwilling to reach a settlement, or the applicant considers the settlement unreasonable, NU stands ready to provide legal aid to the applicant so as to facilitate a formal court hearing. This is also an option in cases where the respondent does not abide by the decisions made.
>
> Following the mediation, NU undertakes to visit the applicant on a monthly basis for three months, so as to monitor the implementation of the shalish decision.[22]

A 2011 study of NU's program to build up women's leadership roles (including in shalish) provides a similarly positive assessment of the organization's work:

---

22 Lena Hasle, *Too Poor for Rights? Access to Justice for Poor Women in Bangladesh: A Case Study* 10–12 (unpublished MSC dissertation for the London School of Economics 2004).

> [I]t seems that this programme is . . . a potentially useful model of a women's leadership building strategy. . . . The efforts of Nagorik Uddyog appear to have resulted in perceptible expansion of women's political space (manifest in greater substantive participation in shalish) and in conjunction with other women's empowerment strategies currently taking place in rural Bangladesh, such efforts could have a real, positive long-term impact on the status of women in Bangladeshi society.[23]

NGO-Assisted Community-Based Organizations (CBOs) Modify Shalish

Some NGOs concentrate on strengthening partner community-based organizations (CBOs) so that they can affect shalish.[24] Part of the rationale is to strengthen access to justice while minimizing NGO engagement and community dependence on NGOs. Under this approach, NGO personnel avoid involvement in creating panels and initiating sessions. They instead concentrate on strengthening citizen capacities to join, pressure, persuade, educate, and otherwise influence traditional shalish bodies. The community members who are trained and supported by NGOs seek to influence preexisting shalish panels.

To varying extents, NGOs engage in monitoring traditional shalish panels even as they seek to co-opt those panels or set up parallel structures. Ain O Salish Kendra (ASK), a women's rights NGO, takes this approach. ASK trains and supports a number of other NGOs to help affiliated CBOs exert influence on shalish and on other local institutions and issues. One such partner organization is the Bangladesh Rural Advancement Committee (BRAC), a very large national NGO that promotes livelihood development, microfinance, and numerous other socioeconomic initiatives in many parts of the country.[25]

Siddiqi summarizes key aspects of this approach, in terms of how ASK aids partner NGOs:

> The organization does not have any offices in the field but works through six [at the time of Siddiqi's summary] partner NGOs. GSJP [ASK Gender and Social Justice Program] staff spend considerable time in the field but their mandate is strictly limited. They do not form alternative shalish committees, nor are they allowed to participate in local shalish. Their role is to observe, to monitor and to persuade. The GSJP seeks to monitor local shalish, track human rights violations in its working areas and increase the legal literacy of the

---

23 Ryan Higgitt, *Women's Leadership Building as a Poverty Reduction Strategy*, 6(1) J. S. Asian Dev. 114 (2011).

24 To make a crude distinction between the two, NGOs are nonprofits that at least partly comprise paid staff, whereas CBOs comprise members of the very populations they serve, represent, or otherwise benefit.

25 In recent years, BRAC has branched out beyond Bangladesh to launch operations in other countries.

> local population. The strategy is to empower through knowledge. ASK focuses on legal education and empowerment in a general sense, working on the assumption that the desired effect on the shalish can be achieved only with an overall shift in ideology.
>
> With the help of its partner NGOs, ASK staff members in the field help to organize a Manobodhikar Songrokkhon Parishad (MSP) [Human Rights Protection Committee], previously known as Ain Shohayota Committees (ASC) [legal assistance committees]. [ASK and its partner NGOs also organize human rights committees exclusively comprising women.] As the name suggests, the responsibilities of MSP members are primarily to monitor the local situation, to intervene in cases where the law has been broken and to facilitate the spread of human rights information. Committee members basically have a watchdog capacity. Members are not necessary [*sic*] drawn from the dominant social groups, at least not exclusively.
>
> Through its Gender and Social Justice program, ASK seeks to challenge and transform local knowledge and moral codes of conduct. The organization's approach is quite distinct—unlike other NGOs involved in remaking the shalish, ASK does not intervene directly in shalish proceedings. Its objective is more long-term—it seeks to persuade the inhabitants in its working areas of the need to transform the existing gendered and unequal structures of power.[26]

As Siddiqi further explains, "ASK proceeds on the assumption that an equitable and representative shalish structure can be created and *sustained* only when there is an overall shift in community norms and practices of power."[27]

This point does not discount other organizations' efforts to alter community dynamics so that women and other disadvantaged populations achieve greater power and more equitable treatment. The ASK approach aims for a lesser degree of NGO engagement so as to facilitate a greater degree of CBO empowerment.

The ways in which such an approach plays out in practice vary among partner NGOs, but usually involve a degree of community organizing by the partner. Alim describes how one partner, BRAC, increased the power of its members by pulling them together into not just small-scale community organizations but also larger-scale (but still local) federations that have a greater likelihood of exercising influence.[28]

Alim analyzes two examples of such operations. In one instance the federation (with a woman leading the way) influenced the deliberations of a

---

26 Siddiqi, *supra* note 8.

27 D. M. Siddiqi, *Ain O Salish Kendra: Twenty Years on the Frontline* 34 (ASK Dec. 2006).

28 A. Alim, *Shalish and the Role of BRAC's Federation: Improving the Poor's Access to Justice*, Social Science Research Network Paper 905745 (2004), available at papers.ssrn.com/sol3/papers.cfm?abstract_id=905745.

shalish regarding an alleged petty theft. In the other, a case of a husband who had illegally taken a second wife, the federation sought police assistance when the shalish failed to reach a resolution. Specifically, this intervention prevented the husband from selling land and leaving his first wife and five children destitute.[29]

NGO Staff Members Conduct Shalish

A number of NGOs utilize individual staff members to settle conflicts between disputants without the involvement of shalish panels. Such efforts—often also called shalish by such groups because of their mediation-oriented nature—can take a number of forms. In some instances, a field or office worker initially interviews one or more disputants and explores the other options of NGO-facilitated shalish or litigation. In others, this kind of shalish is the main mechanism by which the NGO seeks to help resolve a dispute; the NGO retains the option of utilizing its own staff or outside counsel to pursue legal redress.

Thus, at the same time that ASK aids partner NGOs and CBOs in modifying traditional shalish, its Dhaka-based personnel conduct shalish between disputants. Similarly, even as BRAC (sometimes with the assistance of ASK) seeks to strengthen the roles of its partner populations and CBOs in modifying traditional shalish and human rights in their communities, its staff members individually conduct shalish sessions.

Bangladesh Legal Aid and Services Trust (BLAST), a national NGO that undertakes both individual legal aid and more policy-oriented litigation and advocacy, employs this approach exclusively. Staff members engage in shalish but do not become involved in organizing shalish panels or CBOs the way other NGOs' staff members do. The BLAST approach also differs in that, unlike some other NGOs (that rely on outside counsel), BLAST can threaten a recalcitrant party with litigation on behalf of BLAST's client if an agreement is not reached. Thus, BLAST is often closer to arbitration than mediation on the spectrum of what shalish effectively means. This is not to say that BLAST always takes the opposing party to court if shalish fails. But the threat is more immediate than for many other NGOs.

NGOs Aid the Government's Village Court System

Bangladesh has made an effort to build on the advantages of shalish by instituting a formal, officially recognized mediation system. First implemented decades ago, village courts are dispute-resolution bodies that have official status under the laws of Bangladesh[30] but have been moribund in large parts of the country. In connection with the adoption of the Village Courts Act in 2006, there has been renewed donor and government interest in reviving these insti-

---

29 *Id.*, at 42–43.

30 The 1961 Muslim Family Laws Ordinance is a precursor to the village courts. The 1976 Village Courts Ordinance put in place the legal structure that, except for raising the jurisdiction limit from 5,000 to 25,000 taka, largely stayed unchanged in the 2006 Village Courts Act.

tutions. The United Nations Development Programme (UNDP), for example, is conducting a project aiming to "activate" village courts.[31]

Union Parishad chairpersons head village courts. Other Union Parishad members may substitute for them, however. In addition, with the permission of the chairperson, a nonmember may chair the five-person village court panel. The opposing sides of a dispute each select two of the other four members, including one Union Parishad member each. If two parties agree to the jurisdiction of a village court, they are bound by its decision if four out of the five panelists (or if one panelist is absent, three out of four members) agree on a ruling.

In recent years, MLAA has played a role in trying to revive the institution through training and advice. Certainly, Union Parishad chairpersons command a great deal of authority in their communities. *Disputes, Crimes and Pathways of Redress* indicates that community members often seek their help in resolving disputes even in the absence of village courts.[32]

Other NGOs are more skeptical about the village courts' prospects for success. They base this skepticism on the long history of largely fruitless efforts to fortify institutions. They also are concerned about the village courts' potentially politicized or corrupt nature. Other sources lend weight to these doubts by raising questions about local political dynamics, Union Parishad members' biases, and the village courts themselves.[33]

Additional Research Findings

As with so much in the field of law and development, there is a shortage of research that documents the impact of efforts to improve shalish. The studies cited in this chapter provide some preliminary evidence that NGO engagement with shalish can enhance equity in resolving disputes and improve the situations of disadvantaged individuals. One could even, very tentatively, infer that the gender-equitable effects could contribute to poverty alleviation and improved governance. But much more research needs to be done, and not all findings to date have been favorable.

Although the aforementioned 2006-07 Asia Foundation study does not reach firm conclusions, the findings are generally positive. Both beneficiaries and opinion leaders indicate that NGOs that were the foci of the research were generally effective in conducting shalish and otherwise benefit their communities.

---

31 *See* http://www.villagecourts.org/index.php (accessed Sep. 29, 2012).

32 Akmeemana, *supra* note 6.

33 *See*, for example, Bangladesh Ministry of Women's and Children's Affairs (MOWCA), *Background Paper on Good Practices and Priorities to Combat Sexual Abuse and Exploitation of Children in Bangladesh* (MOWCA 2001); T. Haque et al., *In Search of Justice: Women's Encounters with Alternative Dispute Resolution* (Asia Foundation Apr. 2002); and United Nations Development Programme, *Human Security in Bangladesh: In Search of Justice and Dignity* (UNDP Sep. 2002).

Yet, not all research on this matter has yielded positive results. Geirbo and Imam find that even though community members served by BRAC have become aware of dowry being illegal, they continue to pay it. Their research further indicates that deeply ingrained social practices and attitudes tend to persist—to some extent, even among some BRAC NGO workers, which has potentially powerful implications for their shalish-oriented work.[34] A number of the Asia Foundation study's focus groups report that illegal dowry and related problems continue despite the efforts of organizations to provide various kinds of community legal services, including shalish.[35]

Disputes, Crimes and Pathways of Redress provides provocative insights about how widespread Bangladeshis' use of NGO justice services such as modified shalish is. Its findings indicate, inter alia, that far more people identify Union Parishad chairpersons (operating informally, rather than in connection with formally convened village councils) as a first choice in seeking resolution of legal problems, compared to NGO shalish.[36]

As scrupulous as this study was, however, it raises as many questions as it answers about dispute resolution and redress. For example, due to the methodology employed by its survey research, the study identified relatively low rates of gender-specific problems (in a society in which dowry, underage and multiple marriages, physical and psychological abuse of women, and women being cheated out of inheritances and other property are widespread). In addition, especially in view of the aforementioned research regarding the member-matbar-mulla triumvirate and related findings, there remains the issue of whether and to what extent people receive fair treatment from chairpersons (or to what extent that treatment is tainted by gender biases, graft, patronage, and other undue influences on their conduct). There also is the matter of whether the study's design and peer review adequately involved NGO experts.

Still, the study provides a useful basis for further research regarding not only NGOs' and Union Parishad chairpersons' services but also the public's widespread lack of confidence in formal justice sector institutions.[37] The Bank and the personnel involved in initiating and implementing this research should be commended for providing a model for digging deep into how people seek access to justice.

Other Bangladesh-specific studies document NGO efficacy in other regards. One example is Hasle's field research, which includes interviews with NU clients whose shalish agreements were arranged by NU-affiliated panels in 2002. NU's follow-up records indicate that, of a sample of 37 selected by Hasle, 31 agreements were honored. In subsequently interviewing the clients,

---

34 Geirbo & Imam, *supra* note 12.

35 Asia Foundation, *supra* note 20.

36 Akmeemana, *supra* note 6.

37 *Id.*

Hasle found that in all but one case the agreements were "more or less" honored.[38] Siddiqi's research on both NU and ASK similarly document their strategies and efficacy.[39]

The findings of Hasle and Siddiqi are not inconsistent with that of Geirbo and Imam. Many of the disputes that Hasle scrutinized, for example, involved domestic violence that was reportedly halted through shalish interventions. In contrast, Geirbo and Imam researched dowry and related phenomena.

The impact of modifying shalish might best be considered in the context of researching integrated legal services and/or development efforts that include but are not limited to improving how shalish operates. The Asia Foundation's quantitative inquiries into legal services efficacy in Bangladesh, conducted under the auspices of a seven-country study of legal empowerment for the Asian Development Bank in 2000–2001, found indications of poverty-alleviating and good-governance-promoting impact. More specifically, it compared control (that is, nonbeneficiary) populations with those belonging to either Banchte Shekha or Samata, an NGO that focuses on land advocacy, livelihood development, and access to government agricultural services.[40]

The findings indicate that the NGOs' impact included restraining dowry; increasing successful citizen participation in joint actions and in influencing local government decisions; fostering positive community attitudes toward women's rights and participation in governance; increasing use by the poor of government-managed lands that local elites otherwise seize; and dramatically reducing reliance on those elites for dispute resolution. The survey research found similar though more modest impact by MLAA in a number of these regards.[41]

The Foundation findings regarding dowry and other kinds of impact may not be totally consistent with the more qualitative inquiries of Geirbo and Imam. However, these two limited studies looked at different NGOs and communities. Expanded, rigorous research is called for.

Implications for International Development

Efforts to improve TJSs can be as much about social justice and governance as about dispute resolution. There is a tendency to view TJSs in terms of whether and how they settle disputes. The realities of shalish in Bangladesh contradict this view. Shalish in its traditional form often is a means of social control—of

---

38 Hasle, *supra* note 22.

39 D. M. Siddiqi, *Paving the Way to Justice, supra* note 18; *Shalish and the Quest for Gender Justice, supra* note 8; and *Ain O Salish Kendra, supra* note 27.

40 Stephen Golub & Kim McQuay, *Legal Empowerment: Advancing Good Governance and Poverty Reduction*, in *Law and Policy Reform at the Asian Development Bank* 135–49 (Asian Development Bank 2001).

41 *Id.*

men over women, of the relatively wealthy over the impoverished, and of religious and political leaders over their communities. Whether and to what extent these realities apply to traditional systems elsewhere is beyond the purview of this chapter. But the possibility that such systems manifest social control—and the potential to advance social justice by modifying them—should not be overlooked.

NGO engagement—and donor support for it—represents a potentially productive middle ground for efforts to improve TJSs. The experience of NGOs and their CBO partners in Bangladesh suggests that such organizations can productively work to keep the many advantages of TJSs while seeking to improve such systems. This effort represents a programmatic middle ground between simply leaving customary systems to their own devices and seeking to integrate them into the official state justice system. Pursuing this path does not preclude efforts to initiate or strengthen such integration. But given the fact that even after decades of existence, the state's village court system remains largely moribund and in need of "activation" by a UNDP project, and given the degree to which that system likely lends itself to political influence and traditional attitudes, NGO engagement with shalish arguably compares favorably with reliance on that system. This is particularly salient in terms of improving dispute resolution and for the aforementioned considerations regarding social justice. It most likely makes sense to support similar civil society efforts elsewhere.

However, the reality remains that many beneficiaries of NGO modification of TJSs may go from "worse to bad." For example, a farmer may recoup only a portion of the crop proceeds rightly due him, but this is better than nothing. An impoverished woman who in a society that offers more economic opportunities might be able to escape a dysfunctional marriage may opt to return to it by dint of NGO efforts. But this may be preferable to her alternatives outside the marriage: destitution, ostracization, homelessness, or malnourishment for herself or her children.

On a more hopeful note, it should be borne in mind that community dynamics in Bangladesh and elsewhere are not stagnant. The 2011 study on NU reached encouraging conclusions about the progress that the NGO and other women's empowerment strategies are making.[42] This author's observation of NGO-modified shalish in the 1990s found a markedly higher level of engagement by women over the years.

The possibility of litigation can be a powerful incentive for reaching and honoring a TJS agreement. The threat or fear of being taken to court by lawyers associated with an NGO can make an otherwise recalcitrant party cooperate with shalish. Especially when the judiciary is backlogged, corrupt, and otherwise dysfunctional, the expense of litigation and uncertainty of result can persuade a party to avoid becoming enmeshed in the formal wheels of justice.

---

42 Higgitt, *supra* note 23.

Ironically, then, some NGO engagement with shalish implicitly weaves together the country's nonstate and state legal systems. NGOs sometimes take cases straight to court if criminal or otherwise severe violations of a client's rights are at play. More commonly, though, NGO engagement integrates the two systems by holding out the possibility of turning to the judiciary should shalish fail.

On the other hand, under some circumstances, the possibility of going to court may not appeal to the NGO client or may not intimidate his or her opponent. Power imbalances are salient in this regard. An influential person may have resources to afford representation or significant sway in the community, making the client reluctant to go the judicial route.

Are NGOs' potential dual roles in shalish inappropriate? In many instances of shalish, NGOs do not take sides—their influence is on the process as a whole, rather than individual disputes. They convene and moderate in a neutral manner, rather than advocating and litigating in a partisan one. Still, the very fact that some convene sessions in response to one party's request can make her/him a kind of client. And, as discussed above, when they raise the possibility of taking recalcitrant parties to court (and occasionally actually do so), they take a clear stand in their clients' favor. Are these dual roles—neutral convener and partisan advocate—inappropriate? This raises issues of unchecked, unaccountable NGO influence.

The issue may be less problematic than it seems, however. There certainly is a tension between the two roles. And there is room for abuse by NGO personnel. But the balance in many disputes is typically tipped against women and other disadvantaged persons to begin with. There is no assurance that the police or courts redress power imbalances any better than NGOs do; in fact, there are indications to the contrary. Even if NGOs do not always act with absolute integrity or clarity in deciding whom they will support, their net impact is to make for fairer processes that can sometimes advance social justice.

One mechanism for advancing NGO accountability could be the introduction or strengthening of systems by which the organization's management obtains community feedback on whether and how its local personnel are acting responsibly. Although there are examples of such mechanisms in other countries—the dispute-resolution NGO Timap in Sierra Leone, for example—it is beyond the purview of this chapter to explore whether and to what extent similar approaches exist in Bangladesh.

NGO authority lends weight to shalish. The credibility and influence of an NGO can encourage the parties to participate in shalish and to abide by the results. This influence can flow, for example, from an NGO generating donor resources or otherwise bringing benefits to a community that grants the organization a measure of power. Or the NGO may be based in Dhaka or have influential government, donor, or civil society connections there, which suggests to many on a local level that it is a sophisticated, well-connected outfit.

The NGO can act as a countervailing influence to the corruption or politicization that may otherwise affect dispute resolution.

Yet, the degree of this influence is limited in many areas. Local officials' and party activists' political power also generates resources, sometimes far beyond those of an NGO. In addition, they may have criminal or police links that allow them to bring force to bear or otherwise act with impunity. And certainly, not all influential persons in a community necessarily view NGO generation of resources or contacts as unmitigated goods.

To the extent that NGOs do have considerable local influence, this has implications for the trade-off between approaches that prioritize their direct engagement with organizing shalish and those that concentrate on building up CBOs that can act independently. An argument for the former is that such engagement is necessary in most of Bangladesh for the foreseeable future, because change is a slow process and countervailing, conservative social dynamics are too strong for CBOs to counter. The case for the latter approach is that it is ultimately more sustainable and that the NGO remains in the picture to provide advice, training, legal assistance, and other support on an ongoing basis.

The involvement of influential persons can be crucial for shalish. Influential persons on the NGO-modified shalish panels may combine with community mores to create pressure for both parties to reach and honor an agreement. In some cases, long-term NGO engagement in a community on a number of fronts may make such persons' involvement less important. With its years of involvement with literacy, livelihoods, organizing, and other activities benefiting women, Banchte Shekha is a case in point. In some instances, however, NGOs may need to compromise with and try to co-opt influential figures, even if they tend to be conservative in their outlooks, rather than attempt to exclude them from shalish.

Nevertheless, there is a line to walk in such efforts. NGOs are effective to the extent that they mitigate traditional shalishdars' gender biases and other undue influences. The NGOs do this by helping women join the shalish panels and otherwise participate in the process. They also seek to involve community leaders and educated persons—teachers, for example—who may have broader perspectives.

The integration of TJS modification with broader socioeconomic development work holds promise for affecting underlying community dynamics. Shalish is a product of underlying community dynamics. To the extent that improving shalish hinges on affecting those dynamics, it is important to see NGO engagement with shalish as part of an integrated approach to poverty alleviation, improved governance, and social change. This is not to discount the value of straightforward income generation, microfinance, and other operations. But attacking problems such as government corruption and gender inequity requires a long-term, multipronged approach.

This view might seem to weigh in favor of simply supporting socioeconomic development NGOs for service delivery, with legal services NGOs playing supportive (though still crucial) back-up roles. But there are a few reasons to avoid drawing such a stark conclusion. First, insufficient data are available to support it. It would take years of rigorous research to make that judgment. Second, because legal-services NGOs are sophisticated in their legal knowledge and activities, they bring countervailing strengths to the table. Finally, and perhaps most significant, in many situations in Bangladesh the two kinds of NGOs are already cooperating in ways (such as training and other support by the legal services groups to the socioeconomic development ones) that produce integrated approaches.

A cautious approach to strengthening village courts and other government dispute resolution mechanisms is advisable. MLAA's interest in fortifying the village court system deserves respect, given its trailblazing role in community legal services in Bangladesh. UNDP's initiative to work with these bodies also could bear fruit. Nevertheless, it is best to proceed cautiously with government-centered work in Bangladesh and other countries. NGO-assisted shalish merits a greater investment of donor resources.

There are several reasons for such caution regarding village courts. First, the often corrupt and increasingly politicized nature of even the most basic local government functions, together with criminal links to politics, means that the village courts could be similarly infected. Conversely, there is also the more mundane constraint that Union Parishad chairpersons are often too busy to invest time and effort in participating in the process. Third, the problematic history of efforts to energize the system should be taken into account. In addition, MLAA aside, not all NGOs see the village courts as a vehicle for sound dispute resolution.

NGO-assisted shalish merits a greater investment of resources because, when integrated with socioeconomic development efforts, it has the potential to modify underlying community dynamics in ways that reach beyond dispute resolution. The village courts could perpetuate such underlying dynamics to the disadvantage of women and the poor. In a related vein, although *Disputes, Crimes and Pathways of Redress* indicates that Union Parishad chairpersons play important dispute-resolution roles even outside the village courts structure, they may also perpetuate unjust community dynamics.

Intellectual Property

Facilitating Technology Transfer for Development

Roy F. Waldron

In 1994, the Agreement on Trade-Related Aspects of Intellectual Property Rights (TRIPS) established minimum standards for the regulation of many forms of intellectual property (IP), including the right of patent owners to prevent unauthorized persons from using a patented process and making, using, offering for sale, selling, or importing a patented product or a product obtained directly by the patented process.[1] All members of the World Trade Organization (WTO) were required to adopt TRIPS-compliant IP laws, with the exception of least-developed countries (LDCs), which have until 2016 to apply TRIPS provisions for pharmaceutical patents.[2] The most comprehensive and influential international treaty on intellectual property rights, TRIPS is the global baseline for IP protection.

To successfully attract imported technology and to build the necessary preconditions for adapting the imported technology, developing countries needed a supportive environment that would facilitate such transfers, which included strong intellectual property protection and enforcement. To a large extent, this was the rationale behind the negotiation of TRIPS: technology would flow to those developing countries that adopted strong intellectual property protection and enforcement.

Developing countries view technology transfer as part of the bargain in which they agreed to protect intellectual property rights. TRIPS was crafted to create a common understanding of intellectual property rights globally and to provide its signatories (trading partners) with protections and certainties to ensure fair competition through a regime of IP rights. Articles 7 and 66.2 promote the practice of technology transfer, with the goal of ensuring that

---

The author wishes to thank Sharon Reiche and Angela Wasunna, both of Pfizer, for their contributions in the preparation of this chapter. The views expressed are those of the author and do not reflect the policy or position of Pfizer Inc.

1 Agreement on Trade-Related Aspects of Intellectual Property Rights (Apr. 15, 1994), Marrakesh Agreement Establishing the World Trade Organization, Annex 1C, *The Legal Texts: The Results of the Uruguay Round of Multilateral Trade Negotiations* 320 (1999), 1869 U.N.T.S. 299, 33 I.L.M. 1197 (1994), article 28 (hereinafter, TRIPS).

2 *See* World Trade Organization. Declaration on the TRIPS Agreement and Public Health, WT/MIN(01)/DEC/2 (Nov. 20, 2001).

technology holders are assured a favorable environment for investing in developing countries—and transferring their technology.[3]

The objectives section of Article 7 states that the "protection and enforcement of intellectual property rights should contribute to the promotion of technological innovation and to the transfer and dissemination of technology, *to the mutual advantage of producers and users of technological knowledge* and in a manner conducive to social and economic welfare, and to a balance of rights and obligations."[4] The obligation for developed countries to provide incentives to enterprises and institutions to promote and encourage technology transfer to LDC members is found in Article 66.2.[5] To ensure compliance, developed countries are required to submit reports on actions they have taken or plan to take in order to fulfill their commitments under this article.[6]

Despite the reference to technology transfer in Articles 7 and 66.2, TRIPS does not set out a universally recognized definition of technology transfer—leaving it open to legal and policy interpretation. There are many ways to transfer technology. Foreign direct investment, trade, and mobility of human resources are important sources of technology transfer and knowledge spillovers. Imports and exports, scientific collaborations, knowledge-sharing ventures, and capacity building help disseminate technology information from one source to another.[7] Proprietary knowledge may be revealed during licensing agreements and joint ventures with local partners, thus giving rise to the transfer of technology.[8] Additionally, foreign direct investment, a significant indicator of economic development and attractiveness of an economy, leads to technology transfer when multinational enterprises transfer information to their subsidiaries, some of which has the potential to "leak" into the host economy. The host country benefits via the experts, skills, and financial resources that are required to develop and make use of technology, as well as the development of human resources, higher wages, and improvement in corporate governance standards.[9]

---

3 TRIPS, *supra* note 1, Articles 7 and 66.2.

4 *Id.*, at Article 7 (emphasis added).

5 *Id.*, at Article 66.2 ("Developed country Members shall provide incentives to enterprises and institutions in their territories for the purpose of promoting and encouraging technology transfer to least-developed country Members in order to enable them to create a sound and viable technological base").

6 *See* World Trade Organization, Implementation of Article 66.2 of the TRIPS Agreement IP/C/28 (Feb. 20, 2003).

7 *See* Bernard Hoekman, Keith Maskus, & Kamal Saggi, *Transfer of Technology to Developing Countries: Unilateral and Multilateral Policy Options*, Institute of Behavioral Science, Research Program on Political and Economic Change, University of Colorado at Boulder Working Paper PEC2004-0003 (May 2004).

8 *See* Thomas Müller & Monika Schnitzer, *Technology Transfer and Spillovers in International Joint Ventures*, 68 J. Intl. Eco. 456–68 (2006).

9 *See* Maria Maher, Hans Christiansen, & Fabienne Fortanier, *Growth, Technology Transfer and Foreign Direct Investment* (OECD 2011) (prepared for the OECD Global Forum on International Investment: New Horizons and Policy Challenges for Foreign Direct Investment in the

During the 37th Session of the Working Group on Trade and Transfer of Technology (WGTTT),[10] Francis Gurry, the director general of the World Intellectual Property Organization (WIPO), discussed his organization's work on innovation and technology transfer. During his presentation, Gurry quoted Sir Francis Bacon's dictum that "knowledge is power," extrapolating to propose that the sharing of "technological superiority" is a transfer of power.[11] He considered what is required to entice companies to "do away with their competitive power" through technology transfer; in his view, the existence of suitable market conditions and market possibilities in the host country are vital for the transfer of technology to occur.[12]

The Role of Pharmaceutical Intellectual Property and Technology Transfer in Developing Countries

Protection of Intellectual Property Is Critical

As Gurry implied, the private sector considers a variety of factors when deciding whether to engage in technology transfer. To create the necessary conditions to foster confidence to invest in and export new technologies, as well as to develop new technologies in collaboration with developing countries, there must be strong IP protection and effective enforcement in those countries. As an intellectual property–dependent industry, the pharmaceutical industry did not initially engage in technology transfer in developing countries where IP protection was lacking. With TRIPS, a framework was created that encourages the rapid dissemination of ideas and efficient technology transfer, both of which are critical for technology-intensive, high-risk sectors.

The pharmaceutical industry's willingness to invest in critical value-added production and research and development (R&D) facilities in developing countries is directly linked to the strength and effectiveness of their IP systems. By safeguarding property against unauthorized commercial exploitation, effective IP protection provides predictability and, more important, the ability for a company to enter into license agreements and contracts. Because patents provide a legal basis for revealing proprietary information to subsidiaries and licensees, companies are less inclined to engage in technology transactions

---

21st Century, Mexico City, Nov. 26–27, 2001).

10 In 2001, during the WTO's Ministerial Conference in Doha, Qatar, a number of developing countries proposed the establishment of a working group under the umbrella of the WTO General Council to study the relationship between international trade and technology transfer and to make recommendations on ways to increase the flow of technology to developing countries. The proposal was accepted, and the Working Group on Trade and Transfer of Technology (WGTTT) was established. *See* World Trade Organization, Ministerial Declaration WT/MIN(01)/DEC/1 (Nov. 20, 2001), article 37.

11 World Trade Organization, Working Group on Trade and Transfer of Technology. 37th Session, Notes on the Meeting of Nov. 3, 2011, WT/WGTTT/M/37 (Jan. 13, 2012).

12 *Id.*

without effective IP protection.[13] IP protection helps pharmaceutical companies justify investments in the inherently risky, costly, complex, and lengthy R&D and regulatory process, and ensure long-term foreign investor commitment to the local market.

Technology transfers that follow in the wake of strong IP protection also help curtail "brain drain" by generating a more qualified and technically advanced labor force that will be motivated to remain in their home countries. Brain drain is "the departure of educated or professional people from one country, economic sector, or field for another usually for better pay or living conditions."[14] When these skilled workers leave their home country in search of better opportunities in wealthier countries, the developing country fails to benefit from its considerable investment of public funds to educate the person who now brings his or her skills to the developed world.[15] The loss of these workers negatively affects the developing country's ability to absorb technology transfer, because knowledge of scientific and technical information is necessary to accomplish technology transfer and advance development.[16] By providing companies with increased incentives—such as a supportive IP environment—to establish R&D facilities in developing countries, countries may entice local individuals to return or remain in country to capitalize on these opportunities.

IP plays an essential role in technological development and dissemination and provides incentives for innovation in developing countries. Developing countries have the potential to attract not only the transfer of existing technology but also the transfer of new technologies through stronger patent rights.[17] Although the degree to which a country benefits from IP depends on the country's relative strengths and socioeconomic characteristics, in countries with strong and effective IP regimes in place, there is a significant link between increased incentives for local innovation and the transfer of technologies that encourage local innovation and economic growth.[18] By providing the right incentives and removing barriers to the timely launch of innovative medicines, the patients and the private sector benefit.

---

13 *See* Hoekman, Maskus, & Saggi, *supra* note 7.

14 *Merriam-Webster Dictionary*, available at http://www.merriam-webster.com/dictionary.

15 *See* John Barton, *New Trends in Technology Transfer: Implications for National and International Policy*, International Centre for Trade and Sustainable Development Issue Paper No. 18 (Feb. 2007).

16 *See* Keith Maskus & Jerome Reichman ed., *International Public Goods and Transfer of Technology under a Globalized Intellectual Property Regime* 57 (Cambridge U. Press 2005).

17 *See* Walter G. Park & Douglas C. Lippoldt, *Technology Transfer and the Economic Implications of the Strengthening of Intellectual Property Rights in Developing Countries*, OECD Trade Policy Working Paper No. 62, 25 (2008).

18 *Id.*, at 28.

Other Factors Conducive to Technology Transfer

Strong and effective IP protection and enforcement, generally a prerequisite for any out-licensing or joint-venture decision, is only one of many factors influencing a company's decision to engage in technology transfer. Factors such as predictable regulatory standards, government commitment to education, a stable business environment, and alignment with the government's economic development priorities play an essential role.

A reliable and predictable registration process for pharmaceutical products is important in providing motivations and incentives to engage in technology transfer.[19] A heavily regulated sector, the pharmaceutical industry must meet rigorous standards involving safety, quality, and efficacy in order to ensure the welfare of patients. Therefore, when relying on local production, companies frequently transfer their technology to entities based in part on their capacity to meet international quality standards. This in turn contributes to the development of the local pharmaceutical industry.

The presence of a highly skilled workforce is vital to the development, application, utilization, and integration of new technology[20] and makes the investment climate more attractive for foreign investors. Due to their depth of knowledge, these highly trained and educated workers are essential for technology transfer to occur. Through improvements in education and in the operating environment, developing countries are encouraged to promote the knowledge, experience, and skills necessary to enable workers to bring economic value and a competitive advantage to technical companies. These companies, in turn, provide education and training and may bring new information, skills, and technology to host nations.

A country's relative political, economic, and social stability will influence a company's decision whether to transfer technology and is often considered a precondition for technology transfer to occur.[21] Long periods of stability lead to stronger and more successful partnerships because stability lowers the risk of doing business in an unfamiliar environment and provides companies with increased confidence to implement long-term business strategies and assurance that their goals will be sustainable. Economic reforms and other efforts that promote trade, investment, nondiscriminatory policies, legal frameworks, and national infrastructure add to the attractiveness of a country with regard to technology transfer.[22] As governments begin to understand the interrelationship between health care and economic outcomes, investment in health care systems and infrastructures will become a high priority.[23]

19 *See Technology Transfer: A Collaborative Approach to Improve Global Health* (IFPMA 2011).

20 *See* Barton, *supra* note 15.

21 *See Technology Transfer, supra* note 19.

22 *See* Maher, Christiansen, & Fortanier, *supra* note 9.

23 *See Technology Transfer, supra* note 19.

By aligning themselves with a system that promotes technology transfer, developing countries are more likely to create medicines and technologies that address their public health needs and enable local and regional solutions.[24] Technology transfer arrangements can create strong alliances and collaborations that can be leveraged for long-term commercial and economic advantage. A supportive environment that encourages these transactions is a win-win situation for both the private sector and the developing country. The R&D activities of companies can enhance economic and social progress in developing countries. In turn, the development of a robust and dynamic innovation system in a developing country will expand commercial opportunities for companies.

Examples of Technology Transfer in the Pharmaceutical Industry

A goal of technology transfer, in the context of pharmaceuticals, is to promote access to new medicines and technologies for diseases that affect a local population. Access to medicines in developing countries is a high-priority issue in the global health sector, including for multinational pharmaceutical companies.[25] Technology transfer can directly affect research for neglected tropical diseases (NTDs) that primarily occur in developing countries. Many forms of collaboration and alliances have been developed to promote research and treatment of these diseases, and many include a technology transfer element.[26] These types of arrangements, which are becoming more frequent, demonstrate that solutions to societal issues can be found through partnerships and the sharing of knowledge without undermining IP rights.

Pfizer's Research Partnership with Drugs for Neglected Diseases Initiative

According to the World Health Organization (WHO), NTDs affect more than 1 billion people each year and are endemic in 149 countries.[27] For NTDs such as leishmaniasis and human African trypanosomiasis (HAT), infections occur among the poorest people in rural areas. To accelerate the elimination or

---

24 *See* Luis A. Salicrup & Lenka Fedorková, *Challenges and Opportunities for Enhancing Biotechnology and Technology Transfer in Developing Countries,* 24 Biotech. Advances 69–79 (2006).

25 *See* Sofia Gruskin & Zyde Raad, *Are Drug Companies Living Up to Their Human Rights Responsibilities? Moving toward Assessment* (Harvard School of Public Health 2010); Carsten Fink, *Intellectual Property and Public Health: An Overview of the Debate with a Focus on US Policy* (World Bank Development Research Group 2008); Joyce Meng, Expanding Global Access: A Comparative Analysis of Pharmaceutical Corporate Social Responsibility Initiative (unpublished paper 2007); and Greg Martin et al., *Balancing Intellectual Monopoly Privileges and the Need for Essential Medicines,* 3(4) Globalization and Health (2007).

26 James T. Gathii, *Approaches to Accessing Essential Medicines and the TRIPS Agreement,* 15(2) Harv. J. L. & Tech. (2002).

27 *See* the WHO-sponsored Global Health Observatory website's section Neglected Tropical Diseases, http://www.who.int.gho/ (accessed Apr. 2012); and World Health Organization, *Accelerating Work to Overcome the Global Impact of Neglected Tropical Diseases: A Roadmap for Implementation* (WHO 2012).

control of these diseases, Pfizer entered into an agreement with Drugs for Neglected Diseases initiative (DND*i*) in 2009, in which Pfizer agreed to provide DND*i* with access to a Pfizer library of proprietary compounds to screen for new potential targets against leishmaniasis, Chagas disease, and HAT.[28] This arrangement, which partners Pfizer's research infrastructure with DND*i*'s neglected disease expertise, maximizes the chances of identifying promising starting points for drug discovery programs. Although Pfizer owns the IP on these compounds, any novel leads are a candidate for licensing agreements with regard to NTDs. The Pfizer-DND*i* partnership demonstrates that the burden of finding solutions to diseases endemic to developing countries does not rest with a single entity. Through the transfer of technology, duplication of research and repetitiveness of efforts are minimized, resulting in a more streamlined and focused approach that draws on the complementary strengths of each organization. The collaboration has identified promising leads, and DND*i* will continue research, development, and commercialization based on these leads.

GlaxoSmithKline's Vaccine Development Initiative with the Oswaldo Cruz Foundation

In 2009, GlaxoSmithKline (GSK) announced a partnership with the Oswaldo Cruz Foundation (Fiocruz) to develop and manufacture vaccines for public health needs in Brazil.[29] The agreement created an R&D collaboration program at Fiocruz to develop a vaccine for dengue fever, a mosquito-borne viral infection that is the leading cause of serious illness and death among children in Asian and Latin American countries and for which no specific treatment is available.[30] With approximately half of the world's population at risk of contracting dengue fever,[31] this joint R&D initiative will enhance Brazilian capacity to improve the health of patients by protecting them against this disease.

GSK also partnered with Fiocruz in 2009 to provide access to the technology behind GSK's 10-valent conjugate vaccine for pediatric pneumococcal disease, or Synflorix.[32] Under the agreement, GSK supplied Fiocruz with Synflorix until the technology transfer was complete; the vaccine has since been incorporated into Brazil's national immunization program.[33] In sharing knowledge and technology between the two organizations, scientists from GSK and Fiocruz work across facilities in Brazil and Belgium to protect

---

28 *See Pfizer and DNDi Advancing International Research Efforts in the Fight against Neglected Tropical Diseases*, DNDi Press Release (Nov. 18, 2009).

29 *See GSK and Brazil's Fiocruz Form Partnership for New R&D Effort and Increased Vaccine Access*, GSK Press Release (Aug. 17, 2009).

30 *Id.*; World Health Organization, *Dengue and Severe Dengue*, Fact Sheet No. 117 (Jan. 2012).

31 *Id.*

32 *See GSK and Brazil's Fiocruz*, *supra* note 29.

33 *Id.*

children from diseases such as pneumonia, meningitis, and bacteremia.[34] The two organizations extended their partnership in 2010, enabling scientists at Fiocruz and GSK's Tres Cantos facility in Spain to share new ideas, know-how, and research on diseases such as malaria, tuberculosis, Chagas disease, and leishmaniasis.[35]

In collaborations such as these, the transfer of technology and expertise drives discovery and development efforts to produce new and innovative medicines to treat diseases that affect people in developing countries. Antonio de Pádua Risolia Barbosa, deputy director of production at the Immunobiological Technology Institute, or Bio-Manguinhos unit, of Fiocruz, states, "Besides our own innovation and development, we have partnerships with local and global organizations, and we use technology transfer to accelerate the viability of the products for the population."[36]

WIPO Re:Search—Sharing Innovation in the Fight against NTDs

Recognizing the need for progress in neglected disease research and understanding that such research is the collective responsibility of the entire global health community, WIPO Re:Search was formed in 2011 through the efforts of several of the world's leading pharmaceutical companies, WIPO, and BIO Ventures for Global Health (BVGH).[37]

WIPO Re:Search provides three services:

- A comprehensive platform/database, hosted by WIPO, of patent and other proprietary information (for example, clinical trial results, regulatory status) on compounds and technologies available for licensing for NTD research
- A partnership hub, managed by BVGH, providing a forum where interested parties can learn about available licensing opportunities, available funding for research, and networking opportunities in their research fields
- A range of specific supporting activities, such as facilitating licensing agreements and dispute resolution[38]

WIPO Re:Search aims to promote the transfer of knowledge through the facilitation of nontraditional partnerships and by encouraging organizations to share proprietary information publicly. WIPO Re:Search also offers researchers in developing countries access to research facilities and scientists

---

34 *Id.*

35 *See GlaxoSmithKline and Fiocruz Extend Innovative Collaboration to Research and Develop New Medicines for Neglected Tropical Diseases*, GSK Press Release (Nov. 12, 2010).

36 Patricia Van Arnum, *Technology Transfer in Global Health Initiatives*, 7(4) Pharmaceutical Technology Sourcing and Management (Apr. 6, 2011).

37 *See Leading Pharmaceutical Companies & Research Institutions Offer IP and Expertise for Use in Treating Neglected Tropical Diseases as Part of WIPO Re:Search*, WIPO Press Release (Oct. 26, 2011).

38 *See* WIPO Re:Search website, www.wiporesearch.org (accessed Mar. 2012).

working in leading pharmaceutical companies and laboratories, an important step in the technology transfer process. The structure of the consortium demonstrates that solutions to societal issues can be solved through partnerships without undermining IP.

Users of WIPO Re:Search are granted royalty-free licenses to IP for research and development, anywhere in the world, of products and technologies or services for the sole purpose of addressing public health needs for NTDs in LDCs. Users are also granted royalty-free licenses to make or have made such products, technologies, or services. These licenses also allow users to sell these products in LDCs royalty-free. Users are allowed to retain ownership of and apply for registration of IP as they deem fit, but are encouraged to license through WIPO Re:Search new IP rights generated under an agreement made pursuant to membership in the consortium.[39]

WIPO Re:Search leverages expertise to develop new products and technologies, improves research productivity, allows the monetization of technologies and IP assets that would otherwise go unused in the organization's own business, and makes more efficient use of research investments by enhancing the exchange of mutually beneficial knowledge. Through information-sharing consortiums such as WIPO Re:Search, products and technologies can be brought to market faster and more efficiently.

The consortium has received the commitment of more than 50 private and public organizations dedicated to accelerating R&D for NTDs, malaria, and tuberculosis, including Pfizer, GlaxoSmithKline, AstraZeneca, DND*i*, Fiocruz, Medicines for Malaria Ventures (MMV), PATH, and the Walter Reed Army Institute of Research (WRAIR).[40] Although the commitment and willingness of these partners to transfer technology through WIPO Re:Search is a step toward addressing the R&D challenges that affect the developing world, sustained elimination of these diseases is possible only with a commitment by individual countries to ensure access to safe water, proper waste disposal and treatment, basic sanitation, and improved living conditions.[41]

ViiV Healthcare—Joint Venture between Pfizer and GSK

According to the Joint United Nations Programme on HIV/AIDS (UNAIDS), the growth of the global AIDS epidemic appears to have stabilized, and the annual number of new HIV infections has been steadily declining.[42] However, approximately 34 million people worldwide continue to live with HIV,[43] and

---

39 *See WIPO Re:Search: Sharing Innovation in the Fight against Neglected Tropical Diseases*, Guiding Principles (May 2011), available at http://www.wiporesearch.org.

40 *Id.*

41 *See* World Health Organization, *Accelerating Work to Overcome the Global Impact of Neglected Tropical Diseases, supra* note 27.

42 *See* UNAIDS, *Report on the Global AIDS Epidemic* 16 (UNAIDS 2010).

43 *See* UNAIDS website, http://www.unaids.org (accessed Mar. 2012).

more than 7,000 people are newly infected every day.[44] Discrimination and stigmatization remain, and many people continue to lack access to the antiretroviral (ARV) medicines and health care support they require; only one-third of the 15 million people living with HIV in low- and middle-income countries who need treatment are receiving it.[45]

To further efforts to deliver advances in treatment and care for people living with HIV, Pfizer and GSK created a joint venture and established a new specialist HIV company, ViiV Healthcare, in 2009.[46] ViiV Healthcare is focused solely on the research, development, and commercialization of HIV medicines and has a single, sustainable, not-for-profit price for each ARV that it makes available to a wide range of patients in LDCs and sub-Saharan Africa—a total of 69 countries, representing 80% of all people living with HIV/AIDS worldwide.[47] ViiV Healthcare extends royalty-free voluntary licensing of its innovative drugs to generic manufacturers producing and distributing therapies to people living with HIV in LDCs, low-income countries, and all of sub-Saharan Africa. As of 2012, ViiV Healthcare had granted 11 voluntary licenses for its ARVs.[48]

By combining the research efforts and knowledge of Pfizer and GSK, ViiV Healthcare will achieve more for those whose lives are affected by HIV than either company could have achieved alone. Various ViiV initiatives, such as the ViiV Healthcare Effect, strive to strengthen education, support services, local health care capacity, and capabilities through education and collaboration.[49]

Pfizer's Global Health Fellows

Since 2003, more than 300 Pfizer colleagues have participated in the Global Health Fellows Program, an international corporate volunteer program that places Pfizer colleagues in short-term assignments with international development organizations in emerging markets.[50] The objective of the program is to strengthen the ability of health care providers in these countries to care for their patients. Through Pfizer's partnership with more than 40 organizations, colleagues are provided the opportunity to transfer their professional medical and business expertise to optimize local supply chains and business functions

---

44 *See* UNAIDS, *2011–2015 Strategy: Getting to Zero* (UNAIDS 2010).

45 *See* UNAIDS, *supra* note 42, at 7.

46 *See ViiV Healthcare Launches: A New Specialist HIV Company Dedicated to Delivering Advances in HIV Treatment and Care*, ViiV press release (Nov. 3, 2009).

47 *See* ViiV Healthcare website, www.viivhealthcare.com (accessed Mar. 2012).

48 *Id.*

49 The ViiV Healthcare Effect is a portal that introduces the company's approach to partnerships and showcases best practices throughout the world. It provides users the opportunity to hear directly from people creating new solutions on the ground and to learn what has worked and how those efforts can be applied or expanded to support more communities. *See* ViiV Healthcare Effect website, www.viivhealthcareeffect.com (accessed Mar. 2012).

50 *See* Pfizer website, Global Health Fellows, available at http://www.pfizer.com/ghf (accessed Mar. 2012).

and improve health prevention approaches. This program demonstrates that technology transfer encompasses expertise and technical skills.

WHO's TDR Career Development Fellowship Program

In 1975, the Special Programme for Research and Training in Tropical Diseases (TDR), sponsored by the United Nations Children's Fund (UNICEF), the United Nations Development Programme (UNDP), the World Bank, and WHO, was established as a scientific collaboration to coordinate, support, and influence global efforts to combat diseases affecting disadvantaged populations.[51]

TDR founded the Career Development Fellowship on Clinical Research & Development in 2009 with the support of the Bill & Melinda Gates Foundation. Researchers and public health professionals from disease-endemic countries are awarded a 12-month training opportunity with pharmaceutical companies in order to receive specialized in-house training to acquire experience in clinical trial management, R&D project management, regulatory compliance, and good practices.[52] By focusing on human resources development and capacity building, individual fellows are able to maintain their existing capabilities, strengthen their potential, and obtain new skills that are not normally taught in academic centers. Once the fellowship has been completed and the fellows return to their home countries, they have the opportunity to assume a leading role in the global effort on R&D, thereby enhancing the developing country's capacity for product development. In 2009, Pfizer hosted two developing-world clinical researchers as part of the TDR program.[53] In 2011, Eisai, a major Japan-based pharmaceutical company, welcomed a TDR clinical research fellow whose goal is to build the health care capacity of developing countries; Eisai provides the fellow with the opportunity to learn about drug development from the US and Japanese perspective.[54] Upon completion of the fellowship, the fellow returned to his home country, Colombia, to develop and arrange local and regional academic meetings to educate his counterparts in the study of tropical and neglected diseases.[55]

Looking toward the Future: Navigating an Evolving Landscape

The world today is quite different than it was a few decades ago; trade, as well as scientific and education research systems, is highly globalized, and an

---

51 *See* World Health Organization website, TDR, available at http://www.who.int/tdr (accessed Mar. 2012).

52 *See* International Federation of Pharmaceutical Manufacturers & Associations (IFPMA) website, Capacity Building, http://www.ifpma.org/global-health/access/capacity-building.html (accessed Mar. 2012).

53 *See Pfizer Corporate Responsibility Report* (2009), available at http://www.pfizer.com/responsibility (accessed Mar. 2012).

54 *See Eisai Takes Second Clinical Research Fellow from Developing World*, available at http://www.eisai.com (accessed Mar. 2012).

55 *Id.*

increasing number of developing countries are becoming more technologically sophisticated. According to the World Bank's *Global Economic Prospects* report, however, "the world economy has entered a very difficult phase characterized by significant downside risks and fragility," with developing-country growth expected to decline to 5.4 percent and 6.0 percent versus 6.2 percent and 6.3 percent in June 2011 projections.[56]

Developing countries should be encouraged to identify new drivers of growth, one of which is technology transfer. Although technology transfer can be a time-consuming and complex process, given the right incentives and strong interest by developing countries in increasing their access to international technologies, companies from developed countries can assist LDCs in achieving sustained economic change and growth in domestic productivity. Intellectual property, in particular, helps realize the model necessary to transfer technology and should be viewed as a vital tool that can aid in social and economic progress. As countries develop their own assets, they will have greater incentives to respect the IP framework and implement and enforce strong IP regimes that will aid in the facilitation of new types of positive partnerships.

Although not all countries are equally prepared to integrate complex technology into their production chains, the level of complexity on the technology transfer spectrum varies, beginning with knowledge and skills training as the most basic form. Therefore, the transfer of technology should be encouraged in all regions of the developing world, because building local capacity can play a major role in moving LDCs to the next stage of development and significantly affect the pace of innovation within these countries.

---

56 World Bank, *Global Economic Prospects: Uncertainties and Vulnerabilities* (Jan. 2012).

Transforming through Transparency

Opening Up the World Bank's Sanctions Regime

CONRAD C. DALY AND FRANK A. FARIELLO, JR.

The World Bank,[1] whose mission it is to fight against global poverty,[2] is one of the world's premier international financial institutions.[3] The Bank's sanctions system emerges out of the Bank's fiduciary obligation to ensure that the funds that its shareholders contribute are used with attention to economy and efficiency for their intended purposes.[4] As fraud and corruption compromise the effectiveness of development projects[5] and have a perverse and deleterious

---

1 In this chapter, "World Bank" is used to refer collectively to two institutions, the International Bank for Reconstruction and Development (IBRD) and the International Development Association (IDA). IBRD began operations in 1947, with the purpose of providing loans to developing countries, while IDA was founded in 1960 to provide financing on concessional terms to the poorest and least credit-worthy developing countries. The World Bank is part of the World Bank Group, a constellation of institutions including, in addition to IBRD and IDA, the International Finance Corporation (IFC), the Multilateral Investment Guarantee Agency (MIGA), and the International Center for Settlement of Investment Disputes (ICSID).

2 *See* IBRD Articles of Agreement, Article I, Section i (Dec. 27, 1945) ("To assist in the reconstruction and development of territories of members"); and IDA Articles of Agreement, Article I ("The purposes of the Association are to promote economic development, increase productivity and thus raise standards of living in the less-developed areas of the world included within the Association's membership"). The first president of the World Bank, Eugene Meyer, highlighted the place of "the economic development of the world as a whole. . . . [For] economic distress is a prime breeder of war." IBRD, *First Annual Meeting of the Board of Governors: Proceedings and Related Documents*, 15–16 (World Bank 1946).

3 Anne-Marie Leroy & Frank Fariello, *The World Bank Group Sanctions Process and Its Recent Reforms* 1 (World Bank 2012).

4 *See* IBRD Articles of Agreement, Article III, Section 5(b) ("The Bank shall make arrangements to ensure that the proceeds of any loan are used only for the purposes for which the loan was granted, with due attention to considerations of economy and efficiency and without regard to political or other non-economic influences or considerations"); and IDA Articles of Agreement, Article V, Section 6 ("The Association and its officers shall not interfere in the political affairs of any member; nor shall they be influenced in their decisions by the political character of the member or members concerned. Only economic considerations shall be relevant to their decisions, and these considerations shall be weighed impartially in order to achieve the purposes stated in this Agreement"). *See* also World Bank Sanctions Procedures (as adopted Apr. 15, 2012) (hereinafter, Sanctions Procedures), Article 1.01(a).

5 *See*, for example, News & Broadcast, *World Bank, Disclosure of Assets and Income by Public Officials Is Crucial to Curbing Corruption Finds New StAR Study*, Press Release No. 2012/360/FPD (Mar. 28, 2012), available at http://go.worldbank.org/6JFJF7TXA0; Stuart Yikona et al., *Ill-Gotten Money and the Economy, Experiences from Malawi and Namibia* (World Bank 2011), available at http://go.worldbank.org/0PHO7X3QA0. *See* also C. M. Matthews, *Infrastructure Corruption Top of Mind for Public, Private Sectors*, Wall St. J. (Apr. 19, 2012), available at http://blogs.wsj.com/corruption-currents/2012/04/19/infrastructure-corruption-top

effect on systems and societies,[6] they are the target of the Bank's sanctions system. This chapter considers the Bank's recent commitment to opening up its sanctions regime and to making that system more transparent and accountable, highlighting the particularly innovative manner in which the Bank has opened up its system. The desired end of this opening up is a sanctions regime that inspires confidence through the witnessing of the robust deliberative process that underlies it, the promotion of good governance at large, and an increase in stakeholder confidence. Opening up the process both encourages contractors to participate in Bank-financed projects and also garners further support for the fight against poverty by profiting those who play by the rules. The result is a system with significant due process protections that empowers stakeholders at all levels.

This chapter is divided into four parts:

- *First,* this chapter offers an introduction to the nature of the Bank's sanctions regime, highlighting the particular challenges that it faces.[7]
- *Second,* it presents an outline of the development of the sanctions regime, focusing on the system's rapid progression since its foundation in 1996.
- *Third,* it addresses the most recent changes to the system.
- *Fourth,* it examines how this progression is in accord with the Bank's mission of establishing law and justice as developmental ends in and of themselves, with a special emphasis on transparency and accountability for the sake of improving both governance and stakeholder ownership and empowerment.

The chapter concludes with remarks on the relationship between law and development and what that relationship means for the Bank as it seeks to empower those for whom it works as well as to give them a sense of confidence in the Bank and the Bank's systems as a whole.

Introduction to the Bank's Sanctions Regime

Like other international financial institutions,[8] the World Bank has traditionally considered its decisions to exclude an entity or individual from work-

---

-of-mind-for-public-private-sectors/; David Chaikin & J. C. Sharman, *Corruption and Money Laundering: A Symbiotic Relationship* (Palgrave Series on Asian Governance 2009); Dayanath Jayasuriya, *Anti-Money Laundering Efforts, Stock Market Operations and Good Governance,* 1 Qualitative Research in Financial Markets 46–58 (2009).

6 *See id. See* also James D. Wolfensohn, *People and Development: Address to the Board of Governors at the Annual Meetings of the World Bank and the International Monetary Fund,* in *Voice for the World's Poor: Selected Speeches and Writings of World Bank President James D. Wolfensohn, 1995–2005* 50 (World Bank 2005).

7 For a detailed discussion of the historical system's evolution, *see* Leroy & Fariello, *supra* note 3.

8 Consider, for instance, the other multilateral development banks (MDBs), discussed further on. *See infra* note 39. The same is true for many other international organizations, such as the United Nations and the North Atlantic Treaty Organization.

ing on Bank-financed projects or programs as a business decision and has thus subjected those decisions to an administrative regime.[9] That process of exclusion for corrupt or fraudulent behavior is known as "debarment."[10] The principal stated goal of World Bank Group sanctions proceedings is to protect the World Bank Group's funds and not to "punish" respondents: the sanctions imposed do not entail any form of physical coercion, nor even an obligation to repay money to the Bank.[11] From such a perspective, relatively little due process[12] is due to respondents as compared with during civil or criminal proceedings.[13]

There are, however, several factors that complicate the classification of such actions as otherwise-banal business decisions. First, with aggregate new lending commitments of approximately US$43 billion, aggregate outstanding liabilities of US$258 billion, and assets of US$314 billion for fiscal year 2011,[14] and as the Bank directly or indirectly employs tens of thousands of people,[15]

---

9 *See* Leroy & Fariello, *supra* note 3. This model has not gone without criticism. *See*, for example, Alnoor Ebrhaim, *The World Bank Must Fix Its Business Model*, Financial Times (Oct. 5, 2009).

10 *See* Sanctions Procedures, *supra* note 4.

11 The Bank's system allows for five different sanctions—reprimand, conditional nondebarment, debarment, debarment with conditional release, and restitution or remedy—only the last of which imposes the obligation of financial reparation. Sanctions Procedures, *supra* note 4, at Article 9. Of course, these stand apart from the typical contractual remedies available to the Bank under the general conditions.

12 Due process is the legal requirement that the sovereign respect the legal rights that are owed to persons; it is a "central promise [of] assurance that . . . government must operate within the law ('legality') and provide fair procedures." Legal Information Institute (LII), Cornell University, at http://www.law.cornell.edu/wex/due_process. The principle ensures a balancing of sovereign power (or the law of the land), on the one hand, and the rights of the individual, on the other. *See*, for example, *In re Winship*, 397 U.S. 358, 382 (1970) (J. Black, dissenting).

13 As a body of public law, administrative law addresses and controls how government and its agencies govern. *See* William F. Fox, Jr., *Understanding Administrative Law* (4th ed., Lexis 2000). Generally, fewer rights are afforded to respondents in an administrative system than in civil or (especially) criminal proceedings; in administrative proceedings, the interests and prerogatives of the sovereign and the invocation of its discretionary powers are at stake.

14 *See* Moody's *Investors Service Credit Analysis: IBRD (World Bank)* (Feb. 27, 2012), available at http://treasury.worldbank.org/cmd/pdf/Moodys_IBRD_Report_2012.pdf. The Bank also provides financing in the form of development policy loans (DPLs), which provide budget support and other unlinked financing against achievement of defined policy measures rather than to finance specific expenditures. The Bank's sanctions regime does not extend to DPLs because it is not possible to trace the use of loan proceeds. This approach (or the lack of one) has come under increasing criticism. *See*, for example, Independent Advisory Board (IAB), *2010 Annual Report 11-12* (Jan. 2011), available at http://go.worldbank.org/S262CF3KD0 (acknowledging the "significant challenges and difficulties concerning efforts to investigate the extent, if any, of corrupt behaviors that may arise in connection with the implementation of [DPLs]," but encouraging management "to consider ways and means of sharpening the criteria for [DPLs]"). It bears noting that the effect of cross-debarment renders the figures—and the effect of debarment—even greater. *See infra* note 40 et seq. and accompanying text.

15 Moisés Naím & Uri Dadush, *Dr. Kim Comes to Washington*, Huffington Post (Apr. 4, 2012), available at http://www.huffingtonpost.com/moises-naim/kim-world-bank_b_1396618.html.

the stakes of exclusion from Bank-financed projects are substantially higher than those surrounding even the most significant business decisions made by the largest private corporations.[16] Moreover, debarment not only entails substantial financial consequences but also causes considerable public notoriety and reputational damage.[17] Second, debarring an entity has significant market effects, especially when a limited number of entities are capable of performing highly specialized work.[18] Third, the Bank's decision to debar is not one that affects those entities with which the Bank itself would otherwise work, but rather affects the pool of entities from which the borrower might choose to work; that is, the Bank, on the basis of providing project financing, unilaterally decides for the borrowing party that certain entities are not to be dealt with.[19]

---

16 That is to say, the economic implications of exclusion from the possibility of participating in the large potential market of World Bank Group–financed projects are greater than those of being excluded from the activities of any one private actor. For instance, to make a monetary comparison, the market value of Apple in 2011, the world's most valuable company, is around US$337 million, with 12-month sales surpassing the US$100 billion mark. Scott DeCarlo, *The World's 25 Most Valuable Companies: Apple Is Now on Top*, Forbes (Aug. 11, 2011), available at http://www.forbes.com/sites/scottdecarlo/2011/08/11/the-worlds-25-most-valuable-companies-apple-is-now-on-top/.

17 Consider, for instance, the press coverage surrounding the sanctioning of Siemens. See, for example, *Siemens Selects Initial Projects for US$100 million Integrity Initiative*, Siemens AG, Ref. No. AXX20101225e (Dec. 9, 2010), available at http://www.siemens.com/press/en/pressrelease/?press=/en/pressrelease/2010/corporate_communication/axx20101225.htm; Vanessa Fuhrmans, *Siemens Settles with World Bank on Bribes*, Wall St. J. (Jul. 3, 2009), available at http://online.wsj.com/article/SB124655953719287521.html.

18 In this regard, consider, for instance, the debarment of a Siemens subsidiary. *See* News & Broadcast, *World Bank, World Bank Group Debars Limited Liability Company Siemens (OOO Siemens) for Engaging in Fraud and Corruption in a World Bank–Financed Project in Russia*, Press Release No. 2009/168/EXC (Nov. 30, 2009), available at http://go.worldbank.org/VZ1113XEG0. In addition to having a subsidiary entity debarred, Siemens AG paid US$100 million to fight corruption as part of a settlement with the World Bank Group. *See* News & Broadcast, *World Bank, Siemens to Pay $100m to Fight Corruption as Part of World Bank Group Settlement*, Press Release No. 2009/001/EXT (Jul. 2, 2009), available at http://go.worldbank.org/WXRNSDVI40. Siemens, France's Alstom, and Canada's Bombardier are the world's big-three passenger train manufacturers. *See*, for example, Robert Wright, *China to Loosen West's Grip on Rail Sector*, Financial Times (Sept. 13, 2010), available at http://www.ft.com/intl/cms/s/0/83d7e478-bec0-11df-a755-00144feab49a.html#axzz1sKPOrVA4. For the argument that certain private contractors may be too big to debar, *see* Drury D. Steven & Nicholas J. Wagoner, *FCPA Sanctions: Too Big to Debar?* 80 Fordham L. Rev. 775 (2011). *See* also FCPA Compliance and Ethics Blog, *Is Debarment a Viable FCPA Enforcement Option?* (Apr. 19, 2011), available at http://tfoxlaw.wordpress.com/2011/04/19/is-debarment-a-viable-fcpa-enforcement-option/.

19 Others, for reasons such as the absence of privity and the substantial influence that the Bank is capable of exerting, have described the Bank's behavior as "imperialism" or "neocolonialism." Catherine Caufield, *Masters of Illusion: The World Bank and the Poverty of Nations* (Henry Holt & Co. 1996); Jonathan Cahn, *Challenging the New Imperial Authority: The World Bank and the Democratization of Development*, 6 Harv. Hum. Rights J. 159 (1993); Steve Berkman, *The World Bank and the Gods of Lending* (Kumarian Press 2008); Payal Parekh & Oren Weinrib, *Why the Developing World Hates the World Bank*, 122 The Tech 5 (Mar. 12, 2002), available at http://tech.mit.edu/V122/PDF/N11.pdf.

Thus, Bank operational debarments—taken in the absence of any privity—are more than mere run-of-the-mill business decisions about, say, buying pens or paper.[20]

Although none of the aforementioned factors necessarily takes the Bank's regime out of the realm of administrative law, the Bank, in an effort to lead by example, and considering law and justice as developmental ends in and of themselves, affords respondents additional due process protections, more than what are usually required under the general principles of administrative law.[21] Arguments have been made that the World Bank Group's system ought to develop its legal regime based on, alternatively, theories of global constitutionalism,[22] the exercise of international public authority,[23] or the emerging global administrative law (GAL) principles.[24] The Bank has taken a more open-ended approach by working toward a quasi-judicial model inspired by various sources of law from around the world. Such an innovative approach results in a sui generis form that is not dominated by any single tradition (neither common law nor civil law) or by any one national system. In pursuing the objectives of effectiveness and efficiency, the Bank has been equally attentive to ensuring that the process reflects certain fundamental

---

20 It is worth noting that the World Bank Group maintains a separate sanctions system for its own corporate procurement. *See* World Bank Vendor Eligibility Policy (as adopted Jun. 18, 2010), available at http://go.worldbank.org/W40WJB5AA0. To be deemed a responsible vendor with whom the World Bank Group will conduct business, a vendor must meet a range of standards, most of which relate to the financial and organizational capacity of the vendor to deliver or perform the services, as well as its track record in not having seriously violated the terms of a World Bank Group contract in the past. In addition, a vendor must not have committed "any act or offense indicating a lack of integrity or honesty that seriously and directly affects [its] present responsibility . . . , including fraudulent, corrupt, collusive, coercive, or obstructive practices."

21 "'Respondent' means an entity or individual alleged to have engaged in a Sanctionable Practice and who has been designated as such in a Notice." Sanctions Procedures, *supra* note 4, at Article 1.02.

22 *See* Jan Klabbers, Anne Petters, & Geir Ulfstein, *The Constitutionalization of International Law* (Oxford U. Press 2009).

23 *See* Armin von Bogdandy, Philipp Dann, & Matthias Goldmann, *Developing the Publicness of Public International Law: Towards a Legal Framework for Global Governance Activities*, 9 German L.J. 1375, 1377 (2008) ("The legal framework of governance activities of international institutions should be conceived of as international institutional law, and enriched by a public law perspective, i.e. with constitutional sensibility and openness for comparative insights from administrative legal thinking"), and the other articles in the same special issue on public authority and international institutions.

24 *See* Benedict Kingsbury, Nico Krisch, & Richard B. Stewart, *The Emergence of Global Administrative Law*, 16 L. & Contemp. Probs. 15, 17 (2005) (defining global administrative law "as comprising the mechanisms, principles, practices, and supporting social understandings that promote or otherwise affect the accountability of global administrative bodies, in particular by ensuring they meet adequate standards of transparency, participation, reasoned decision, and legality, and by providing effective review of the rules and decisions they make"), and the other articles in the same symposium. *See* also articles in the symposium Global Administrative Law in the Operations of International Organizations in 6 Intl. Org. L. Rev. (2009); Pascale Hélène Dubois & Aileen Elizabeth Nowlan, *Global Administrative Law and the Legitimacy of Sanctions Regimes in International Law*, 36 Yale J. Intl. L. 15–25 (2010).

principles and values associated with the rule of law from around the world.[25] In so doing, it is particularly mindful of the varied—and ever-evolving—legal traditions and conceptions of its members.[26] Such a creative approach gives the Bank's system a certain formality while allowing it to retain a necessary flexibility.[27] That flexibility is particularly useful in dealing with parties coming from different developmental backgrounds. The unique mix of formality and flexibility is a development of the Bank's legal heritage that goes beyond traditional understandings of either civil or common law.[28] This legal innovation—with its sensitivity to culture and tradition and its implementation of robust due process guarantees—is particularly important in a world where international organizations (IOs) are increasingly helping to form international law.[29]

The system's evolution, with its progressive permutations and additions, has made the regime increasingly robust and juridical. Although it was not the intention of the framers that the Bank's system be overly "legalistic,"[30] such an evolution is an almost-inevitable by-product of a two-tiered adversarial process that allows for legal representation and, more recently, publication of reasoned decision making.[31] The Bank has instituted these structural changes in the spirit of due process and of rule of law. Although this judicialization has had the unintended consequence of increasing the system's intricacy—a

---

25 Leroy & Fariello, *supra* note 3, at 6–7. Elements of the rule of law are embedded in the writings of modern and Western political philosophers such as Locke, Montesquieu, Ricardo, and Weber. More broadly, a concept of the rule of law is inherent in natural law ideals as expressed by Aristotle and Aquinas, as well as in religiously inspired legal systems such as Islamic sharia. As far back as the third century B.C., the Chinese legal thinker Han Fei promoted the view that laws had to be predictable, public, and consistent.

26 *See supra* note 25 and accompanying text. *See* Karen Gottschang Turner, *Rule of Law*, in *The Oxford International Encyclopedia of Legal History* vol. V, 164 (Stanley N. Katz ed., Oxford U. Press 2009).

27 For an instance of such duality considered in the US national context of prosecution and prosecutorial discretion, *see* Nathan Piwowarski, *Prosecutorial Discretion and the Rule of Law: Is It Time for a Little Formalism? (Or, Mr. Prosecutor: How Formalists Learned to Stop Worrying and Love Discretion)*, King Scholar Senior Seminar Paper, Michigan State University College of Law (2007), available at http://www.law.msu.edu/king/2007/index.html.

28 Robert D. Cooter & Hans-Bernd Schafer, *Solomon's Knot: How Law Can End the Poverty of Nations* 94–95 (Princeton U. Press 2012).

29 *See*, for example, José E. Alarez, *International Organizations as Law-Makers* (Oxford U. Press 2005).

30 *See*, for example, Dick Thornburgh, Ronald L. Gainer, & Cuyler H. Walker, *Report Concerning the Debarment Processes of the World Bank* (Aug. 14, 2002 [Rev.]), available at http://go.worldbank.org/1O93GTKH40 (hereinafter, Second Thornburgh Report) at 27 ("[I]t should be kept in mind that the Sanctions Committee procedures are designed and intended to be very informal and avoid unnecessary legal complexities. For that reason, circumspection should be employed in evaluating former judges and litigating attorneys—persons whose careers have been steeped in the mastery of formal hearing procedures of particular national jurisdictions and who are thus more likely than others (for example those whose primary experience has been with informal arbitration proceedings or administrative proceedings) to exhibit a penchant for procedural formality and rigidity").

31 Leroy & Fariello, *supra* note 3, at 28.

weight that weighs most heavily on lesser-capacity respondents—that same augmentation of due process protections has the benefit of assuring all respondents ever-greater protection, therein helping to ensure that respondents have an opportunity to have their full and fair day in court. Respondents need not fear lengthy proceedings; despite its evolution toward greater due process, the Bank's sanctions process remains far more expeditious than national court systems.[32]

The Innovative History of the Bank's Ever-Expanding Sanctions Regime

Year by year, the Bank's system has become more expansive and innovative, providing an ever more complete means of protecting the Bank and the projects that it finances from the deleterious effects of fraud and corruption. Initiated in 1996,[33] the implementation of the Bank's sanctions regime coincided with an increased focus on corruption as a development issue.[34] Since its inception, the Bank's sanctions regime has grown dramatically: in 1999, only corruption, fraud, and collusion were referred to in the Procurement and Consultant Guidelines.[35] In 2004, "coercive practice" was added to this list of "sanctionable practices," therein prohibiting the threatening of competing bidders, government officials, or others.[36] In 2006, a fifth rubric of "obstructive practices" was added to the guidelines and targets actions that impede an investigation, such as destroying evidence or threatening witnesses.[37] Moreover, the regime was expanded beyond fraud and corruption in the limited area of the procurement context alone to cover all fraud and corruption that may occur in connection with the use of Bank financing in the preparation and/or implementation of Bank-financed projects at large.[38] These reforms were accompanied by new

32 On average, a sanctions case (excluding investigation) takes approximately one year. When a case is not appealed to the Sanctions Board, the median time for sanctions proceedings is about six months.

33 Second Thornburgh Report, *supra* note 30, at 12.

34 *See* Leroy & Fariello, *supra* note 3, at 9.

35 All current and historical guidelines are available at the World Bank website. *See* World Bank, Guidelines: Selection and Employment of Consultants by World Bank Borrowers, section 1.22 (Oct. 1, 2006), available at http://go.worldbank.org/U9IPSLUDC0 (hereinafter, Consultant Guidelines); World Bank, Guidelines: Procurement under IBRD Loans and IDA Credits, section 1.14 (May 1, 2010), available at http://go.worldbank.org/1KKD1KNT40 (hereinafter, Procurement Guidelines).

36 *Reform of the World Bank's Sanctions Process* (Jun. 28, 2004), *Policies Guiding INT's Work,* World Bank, available at http://go.worldbank.org/VVY6KYS720.

37 *Expansion of Sanction beyond Procurement and Sanctioning of Obstructive Practices* (Jul. 28, 2006), *Policies Guiding INT's Work,* World Bank, available at http://go.worldbank.org/VVY6KYS720.

38 *See* President's Memorandum to the Executive Directors, *Sanctions Reform: Expansion of Sanctions Regime beyond Procurement and Sanctioning of Obstructive Practices* (Jun. 12, 2006). Concurrently, amended sanctions procedures were adopted, reflecting both the 2004 and the 2006 rounds of sanctions reform.

harmonized definitions of the first four sanctionable practices, as used by all of the five major multilateral development banks (MDBs).[39]

In 2010, in a move that further expanded the system, the Bank signed a cross-debarment accord with the other four major MDBs,[40] allowing for the signatories to cross-debar firms and individuals found to have engaged in wrongdoing in MDB-financed development projects.[41] Not only did this agreement establish the first four sanctionable practices as common among the five MDBs (as already noted); it also codified a common standard of proof, namely, the "more likely than not"[42] standard.[43]

The Bank is constantly monitoring the implementation of its sanctions framework with a view to improving its effectiveness and efficiency, in dialogue with all internal actors as well as with the other major MDBs and other IOs. Similarly, the Bank is always looking for inspiration to improve transparency and fairness.

This chronological development has been presented without any reference to the infrastructural developments; a few notes ought to be made. The system began in 1998 with relatively few structural due process checks and bal-

---

39 *See* Uniform Framework for Preventing and Combating Fraud and Corruption, International Financial Institutions Anti-corruption Task Force (Sep. 2006), available at http://go.worldbank.org/VVY6KYS720. The agreement includes the African Development Bank, the Asian Development Bank, the European Bank for Reconstruction and Development, the Inter-American Development Bank Group, and the World Bank Group.

40 *See* News & Broadcast, *World Bank, Cross-Debarment Accord Steps Up Fight against Corruption* (Apr. 9, 2010), available at http://go.worldbank.org/B699B73Q00. *See* also *Integrity Vice Presidency Annual Report, Fiscal Year 2008: Protecting Development's Potential* 2 (World Bank INT 2009), available at http://go.worldbank.org/T40HHT3RF0.

41 *See World Bank, Cross-Debarment Accord Steps Up Fight against Corruption, supra* note 40; *Integrity Vice Presidency Annual Report, Fiscal Year 2008, supra* note 40. *See* also Stephen S. Zimmermann & Frank A. Fariello, *Coordinating the Fight against Fraud and Corruption: Agreement on Cross-Debarment among Multilateral Development Banks,* in *International Financial Institutions and Global Legal Governance* (Hassane Cissé, Daniel D. Bradlow, & Benedict Kingsbury ed., World Bank 2011). Cross-debarment is permitted for any of the first four sanctionable practices, namely, corruption, fraud, collusion, and coercive practices.

42 *See* Sanctions Procedures, *supra* note 4, at Article 8.01(b)(i). *See* also Anne-Marie Leroy, *Advisory Opinion on Certain Issues Arising in Connection with Recent Sanctions Cases,* No. 2010/1 (Nov. 15, 2010), paragraphs 45–51, in the *UN Juridical Yearbook 2012* ("The standard of proof is predicated on the same basic considerations that underlay the omission of an explicit mens rea requirement from most of the definitions, namely the administrative nature of the proceedings and INT's lack of investigative tools. This standard of proof is understood as being equivalent to the 'preponderance of the evidence,' essentially the standard to be found in civil cases in most jurisdictions. When this nomenclature was adopted in 2004, it was felt that the phrase 'more likely than not' would be more understandable to non-lawyers. However, the 'more than 50%' approach may not be the most useful or appropriate either at the EO stage or at the Sanctions Board stage. Firstly, it suggests a formulaic approach to the evidence while . . . the Sanctions Procedures calls for a discretionary approach. [Secondly . . .], the EO's assessment of the evidence requires special considerations, given that he or she is looking at only one side of the case. The EO is actually charged with assessing the sufficiency of the evidence"),

43 *World Bank, Cross-Debarment Accord Steps Up Fight against Corruption, supra* note 40.

ances; an entirely internal sanctions committee reviewed allegations of fraud and corruption and recommended an appropriate sanction to the president of the Bank, who made the actual decision.[44] In 2001, a nascent yet independent prosecutorial and investigatory branch, the Integrity Vice Presidency (INT), was established, therein consolidating functions that had been spread across various units of the Bank.[45] INT was one of the first specialized units created specifically to address fraud and corruption allegations and integrity issues at an international level.[46] The system evolved into its current two-tiered process in 2007, with an initial determination made by the Evaluation and Suspension Officer (EO) and with the possibility of a de novo review by the World Bank Sanctions Board.[47] Further modifications were made to assure the independence and adequacy of the various actors,[48] and measures for controlling lingering vulnerabilities at either end of the sanctions process were added.[49] Additional added features include the means of sanctioning corporate affiliates[50] and the possibility of resolving disputes through settlement (termed as "negotiated resolution agreements" and "deferral agreements," depending on the type of settlement).[51]

Given that the regime is inherently an administrative one, the Bank's sanctions system has evolved into one that affords respondents substantial

---

44 *See* Leroy & Fariello, *supra* note 3, at 10. *See* also Ko-Yung Tung, General Counsel, World Bank, The World Bank's Institutional Framework for Combating Fraud and Corruption, remarks delivered at the Seminar on Monetary and Financial Law International Monetary Fund (May 8, 2002).

45 The then Department of Institutional Integrity was given institutional independence and reported directly to the president. *See*, for example, Ko-Yung Tung, remarks delivered at the Seminar on Monetary and Financial Law International Monetary Fund (May 8, 2002).

46 Although the UN Office of Internal Oversight Services was created somewhat earlier (1994), that office has a much more general mandate than does INT. *See* UN Office of Internal Oversight Services at http://www.un.org/Depts/oios/.

47 *See* Leroy & Fariello, *supra* note 3, at 10–11.

48 *See*, for example, Paul A. Volcker et al., *Independent Panel Review of World Bank Group Department of Institutional Integrity* (Sep. 13, 2007) (recommending, among other things, that INT be elevated to the status of a vice presidency with reporting lines directly to the president, as well as the creation of the external Independent Advisory Board to facilitate oversight of INT).

49 Inefficiencies and lingering vulnerabilities undermined the effectiveness of the system, both at the "front end" (for example, firms under investigation remain eligible to bid for Bank-financed contracts) and at the "back end" (for example, sanctioned firms were normally released from debarment without any demonstration of rehabilitation). These weaknesses led to the implementation of, first, in May 2009, the possibility for INT to request early temporary sanctions for the time prior to the commencement of formal proceedings, and, second, the institution of the Integrity Compliance Office, which provided guidance to sanctioned parties and monitored implementation of respondents' compliance programs. For more, *see* Leroy & Fariello, *supra* note 3, at 12–17. The drive for greater efficiency also led the Bank to consider and then pilot negotiated resolutions to sanctions cases (aka settlements) in lieu of full-blown sanctions proceedings.

50 *See* Leroy & Fariello, *supra* note 3, at 17–18.

51 Sanctions Procedures, *supra* note 4, at Article XI. *See* Leroy & Fariello, *supra* note 3, at 20–22.

procedural protections.[52] Indeed, in a comparative study with the other major MDBs and with other IOs, the Bank's procedures are substantially more elaborate.[53] The Bank, with different needs and with a greater variety of interests than most other IOs, has deemed such provisions to be well merited: on the one hand, the Bank funds a diversity of projects in a diversity of places, implicating stakeholders around the world; on the other hand, more than half of respondents are sanctioned by default because they do not respond in any way to notices of sanctions proceedings, and only one-third of respondents appeal the EO's recommended sanction.[54] Moreover, recognizing that due process standards are not ubiquitous,[55] the Bank has not created a one-size-fits-all system: although operating within the expeditious contours of an administrative model, the Bank has developed a series of gradations within its regime. Thus, at one end of the spectrum, the system allows for more expedient processing when allegations are less serious and when the corresponding due process requirements are less onerous; at the other extreme, when allegations are considerably weightier, the full system, with all of its incumbent due process guarantees, is engaged. Such legal innovations allow the Bank to more attentively engage respondents while fulfilling its fiduciary duty.

The Commitment to Transparency: An Ever-Improving System

The Bank's decision to increase due process protections for respondents in its sanctions regime is doubly beneficial. First, it ensures that the Bank appropriately fulfills its fiduciary duty under its Articles of Agreement.[56] Second, it corresponds with the Bank's emerging role of seeking to encourage not only economic development but also the growth of socially accountable societies founded on and embracing law and justice.[57] As this edition of the *World Bank*

---

52 See Fox, *supra* note 13. *See* also, Second Thornburgh Report, *supra* note 30 at 2 et seq.

53 *See* Zimmermann & Fariello, *supra* note 41.

54 Dubois & Nowlan, *supra* note 24, at 21–22.

55 *See* discussion of due process at note 12. The US Supreme Court has said that due process, "unlike some legal rules, is not a technical conception with a fixed content unrelated to time, place and circumstances." *Matthews v. Eldridge*, 424 U.S. 319, 334 (1975) (quoting *Cafeteria Workers v. McElroy*, 367 U.S. 886, 895 [1961], describing the flexibility of due process). The court highlighted the flexibility of the notion by continuing that its protections are required only when the "particular situation demands" (quoting *Morrissey v. Brewer*, 408 U.S. 471, 481 [1972]).

56 IBRD Articles of Agreement, *supra* note 4, at Article III, Section 5(b), and IDA Articles of Agreement, *supra* note 4, at Article V, Section 1(g).

57 *See* News & Broadcast, World Bank, *The Global Partnership for Social Accountability: A New Mechanism to Support Civil Society Organizations*, Press Release No. 2012/406/WBI (Apr. 19, 2012), available at http://go.worldbank.org/1393388IP0; Hassane Cissé, *Conflict, Fragility and Development in a Globalized World: Challenges and Implications for the Law of the Future*, 4th HiiL Law of the Future Conference (Jun. 23, 2011) ("[D]iverse . . . forms of violence result in fragility, or the weakening, diminishing and destruction of institutions that would otherwise contain conflicts and resolve injustice peacefully. This definition of fragility constitutes the flip side of what has been defined as 'rule of law'"); Q&A with Hassane Cissé, *Global Forum: How Open Data Links Rule of Law to Economic Growth*, East African (Apr. 9–15, 2012)

Legal Review so clearly shows, and as this chapter emphasizes with regard to a specific facet of the Bank's activities, law and justice are not merely means to an end but are themselves ends, albeit ends that will further other developmental ends, such as economic growth.[58] Such theories of inclusive development are not new,[59] although they are (relatively) new in their implementation.[60]

The Bank's vision of inclusive growth and development—that is, broad-based investment in human beings[61]—is one that the Bank has embraced at large.[62] This vision is apparent in the World Bank Inspection Panel, which ensures that a voice is afforded to those affected by Bank-financed projects in which there has been a breach of Bank protocol.[63] The vision dovetails with

---

("Business actors need to trust [governmental and social] institutions, and especially judicial institutions. The system has to be robust, efficient and respond to people's needs. If business people don't trust that rulings will be timely and just, they will find other ways to solve disputes. More often than not, they will prefer to bypass the justice system and buy outcomes—in other words, resort to corruption. This spills over beyond the business sector and becomes a social problem, setting the clock back for development. . . . A working system has to be fair, transparent, accessible to everyone, and timely. . . . Only then can we have tools to hold government accountable, so that concepts like the rule of law, justice, social inclusion, empowerment and accountability move beyond simple words to become reality, and part and parcel of the development process"). *See* also Justin Yifu Lin, *Demystifying Success: The New Structural Economics Approach* (World Bank Apr. 2011); Siobhán McInerney-Lankford & Hans-Otto Sano, *Human Rights Indicators in Development: An Introduction* (World Bank 2010).

58 *See*, for example, Justin Yifu Lin and Célestin Monga, *The Growth Report and New Structural Economics* (World Bank 2010); Q&A with Hassane Cissé, *supra* note 57 ("Development goes beyond providing economic growth. It has to address equity, equality and justice, and these are at the heart of the rule of law. If these are not dealt with, you don't have the foundation for economic development"). *See* also Cooter & Schafer, *supra* note 28.

59 For example, *see* David M. Trubek & Marc Galanter, *Scholars in Self-Estrangement: Some Reflections on the Crisis in Law and Development Studies in the United States*, 4 Wis. L. Rev. 1062 (1974); Richard A. Posner, *Creating a Legal Framework for Economic Development*, 13 World Bank Research Observer 1 (1998); Hernando de Soto, *The Other Path. The Economic Answer to Terrorism* (Basic Books 1989); Amartya Sen, *Development as Freedom* (Knopf 1999); Kaushik Basu & Ravi Kanbur ed., *Arguments for a Better World: Essays in Honor of Amartya Sen* (Oxford U. Press 2009). *See* also Cooter & Schafer, *supra* note 28.

60 Although the Bank has long acknowledged the important role of civil society and has worked with civil society organizations for decades, having, for example, established what would be called the Civil Society Fund in 1983, the Bank has stepped up efforts and is committed to such activities and to such development. *The Global Partnership for Social Accountability*, *supra* note 57. *See* also Lin and Monga, *supra* note 58.

61 *See* Elena Ianchovichina, Susanna Lundstrom, & Leonardo Garrido, *What Is Inclusive Growth?* PRMED Knowledge Brief (Feb. 10, 2009), available at http://go.worldbank.org/LG5Z4L6LR0. *See* also Jim Yong Kim, *My Call for an Open, Inclusive World Bank*, Financial Times (Mar. 28, 2012).

62 World Bank, *The Growth Report: Strategies for Sustained Growth and Inclusive Development* (World Bank 2008); Lin and Monga, *supra* note 58, at 14 ("Long-term sustainable and inclusive growth is the driving force for poverty reduction in developing countries, and for convergence with developed economies").

63 Inspection Panel, World Bank, at http://www.inspectionpanel.org/. The Inspection Panel is an independent, "bottom-up" accountability and recourse mechanism that investigates IBRD/IDA-financed projects to determine whether the Bank has complied with its operational policies and procedures (including social and environmental safeguards), and to address related issues of harm.

the selection of Dr. Jim Yong Kim,[64] a medical doctor and developmentalist, as president rather than the more traditional choice of an economist or of a politician.[65] Similarly, it is a motivating factor behind the Global Forum for Law, Justice and Development, of which the Bank will serve as Secretariat, and which aims to support the development of strong legal and judicial institutions by sharing and generating knowledge through international collaboration.[66] In the spirit of improving social accountability,[67] among other things, the Bank has worked vigorously to develop means of measuring success beyond traditional economic metrics; critically, it is tying these new measures to governance and anticorruption strategies.[68] The key tool therein is transparency; as US Supreme Court justice Louis Brandeis once quipped, "Sunlight is . . . the best disinfectant."[69]

---

64 *See*, for example, *Obama Nominates Dartmouth President Jim Yong Kim to Lead World Bank*, Time (Mar. 23, 2012) ("Officials believe [Kim's] experience will help counter criticism from developing countries that have grown weary of the U.S. stranglehold on the World Bank presidency"). *See* also News & Broadcast, World Bank, *World Bank's Executive Directors Select Dr. Jim Yong Kim 12th President of the World Bank Group*, Press Release No. 2012/395/SEC (Apr. 16, 2012), available at http://go.worldbank.org/AX89KWI2H0.

65 Annie Lowrey, *College President Is Obama's Pick for World Bank Chief*, NY Times (Mar. 23, 2012), available at http://www.nytimes.com/2012/03/24/business/global/dartmouth-president-is-obamas-pick-for-world-bank.html. Kim's acceptance is striking because he has openly—and articulately—challenged "[t]he idea that robust economic growth will automatically lead to a better life for everybody" and has even gone so far as to argue that "the structure and current rules of today's market-led economic globalization [that is, in 2000] widen the chasm between the privileged and the destitute, imperiling the lives of the world's poor." *See* Jim Yong Kim et al. ed., *Dying for Growth: Global Inequality and the Health of the Poor* 7, 3 (Common Courage Press 2000). A better metric for the success of development, Kim et al. argue, is "[f]ocusing on health rather than other traditional indicators of wealth." Kim's unorthodox background led both to considerable criticism of his nomination (*Hats Off to Ngozi: A Golden Opportunity for the Rest of the World to Show Barack Obama the Meaning of Meritocracy*, The Economist [Mar. 31, 2012]) and to much praise (Thomas J. Bollyky, *How to Fix the World Bank*, NY Times [Apr. 8, 2012]); Gillian Tett, *Right Time for a World Bank Renaissance Man*, Financial Times [Mar. 30, 2012]). Kim has responded to criticism by saying that his thoughts in 2000 are not applicable: "Our concern [in 2000] was that the vision was not inclusive enough, that it wasn't, in the bank's words, 'pro-poor.' The bank has shifted tremendously since that time, and now the notion of pro-poor development is at the core of the World Bank." Annie Lowrey, *Obama Candidate Sketches Vision for World Bank*, NY Times (Apr. 9, 2012). Kim has also noted that his top priority is "spurring economic growth that creates jobs." Nicole Kekeh, *Dr. Kim Wins Top Job at the World Bank*, Forbes (Apr. 17, 2012), available at http://www.forbes.com/sites/worldviews/2012/04/17/dr-kim-wins-top-job-at-the-world-bank-promises-inclusive-leadership/.

66 Charter of the Global Forum for Law, Justice and Development.

67 *See*, for example, World Bank president Robert Zoellick's comments on the need to "democratize development" in his Peterson Institute for International Economics speech, *The Middle East and North Africa: A New Social Contract for Development* (Apr. 6, 2011), available at http://go.worldbank.org/QQ10SJQOJ0; *see* also Robert Zoellick's talk at the conference "Supporting Social Accountability for Better Results" (Apr. 19, 2012).

68 *The Global Partnership for Social Accountability*, *supra* note 57. *See* also Governance and Anticorruption Key Principles, Governance & Anticorruption, World Bank, available at http://go.worldbank.org/32PINXVIJ0; *Beyond Transparency: What's Next? Governance for Development*, available at http://blogs.worldbank.org/governance/beyond-transparency-what-s-next.

69 *Other People's Money and How the Bankers Use It* 13 (Frederick A. Stokes Co. 1913).

In this vein, the Bank is contemplating further reforms to its sanctions regime, with particular emphasis on improving transparency and participation—both of the sanctions process itself and of the policy making that surrounds it—as well as due process protections, and exploring ways to afford better access to low-capacity respondents. Although there is more to be done, the Bank has attempted to remain true to its calling to empower the disempowered. This cyclical process results in ever-greater legitimacy of the Bank and its sanctions regime, as well as in greater efficiency and effectiveness.

The Legal Orientation of the Bank's Sanctions Regime: Toward Ever-Better Governance

The Bank's current system draws from different legal disciplines, not reflecting any single national system, or even any single legal tradition—indeed, that is the point. With stakeholders around the world, the World Bank continually strives to remain both global and worldly—that is, to represent the communities of the world while remaining not merely relevant but vibrant in a developmental sea populated by multiple players of all sizes.[70] In developing its own system, the Bank draws from both common law and civil law traditions, as well as looking to national systems for inspiration. The Bank's incorporation of elements on the basis of efficiency and effectiveness has allowed it to create its own sui generis tradition, a tradition that operates best in this transnational space where IOs are increasingly developing the meaning of international law.[71] Moreover, legal diversification has the added bonus of allaying potential perceptions that the Bank is biased in favor of any given national system. This sui generis system is a major legal innovation that allows the Bank, notwithstanding its size, to bring an impressive degree of particularity, precision, and attention to its dealings with varied stakeholders.

To understand the orientation and nature of the Bank's sanctions system, one must understand that the ultimate aim of the system is not to punish but rather to correct and rehabilitate: the system seeks to reintroduce those entities that have been implicated in fraudulent or corrupt behavior back into the market after a certain minimum period of debarment and upon adoption of adequate and effective policies and measures to guard against future misconduct.[72] Thus, the system's baseline sanction is "debarment with conditional

---

70 *See*, for example, Robert B. Zoellick, *Why We Still Need the World Bank: Looking beyond Aid*, Foreign Affairs (Mar./Apr. 2012), available at http://go.worldbank.org/45JDG1N1E0.

71 *See* Alarez, *supra* note 29.

72 *See* Leroy & Fariello, *supra* note 3, at 15. The nuance is subtle yet important, and it has been overlooked by many observers. For an example of the confusion, *see* Dionne Searcey & David Crawford, *World Bank Punishes Units of Alstom SA for Bribery*, Wall St. J. (Feb. 23, 2012), available at http://online.wsj.com/article/SB10001424052970203918304577238943984834040.html; and Greg McArthur, *Meet the World Bank's Anti-bribery Cop*, The Globe and Mail (Feb. 7, 2012), available at http://m.theglobeandmail.com/report-on-business/industry-news/the-law-page/meet-the-world-banks-anti-bribery-cop/article2330154/?service=mobile. Notwithstanding the Bank's desire to rehabilitate vendors, the Bank recognizes its role in

release": in other words, the sanctioned party will be excluded from the possibility of participating in Bank-financed projects for a period of time, and, on condition of proper implementation of appropriate compliance measures, allowed to bid once more.[73] Operating—as one would expect from bankers—on the understanding that corruption taints the market but that the free market is generally good for all involved, the aim is one of release from debarment and reintegration within the Bank's (otherwise open) bidding system. Compliance with such measures, as well as the system's objective of rehabilitation and reintroduction, is facilitated through the guidance offered by the integrity compliance officer (ICO), whose office also monitors and decides whether conditions have been satisfied.[74]

The Bank, as much as any other organization, strives toward good governance—that is, the process of effectively addressing shared problems through group decision making.[75] Good governance comes only through good rapport and good communication between those governing and those who are governed.[76] Critical to such a process are the principles of both transparency and accountability.[77] Transparency, which is premised on free access to information, guards against the particular problems of capture and conflicts of interest.[78]

---

supporting the rule of law; to this end, if INT substantiates findings of fraud or corruption, the Bank will refer cases to national authorities for prosecution. *See*, for example, *Referrals Made to Governments in FY 10–11, Integrity Vice Presidency Annual Report, Fiscal 2011* 44 (World Bank INT 2011), available at http://go.worldbank.org/T40HHT3RF0; *see* also FAQs, Fraud & Corruption, World Bank, at http://go.worldbank.org/JF938Z5CU0.

73 *See* Leroy & Fariello, *supra* note 3, at 14–17.

74 Similarly, the integrity compliance officer (ICO) decides whether conditions established by the sanctions board or EO as part of a conditional nondebarment sanction have been satisfied. The conditions imposed are likely to be similar to those imposed under debarment with conditional release, including, for example, adoption or improvement of an integrity compliance program and/or other remedial actions related to the relevant misconduct. *See* Sanctions Procedures, *supra* note 4, at Article 9.03 (Compliance with Conditions for Nondebarment and Release from Debarment). The ICO was created in 2010. *See* INT, Sanctions and Compliance, at http://go.worldbank.org/G9UW6Y0DC0.

75 *See*, for example, Wesley Carrington, Jim DeBuse, & Hee Jin Lee, *The Theory of Governance & Accountability* (U. of Iowa Center for International Finance and Development 2008).

76 Huma Haider, Claire Mcloughlin, & Zoë Scott, *Topic Guide on Communication and Governance* (CommGAP & GSDRC 2011), available at http://go.worldbank.org/7BUHFCCQ70.

77 *See*, for example, Carrington, DeBuse, & Lee, *supra* note 75; Haider, Mcloughlin, & Scott, *supra* note 76. *See* also Caroline Freund & Mélise Jaud, *Democratic Transitions: Successful, Gradual, and Failed*, in *Accountability and Transparency, World Bank Economists' Forum 2012* (May 9, 2012); Ryan Booth, Deon Filmer, & Jamele Rigolini, *Does Electoral Competition Raise Accountability?*, in *Accountability and Transparency, World Bank Economists' Forum 2012* (May 9, 2012); Marco Larizza, Ryan Jabonski, & Audrey Sacks, *Electoral Competition and Access to Information on Public Service Provision: Evidence from Sierra Leone*, in *Accountability and Transparency, World Bank Economists' Forum 2012* (May 9, 2012); Carolin Geginat, Adrian Gonzalez, & Valentina Saltaine, *Access to Information in Business Regulation*, in *Accountability and Transparency, World Bank Economists' Forum 2012* (May 9, 2012).

78 "Capture" refers to the manipulation of policy formation and/or to the distortion of the rule-making process that results in substantial individual gain to the detriment of society or the nation at large; a classic example comes from the profits that accrue to oligarchs of resource-rich countries rather than to the countries and to their citizens. In this context, a "conflict of

Accountability, which contemplates the relationship between the organization and its stakeholders, ensures that the organization remains attentive to the needs and interests of its stakeholders and holds managers responsible for deviations thereof.[79] However, accountability can operate only in a transparent environment.[80]

The World Bank Group as a whole has committed itself to furthering the objectives of good governance, transparency, and accountability.[81] Notably, the World Bank Group has decided that its internal documents should be made available to the public: adopted at a World Bank Group–wide level under the 2010 Access to Information Policy, all information not on a list of exceptions is disclosed to the public (rather than only information corresponding to a positive list).[82]

The sanctions system was construed as an exception to the open information norm and thus stands apart: understanding that the nature of information concerning the sanctions system is fundamentally different from information generally in the Bank's possession, and recognizing the need to assure the objectiveness of the deliberative process apart from the potential disruptive effect of media attention, the Bank walled off the sanctions system.[83] Thus, in short, the general presumptions underlying the Access to Information Policy do not apply to the sanctions regime.

Notwithstanding the exception that was carved out for the sanctions process, it is undesirable if not untenable to maintain the system behind a veil of

---

interest" occurs where there is self-interest competing with a communal interest. *See* Roberta S. Karmel & Claire R. Kelly, *The Hardening of Soft Law in Securities Regulation*, 34 Brook. J. Intl. L. 883, 946 (2009). *See* also Geginat, Gonzalez, & Saltaine, *supra* note 77; Joel Hellman & Daniel Kaufmann, *Confronting the Challenge of State Capture in Transition Economies*, Fin. & Dev. (IMF September 2001), available at http://www.imf.org/external/pubs/ft/fandd/2001/09/hellman.htm.

79 *See*, for example, Helen Darbishire, *Proactive Transparency: The Future of the Right to Information?* CommGAP, World Bank, available at http://go.worldbank.org/7BUHFCCQ70. *See* also UN DESA DPADM, *Transparency and Accountability in the Public Sector in the Arab Region*, in Concept Paper 2: Transparency and Accountability in Public Financial Administration, RAB/01/006 (Mar. 2004). For a discussion of the evolution of accountability in public organizations and what the term has come to mean, *see* B. G. Peters in *Restoring Accountability Research Studies, Vol. 3: Linkages, Responsibilities and Accountabilities* (D. Savoie ed., Public Works and Government Services Canada 2006).

80 *Id.*

81 In the words of former World Bank president Robert Zoellick, "Accountability and transparency are important pillars of the World Bank's work." Inspection Panel, available at http://www.inspectionpanel.org/. *See* also Lisa Bhansali, *Defining Our Path to the "Rule of Law,"* Governance for Development, World Bank (Apr. 17, 2012), available at http://blogs.worldbank.org/governance/defining-our-path-to-the-rule-of-law.

82 *See* The World Bank Policy on Access to Information (Jul. 1, 2010), paragraph 13, available at http://go.worldbank.org/LN06W7ZCB0. *See* also Disclosure Policy Review & Global Consultations, World Bank, available at http://go.worldbank.org/FSBLXEWJ50.

83 One of the categorical exceptions in which most information is kept confidential is "other disclosure regimes," which includes the Bank's sanctions regime.

secrecy;[84] therefore, the regime's actors have worked steadily toward the goal of ever-greater transparency. A series of events in 2011 is particularly revealing. In January 2011, the first notable step to enhance transparency was taken with the updating and making public of the Bank's Sanctioning Guidelines.[85] These guidelines, which attempt to balance predictability with sufficient and equitable flexibility, afford clarity about the imposition of sanctions and offer guidance to INT in its negotiation of settlements.[86] In November 2011, the Bank released, for the first time, a detailed information note describing the entire sanctions regime.[87] This note gives the public an understanding of the system as a whole, making public the system's internal relations and operations, information that was previously largely unknowable to outsiders. An even bigger step came in December 2011, when the Bank published both the undisputed first-tier determinations (that is, those of the EO),[88] and, in decisions that are fully reasoned and include relevant facts and the applied legal reasoning,[89] the decisions of the system's appellate body (that is, those of the Sanctions Board).[90] These developments evince the Bank's commitment to making fairness, transparency, and accountability key tenets of the World Bank Group's sanctions reform agenda[91]—indeed, the Bank continually explores ways to further transparency and accountability.

It should be cautioned that, although the actors of the sanctions system are seeking to make the system more open, total disclosure is not contemplated. For instance, disclosure is limited to undisputed EO determinations and to Sanctions Board decisions, not to all documents or products of the system. Thus, for the sake of the deliberative process, confidentiality is maintained throughout the process, with disclosure of undisputed determinations and decisions made only when they are final. Similarly, INT maintains a "positive list" approach that is intended to cover information that could "be harmful to innocent persons; undermine the work of these groups; or could interfere with

---

84 Such notions are in keeping with general notions of due process, for example, Article 6, Section 1, of the European Convention on Human Rights ("In the determination of his civil rights and obligations or of any criminal charge against him, everyone is entitled to a fair and public hearing within a reasonable time by an independent and impartial tribunal established by law. Judgment shall be pronounced publicly").

85 World Bank Group Sanctioning Guidelines (Jan. 1, 2011), Key and Reference Documents, World Bank, available at http://go.worldbank.org/CVUUIS7HZ0.

86 Sanctions Regime—The 2008–2010 Reforms, World Bank, available at http://go.worldbank.org/P7Z3PKTXP0. *See* also Leroy & Fariello, *supra* note 3, at 19.

87 The World Bank Group's Sanctions Regime: Information Note, available at http://go.worldbank.org/CVUUIS7HZ0.

88 *See* Sanctions Procedures, *supra* note 4, at Article 10.01(b); Evaluation and Suspension Officer Determinations in Uncontested Proceedings, World Bank, available at http://go.worldbank.org/G7EO0UXW90.

89 *Sanctions Board Law Digest*, World Bank, available at http://go.worldbank.org/S9PFFMD6X0.

90 *Id.*

91 *See*, for example, Notes from the Sanctions Board Chair, in *Sanctions Board Law Digest*, *supra* note 89.

the work of the groups that play an independent role within the institution."[92] Thus, although the actors have taken the initiative of making the sanctions system as accessible as possible, the entirety of the process is not made public.

In effect, the result of this transparency is an increase in both empowerment and confidence for stakeholders and external participants. Publication of the *Sanctions Board Law Digest* is an excellent illustration: the *Digest* fosters greater access to and awareness of the public while resulting in greater certainty and deterrence due to the regime's heightened visibility.[93] At the same time, the *Digest* offers illustrations of the legal principles at play and how they are to be applied.[94] The transparency resulting from offering to the public the decision-making process—the logic, its application, and the context for judgment—serves as a mechanism for accountability for all the various actors in the system. Instruments like the *Digest* also enforce the notion of independence, a notion central to a properly functioning dispute-resolution system.[95] On the flip side, appeals for abuse of discretion keep both Bank Management and the ICO (who monitors implementation of the compliance systems) accountable. As a result, stakeholders have not only reason to be confident in the Bank and in its actors but also the tools necessary for ensuring continued high standards of quality, and Bank adherence to those standards and to the rules that shape them.

---

92 *See* INT, *The Disclosure of Information Policy of the Integrity Vice Presidency* (Feb. 3, 2011), available at http://go.worldbank.org/J65IMLGAX0. The positive list is limited to (1) redacted final investigation reports (FIRs) that set out findings and recommendations at the conclusion of INT's external investigations and may be followed by sanctions proceedings; (2) redacted Detailed Implementation Review reports (DIRs) of integrity risks in WBG-financed projects, and assessments of measures designed to prevent them; (3) INT's annual report; (4) reports and other information generated as part of INT's preventive efforts, for example, thematic reviews, "lessons learned" publications, training, and capacity-building materials; (5) policy papers; and list of debarred companies.

93 *See* President's Introduction, in *Sanctions Board Law Digest*, *supra* note 89 ("Sanctions protect Bank Group funds and member countries' development projects by excluding proven wrongdoers from our operations and financing. Sanctions also deter other participants or potential bidders in Bank Group–financed operations from engaging in fraud, collusion, or corruption. By holding companies and individuals accountable through a fair and robust process, the Bank Group's sanctions system promotes integrity and levels the playing field for those committed to clean business practices").

94 *See* Notes from the Sanctions Board Chair, in *Sanctions Board Law Digest*, *supra* note 89.

95 In both common and civil law traditions, emphasis is placed on rule of law principles, notably that of separation of powers and its incumbent notion of judicial independence. The notion of separation of powers was first discussed by Locke, *Second Treatise on Government* chapter XII, section 143 (1690). However, Montesquieu is the best-known theorist who has treated the topic. Montesquieu, *L'esprit des lois* vol. 1, book XI, chapter 6, page 219 (1749). Because the judiciary is generally understood as the "weakest" branch of government, it is widely accepted that it must have the most substantial structural independence from undue influence. In the words of US Supreme Court chief justice Marshall, "The greatest scourge an angry Heaven ever inflicted upon an ungrateful and a sinning people, was an ignorant, a corrupt, or a dependent judiciary." Quoted in John B. Cassoday, John Scott, & John Marshall, *The American Lawyer* vol. VII, 60 (Stumpf & Steurer 1899).

The move toward transparency is good practice and is in keeping with general rule of law dictates.[96] Moreover, it is hoped that such confidence will further encourage worldwide participation in the combat against fraud and corruption and in the development of law and justice. Opening up the sanctions system demonstrates both to those "in the docket" as respondents and to external observers that the Bank has a robust and deliberative sanctions system. This kind of a system inspires trust and confidence, thereby encouraging engagement with the Bank at all levels, be it at the level of the sanctions process or in deciding whether to do business with the Bank.

Conclusion

Poverty persists and economies stagnate or fail when innovation and growth lag.[97] Law and justice offer the infrastructure to nurture the trust and certainty that in turn promote innovation and growth.[98] However, economic growth should not be considered a panacea for social problems, nor should the benefits of providing law and justice be understood as merely the handmaid of economic growth.[99] Just law encourages social cohesion, equality, citizen empowerment, and justice—"[a]fter all, the law is, or ought to be, but the handmaid of justice"[100] and "an unjust law is no law at all."[101] More sophisticated and more formal legal systems expand economic opportunities by creating trust among strangers and expectations of generalized reciprocity,[102] therein encouraging the building of communities of hope, trust, and prosperity. Development, therefore, cannot be read as advancing economic development in the strictest sense of the term; a sense of ownership and empowerment must also be nurtured. Accordingly, more attention must be paid to strengthening governance. To achieve such an end, legal and governance institutions must be developed, and a sense of the importance of the rule of law must be fostered.[103] However, such development can occur only if stakeholders believe

96 "The rule of law can be defined as a system in which the laws are public knowledge, are clear in meaning, and apply equally to everyone." Thomas Carothers, *The Rule of Law Revival*, 77 Foreign Affairs 96 (1998).

97 Cooter & Schafer, *supra* note 28, at 5. *See* also Niall Ferguson, *Civilization: The West and the Rest* (Penguin 2011).

98 Cooter & Schafer, *supra* note 28, at 1–26. *See* also Ferguson, *supra* note 97; Daron Acemoglu & James A. Robinson, *Why Nations Fail: The Origins of Power, Prosperity, and Poverty* (Random House 2012).

99 *See* Carothers, *supra* note 96, at 95–105. *See* also Philip Alston, *The Myopia of the Handmaidens: International Lawyers and Globalization*, 3 Euro. J. Intl. L. 423–48 (1997); Shirley V. Scott, *International Lawyers: Handmaidens, Chefs, or Birth Attendants? A Response to Philip Alston*, 9 Euro. J. Intl. L. 750–56 (1998). *See* also Jim Yong Kim et al. ed., *Dying for Growth: Global Inequality and the Health of the Poor* 7, 3 (Common Courage Press 2000).

100 Lord Penzance, *Combe v. Edwards* (1878), L. Reports 3 P.D. 142.

101 St. Augustine of Hippo.

102 Cooter & Schafer, *supra* note 28, at 82 et seq.

103 *See*, for example, Lisa Bhansali, *Defining Our Path to the "Rule of Law," Governance for Devel-*

that the systems are accountable, which in turn requires transparency. Leading by example, the World Bank is adhering to social accountability by making its sanctions regime increasingly transparent and robust.

Internationally, the Bank plays an active role[104] in combating the "cancer of corruption."[105] However, for enduring change to occur there must be not only outside support but also the will to reform; that will can come only from within the community.[106] Merely enacting good laws does little without substantial investment and corresponding changes in implementation and enforcement that nurture mutual trust.[107] Realizing as much from its extensive experience in rule of law and justice reform projects,[108] the Bank emphasizes transparency and accountability across its work, and in its own sanctions regime in particular, is intended to create a sense of trust, confidence, and ownership, that (it is hoped) will elicit that ever-so-essential will for change.

The Bank has further bolstered transparency's transformative effect by crafting an innovative sui generis system that allows it to attentively and

---

opment, World Bank (Apr. 17, 2012), available at http://blogs.worldbank.org/governance/defining-our-path-to-the-rule-of-law.

104 In taking up this area, the Bank has overcome the strictest interpretations of the "political prohibition" that bars it from interfering in the political affairs of its members. The IBRD Articles of Agreement contain a provision that states that "[t]he Bank and its officers shall not interfere in the political affairs of any member; nor shall they be influenced in their decisions by the political character of the member or members concerned." *See* IBRD Articles of Agreement, Article IV, Section 10. IDA Articles of Agreement contain an identical provision. *See* IDA Articles of Agreement, Article V, Section 6. Almost-identical provisions are contained in the Agreement Establishing the Inter-American Development Bank, Article VIII, Section 5(f); the Articles of Agreement of the Asian Development Bank, Chapter VI, Article 36; and the Agreement Establishing the African Development Bank, Chapter V, Article 38. In contrast, the constituent documents of EBRD and EIB do not contain any such restriction. *See* also Hassane Cissé, *Should the "Political Prohibition" in Charters of International Financial Institutions Be Revisited? The Case of the World Bank*, in *International Financial Institutions and Global Legal Governance* (Hassane Cissé, Daniel D. Bradlow, & Benedict Kingsbury ed., World Bank 2011).

105 Wolfensohn, *supra* note 6, at 50. *See* also Transparency International USA, *World Bank–Siemens Agreement Sends Strong Signal* (Jul. 2, 2009), available at http://www.transparency-usa.org/news/documents/TIUSASiemensRelease7.2.09.pdf. For example, the Bank is keenly engaging with national authorities. *See*, for example, News & Broadcast, World Bank, *World Bank Welcomes Norwegian Convictions of Three Former Employees of Norwegian Company "Norconsult" in Bribery Case in Tanzania*, Press Release No. 2012/029/INT (Jul. 22, 2011), available at http://go.worldbank.org/VO2EW48OO0.

106 *See* Carothers, *supra* note 96, at 96.

107 *Id.*, at 104.

108 Compare, for example, the great increase in projects over the course of the years: *Initiatives in Legal and Judicial Reform 2002* (World Bank 2002) (listing 330 Bank-financed projects related to legal and judicial reform, including a US$58 million loan to Russia), available at http://go.worldbank.org/PJHSQT4RA0; *Initiatives in Legal and Judicial Reform 2004* (World Bank 2004) (approximating the number of Bank-financed projects related to legal and judicial reform at 600), available at http://go.worldbank.org/PJHSQT4RA0; *Initiatives in Justice Reform 2009* (World Bank 2009) (noting that the Bank's current justice sector assistance and reform portfolio comprises nearly 2,500 justice reform activities in developing or transition countries), available at http://go.worldbank.org/PJHSQT4RA0.

expeditiously engage respondents of all shapes and sizes. Until recently, those borrowing from the Bank had their freedom restricted: not only did borrowers not understand the nature of the Bank's debarment system; they also had limited decision-making powers as the Bank decided on whether certain contractors were employable. The opening up of the Bank's sanctions regime gives increased confidence to borrowers and contractors alike, as they can see the robust and deliberative nature of the Bank's system; this opening up also will make the sanctions system more predictable and accessible.

Of course, the sanctions system—as with any judicial recourse—remains a contingency: it is the unhappy alternative, not the desired route. That said, confidence in the system is of enduring importance to bolstering the rule of law, as obscuring the nature of that system can have a chilling effect: for those entities doing business with the Bank, not knowing the basis on which the Bank debarred, and yet remaining subject to the possibility of a public shaming, detracted from the Bank's legitimacy, as well as adding a degree of uncertainty and hassle to working with the Bank. Opening up the sanctions system builds confidence in that system, empowers stakeholders, and has the correlative benefit of building confidence in doing business with the Bank. In matters of governance and of rule of law, the Bank is practicing what it preaches, thereby assuring stakeholders that, in doing business with the Bank, they are not throwing caution to the wind. Such relations improve the political economy of Bank-financed development projects.

* * *

Left unchecked, fraud and corruption have broad, corrosive, and lingering effects on countries and on communities; they undermine the effectiveness of development projects and erode confidence in systems and in societies.[109] The consequence of unchecked corruption is an increase in corruption, as well as a general lack of public confidence in democratic processes, slowed economic growth, the deepening of inequality, and a general breakdown in social norms of sensitivity.[110] Shoring up the rule of law helps temper corruption and crime.[111] The Bank's sanctions regime plays a key role in combating fraud and

---

109 *See* Governance and Anticorruption (GAC) Implementation Plan, OPCS, World Bank (Sep. 28, 2007), available at http://go.worldbank.org/ZFUWCFJQ80; FAQs, Fraud & Corruption, World Bank, at http://go.worldbank.org/JF938Z5CU0. *See* also Wolfensohn, *supra* note 6, at 50; Yikona et al., *supra* note 5; Chaikin & Sharman, *supra* note 5; Jayasuriya, *supra* note 5, at 46–58.

110 *Id.* For instance, the growth of corruption in South Africa resulted in citizens not knowing how to report corruption and, even more alarmingly, in the general belief that reporting would not be beneficial and fear of the consequences of reporting. *See* Hennie van Vuuren, *Small Bribes, Big Challenges: Extent and Nature of Petty Corruption in South Africa*, 9 S. Afr. Crime Quarterly (2004). In an interesting though counterintuitive and somewhat questionable conceptualization, Cooter & Schafer argue that certain corruption can serve a beneficial purpose insofar as it subverts laws that impede economic growth; unfortunately, no consideration is made of the subversive rule of law effects of this "good" corruption. Cooter & Schafer, *supra* note 28, at 168–72.

111 *See* Carothers, *supra* note 96, at 99.

corruption around the world, and it is hoped that the opening up of the process to stakeholders will help to combat corruption further.

The international community has recognized that "[c]ommunity development draws on existing human and material resources in the community to enhance self-help and social support, and to develop flexible systems for strengthening public participation. . . . This requires full and continuous access to information, learning opportunities . . . , as well as funding support."[112] By developing an effective and innovative sanctions system, and in making that system transparent, the Bank is stepping up its efforts to fight fraud and corruption, with the ultimate goal of strengthening and empowering communities. The World Bank's dream is of a world without poverty; impoverishment, however, can come in many forms, and, so the Bank—and the actors in its sanctions regime—is expanding the battlefront.

112 The Ottawa Charter for Health Promotion (Nov. 21, 1986).

Human Rights and Development

Regime Interaction and the Fragmentation of International Law

Siobhán McInerney-Lankford

Human rights and development interact in a range of ways, and so too do the legal and policy frameworks, or regimes, that govern each.[1] In this chapter, "regimes" are defined as "sets of norms, decision-making procedures, and organizations coalescing around functional issue-areas."[2] This chapter considers the connections between human rights and development from the perspective of public international law as "regime interaction," focusing specifically on the links between human rights law and development policy. It departs from the premise of the centrality of law as a defining feature of human rights[3] and legal accountability as a key contribution of human rights and development.[4] It espouses the view that more attention is due to human rights law and human rights obligations in the context of development.[5] From this the chapter considers the degree to which human rights are integrated explicitly into development policies and programs and the extent to which human rights are recognized as law in those contexts.[6]

The views expressed in this article are those of the author and do not necessarily reflect the views of the Board of Executive Directors of the World Bank or the governments they represent. The author thanks Mac Darrow, Olufemi Elias, Nathan Lankford, Victor Mosoti, Hans-Otto Sano, Andres Rigo Sureda, and Chantal Thomas for comments on earlier drafts of this article, and Behnaz Bonyadian, Christian Jimenez-Tomas, and Laura Lalime-Mowry for research assistance. Responsibility for errors or omissions remains with the author.

1 M. Young, *Regime Interaction in International Law: Facing Fragmentation* (Cambridge U. Press 2012).

2 M. Young, *Introduction*, in Young, *id.*, at 9. The term is understood to cover both the formal or binding legal frameworks governing a particular area or issue, including treaties, norms, legislation, rules, and regulations, and softer measures such as policies, statements, programs, processes, and directives. Nevertheless, the term "regime" is a nonlegal term with no fixed definition that has generated a vast body of literature in both international relations and public international law. *See*, for example, S. Krasner ed., *International Relations* (Cornell U. Press 1983).

3 D. Forsythe, *Human Rights Studies: On the Dangers of Legalistic Assumptions*, in *Methods of Human Rights Research* (F. Coomans, F. Grünfeld, & M. Kamminga ed., Intersentia 2009). Despite the author's thesis and cautions, he acknowledges that "law has remained central to the notion of human rights. That is because, . . . it is law that authoritatively defines a society's understanding of what are human rights at a given point in time."

4 *See* S. McInerney-Lankford, *Human Rights and Development: A Comment on Challenges and Opportunities from a Legal Perspective*, 1(1) J. of Human Rights Practice 74–75 (2009).

5 For a critical view of the value of international human rights treaties, *see* O. Hathaway, *Do Human Rights Treaties Make a Difference?* 111 Yale L. J. 1935–2042 (2002).

6 This chapter considers the potential influence of human rights on development, rather than

In particular, this chapter explores the place of international human rights obligations and human rights treaties in development policies and assesses the impact of this role in operational terms.[7] It notes that, despite growing recognition of human rights as the subject of binding international law obligations on the part of development agencies and banks, and despite increased emphasis on policy coherence, the trend across development is far from uniform and in many respects is inconsistent and divergent.[8] The chapter argues that the relationship between human rights and development policy can be analyzed as regime interaction. This interaction exemplifies the fragmentation of international law, most evident in the uneven integration of human rights law obligations into development policies and processes.

This chapter contends that the growing recognition of human rights in legal and operational terms could advance international policy coherence and mediate risk. It also suggests that the ability of international development institutions and their regimes to adapt to evolving international norms could be expanded to human rights.[9] It argues for the place and relevance of human rights in development regimes rather than suggesting particular ways in which potential norm conflicts between the regimes should be resolved. It therefore invites consideration of the relationship of human rights and development in terms of regime interaction and suggests a frame for future consideration of norm interaction.

The Relationship of Human Rights and Development

Human rights and development connect in a range of ways. The following discussion does not review in detail the conceptual discussions developed elsewhere but rather sets the context for the ensuing discussion of how human rights are reflected in development policy frameworks or regimes to facilitate a discussion of how those regimes interact and the place of legal obligations within that relationship.

Human rights and development are different: achieving a positive result in a given field, such as health, is not the same as realizing the right to health; nor will such a result "automatically promote respect for the corresponding right and imbue the rights-holder and duty-bearers with a long-term guarantee [or] set of structural claims."[10] Yet, at some intuitive level, human rights

---

the reverse, although it assumes the two-way nature of the relationship between the two. *See* World Bank, *Development and Human Rights: The Role of the World Bank* (World Bank 1998).

7 This approach departs from the view that "when we speak of universal human rights, it is international law that defines them in a positivistic sense, for better or worse." Forsythe, *supra* note 2, at 61.

8 P. Uvin, *Human Rights and Development* 47 (Kumarian Press 2004).

9 A. Rigo Sureda, *The Law Applicable to the Activities of International Development Banks*, in *Receuil des cours* 217 (Martinus Nijhoff 2005).

10 Anand Grover, *Report of the Special Rapporteur on the Right of Everyone to the Enjoyment of the Highest Attainable Standard of Physical and Mental Health*, A/HRC/17/25 (Apr. 12, 2011),

and development share affinities. In substantive ways, they occupy many of the same sectors or spheres, and in certain types of operations, development bears distinct similarities to human rights.

The "normative and institutional pluralism"[11] that exists between human rights and development results in overlapping activities and mutual influence among their governing regimes, such that the demarcation between them is sometimes difficult to draw.[12] It may even be said that the overlap between the two areas or regimes is increasing and that the range of development policies and activities now affecting areas governed by human rights treaties is growing. Some practitioners have even observed that there has not been an evolution in the thinking on matters related to human rights to correlate with the expansion in the mandate of development institutions.[13]

Moreover, "complex problems have ramifications in many specialized directions."[14] Attempts at strict demarcations between different regimes or competencies fail to register the complex realities of international human rights and development, giving rise to both an increased potential for conflicting norms in international law and a "situation of ongoing institutional diversity and pluralism and the day-to-day and relatively mundane occurrences of overlapping forms and inter-regime activity."[15] This is particularly true because development and human rights share consistent goals[16] but pursue them differently, and their agendas overlap extensively[17] and in mutually reinforcing ways.[18]

---

paragraph 50, quoting P. Uvin, *Human Rights and Development* 52–53 (Kumarian Press 2004).

11 M. Young, *Regime Interaction in Creating, Implementing and Enforcing International Law*, in Young, *supra* note 1, at 86.

12 On the overlap of domains of activity and regulatory processes at the international level, *see* B. Kingsbury, *Introduction: Global Administrative Law in the Institutional Practice of Global Regulatory Governance*, in *World Bank Legal Review* vol. 3 (H. Cissé, D. Bradlow, & B. Kingsbury ed., World Bank 2012).

13 Sureda, *supra* note 9, at 217.

14 Judge Weeramantry dissenting, *Use of Nuclear Weapons in Armed Conflict Advisory Opinion* (1999) (I) ICJ Rep. 66.

15 Young, *supra* note 11, at 85.

16 United Nations Development Programme (UNDP), *Human Rights and Human Development*, in *Human Development Report 2000*, sections 19–28 (UNDP 2000). *See* S. Jahan, *Millennium Development Goals and Human Rights* (2002), available at http://www.inwent.org/ef-texte/human_rights/jahan.htm. *See* also *Report of the Millennium Project, Investing in Development: A Practical Plan to Achieve the Millennium Development Goals*, which characterizes the MDGs as human rights: "[The MDGs] are also basic human rights—the rights of each person on the planet to health, education, shelter, and security as pledged in the Universal Declaration of Human Rights and the UN Millennium Declaration" (page 1), available at http://www.unmillenniumproject.org/reports/fullreport.htm.

17 P. Alston, *Ships Passing in the Night: The Current State of the Human Rights and Development Debate Seen through the Lens of the Millennium Development Goals*, 27(3) Hum. Rights Q. 758.

18 OHCHR, *Frequently Asked Questions on Human Rights Based Approach to Development Cooperation* (UN 2006), and UNDP, *Human Development Report 2003: Millennium Development Goals: A Compact among Nations to end Human Poverty* (UNDP 2003). *See* also J. L. Roy, *Implementing the*

Examples of this convergence can be identified in the areas of social protection, education, governance, and health, as well as in thematic terms through activities aimed at the protection of women, indigenous peoples, children, and persons with disabilities. The Millennium Development Goals (MDG) illustrate the proximity and compatibility of human rights and development, even if they are critiqued for their silence on human rights[19] and their failure to address inequalities and the plight of the most vulnerable.[20]

At a deeper level, human rights and development may be viewed as converging in shared principles such as equality, participation, accountability, transparency, and voice, as well as in attention to vulnerable groups, all of which are principles that have become hallmarks of good development practice.[21] Both development and the international human rights frameworks give expression to these principles in different ways that evince a convergence of a more deliberate and strategic sort.

However, in general legal and policy terms, the international frameworks governing human rights and development occupy separate spheres governed by distinct regimes. Nowhere is this more apparent than in relation to legal obligations.[22]

International human rights are the purview of treaty frameworks such as the International Covenant on Civil and Political Rights (ICCPR)[23] and the International Covenant on Economic, Social and Cultural Rights (ICESCR),[24] along with a range of other universal instruments and their protocols governing issues such as gender discrimination,[25] child rights,[26] disabilities,[27]

Millennium Development Goals: Our Human Rights Obligation, 15(1) Libertas, who opines, "many of the MDGs can be reinforced by the binding human rights obligations of states."

19 Alston, *supra* note 17, at 796. *See,* generally, OHCHR, *Claiming the Millennium Development Goals: A Human Rights Approach* (United Nations 2008), available at http://www2.ohchr.org/SPdocs/Claiming_MDGs_en.pdf.

20 *See,* for example, M. Langford, *A Poverty of Rights: Six Ways to Fix the MDGs,* 41(1) IDS Bulletin 87 (Jan. 2010).

21 S. McInerney-Lankford & H.-O. Sano, *Human Rights Indicators in Development: An Introduction* 31–36 (World Bank 2010).

22 *Id.,* at 36–40.

23 International Covenant on Civil and Political Rights (ICCPR), UN GA Res. 2200A (XXI), 21 UN GAOR Supp. No. 16, at 52, UN Doc. A/6316 (1966), 999 UNTS 171 (entered into force Mar. 23, 1976).

24 International Covenant on Economic, Social and Cultural Rights (ICESCR), UN GA Res. 2200A (XXI), 21 UN GAOR Supp. No. 16, at 49, UN Doc. A/6316 (1966), 993 UNTS 3 (entered into force Jan. 3, 1976).

25 Convention on the Elimination of All Forms of Discrimination Against Women (CEDAW), UN Doc. A/34/46, at 193 (1979), 1249 UNTS 14 (entered into force Sep. 3, 1981).

26 Convention on the Rights of the Child (CRC), UNTS 3, 28 I.L.M. 1456 (entered into force Sep. 2, 1990).

27 Convention on the Rights of Persons with Disabilities (ICRPD), A/RES/61/106 (adopted Jan. 24, 2007).

torture,[28] and migrant workers.[29] This is complemented by regional human rights law frameworks and monitoring systems in Europe (ECHR,[30] the Charter of Fundamental Rights of the EU[31]), the Americas,[32] and Africa.[33]

Development, for its part, is defined more by broad-based goals such as the MDGs and general statements, strategies, programs, and policy frameworks of development institutions, which do not generally incorporate international legal norms[34] directly or explicitly. Philip Alston has noted the resistance to human rights in the context of the MDGs, attributing it to the fact that human rights are "a quintessentially legal domain and thus not one which is suitable for use in a general development studies context."[35] Thus, the binding legal frame of development cooperation tends to operate either at the level of the constitutive instruments of development agencies or at the transactional level of individual legal agreements underpinning particular operations. Although each of these instruments is an international agreement[36] subject to public international law,[37] the bulk of the development policy framework is not the domain of international legal norms, is not usually framed in terms of treaties, and does not readily admit a place for treaty obligations such as those flowing from human rights treaties.

Moreover, despite the more recent emphasis on accountability in development frameworks,[38] these frameworks do not involve legal accountability of

---

28 Convention Against Torture and Other Cruel, Inhuman or Degrading Treatment or Punishment (CAT) (Dec. 10, 1984), 1465 UNTS 85 (entered into force Jun. 26, 1987).

29 International Convention on the Protection of the Rights of All Migrant Workers and Members of Their Families, CPRMW (Dec. 18, 1990), UN GA Res. 45/158 (annex), 30 I.L.M. 1521 (1991) (entered into force Jul. 1, 2003).

30 *See* http://www.hri.org/docs/ECHR50.html.

31 Official Journal of the European Union C 83/389, available at http://eurlex.europa.eu/LexUriServ/LexUriServ.do?uri=OJ:C:2010:083:0389:0403:en:PDF.

32 American Convention on Human Rights (Pact of San Jose), OAS Treaty Series No. 36, 1144 UNTS 123 (entered into force Jul. 18, 1978), available at http://www.oas.org/juridico/english/treaties/b-32.html.

33 African Charter on Human and Peoples' Rights, OAU Doc. CAB/LEG/67/3 rev. 5, 21 I.L.M. 58 (1982) (entered into force Oct. 21, 1986).

34 By norms, this chapter refers to legally binding rules that create rights and obligations between subjects of international law.

35 P. Alston, *What's in a Name: Does It Really Matter if Development Policies Refer to Goals, Ideals or Human Rights?* 22 SIM Special 101 (1997).

36 Because these international agreements are entered into by UN members, the agreements are subject to the registration requirement of Article 102 of the UN Charter. *See* A. Broches, *Theory and Practice of Treaty Registration with Particular Reference to Agreements of the International Bank*, in *Selected Essays World Bank, ICSID, and Other Subjects of Public and Private International Law* 99 (Martinus Nijhoff 1995). All treaties and international agreements registered with the United Nations are available at http://treaties.un.org/.

37 I. Shihata, *The World Bank Legal Papers* 151 (Martinus Nijhoff 2000), in discussing the World Bank general conditions, confirms that the Bank's loan and guarantee agreements are international agreements that, although insulated from domestic law, are subject to public international law.

38 For example, Global Monitoring is a monitoring framework focused on "how the world is

the sort associated with treaties such as human rights treaties, and arguably cannot therefore empower poor or marginalized groups to claim their rights in the development process and bridge the gap between global standards and local circumstances.[39] Indeed, some people have argued that accountability itself cannot be separated from contests over the realization of rights and the distribution of resources.[40]

In general terms, therefore, human rights and development are governed by distinct regimes, including separate legal frameworks, that interact only occasionally and in ways that are far from clear. Only very rarely do human rights law obligations, such as those emanating from human rights treaties, receive formal recognition in the development regimes, and even then the operational consequences of such obligations are not always apparent. This chapter draws on the well-known concept of fragmentation of international law to analyze the relationship between human rights and development and the interaction of the legal and policy regimes that govern each.[41]

The fragmentation of international law is generally understood to refer to the way in which international law is split into "highly 'specialized boxes' that claim relative autonomy from each other and from the general law."[42] It is the subject of extensive academic commentary,[43] viewed by many as a product of the expansion and diversification of public international law and connected with the proliferation of special regimes. Some view fragmentation as a problem that undermines the general law and the systemic nature of international law,[44] while others view it as inevitable, perhaps even capable of strengthening special regimes.[45] Some of the literature focuses on the resolution of conflict between the norms of various special regimes,[46] whereas other work explores

---

doing in implementing the policies and actions for achieving the MDGs and related development outcomes. It is a framework for accountability in global development policy." *See* http://go.worldbank.org/AECE2VJFU0 .

39 *See* P. Newell & J. Wheeler, *Rights, Resources and the Politics of Accountability* (Institute of Development Studies 2006).

40 *Id.*

41 The putative causes of this fragmentation are discussed in more detail below.

42 ILC Study Group, *Conclusions of the Work of the Study Group on the Fragmentation of International Law: Difficulties Arising from the Diversification and Expansion of International Law,* UN Doc. A/CN.4/L.682 256 (2006).

43 P. M. Dupuy, *The Danger of Fragmentation or Unification of the International Legal System and the International Court of Justice,* 31 N.Y.U. J. Intl. L. & Pol. 791–807 (1999); J. Pauwleyn, *Bridging Fragmentation and Unity: International Law as a Universe of Inter-connected Islands,* 25 Mich. J. Intl. L. 903–17 (2004); K. Wellens & R. Vinaixa ed., *L'influence des sources sur l'unité et la fragmentation du droit international* (Bruylant 2006). The 105th Meeting of the American Society of International Law addressed some similar themes in *Harmony and Dissonance in International Law* (2011).

44 M. Koskenniemi & P. Leino, *Fragmentation of International Law? Postmodern Anxieties,* 15 Leiden J. Intl. L. 553 (2002), discuss a range of views on the various risks of fragmentation.

45 B. Simma, *Fragmentation in a Positive Light,* 25 Mich. J. Intl. L. 845 (2004).

46 For example, M. Milanović, *Norm Conflict in International Law: Whither Human Rights?* 20

the ways in which norms and institutions from disparate regimes overlap and interact.[47] This chapter adopts the latter approach, applying it to the interaction of regimes governing human rights and development.

Human Rights and Development: Regime Interaction and Policy Coherence

What, then, is the nature of the interaction between the regimes governing human rights and development?[48] Where and how do the regimes interact at the level of legal and policy discourse? In particular, how are human rights reflected in the development policy frameworks of bilateral and multilateral donors? This section outlines the various levels of formal interaction between the development and human rights regimes in high-level political statements and soft law, as well as the individual policies of particular agencies and institutions. From there, it assesses the nature and quality of the transposition of human rights, whether in general references, as principles, or as legal obligations with direct operational implications.

International Political Statements and Soft Law

Soft law measures dating from the 1960s link human rights and development. These recognize that failure to reach development goals impedes the realization of human rights and that "the achievement of lasting progress in the implementation of human rights is dependent upon sound and effective national and international policies of economic and social development."[49] Perhaps the most direct attempt at linking human rights and development emerges in the right to development. In 1986, the UN General Assembly adopted the Declaration on the Right to Development,[50] which pronounces the right to development as a new human right, one of the so-called third generation of human rights. At the same time these initiatives were under way at the international political level, philosophers such as Amartya Sen and Martha Nussbaum were forging links between human rights and development. Sen's concept of development as freedom, under which the essential goal of development is expanding substantive human freedoms, or "capabilities," has a natural affinity with human rights and human rights–based approaches to development, particularly in its emphasis on the importance of voice for marginalized groups.[51]

Duke J. Comp. & Intl. L. 69 (2009).

47 M. Young ed., *Regime Interaction in International Law* (Cambridge U. Press 2012).

48 For a definition of regimes, *see* Young, *supra* note 1.

49 Proclamation of Teheran, Final Act of the International Conference on Human Rights, Teheran, Apr. 22 to May 13, 1968, UN Doc. A/CONF. 32/41, at 3 (1968).

50 Declaration on the Right to Development, A/RES/41/128 (Dec. 4, 1986). *See* also S. Marks, *Emerging Human Rights: A New Generation for the 1980's*, 33 Rutgers L. Rev. 435 (1981); S. Marks, *The Human Right to Development: Between Rhetoric and Reality?* 17 Harv. Hum. Rights J. 137 (2004).

51 A. Sen, *Development as Freedom* (Oxford U. Press 2000).

The Declaration on the Right to Development underscores the links between human rights and development by "[r]ecognizing that the human person is the central subject of the development process and that development policy should therefore make the human being the main participant and beneficiary of development." Article 1 states, "The right to development is an inalienable human right by virtue of which every human person and all peoples are entitled to participate in, contribute to, and enjoy economic, social, cultural and political development, in which all human rights and fundamental freedoms can be fully realized."

In 1993, the Vienna Declaration and Programme of Action, in addition to reaffirming the right to development, asserted that "[d]emocracy, development, and respect for human rights and fundamental freedoms are interdependent and mutually reinforcing."[52]

Although such measures represent efforts to connect human rights and development cohesively, they also underscore the fragmentation of international law by not being binding and by the fact that they do not connect human rights obligations operationally with development.[53] The marginality of the right to development in normative terms and the vagueness surrounding content and meaning in the operational frameworks of development agencies are evidence of the separateness of the human rights and development frameworks rather than an example of their convergence.

In 2000, the global community adopted the Millennium Declaration, which contains commitments to respect human rights and uphold the Universal Declaration of Human Rights.[54] This was followed by the 2010 Millen-

---

52 Vienna Declaration and Programme of Action, A/CONF.157/23 (Jul. 12, 1993; adopted by the World Conference on Human Rights on Jun. 25, 1993), paragraph 8.

53 The discourse around the right to development has often been a polarized one, generating sharp differences between developed and less developed countries in the context of demands for redressing economic imbalances and a new international economic order. For a thoughtful review of the history and implications of the right to development, *see* I. Bunn, *The Right to Development: Implications for International Economic Law,* 15 Am. U. Intl. L.J. 1425 (2000). On the right to development more generally, *see* S. Choudhury, *The Right to Development in International Law* (Martinus Nijhoff 1992).

54 Section V of the Millennium Declaration, on human rights, democracy, and good governance, reads:

> 24. We will spare no effort to promote democracy and strengthen the rule of law, as well as respect for all internationally recognized human rights and fundamental freedoms, including the right to development.
>
> 25. We resolve therefore:
>
> • To respect fully and uphold the Universal Declaration of Human Rights.
>
> • To strive for the full protection and promotion in all our countries of civil, political, economic, social and cultural rights for all.
>
> • To strengthen the capacity of all our countries to implement the principles and practices of democracy and respect for human rights, including minority rights.
>
> • To combat all forms of violence against women and to implement the Convention on the Elimination of All Forms of Discrimination against Women.

nium Summit Outcome document, *Keeping the Promises: United to Achieve the Millennium Development Goals*,[55] which contains several references to human rights and international law instruments, reaffirming full respect for international law and principles[56] and for all human rights, including the right to development.[57] It also notes that gender equality and women's full enjoyment of human rights are essential to economic and social development, including the achievement of the MDGs.[58] Agencies such as the UN Office of the High Commissioner for Human Rights (OHCHR) have continued to emphasize the importance of human rights to development as part of a broader agenda of international policy coherence.[59] This was affirmed by the UN High Commissioner for Human Rights in the context of the right to development: "We must foster policy coherence and systemic integration of human rights, including the right to development, across sectors, across institutions and across layers of governance. Human aspirations for well-being can be realized only when there is a strong accountability framework."[60]

In the area of aid effectiveness, although the 2005 Paris Declaration on Aid Effectiveness[61] does not contain any explicit reference to human rights as a cross-cutting theme,[62] it does confirm five core principles deemed essential to improving the effectiveness of development assistance and contributing to meeting the MDGs: ownership, alignment, harmonization, managing for results, and mutual accountability to improve the quality of aid and its impact on development. In 2008, the Accra Agenda for Action (AAA) proclaimed respect for human rights as a cornerstone for achieving enduring impact on the

---

- To take measures to ensure respect for and protection of the human rights of migrants, migrant workers and their families, to eliminate the increasing acts of racism and xenophobia in many societies and to promote greater harmony and tolerance in all societies.
- To work collectively for more inclusive political processes, allowing genuine participation by all citizens in all our countries.
- To ensure the freedom of the media to perform their essential role and the right of the public to have access to information.

55 Integrated and Coordinated Implementation of and Follow-Up to the Outcomes of the Major UN Conferences and Summits in the Economic, Social, and Related Fields. Follow-up to the Outcome of the Millennium Summit, A/65/L.1 (Sep. 17, 2010).

56 Paragraph 2, 2010 Millennium Summit Outcome document.

57 Paragraph 3, 2010 Millennium Summit Outcome document.

58 Paragraph 12, 2010 Millennium Summit Outcome document.

59 *See* below for a discussion of international policy coherence.

60 Closing Statement by the High Commissioner for Human Rights at UN General Assembly Event to Commemorate the 25th Anniversary of the United Nations Declaration on the Right to Development (Nov. 8, 2011), available at http://www.ohchr.org/en/NewsEvents/Pages/DisplayNews.aspx?NewsID=11583&LangID=E.

61 *See* http://www.oecd.org/dataoecd/11/41/34428351.pdf and http://ec.europa.eu/development/icenter/repository/SEC_PDF_2009_1137_F_ACTE_PCD_EN.pdf (2009).

62 Paragraph 42 of the 2005 Paris Declaration on Aid Effectiveness notes the need for "harmonisation efforts on other cross cutting issues such as gender equality and other thematic issues."

lives and potential of poor women, men, and children, stating that it is "vital that all our policies address these issues in a more systematic and coherent way."[63]

In paragraph 13(c), the AAA goes further: "Developing countries and donors will ensure that their respective development policies and programmes are designed and implemented in ways consistent with their agreed international commitments on gender equality, human rights, disability and environmental sustainability." The 2011 outcome document from the Fourth High-Level Forum on Aid Effectiveness in Busan explicitly preserves the commitments of the AAA and, like the AAA, contains provisions on human rights. In addition, it provides for the right to development and confirms that the "common principles which—consistent with our agreed international commitments on human rights, decent work, gender equality, environmental sustainability and disability—form the foundation of our cooperation for effective development."[64]

The trend among such high-level statements and declarations is clearly in favor of recognizing human rights more explicitly and in terms of obligations and international commitments. This movement promotes a vision of development and human rights that supports international policy coherence and that recognizes the potential impacts of actions in one policy realm on other areas. At the level of general political statements, therefore, the trend increasingly recognizes the relevance of human rights law obligations to development cooperation, including aid effectiveness.

Development Policies

At an institutional level, the policies of many development agencies and banks reflect the points of convergence, albeit in different ways. This section traces the links between human rights and development in these policies, noting the ways in which they approach the question of human rights as the subject of binding international law obligations.

References to Human Rights

Some policies contain general or preambular references to human rights, but the operational implications of these references remain unclear. Such references might cite the importance of human rights in the development process or include provisions regarding the respect of human rights of particular groups; some even go so far as to define human rights by reference to the relevant international legal instruments. Examples are found in the indigenous peoples

---

63 Accra Agenda for Action, paragraph 3.

64 Busan Partnership for Effective Development Cooperation, Outcome Document (Dec. 1, 2011), paragraph 11, available at http://www.aideffectiveness.org/busanhlf4/images/stories/hlf4/OUTCOME_DOCUMENT_-_FINAL_EN.pdf. *See* also references to human rights and rights-based approaches in relation to the Millennium Declaration (paragraph 3) and the role of CSOs (paragraph 22).

policies of a number of multilateral development banks, such as the World Bank[65] and the Inter-American Development Bank (IDB). The IDB Operational Policy on Indigenous Peoples makes numerous references to indigenous peoples' rights,[66] defined as "the rights of indigenous peoples and individuals, whether originating in the indigenous legislation issued by States, in other relevant national legislation, in applicable international norms in force for each country, or in the indigenous juridical systems of each people, hereinafter collectively referred to as the 'applicable legal norms.'"[67] The policy enumerates the relevant international and regional human rights instruments, also making reference to the jurisprudence of international human rights bodies.[68]

Human Rights as General Principles

The frameworks of some agencies evidence a more strategic engagement with human rights, acknowledging their importance for development policy and practice[69] and highlighting the links between human rights and sustainable

---

65 Operational Policy on Indigenous Peoples 4.10, the preamble of which reads: "This policy contributes to the Bank's mission of poverty reduction and sustainable development by ensuring that the development process fully respects the dignity, human rights, economies, and cultures of Indigenous Peoples."

66 http://idbdocs.iadb.org/wsdocs/getdocument.aspx?docnum=691261.

67 *Id.*, paragraph 1.2.

68 Page 1, footnote 4 , IDB Operational Policy on Indigenous Peoples, reads:

> [T]hose international norms in force for each country are defined as follows: International legislation includes, as in force for each country, the United Nations Universal Declaration of Human Rights (1948), the International Covenant on Civil and Political Rights (1966), the American Convention on Human Rights (1969), the International Covenant on Economic, Social, and Cultural Rights (1976), the International Convention on the Elimination of all Forms of Racial Discrimination (1966), the Convention on the Rights of the Child (1990), the International Labor Organization (ILO) Convention 107 concerning the Protection and Integration of Indigenous and Other Tribal and Semi-Tribal Populations in Independent Countries (1957), ILO Convention 169 concerning Indigenous and Tribal Populations in Independent Countries (1989), Agenda 21 adopted by the United Nations Conference on Environment and Development (UNCED) (1992), and the International Convention on Biological Diversity (1992), as well as the corresponding international jurisprudence of the Inter-American Court of Human Rights or similar bodies whose jurisdiction has been accepted by the relevant country. Other international instruments currently in preparation, such as the draft United Nations Declaration on the Rights of Indigenous Peoples and the draft American Declaration on the Rights of Indigenous Peoples, establish aspirational principles that may be taken into account to the extent that these instruments are finalized and subscribed by the relevant country.

The UN Declaration on the Rights of Indigenous Peoples was adopted by the UN General Assembly in September 2007.

69 NZAid, Human Rights Policy Statement, 4 (2002), available at http://www.nzaid.govt.nz/library/docs/nzaid-human-rights-policy.pdf; Danish Ministry of Foreign Affairs, Democratisation and Human Rights for the Benefit of the People: Strategic Priorities for Danish Support for Good Governance, page 3 (2009), available at http://www.um.dk/NR/rdonlyres/D04B984F-41A2-4E7E-81C1-A35C09F95964/0/DraftDHRstrategyFINALVERSION030309.pdf. Denmark's general policy on development, "The Right to a Better Life," was adopted in 2012. The first of five strands of the strategy is freedom, democracy, and human rights. Available at http://um.dk/en/danida-en/goals/strategy/.

development.[70] Others draw connections between the international human rights law framework and the MDGs[71] and compliance with human rights principles and improvements in MDG-oriented development.[72] Several agencies have well-established human rights mainstreaming policies[73] or policies founded on a rights perspective.[74] Such policies promote the integration of human rights into country programs or existing aid interventions across sectors or promote the rights of certain groups such as children, women, minorities and indigenous peoples, or persons with disabilities.

Human Rights–Based Approaches

Some governments have adopted human rights–based approaches to development.[75] At the global level, the United Nations is the most prominent example of a general rights-based approach to development,[76] founded directly on the legal obligations enshrined in the UN Charter, the Universal Declaration, and

70 *Human Rights and Australia's Aid Program*. From an aid perspective, development and human rights are interdependent and mutually reinforcing. For development to be sustainable, individuals in developing countries must have secure and long-term access to the resources required to satisfy their basic needs, be they economic, social, cultural, civil, or political.

At the broadest level, therefore, the entire Australian aid program contributes to the realization of human rights. *See* http://www.ausaid.gov.au/keyaid/humanrights.cfm.

71 Netherlands Ministry of Foreign Affairs, *Human Dignity for All: A Human Rights Strategy for Foreign Policy*. There are major similarities between the MDGs and the objectives of the human rights instruments. Both aim to eliminate hunger, improve access to education and health care, and improve the position of women, children, and other vulnerable groups. All the MDGs also have an equivalent in the international human rights instruments, particularly the International Covenant on Economic, Social, and Cultural Rights (ICESCR), the Convention on the Elimination of All Forms of Discrimination against Women (CEDAW), and the International Convention on the Rights of the Child (CRC).

72 BMZ, Human Rights in German Development Policy, *BMZ Strategy Paper* 4 (2011), at section 2.3; *see* also Germany's Development Policy Action Plan on Human Rights (2008–10).

73 *See*, for example, F. Uggla, *Mainstreaming at Sida: A Synthesis Report* 7, Sida Studies in Evaluation No. 5 (2007), available at http://www.oecd.org/dataoecd/0/40/39070485.pdf and http://www.sida.se/English/.

74 Sweden's policy for democratic development and human rights in Swedish development cooperation, 2010–14. Memorandum Appendix to Government Decision 2010-01-2 (UF2009/33076/UP). "With this policy, the Government is raising its level of ambition and clarifying its aims concerning Swedish development cooperation in working towards the goal of democratic development and greater respect for human rights in developing countries." Contrasting a rights-based approach and a rights-based perspective, *see* L. Munro, *The "Human Rights-Based Approach to Programming": A Contradiction in Terms?* in *Rights-Based Approaches to Development Exploring the Potential and the Pitfalls* 187–206 (S. Hickey & D. Mitlin ed., Kumarian Press 2009). According to Munro, a rights-based approach insists that everything the organization does be based on human rights, whereas a rights-based perspective is less absolute.

75 For instance, a key aim of Germany's Development Policy Action Plan on Human Rights (2008–10) is "systematically integrating a human rights based approach into development." Available at http://www.bmz.de/en/service/infothek/fach/konzepte/konzept167.pdf?follow=adword.

76 *See*, especially, UNICEF's rights-based approach to programming, Munro, *supra* note 74, at 193–202. For a critical review of human rights–based approaches in development, *see* M. Darrow & A. Tomas, *Power, Capture and Conflict: A Call for Human Rights Accountability in Development Cooperation*, 27 Hum. Rights Q. 471–538 (2005).

the core UN human rights treaties. The 2003 UN Interagency Common Understanding of a Human Rights–Based Agreement[77] was adopted by the UN Development Group (UNDG) to ensure the consistent application of a human rights–based approach by UN agencies, funds, and programs at global and regional levels, especially at the country level in relation to the UN Common Country Assessments/UN Development Assistance Frameworks (CCA /UNDAF), which were established to strengthen the coherence and effectiveness of the UN system's contribution to countries' development efforts. The Common Understanding establishes a set of principles that guide and define a human rights approach; it confirms the central importance of the international human rights treaty framework in all development cooperation programs.[78] The secretary-general's 2002 reform program included a decision, known as "Action 2," to mainstream human rights across country programs.[79] Action 2 was followed by further reform programs in 2005[80] and backed by the commitment of world leaders at the 2005 UN World Summit[81] to mainstream human rights within their national policies and in the development programs of the United Nations. Several UN agencies have led efforts to catalog their experiences and guidance on integrating human rights and rights-based approaches.[82] In November 2009, the UNDG established a Human Rights

---

77 The Human Rights Based Approach to Development Cooperation Towards a Common Understanding Among UN Agencies, available at http://www.undg.org/archive_docs/6959-The_Human_Rights_Based_Approach_to_Development_Cooperation_Towards_a_Common_Understanding_Among_UN.pdf.

78 Those principles are

> 1. All programmes of development co-operation, policies and technical assistance should further the realisation of human rights as laid down in the Universal Declaration of Human Rights and other international human rights instruments.
>
> 2. Human rights standards contained in, and principles derived from, the Universal Declaration of Human Rights and other international human rights instruments guide all development cooperation and programming in all sectors and in all phases of the programming process.
>
> 3. Development cooperation contributes to the development of the capacity to meet their obligations and/or of "'rights-holders" to claim their rights.

79 Secretary-General, *Strengthening of the United Nations: An Agenda for Further Change*, A/57/387 (Sep. 9, 2002), from which the strengthening and mainstreaming of human rights in the UN have come to be known as "Action 2." Action 2, related to strengthening UN support for the promotion and protection of human rights worldwide, was adopted by UNDG, ECHA, and OHCHR in 2003 pursuant to the secretary-general's report. Its main goal is to develop the capacity of UN humanitarian and development operations to strengthen national human rights promotion and protection systems consistent with international norms and principles. *See* http://www.un.org/events/action2/.

80 Paragraph 126 contains the commitment to integrate the promotion and protection of human rights into national policies and support the further mainstreaming of human rights throughout the UN system. *See* also Secretary-General, *In Larger Freedom: Towards Security, Development and Human Rights for All* (UN 2005), available at http://www.un.org/largerfreedom/.

81 2005 World Summit Outcome: Resolution adopted by the UN GA A/RES/60/1.

82 UNICEF Guidelines for Human Rights Based Programming Approach CF/EXD/1998-04 (Apr. 21, 1998), available at http://www.fao.org/righttofood/kc/downloads/vl/docs/212951.pdf; UNDP, *Human Rights in UNDP: A Practice Note* (Apr. 2005), available at http://

Mainstreaming mechanism, supported by a multidonor trust fund, to coordinate UN systemwide work on human rights in development cooperation.

Human Rights Obligations as a Policy Frame

Some policies integrate human rights explicitly in terms of international law obligations. In these policies, human rights have potentially far-reaching implications because the policies rely on the legally binding quality of human rights to ground their approach, even if the references are more general and operate as an overall frame. For example, a tenet of the Austrian Development Cooperation (ADC) Human Rights Policy Document (2006) establishes "[h]uman rights as a normative principle, as a programming principle, and as an instrument for evaluating interventions." The ADC policy states: "A stronger link between these two areas offers a legally based framework and a planning instrument for policies and programs. It steers the focus in poverty reduction away from the needs of the poor towards the obligations of the state and the capabilities/potential of citizens to demand their rights." Like a number of other bilateral aid agencies, the Swedish International Development Cooperation Agency (SIDA) has a well-established practice of mainstreaming human rights.[83] In keeping with this practice, Sweden's policy for democratic development and human rights in Swedish development cooperation[84] highlights the human rights perspective,[85] which it defines based on the UN Universal Declaration of Human Rights and international and regional human rights conventions, and further confirms that "[a]lthough contradictions or tension may exist between different rights, states cannot choose to disregard certain of their obligations under international law."[86]

New Zealand's International Aid and Development Agency document Human Rights Policy Statement (2002) and its Human Rights Implementation Plan of Action 2004–09 similarly confirm the role of donor and partner human rights treaty obligations in linking human rights and development. Likewise, the policy of German development cooperation rests on common human rights law obligations. Germany's Development Policy Action Plan

---

www.undp.org/governance/docs/HRPN_English.pdf. The UNDP Strategic Plan, 2008–11 makes numerous references to human rights and clarifies the role of the program: "16. Underscores that while UNDP should uphold universal United Nations norms and standards, including those related to human rights, UNDP does not have any normative or monitoring role with regard to human rights." *UNDP Strategic Plan, 2008–2011: Accelerating Global Progress on Human Development*, DP/2007/43/Rev.1, 4 (May 22, 2008). More generally, *see* E. Mandeville, *United Nations Development Programme*, in *Encyclopedia of Human Rights* 150–57 (D. Forsythe ed., Oxford U. Press 2009).

83 *See*, for example, Uggla, *supra* note 73.

84 Memorandum Appendix to Government Decision 2010-01-2 (UF2009/33076/UP). "With this policy, the Government is raising its level of ambition and clarifying its aims concerning Swedish development cooperation in working towards the goal of democratic development and greater respect for human rights in developing countries."

85 *See* Munro, *supra* note 74.

86 SIDA, *Memorandum Appendix to Government Decision* 2010-01-2, 6.

on Human Rights 2008–2010 highlights the shared obligations of donors and partners under human rights treaties:

> Human rights provide us with legally binding standards to which we, in common with our partner countries, have committed ourselves inside and outside our borders. We have jointly ratified international human rights treaties and so it is our joint responsibility to work for the respect, protection and fulfillment of human rights. By meeting our obligations, we want to help our partners specifically and effectively to meet theirs.[87]

The 2011 BMZ strategy paper Human Rights in German Development Policy supports this view, affirming that human rights form the overarching framework for development policy. It states that the implementation of human rights conventions is a legally binding obligation and that this "provides the binding frame of reference for Germany's development cooperation with partner countries."[88]

Among multilaterals, the UN system's human rights approach[89] and UN guidance in development activities are broadly based on human rights treaty obligations,[90] even if the broader question of the UN's own human rights obligations remains contested.[91] A sophisticated example is UNICEF's human rights–based programming approach, which treats the Convention on the Rights of the Child (CRC) as a central programming document, relying on it directly and explicitly. In addition, although the Committee on the Rights of the Child is the monitoring body established by the CRC, and although UNICEF does not have a formal role in monitoring CRC compliance, UNICEF has, over time, become active in all stages of the reporting process. In this respect, the UNICEF example illustrates the possibility of institutional coordination between development programming and treaty monitoring activities.

The position of other international organizations has similarly signaled broader recognition of the role of human rights in development. The OECD Development Assistance Committee's (2007) *Action-Oriented Policy Paper on Human Rights and Development* (AOPP) is predicated on a vision of human rights as integral to development and of human rights and equitable, sustainable development being mutually reinforcing. This approach is squarely

---

87 BMZ, *Development Policy Action Plan on Human Rights 2008–2010*, 4. The policy also includes a comprehensive list of human rights treaty resources (18–19).

88 BMZ Human Rights in German Development Policy, *BMZ Strategy Paper* 4, introductory summary, paragraph 2 (2009).

89 *See supra* note 77.

90 *See*, for example, UNDAF guidelines available at www.undg.org. Within the UNDG, implementing a human rights–based approach to development programming is the focus of the Human Rights Mainstreaming Mechanism (HRM); *see* also the UN Common Learning Package on Human Rights–Based Approach.

91 For a thorough and thoughtful analysis of this question in the context of the UN's development operations, *see* M. Darrow & L. Arbour, *The Pillar of Glass: Human Rights in the Development Operations of the United Nations*, 103 Am. J. Intl. L. 446 (2009).

based on the international human rights law framework: "Human rights constitute a unique, internationally shared and accepted normative framework, reflecting global moral and political values. International human rights law has evolved to protect and safeguard the integrity and dignity of the person, by establishing legal obligations on states." The first of 10 principles, intended to serve as a basic orientation on human rights in key development areas and activities where donor harmonization is of particular relevance, states: "Build a shared understanding of the links between human rights obligations and development priorities through dialogue."

Another acknowledgment of the place of human rights obligations in development policy, albeit indirectly and from a private sector perspective, is the International Finance Corporation (IFC) Policy on Enviromental and Social Sustainability, which is part of the IFC Sustainability Framework.[92] The 2012 policy recognizes the responsibility of business to respect human rights independently of state duties to respect, protect, and fulfill human rights.[93] In a footnote to the term "human rights," the policy states that "for the purposes of this Policy, IFC shall be guided by the International Bill of Rights and the eight core conventions of the International Labour Organization."[94]

Human Rights as Operational Norms in Development Policy Frameworks

Despite the broad support for human rights adduced in the policies reviewed above, not all such provisions translate into a reliance on human rights in a direct operational sense. Indeed, not all agencies with human rights–related policies accept that they are under a legal obligation to promote and respect human rights, and intrinsic arguments for including human rights in development cooperation are not always limited to legal ones.[95] Subtle differences in terminology are also discernible in some policies' treatment of human rights in terms of responsibilities rather than in more definite legal terms such as obligations with specific policy consequences resulting from their invocation.

The policies of a number of agencies and institutions are distinguished by the strength of the legal and policy provisions integrating human rights, with the potential for significant operational implications. At their strongest, such policies emphasize human rights as a shared legal framework, highlighting both partner and donor obligations under international human rights law and offering concrete operational entry points for their application in development activities.

---

92 http://www1.ifc.org/wps/wcm/connect/Topics_Ext_Content/IFC_External_Corporate_site/IFC+Sustainability/Sustainability+Framework.

93 IFC Policy on Environmental and Social Sustainability (Jan. 1, 2012), paragraph 12, available at http://www1.ifc.org/wps/wcm/connect/7540778049a792dcb87efaa8c6a8312a/SP_English_2012.pdf?MOD=AJPERES.

94 *Id.*

95 OECD DAC, *Integrating Human Rights into Development: Donor Approaches, Challenges and Experiences* 29 (OEDC 2006), study by L.-H. Piron & T. O'Neil.

The European Union provides an example of a policy approach connecting the dictates of the international human rights law frameworks and the policy requirements applicable in development cooperation. Although its trade and external policies have been critiqued for internal incoherencies,[96] for their potential negative impacts on human rights in developing countries,[97] and for failing to fully integrate human rights, the EU has, since 1995, adopted "a distinct policy" on human rights in its external relations. As a result a human rights clause[98] is introduced into all trade and development agreements with third countries or nonmembers,[99] making the protection of human rights an essential element of any trade and development agreement.[100] As with a number of the bilateral examples discussed above, the centrality of human rights to EU development cooperation draws explicitly on legal commitments that are both internal and external to the EU itself,[101] anchoring human rights operationally in development through the treaty obligations of member states.[102] Thus, Article 9 of the Cotonou Agreement makes the respect of human rights an essential element of the agreement, basing that clause explicitly on international obligations and commitments concerning respect for human rights.[103]

---

96 B. Mahnkopf, *EU Multilateral Trade Policy: Neither Coherent nor Development Friendly*, Global Labour University Working Paper No. 2 (Feb. 2008).

97 J. Nwobike, *The Application of Human Rights in African Caribbean and Pacific–European Union Development and Trade Partnership*, 6(10) German L.J. 1381 (2005). Examples include the future potential human rights impact (ex ante study) of EU economic partnership agreements on dairy and honey farmers in Zambia and the right to food of milk and maize farmers in Uganda (2009).

98 "The essential element" of an agreement, or the "human rights essential element clause." *See* EU Council Decision 7255/95. *Human Rights Clauses in Community Agreements with Nonmember Countries* (May 24, 1995). *See* also Commission Communication on the Inclusion of Respect for Democratic Principles and Human Rights in Agreements between the Community and Third Countries COM (95) 216 (May 23, 1995).

99 M. Cremona, *Human Rights and Democracy Clauses in the EC's Trade Agreements*, in *The European Union and World Trade Law after the GATT Uruguay Round* (N. Emiliou & D. O'Keefe ed., Wiley 1996); E. Reidel & M. Will, *Human Rights Clauses in External Agreements of the EC*, in *The EU and Human Rights* (P. Alston ed., Oxford U. Press 1999).

100 *See* also Cotonou Agreement—partnership agreement between the EC and ACP countries, concluded in 2000, a revised version of which entered into force on July 1, 2008. Negotiations for a second round of revisions were concluded on March 19, 2010.

101 http://www.ihrnetwork.org/eu-development-policies_215.htm. Internal commitments are based on the Treaty on European Union and were confirmed in the Treaty of Amsterdam and the EU Charter of Fundamental Rights and the European Instrument for Democratization and Human Rights (2006).

102 According to the International Human Rights Network, "Human rights are central to EU Development Cooperation matching similar commitments to its humanitarian aid and Common Foreign and Security Policy. The policies flow from the legal obligations of its Member States, as well as from EU treaty provisions which recognize human rights as common values underpinning EU partnership and dialogue with third countries." *See* http://www.ihrnetwork.org/eu-development-policies_215.htm.

103 Article 9 of the Cotonou Agreement provides:

Essential Elements and Fundamental Element

> 1. Cooperation shall be directed towards sustainable development centered on the human person, who is the main protagonist and beneficiary of development; this entails

The centrality of human rights treaties is similarly reflected in the 2007 EU European Instrument for Democracy and Human Rights. This instrument establishes a mechanism under which the community provides assistance within the framework of the community's policy on development cooperation and economic, financial, and technical cooperation with third countries, consistent with EU foreign policy as a whole, contributing to the development and consolidation of democracy and the rule of law and of respect for all human rights and fundamental freedoms.[104] The instrument draws directly from international and regional human rights legal frameworks,[105] and its aims are squarely based on human rights[106] and the international and regional legal frameworks that enforce them.[107] Other developments in the EU context reveal the increasing relevance of international human rights standards

---

respect for and promotion of all human rights. Respect for all human rights and fundamental freedoms, including respect for fundamental social rights, democracy based on the rule of law and transparent and accountable governance are an integral part of sustainable development.

2. The Parties refer to their international obligations and commitments concerning respect for human rights. They reiterate their deep attachment to human dignity and human rights, which are legitimate aspirations of individuals and peoples. Human rights are universal, indivisible and inter-related. The Parties undertake to promote and protect all fundamental freedoms and human rights, be they civil and political, or economic, social and cultural. In this context, the Parties reaffirm the equality of men and women. . . . Respect for human rights, democratic principles and the rule of law, which underpin the ACP-EU Partnership, shall underpin the domestic and international policies of the Parties and constitute the essential elements of this Agreement. . . . These areas will also be a focus of support for development strategies. The Community shall provide support for political, institutional and legal reforms and for building the capacity of public and private actors and civil society in the framework of strategies agreed jointly between the State concerned and the Community.

104 Regulation (EC) No. 1889/2006 of the European Parliament and of the Council of December 20, 2006, on establishing a financing instrument for the promotion of democracy and human rights worldwide, 29.12.2006 EN *Official J. of the European Union L.* 386/1.

105 Paragraph 7 provides: "The Community's contribution to the development and consolidation of democracy and the rule of law, and of respect for human rights and fundamental freedoms is rooted in the general principles established by the International Bill of Human Rights, and any other human rights instrument adopted within the framework of the United Nations, as well as relevant regional human rights Instruments."

106 Paragraph 2(a) provides: "Such assistance shall aim in particular at (a) enhancing the respect for and observance of human rights and fundamental freedoms, as proclaimed in the Universal Declaration of Human Rights and other international and regional human rights instruments."

107 Paragraph 2(b) provides: "Such assistance shall aim in particular at (a) enhancing the respect for and observance of human rights and fundamental freedoms, as proclaimed in the Universal Declaration of Human Rights and other international and regional human rights instruments." However, it is worth noting that the recent EU Communication on the MDGs does not highlight the role of human rights frameworks in any significant way, other than to mention that "[MDGs] emphasize the importance of a Human Rights based approach to development." European Commisssion, *A Twelve-Point EU Action Plan in Support of the Millennium Development Goals, Communication from the Commission to the European Parliament, the Council, the European Economic and Social Committee and the Regions*, 6 (2010). *See* also Annual Action Programme 2011 for the European Instrument for the Promotion of Democracy and Human Rights Worldwide (EU Commission Mar. 29, 2011).

in fostering sustainable development in EU trade policy. Examples include the European Parliament resolution that encourages greater cooperation at the multinational level between the World Trade Organization (WTO) and the main UN institutions in the human rights field. This resolution states that the Parliament considers that closer links with the Office of the United Nations High Commissioner for Human Rights via special procedures would be particularly useful to provide a multilateral trade framework that would enhance respect for human rights and considers, similarly, that the high commission's expertise could be taken into account by WTO panels and the appeals body when cases of serious breaches of human rights are observed. In addition, the Parliament's resolution considers that the Human Rights Council's universal periodic review should be a useful tool to monitor compliance with human rights provisions in international trade agreements and supports the practice of including legally binding human rights clauses in the EU's international agreements.[108]

The EU development policy landscape was further defined by new policies on the future of development policy and the instrument of budget support in October 2011. *Increasing the Impact of EU Development Policy: An Agenda for Change* seeks to focus aid on fewer countries and fewer sectors while prioritizing human rights, democracy, and other key elements of good governance.[109] The EU Commission's 2011 position on budget support to third countries[110] reiterates the linkage between human rights and development, indicating that its proposed approach "would lead to enhanced importance of human rights, democracy and good governance trends in determining the mix of instruments and aid modalities at country level."[111]

The European Investment Bank (EIB) provides another example of broad legal and policy commitment to human rights. As an EU institution, EIB is bound by the EU Charter of Fundamental Rights and takes the charter as a point of departure.[112] EIB policy integrates an approach to human rights focused on respect for environmental, social, and economic rights and takes

---

108 European Parliament resolution of November 25, 2010, on human rights and social and environmental standards in international trade agreements (2009/2219 [INI]). For a critical view of the traditional models on the value added of human rights in trade, *see* A. Lang, *The Role of the Human Rights Movement in Trade Policy-Making: Human Rights as a Trigger for Policy Learning*, 5 New Zealand J. Pub. Intl. Law. 77–102 (2007).

109 European Commission, *Increasing the Impact of EU Development Policy: An Agenda for Change* (EU Commission Oct. 13, 2011), available at http://ec.europa.eu/europeaid/what/development-policies/documents/agenda_for_change_en.pdf.

110 European Commission, *The Future Approach to EU Budget Support to Third Countries* (EU Commission Oct. 13, 2011).

111 The policy provides that "the EU should assess whether pre-conditions exist to entrust Good Governance and Development Contracts to a partner country, i.e.; whether fundamental values of human rights, democracy and rule of law or a clear path towards international standards exist and whether such a Contract could clearly act as a driver to accelerate this movement."

112 http://www.eib.org/about/news/business-and-human-rights.htm.

human rights considerations into account in its project evaluations. The EIB is reviewing its existing project social performance standards in light of the principles of the UN Respect, Protect, and Remedy framework[113] and will update existing project guidelines and operational practices based on the outcome of that review.

The direct links between human rights and development frameworks are evident in the 2005 framework document of the New Economic Partnership for Africa's Development (NEPAD),[114] which contains several references to human rights as a foundation,[115] objective, and responsibility of the mechanism. It recognizes that "development is impossible in the absence of true democracy, respect for human rights, peace, and good governance."[116] The African Peer Review Mechanism (APRM),[117] which operates as part of the NEPAD, links the final stage of its review to existing human rights mechanisms such as the African Commission on Human Rights.[118] In this, the African-led policy is an example of a framework that explicitly links development with human rights and human rights obligations as well as the regional institutional mechanism that monitors them.[119]

Some donors specify that human rights obligations operate as minimum legal standards against which their development activities are judged for consistency. In these instances, human rights treaty obligations are operationally connected with the core of development cooperation policies and activities. An example of this is Canada's 2008 Official Development Assistance Accountability Act, which contains a human rights clause requiring development operations financed by Canada to be consistent with international human rights standards.[120]

---

113 *See infra* note 164.

114 http://www.nepad.org/home/lang/en.

115 *Id.*, paragraph 180. The NEPAD has, as one of its foundations, the expansion of democratic frontiers and the deepening of the culture of human rights. A democratic Africa will become a pillar of world democracy, human rights, and tolerance. The resources of the world currently dedicated to resolving civil and interstate conflict could therefore be freed for more rewarding endeavors.

116 *Id.*, paragraph 79.

117 An important accountability-related mechanism to the NEPAD, the APRM is an instrument voluntarily acceded to by member states of the African Union (AU) as an African self-monitoring mechanism. The APRM is central to the NEPAD process for the socioeconomic development of Africa.

118 The APRM base document, available at http://www.chr.up.ac.za/hr_docs/aprm/docs/book3.pdf, Article 25, states: "Six months after the report has been considered by the Heads of State and Government of the participating member countries, it should be formally and publicly tabled in key regional and sub-regional structures such as the Pan-African Parliament, the African Commission on Human and Peoples' Rights, the envisaged Peace and Security Council and the Economic, Social and Cultural Council (ECOSOCC) of the African Union."

119 *See* analogies with the IDB policy linkages to the Inter-American Court of Human Rights discussed in the subsection *References to Human Rights*.

120 Canada, 2008 Official Development Assistance Accountability Act, which came into force on June 28, 2008, states in Section 4(1): "Official development assistance may be provided only if

The European Bank for Reconstruction and Development (EBRD) adopts a similar approach, establishing direct operational implications for human rights obligations in development activities. Unlike other multilateral development banks (MDBs), the Agreement Establishing the EBRD sets forth a political mandate for the EBRD to further the transition to multiparty democracy and to encourage a respect for human rights, making an explicit provision for human rights in its preamble.[121] Thus, "the preamble and the phrasing of Article 1 seem to imply that the founding members expected that the EBRD in its operations would be sensitive to the human rights of residents in the countries of its operation."[122] Building on its foundational agreement, the EBRD's 2008 Environmental and Social Policy incorporates human rights as a minimum standard defined in accordance with human rights instruments. "The EBRD will not knowingly finance projects that would contravene obligations under international treaties and agreements related to environmental protection, human rights and sustainable development as identified through project appraisal."[123] The fact that the baseline underpinning this policy is rooted in human rights treaties has not insulated the EBRD from NGO criticism that the Bank's commitment to human rights is weak in practice.[124]

A similar example is found in the Council of Europe Development Bank (CEB), administered under the authority of the Council of Europe, which has the protection and promotion of human rights as one of its principal aims.

---

the competent minister is of the opinion that it (a) contributes to poverty reduction; (b) takes into account the perspectives of the poor; and (c) is consistent with international human rights standards."

121 The preamble of the agreement establishing the EBRD provides that contracting parties are:

> [c]ommitted to the fundamental principles of multiparty democracy, the rule of law, respect for human rights and market economics; . . . Welcoming the intent of Central and Eastern European countries to further the practical implementation of multiparty democracy, strengthening democratic institutions, the rule of law and respect for human rights and their willingness to implement reforms in order to evolve towards market-oriented economies.
>
> Article 1 provides:

Purpose

> In contributing to economic progress and reconstruction, the purpose of the Bank shall be to foster the transition towards open market-oriented economies and to promote private and entrepreneurial initiative in the Central and Eastern European countries committed to and applying the principles of multiparty democracy, pluralism and market economics.

122 A. McAuley, *European Bank for Reconstruction and Development*, in *Oxford Encyclopedia of Human Rights* vol. 2, 169, 171 (D. Forsythe ed., Oxford U. Press 2009).

123 EBRD, Environmental and Social Policy, paragraph 9. Paragraph 37 specifies that EBRD's country and sector strategies should summarize the principal environmental, human rights, gender equality, and other social issues in the relevant country or sector and sets out the EBRD's proposals for taking these issues into account in its operations, where appropriate. *See* http://www.ebrd.org/pages/about/principles/sustainability/policy.shtml.

124 For a brief discussion of such critiques, *see* A. McAuley, *The European Bank for Reconstruction and Development*, in *Oxford Encyclopedia of Human Rights* 172 (D. Forsythe ed., Oxford U. Press 2009).

The CEB is institutionally grounded in human rights, and the secretary general of the Council of Europe is required to review all project applications to assess whether they conform to the political and social aims of the Council of Europe. Thus, the CEB's human rights framework includes loan regulations that require projects to conform to provisions of the Convention for the Protection of Human Rights and Fundamental Freedoms and the European Social Charter.[125] In addition, the CEB Environmental Policy, which describes the environmental and social principles that guide its project-related operations, connects socially and environmentally sustainable development to human rights and mandates that "the CEB will not knowingly finance projects which are identified as undermining human rights."[126] In a similar vein, albeit domestically rather than externally focused, the Council of Europe Parliamentary Assembly adopted a resolution inviting its 47 member states to be guided by OHCHR's 2006 Principles and Guidelines on a Human Rights Approach to Poverty Reduction in their policymaking and budget decisions.[127]

Human Rights and Development: Initial Observations on Regime Interaction

As the foregoing review illustrates, the interaction of human rights and development regimes is significant and increasing but widely divergent. It is difficult, however, to discern an automatic consequence from the mere mention of human rights (or even human rights obligations) in a development policy framework. Even the adoption of a human rights policy or human rights mainstreaming approach does not necessarily have immediate or concrete operational consequences. Not every such policy or provision requires particular forms of assessments or analyses, nor will each generate specific guidelines or parameters in financing decisions or dialogues.

The review reveals the limited engagement of most development policy frameworks with human rights as binding legal obligations. In many instances, human rights are referred to in general or preambular terms; in others, they receive mention as principles or cross-cutting themes—none of which has a clear legally binding underpinning. Moreover, more explicit and elaborate articulations of the links between human rights and development, such as in

---

125 CEB, Policy for Loan and Project Financing, adopted June 2006 under Administrative Council Resolution 1495, Council of Europe, Paris, available at http://www.coebank.org/Upload/legal/en/ppfp_english.pdf. These CEB contractual covenants are a unique feature: CEB can suspend, cancel, and/or demand early reimbursement of a loan if a project's implementation leads to a human rights violation. (*See*, for example, Article 3.3(g)(iii) of the CEB loan regulations.)

126 CEB, Environmental Policy, available at http://www.coebank.org/Upload/infocentre/brochure/en/environmental_policy.pdf#search=%22environmental%22.

127 Council of Europe Parliamentary Report and Draft Resolution, Doc. 12555, *Combating Poverty* (Mar. 28, 2012), paragraph 7, provides: "The Assembly strongly supports the Principles and Guidelines for a Human Rights Approach to Poverty Reduction Strategies proposed by the Office of the United Nations High Commissioner for Human Rights (UNHCHR) and invites member states to take due account of the Guidelines in their public policymaking and relevant budgetary decisions."

the declaration of the right to development and the various resolutions built upon it, are not legally binding. Most of the policy examples that integrate human rights obligations do so in ways confined to particular policies, themes, or groups, or in a manner so general that their specific impacts are hard to identify. The operational impacts of human rights legal obligations are only beginning to be explored in policies like those of the European Union or Canada, where human rights obligations are operative in a direct legal and policy sense and they trigger some immediate consequence or action.

In addition, although the trend in both political statements and development policies appears to be greater integration of human rights in development policy and a gradual recognition of the potential relevance of human rights obligations in development contexts, the majority of development policy frameworks evidence the separability of human rights and development and the fragmentation of international law.

Human Rights, Development, and the Fragmentation of International Law

Fragmentation of International Law: Causes and Consequences

Why are there such significant divergences and disconnects between human rights and development? Why do these disconnects persist when the same countries are parties to the human rights treaties and members of development agencies and banks?[128] The reasons are similar to those underpinning the fragmentation of law in general. Some practitioners opine that not only has there never been a single global legislature or appellate court to mold a unified body of law, but there has never been a uniform will for such a system. Instead, states have implicitly or explicitly conceived of particular issues and problems and responded by agreeing to new laws and supporting international organizations.[129] Some observers go further and argue that the "unwieldy and intransigent nature of regimes is often intentional and may reflect a wish by powerful states to protect their dominance."[130] Other reasons for fragmentation and impediments to coherent regime interaction include lack of coordination at the domestic level, states adopting inconsistent national positions across different international fora, and a lack of transparency within particular regimes.[131]

128 On the diversity of policy formulations that emanate from international organizations, *see* Alston, *supra* note 17, at 95–106, who argues that diversity can be explained by "a desire to maintain as much policy flexibility as possible. This helps to accommodate a broad array of approaches on the part of different governments, gives the organization itself considerable leeway to define or redefine its priorities, and makes it easier to move away from failed policies towards new ones" (97).

129 M. Young, *Introduction*, in Young, *supra* note 1, at 2.

130 *Id.*, at 10.

131 Young, *supra* note 1, at 95.

The specific reasons for the divergences between human rights and development regimes are thus complex and multifaceted, varying across institutions and over time.[132] They are often connected with historically entrenched understandings of institutional roles and mandates[133] and linked to the predominance of different disciplines, evidence bases, premises, and values within those different regimes.[134] "Functional differentiation leads to path dependency, higher transaction costs, 'tunnel vision' and even solipsistic and imperial tendencies within regimes."[135] The separateness may be rooted in legal factors, such as the emergence of the relevant frameworks at different times; the fact that laws (treaties) are implemented by different institutions with different powers of enforcement and relative strengths; the absence of a uniform ratification of the laws (treaties) by all member states;[136] and the fact that the laws aim to fulfill particular sets of preferences within the international legal system that may not be in harmony.[137]

In the case of development agencies, these factors are underscored by established legal interpretations of constitutive instruments, which in some cases include strong political prohibitions that have special relevance for human rights.[138] Governments take very different positions on human rights, even more so when human rights are connected with development interventions or aid resource allocations. Indeed, the reluctance to connect development cooperation policies and activities with human rights legal obligations may be attributable to the clarity, enforceability, and lack of flexibility such obligations impose. They may also be reinforced by perceptions of human rights obligations as less amenable to measurement or less empirically based.

What are the consequences of such fragmentation? What practical problems or risks does it generate, and how do these translate for human rights in the context of development?

---

132 S. McInerney-Lankford, *Human Rights and Development: Some Institutional Perspectives,* 25(3) Netherlands Q. Hum. Rights 459 (2007).

133 Y. Yokata, *Non-political Character of the World Bank,* 20 Japanese Ann. Intl. L. 39 (1976).

134 *See* D. Seymour & J. Pincus, *Human Rights and Economics: The Conceptual Basis for Their Complementarity,* 4 Dev. Pol. Rev. 387–405 (2008).

135 Young, *Introduction,* in Young, *supra* note 1, at 11.

136 *See* discussion of parallel membership below.

137 Young, *supra* note 1, at 88–89.

138 *See,* for example, in relation to the IBRD, I. Shihata, *Political Activity Prohibited,* in *World Bank Legal Papers* 219–44 (Martinus Nijhoff 2000); I. Shihata, *The Exclusion of Political Consideration in the Bank's Articles—Its Meaning and Scope in the Context of the Institutional Evolution,* in *The World Bank in a Changing World: Selected Essays* 62–78 (Martinus Nijhoff 1995). Also relevant in this context is I. Shihata, *Human Rights, Development and International Financial Institutions,* in *The World Bank in a Changing World: Selected Essays and Lectures Volume II* 553–78 (Martinus Nijhoff 1995), to be contrasted with EBRD, *Political Aspects of the Mandate of the European Bank for Reconstruction and Development* (1991), available at http://www.ebrd.org/pages/research/publications/institutional/procedures.shtml, and *Political Aspects of the Mandate of the European Bank for Reconstruction and Development in Relation to Ethnic Minorities* (1991), available at http://www.ebrd.org/pages/research/publications/institutional/ethnic.shtml.

Although some commentators have argued that fragmentation is inevitable[139] and endemic to international law,[140] and others note the ways in which it may benefit specialized regimes,[141] many point to the risks of systemic ambiguity and incoherence. The first and most obvious consequence of fragmentation is the undermining of coherence in international law in general and international policy coherence in particular.[142] Policy coherence aims to prevent duplication and avoid contradiction in government policy actions by promoting consistency across related subject matters and assessing the impacts of diverse areas of international policy on one another.[143] It operates both vertically —ensuring that states implement treaty obligations through laws, policies, and processes—and horizontally—ensuring that state policies across sectors, departments, or ministries are consistent or compatible with one another.

Promoting international policy coherence is an objective of growing importance for international development agencies and organizations. In the context of development, this objective aims to "ensure that government policies are mutually supportive of the countries' development goals."[144] It implies "strengthening synergies and weeding out inconsistencies between non-aid policies and development objectives."[145] The EU has made policy coherence a point of emphasis in development, particularly since the Lisbon Treaty;[146] in

---

139 A growing body of literature is emerging on global administrative law that addresses, among other themes, the constraints and enduring reasons for "nonconvergence" and assesses the normative case for and against the promotion of a unified field of global administrative law; *see*, for example, B. Kingsbury, N. Krisch, & R. Stewart, *The Emergence of Global Administrative Law*, 68 L. & Contem. Probs. 15 (2005); and B. Kingsbury, *Introduction: Global Administrative Law in the Institutional Practice of Global Regulatory Governance*, in *World Bank Legal Review International Financial Institutions and Global Legal Governance* 3–33 (World Bank 2011).

140 S. Humphreys, *Technology Transfer in Three Regimes*, in Young, *supra* note 1, at 195, citing the ILC Study Group, *supra* note 42.

141 B. Simma, *Fragmentation in a Positive Light*, 25 Mich. J. Intl. L. 845 (2004).

142 *See*, for example, M. Salomon, *Global Responsibility for Human Rights* 106 (Oxford U. Press 2007).

143 http://www.oecd.org/document/54/0,2340,cn_2649_33721_35320054_1_1_1_1,00.html. This idea has relevance to efforts in the UN human rights mechanisms to enhance coherence and harmonization among treaty bodies; see *UN Report of the Working Group on Harmonisation of Working Methods of Treaty Bodies* (Jan. 9, 2007); *Report on Working Methods of the Human Rights Treaty Bodies Relating to State Party Reporting Processes: Note by the Secretariat*, HRI/MC/2007/4 (Jun. 1, 2007); and *Report on the Implementation of Recommendations of the 5th Intercommittee Meeting and the 18th Meeting of Chair Persons, Note by the Secretariat*, HRI/MC/2007/6 (May 29, 2007).

144 OECD, Declaration on Policy Coherence for Development, C/MIN(2008)2/FINAL (Jun. 4, 2008).

145 European Commission, *EU 2011 Report on Policy Coherence for Development*, Commission Staff Working Paper (Dec. 15, 2011).

146 Article 208 of the Lisbon Treaty requires that "[t]he Union shall take account of the objectives of development cooperation in the policies that it implements which are likely to affect developing countries." Some observers have voiced criticism of the implementation of this objective, including in relation to human rights. *See* http://coherence.concordeurope.org/pdf/Concord_Report_15_AW_LORES.pdf. *See* also *EU Report on Policy Coherence for Development* (2007), available at http://ec.europa.eu/development/icenter/repository/Publication_Coherence_DEF_en.pdf.

May 2010, the European Parliament created the Standing Rapporteur on Policy Coherence for Development, responsible for facilitating interaction between the parliamentary committee on development and other committees. Policy coherence for development focal points have also been appointed within the European Commission Directorates-General and the External Action Service.

In 2008, the ministers of Organization for Economic Cooperation and Development (OECD) countries issued a Declaration on Policy Coherence for Development, which acknowledges the increased economic interdependence among countries, as well as between development policies and other areas of public policy.[147] Although it does not mention human rights, the declaration stresses the importance of policy coherence in achieving internationally agreed-upon development goals, including those contained in the Millennium Declaration,[148] which includes commitments related to human rights. The OECD launched an international platform for policy coherence in development:[149] "OECD countries recognize the need for greater coherence in policies across sectors that affect developing countries. Aid alone cannot address the needs of the developing world. Policies in areas like agriculture, trade, investment, migration and others have a profound impact on developing countries, yet they often work at cross-purposes."

Fragmentation and policy incoherence are apposite in the context of human rights, including threats to "the quality and coherence of international law as a whole and resulting in serious conflicts and tensions between programmes and principles."[150] Such fragmentation has potential impacts on the levels of protection afforded by international human rights law through the emergence of "special normative regimes in various areas of technical cooperation described as 'self contained' in order to highlight their operation outside the general international law."[151] This in turn potentially leads to "the erosion of international law, conflicting jurisprudence, forum shopping and the loss of legal security";[152] some argue that it undermines the international rule of law.[153]

It is not inconceivable that development and human rights regimes yield different interpretations of the same rule of international law, which risks gen-

---

147 OECD, Policy Coherence for Development.

148 For example, paragraph 4. Paragraph 9 contains states' pledge to "ensure the implementation, by States Parties, of treaties in areas such as arms control and disarmament and of international humanitarian law and human rights law." *See* also paragraphs 24–26 and 30.

149 http://www.oecd.org/department/0,3355,en_2649_18532957_1_1_1_1_1,00.html.

150 I. Brownlie, *The Rights of Peoples in Modern International Law*, in *The Rights of Peoples* 1, 15 (J. Crawford ed., Clarendon Press 1988).

151 B. Simma, *Self Contained Regimes*, 15 Netherlands Yearbook Intl. L. 111, 136 (1985); Koskenniemi & Leino, *infra* note 154, at 560.

152 ILC Study Group, *supra* note 42, paragraph 9.

153 M. Scheinin, *Human Rights Treaties and the Vienna Convention on the Law of Treaties—Conflicts or Harmony*, in *The Status of International Treaties on Human Rights* 43–45 (Venice Commission ed., Council of European Publishing 2006).

erating confusion and even injustice.[154] This has led some observers to point to the risk of a lower standard of protection due to a special regime not taking into account more detailed guidance or robust protection provided for in general law or by other organizations.[155] Others point to the failure to assess human rights impacts of policy measures, noting the potentially detrimental consequences for human rights in developing countries.[156]

The growth of development law or policy-making processes alongside the proliferation of human rights law and standards exemplifies the phenomenon of the fragmentation of international law. The growing reach of development policy and transgovernmental regulation[157] into areas governed by human rights treaties increases the likelihood of regime interaction between human rights and development, as evidenced in the substantive and policy overlaps described above. The potential for norm conflict is a growing problem inherent in the fragmentation of international law due to the partial and poorly understood points of convergence between human rights and development regimes and the lack of clarity around operational implications of human rights provisions in development frameworks. This situation is heightened by the neglect of human rights obligations and the absence of a clear, governing legal baseline where regimes do interact and their norms conflict.

The fragmentation in general and these specific consequences in particular generate a risk of accountability gaps[158] for human rights in development processes and outcomes.[159] Although rights and accountability interact in complex ways in any setting, and although they play an especially complex and dynamic role in development,[160] the point here is that neglecting rights

---

154 M. Koskenniemi & P. Leino, *Fragmentation of International Law? Postmodern Anxieties,* 15 Leiden J. Intl. L. 553 (2002), discuss a range of views on the various risks of fragmentation.

155 As in the case of *Van Alphen v. The Netherlands*, where the partially dissenting judges inquired as to whether it was "permissible today for the Europe Convention on Human Rights to provide a lower level of protection than that which is recognized and accepted in other organizations."

156 M. Salomon, *Global Responsibility for Human Rights* 106 (Oxford U. Press 2007). *See* also her related discussion of disparate and contradictory trends in of international legal regimes and the need for international policy coherence; *id.*, 150, 156.

157 Kingsbury et al., *supra* note 139, at 16.

158 There is a growing body of literature on the theme of accountability in the context of global governance and constitutionalism; *see* G. de Búrca & J. Scott ed., *Law and New Governance in the EU and the US* (Hart Publishing 2006).

159 On this theme as applied to the World Bank, *see* D. Clark, *The World Bank and Human Rights: The Need for Greater Accountability,* 15 Harv. Hum. Rights J. 205 (2002); S. Skogly, *The Human Rights Obligations of the World Bank and the International Monetary Fund* (Cavendish Press 2001); D. Bradlow, *The World Bank, the IMF and Human Rights,* 6 Transnatl. L. & Contemp. Probs. 48–89 (1996); D. Bradlow & C. Grossman, *Limited Mandates and Intertwined Problems: A New Challenge for the World Bank and the IMF,* 17 Hum. Rights Q. (1995); D. Bradlow, *The World Bank, the IMF and Human Rights,* 6(1) Transnatl. L. & Contemp. Probs 48 (1996); M. Darrow, *Between Light and Shadow: The World Bank, the IMF and International Human Rights Law* (Hart Publishing 2003); W. van Genugten, P. Hunt, & S. Mathews, *World Bank, IMF and Human Rights* (Wolf Legal Publishers 2003).

160 Newell & Wheeler, *supra* note 39, at 7.

altogether in development will significantly undermine accountability. That is, the potential to advance accountability for development or access to resources or basic services is difficult to advance in a context in which rights are not explicitly acknowledged. The identification of such gaps is symptomatic of broader concerns that exist about accountability and legitimacy in the context of globalization, the expansion and scope of authority of multilateral organizations, and the increase in numbers of NGOs.[161] Thus, human rights accountability may be difficult to locate and uphold where human rights law obligations are not integrated into development policies[162] in a way that states—as donors or clients—can pursue development activities without systematic assessments of the human rights consequences of these and without formal legal recourse where those consequences are negative in respect to both process and outcomes.[163]

Arguing for Coherence Based on Human Rights Obligations

The trend of increasingly explicit recognition of human rights obligations and instruments may have positive potential for human rights protection in development. This suggestion is supported by the increased emphasis on international policy coherence, in particular, coherence based on states' human rights obligations. Indeed, the UN Guiding Principles on Business and Human Rights, adopted by states in the UN Human Rights Council, include a principle on ensuring policy coherence: "8. States should ensure that governmental departments, agencies, and other state-based institutions that shape business practices are aware of and observe the State's human rights obligations when fulfilling their respective mandates, including by providing them with relevant information, training and support."[164] This section assesses the value of coherence and regime interaction in international law in relation to human rights and development. It focuses on international human rights treaties[165] to suggest how the pursuit of international legal coherence could be approached and why it might benefit development regimes.

---

161 R. Grant & R. Keohane, *Accountability and Abuses of Power in World Politics,* 99(1) Am. Pol. Science Rev. 29 (Feb. 2005).

162 This point does not, however, ignore other important forms of accountability, such as social accountability. Nor does it assume that legal accountability mechanisms are the sole or most effective means of ensuring that people can claim and realize their rights.

163 On this theme, *see* P. Twomey, *Human Rights–Based Approaches to Development: Towards Accountability,* in *Economic, Social and Cultural Rights in Action* 45–69 (M. A. Baderin & R. McCorquodale ed., Oxford U. Press 2007).

164 John Ruggie, *Report of the Special Representative of the Secretary-General on the Issue of Human Rights and Transnational Corporations and Other Business Enterprises: Guiding Principles on Business and Human Rights: Implementing the United Nations "Protect, Respect and Remedy" Framework,* A/HRC/17/31 21 (Mar. 2011).

165 In this it does not disregard the potential source of obligations in custom or general principles of law, but focuses on treaties as the most visible and clear source of such obligations for the purposes of the present discussion. For a more elaborate discussion of this argument, *see* S. McInerney-Lankford, *International Financial Institutions and Human Rights: Select Perspectives on Legal Obligations,* in *International Financial Institutions and International Law* 239

Principle 8 of the UN Guiding Principles on Business and Human Rights elaborates on the importance of both vertical and horizontal policy coherence based on government's human rights obligations. "Vertical policy coherence entails States having the necessary policies, laws and processes to implement their international human rights law obligations. Horizontal policy coherence means supporting and equipping departments and agencies, at both the national and sub-national levels, that shape business practices . . . to be informed of and act in a manner compatible with the Governments' human rights obligations."[166]

Principles of international law may promote strategic regime interaction and advance policy coherence between human rights and development in relevant ways. For instance, the principle of systemic integration,[167] derived from Article 31(3)(c) of the Vienna Convention on the Law of Treaties,[168] states that in addition to the treaty's context, "any relevant rules of international law applicable in relations between parties" should be taken into account under the general rule of interpretation of treaties. This principle is, according to some, "the most influential principle in terms of reception of international law,"[169] and one that could be used more generally to argue for taking relevant binding human rights obligations into account in certain development contexts. In particular, this principle might support the integration of relevant human rights obligations at the levels of strategies, programs, processes, or projects as "relevant rules of international law applicable between the parties." This

---

(D. Bradlow & D. Hunter ed., Kluwer International 2010).

166 *Guiding Principles, supra* note 164, at 11–12.

167 C. McLachlan, *The Principle of Systemic Integration and Article 31(3)(c) of the Vienna Convention*, 54 ICLQ 279–320 (2005).

168 Vienna Convention on the Law of Treaties (VCLT), UNTS Vol. 1155 (entered into force Jan. 27, 1980).

169 Forowicz, 13. Vienna Convention on the Law of Treaties (VCLT), Article 31:

> General rule of interpretation:
>
> 1. A treaty shall be interpreted in good faith in accordance with the ordinary meaning to be given to the terms of the treaty in their context and in the light of its object and purpose.
>
> 2. The context for the purpose of the interpretation of a treaty shall comprise, in addition to the text, including its preamble and annexes:
>
> a. Any agreement relating to the treaty which was made between all the parties in connexion with the conclusion of the treaty;
>
> b. Any instrument which was made by one or more parties in connexion with the conclusion of the treaty and accepted by the other parties as an instrument related to the treaty.
>
> 3. There shall be taken into account, together with the context:
>
> a. Any subsequent agreement between the parties regarding the interpretation of the treaty or the application of its provisions;
>
> b. Any subsequent practice in the application of the treaty which establishes the agreement of the parties regarding its interpretation;
>
> c. Any relevant rules of international law applicable in the relations between the parties.
>
> 4. A special meaning shall be given to a term if it is established that the parties so intended.

would apply only when the human rights treaty in question was ratified by the state involved and would be delimited also by subject matter relevance.

Countries are both parties to human rights treaties and members of development organizations, and what they do in each realm has potential relevance to the other.[170] Without arguing for this principle as a prerequisite for regime interaction, the existence of parallel membership[171] between the regimes governing human rights and development is a factor in assessing the relevance of human rights to development and the relationship between their norms.

Binding human rights treaty obligations could be relied upon substantively and in the interpretation of a range of development measures in areas covered by a particular human rights treaty provision. In the case of ambiguity or conflict, a human rights treaty obligation and its accompanying interpretation and elaboration by the relevant expert treaty body could provide policy guidance grounded in the law. Human rights offer an established legal foundation upon which to base international policy coherence:

> The fact that both donors and partner countries have ratified the international human rights treaties provides a uniquely valuable reference point for harmonisation efforts. A mutually agreed, universal normative framework already exists, supported not only by political commitment, but also by the force of legal obligation. As well, at the operational level, there is growing convergence in the integration of human rights in development.[172]

The foregoing does not deny the influence of cultural relativism, divergent interpretations of human rights norms, and differences among the social orders across countries and regions, which can be accentuated with respect to rights. In "a pluralist international society in which human rights are not protected at all or only minimally protected the social basis for global administrative law based on individual rights is largely absent."[173] What is contended here is that the legal basis for integrating human rights into development, and possibly other spheres of international regulation, does exist in the shared human rights treaty obligations of states.

What are the practical benefits of such integration for development?

---

170 On the related question of the law binding international organization as subjects of international law, the International Court of Justice (ICJ) has long established that such organizations are "bound by any obligations incumbent upon them under general rules of international law, under their constitutions or under international agreements to which they are parties." *Interpretation of the Agreement of 25 March 1951 between WHO and Egypt*, Advisory Opinion, 1980 ICJ Reports, at 89–90.

171 Young, *supra* note 1, at 94–96.

172 OECD DAC Human Rights Task Team, *Human Rights and Aid Effectiveness*, DAC Update 3 (Apr. 2007).

173 Kingsbury et al., *supra* note 139, at 46.

Coherence and Legal Accountability

Some might argue that coherence is a benefit in and of itself and that it underpins the international rule of law and legal certainty upon which every specialized body of international law depends.[174] This chapter suggests that pursuing such coherence based on the principle of systemic integration could ensure the consideration of human rights treaty obligations and thereby promote legal accountability for human rights in development processes and outcomes. Strengthening accountability by framing development in terms of legal entitlements[175] would help ensure that development benefits the poorest and most vulnerable, thereby promoting poverty reduction goals too. Anchoring relevant aspects of development regimes in applicable human rights treaty obligations could mitigate incoherence by providing a relatively clear legal and normative baseline for assessment.

Thus, coherence around binding human rights treaty obligations would support states parties (whether as donors, partners, or merely members of development agencies and banks) upholding their human rights obligations and ensure accountability for human rights in development processes and outcomes. Such a renewed consideration of applicable legal norms could strengthen accountability more generally[176] by reinforcing legal accountability in frameworks that are more usually the purview of broad policy commitments, programs, and processes than of treaties.[177]

Do No Harm/Do Good

A more strategic engagement of development and human rights regimes might ensure that development policies and activities adapt to evolving international norms such as human rights.[178] In particular, it would help ensure that states "do no harm" and that, at a minimum, states engaged in development bilaterally or through multilateral agencies consider their obligations and endeavor not to undermine human rights standards.[179] That is, the integration of relevant human rights standards based on international human rights law obligations could support the prevention and mitigation of undue

174 *See supra* notes 153 and 154.

175 P. Gready, *Rights-Based Approaches to Development: What Is the Value-Added?*, 18(6) Dev. in Practice 737 (Nov. 2008).

176 On the theme of accountability in globalized lawmaking and the emerging principles and requirements of global administrative law, *see* Kingsbury et al., *supra* note 139, at 44–45 and 58–59.

177 International trade agreements and environmental treaties do feature somewhat more prominently in development policies; *see* World Bank OP 4.01—Environmental Assessment (Jan. 1999), available at http://go.worldbank.org/RUEQVWD550.

178 Sureda, *supra* note 9, at 217.

179 This point is eloquently made by Andres Rigo Sureda, former deputy general counsel of the World Bank: "The IBRD is rightly concerned with its borrowers respecting the treaties that bind them in the course of its operations. In its work, there should not be any question that the IBRD is bound to respect them. [It] itself should not be instrumental in creating opportunities for the violation of human rights." *Supra* note 9, at 218.

harm, especially of a social and environmental nature. In this, human rights obligations, such as the obligation to respect, would serve as a minimum standard against which development policies and activities could be assessed to ensure against harm in both processes and outcomes.

An apposite example of such a standard emerges in the UN Guiding Principles on Business and Human Rights.[180] Principle 13 states:

> The responsibility to respect human rights requires that business enterprises:
>
> a. Avoid causing or contributing to adverse human rights impacts through their own activities, and address such impacts when they occur;
>
> b. Seek to prevent or mitigate adverse human rights impacts that are directly linked to their operations, products or services by their business relationships, even if they have not contributed to those impacts.

Although the principles are primarily an elaboration of business enterprises' responsibilities rather than state legal obligations, they offer conceptual and practical guidance by analogy.

The different regimes might benefit from interaction and mutual definition. There may be potential for mutual reinforcement among norms derived from human rights and development regimes[181] such that human rights obligations of donors and partners could inform development policy and its monitoring and evaluation frameworks,[182] or development cooperation activities could advance the realization of human rights (particularly economic and social rights).[183] For instance, one could argue that a state party's obligations under Article 12 of the ICESCR, protecting the right to health,[184] might be rele-

---

180 *See Guiding Principles on Business and Human Rights*, *supra* note 164; and UN OHCHR, *Corporate Responsibility to Respect Human Rights: An Interpretative Guide* 15–22 (advance unedited version, Nov. 2011).

181 *See* M. Robinson & P. Alston, *The Challenges of Ensuring the Mutuality of Human Rights and Development Endeavours*, in *Human Rights and Development: Towards Mutual Reinforcement* (M. Robinson & P. Alston ed., Oxford U. Press 2005).

182 The fact that the monitoring and internal reviews of the UN Development Programme (UNDP), World Bank, and International Monetary Fund (IMF) do not take the established system of international human rights monitoring into account is noted as a concern by P. Alston, *Ships Passing in the Night: The Current State of the Human Rights and Development Debate Seen through the Lens of the Millennium Development Goals*, 27(3) Hum. Rights Q. 755, 814 (2005).

183 *See* an analogous argument on the potential for a positive role for a development agency (World Bank) to support the realization of the right to food. G. van Hoof & B. G. Tahzib, *Supervision with Respect to the Right to Food and the Role of the World Bank*, in *International Law and Development* 334 (Paul de Waart, Paul Peters, & Eric Denters ed., Martinus Nijhoff 1988).

184 Article 12 of the ICESCR provides:

> 1. The States Parties to the present Covenant recognize the right of everyone to the enjoyment of the highest attainable standard of physical and mental health. 2. The steps

vant to the design and implementation of a development project, program, or strategy in the health sector.[185] In particular, Article 12 could inform both minimum standards for process and outcomes by reference to the core obligation to ensure minimum essential levels of the right to health.[186] One could argue further that general comment 14, issued in 2000 by the Committee on Economic, Social, and Cultural Rights on the right to the highest attainable standard of health, could provide relevant guidance to a state party engaged in development cooperation activities in the health sector.[187] For instance, guidance could be drawn from the four dimensions established by the committee: availability, accessibility, acceptability, and quality.[188] The right to health might inform a program's focus on nondiscrimination and equality and the rights of the most vulnerable groups. It might also provide specificity in terms of both freedoms and entitlements, as well as precision in terms of more particular entitlements implied by the right, such as maternal and reproductive health; water; prevention, treatment, and control of diseases; and a healthy workplace and environment.[189]

One outcome of the regime interaction described above would be to facilitate the adaptation of development to evolving international norms such as human rights. This would help "transform development priorities from being measured in macroeconomic terms by focusing on the needs and interests of specific human groups."[190] Or, to argue this point further, this would move development from a matter of needs and trade-offs to one of rights and obligations. In this way, a more explicit integration of rights would focus on poor people's ability to realize the rights to resources and enhance accountability in development.[191] At a less formal legal level, it can be argued that human rights

---

to be taken by the States Parties to the present Covenant to achieve the full realization of this right shall include those necessary for:

(a) The provision for the reduction of the stillbirth-rate and of infant mortality and for the healthy development of the child; (b) The improvement of all aspects of environmental and industrial hygiene; (c) The prevention, treatment and control of epidemic, endemic, occupational and other diseases; (d) The creation of conditions which would assure to all medical service and medical attention in the event of sickness.

185 Grover, *supra* note 10, paragraphs 24, 49.

186 *Id.*, paragraph 19.

187 See Committee on Economic, Social and Cultural Rights, General Comment No. 14, Substantive Issues Arising in the Implementation of the International Covenant on Economic, Social and Cultural Rights, The Right to the Highest Attainable Standard of Health (Article 12 of the International Covenant on Economic, Social and Cultural Rights), E/C.12/2000/4 (Aug. 11, 2000).

188 *See* also E. Reidel, *The Human Right to Health: Conceptual Foundations*, in *Realizing the Right to Health* vol. 3, 28–30 (M. Robinson & A. Clapham ed., Swiss Human Rights 2009).

189 Paul Hunt, *Report of the Special Rapporteur on the Right of Everyone to the Enjoyment of the Highest Attainable Standard of Physical and Mental Health*, E/CN.4/2003/58, paragraph 25 (Feb. 13, 2003).

190 M. Koskenniemi, *Hegemonic Regimes*, in Young, *supra* note 1, at 322.

191 Newell & Wheeler, *supra* note 39, at 1, place accountability at the intersection between rights and resources.

principles such as participation, inclusion, and transparency in respect to regime interaction and in the structures and processes that govern development can promote accountability within it.[192]

Specificity and Technical Guidance

In the context of development as a shared,[193] stable, bounded structure of treaties with substantial and in some cases near-universal ratification,[194] the human rights law framework includes a number of key strengths. These offer a legitimate[195] and delimited legal and normative baseline founded on the voluntarily undertaken commitments of states that bind them under international law. Human rights treaties are binding international agreements, and, like trade agreements or environment treaties, human rights treaties generate legally binding norms and enjoy high levels of ratification.[196] However, human rights treaties predate many of these other treaties and have well-established bodies of interpretation and jurisprudence to support them. Beyond their normative power and legally binding nature, such treaties introduce a measure of specificity with regard to substantive and procedural standards—their provisions have been the subject of extensive commentary through the interpretations of treaty monitoring bodies,[197] the individual complaints brought under those treaties,[198] and, in the case of the regional human rights bodies, binding court rulings.

In recent years, the UN human rights treaty bodies have enhanced the accuracy and consistency of interpretation by supporting the development of human rights indicators by the Office of the High Commissioner for Human Rights (OHCHR).[199] The framework adopted by the OHCHR offers method-

---

192 *See,* for example, Young, *supra* note 1, at 107.

193 AOPP, Principle 1, paragraph 40(1).

194 *See,* for example, the Convention on the Rights of the Child, which is ratified by all but three countries in the world (the United States, Somalia, and South Sudan); of those nonstate parties, the United States has signed the treaty and is, according to Article 18 of the VCLT, therefore obliged not to act against the object and purpose of the treaty. On the role and strengths of international human rights treaties, *see* B. Simma & P. Alston, *The Sources of Human Rights Law: Custom, Jus Cogens and General Principles,* 12 Australian Yearbook of Intl. L. 81–108 (1992).

195 Grant & Keohane note that the standards of legitimacy against which power wielders can be held accountable derive from different sets of norms, and that legitimacy derives from conformity with human rights norms; *supra* note 161, at 35.

196 http://www2.ohchr.org/english/bodies/ratification/index.htm.

197 UN Human Rights Treaty Bodies, http://www2.ohchr.org/english/bodies/treaty/index.htm.

198 http://www2.ohchr.org/english/bodies/petitions/index.htm. Five of the human rights treaty bodies (CCPR, CERD, CAT, CEDAW, and CRPD) may, under particular circumstances, consider individual complaints or communications from individuals.

199 This work was initiated in 2005 at the request of the intercommittee meeting of UN human rights treaty bodies to help it assess the use of statistical information in states parties' reports in assessing the implementation of human rights. *See Report on Indicators for Monitoring Compliance with International Human Rights Instruments,* HRI/MC/2006/7; a report was issued in 2011 that applied the analysis to economic, social, and cultural rights (*Report of the UN High Com-*

ological, institutional, and practical considerations for the effective use of human rights indicators. The OHCHR has developed a series of indicators for approximately 12 human rights, covering economic, social, and cultural rights as well as civil and political rights.[200] These indicators may be of particular use for development in supporting the measurement of economic, social, and cultural rights by charting progress, stagnation, and retrogression, as well as patterns of discrimination and marginalization.[201] Indeed, beyond being positively received and used within the UN system, other agencies and human rights bodies,[202] and NGOs, the indicators have been employed by certain governments in national development plans.

Connected with the advances in empirical approaches and measurement methodology on human rights indicators and benchmarks, there is a growing body of work on human rights impact assessment (HRIA).[203] HRIAs have been developed across a range of sectors, supporting the case for both the feasibility of bringing human rights law to bear in other areas of law and the possibility of generating concreteness and specificity to back the normative underpinning of human rights. In particular, such assessments advance the possibility of identifying rights and duties in a range of contexts and help specify both the human rights claims of rights holders and the corresponding human rights obligations of duty bearers. Such assessment can also identify the immediate, underlying, and structural causes of nonrealization of human rights, as well as offer recommendations on mitigation and approaches for redress,[204] monitoring, and evaluation.

Conclusions

As suggested above, the fragmentation of international law may be as endemic as it is pervasive, and it may even constitute a semideliberate state of affairs. The specificity of roles of different international regimes and their institutions should be respected for legal, technical, and political reasons; this may be required to afford institutions a necessary measure of flexibility and allow them to leverage their comparative advantages in their respective fields of competence. A host of legal challenges attendant on a project of pursuing

---

missioner on Human Rights, E/2011/90). *See* http://www.ohchr.org/EN/Issues/Indicators/Pages/documents.aspx.

200 *Report on Monitoring and Promoting the Implementation of Human Rights,* HRI/MC/2008/3.

201 *Report of the UN High Commissioner on Human Rights,* E/2011/90, paragraphs 23–24.

202 For example, the European Union Fundamental Rights Agency. Also relevant is the work on human rights benchmarks commissioned by the EU Parliament Subcommittee, *Briefing Paper: Human Rights Benchmarks for EU External Policy,* EXPO/B/DROI/2011/15, available at http://www.europarl.europa.eu/committees/fr/studiesdownload.html?languageDocument=EN&file=67511.

203 *See,* for example, S. Walker, *The Future of Human Rights Impact Assessments of Trade Agreements* (Intersentia 2009).

204 Grover, *supra* note 10, paragraph 22.

coherence have been expertly documented by the ILC Study Group, among others. These include the absence of a hierarchy among norms;[205] the fact that the Vienna Convention on the Law of Treaties does not provide clear guidance on the meaning of "systemic integration" or on how to reconcile conflicting norms; and the lack of an international legislature or appeals court to resolve conflicts around norms and their interpretation. The questions and challenges arising from international bodies reviewing the actions of other international organizations are myriad,[206] and their complexity is evident in the EU-European Convention on Human Rights context,[207] with no sense that they would be any less fractious or challenging in the context of human rights agencies and development organizations. The general limits on competences and resources of various international agencies may be heightened in respect to human rights obligations when institutions operate subject to political prohibitions[208] that have historically been interpreted to bar human rights considerations.[209]

At a technical level, the body of knowledge on human rights measurement methodology, although growing, is incomplete despite significant progress in areas such as human rights impact assessments and human rights indicators. Human rights assessment itself is controversial: it is attended by risks of politicization, annexation, and externalization and, many argue, impossible to undertake in a completely neutral or objective manner. Resources are a relevant consideration here as well: HRIAs are costly and time-consuming, and monitoring and implementation require substantial institutional commitments and large amounts of data.

For development agencies that do not operate from a normative base and do not fulfill an enforcement role with respect to human rights norms, the fact that the instrumental case for human rights in development has yet to be persuasively established presents an additional challenge. That is, although risk-based arguments related to "do no harm" can be made, the empirical basis for arguing that integrating human rights increases development effectiveness is less clear. This is compounded by the relatively small number of quality human rights indicators developed, the dearth of human rights data (especially

---

205 ILC Study Group, *supra* note 42, at paragraph 31.

206 Kingsbury et al., *supra* note 139, at 45.

207 *See,* for example, C. Costello, *The Bosphorus Ruling of the European Court of Human Rights: Fundamental Rights and Blurred Boundaries in Europe,* 6(1) Hum. Rights L. Rev. 87–130 (2006); T. Lock, *EU Accession to the ECHR: Implications for the Judicial Review in Strasbourg,* 35 European L. Rev. 777 (2010).

208 For example, IRBD Articles of Agreement, Article IV, Section 10, and Article III, Section 5 (Dec. 27, 1945), available at http://siteresources.worldbank.org/EXTABOUTUS/Resources/ibrd-articlesofagreement.pdf. Similar provisions exist in the constituent instruments of a number of other development banks, such as the Inter-American Development Bank and the African Development Bank.

209 Ibrahim Shihata, *The World Bank and Human Rights,* in *The World Bank in a Changing World Selected Essays and Lectures* vol. 2, 567 (Martinus Nijhoff 1991); similarly, *see* Ibrahim Shihata, *Human Rights and International Financial Institutions,* in *id.*, 553.

in developing countries), and the difficulty of establishing causation or attribution between human rights requirements and development outcomes.

Nevertheless, despite the legal, political, and practical challenges of arguing for the integration of human rights obligations into development regimes, and despite the elusive nature of coherence in the international legal system, the core relevance of human rights to development must be recognized, and the legal treaty obligations underpinning human rights are one reason to do so. These treaty obligations form part of the body of evolving international norms that have practical relevance and legal pertinence for development regimes such that the latter should interact with, and adapt to, them. Interaction between human rights and development regimes could be mutually beneficial, potentially strengthening aspects of each regime. At the very least, human rights should not be ignored in development frameworks, in respect of a minimum no-harm threshold. The overall benefit of such interaction and systemic integration would be enhanced by accountability for human rights in development, at least at the macrolevel of regimes, through a more formal type of "hierarchical, supervisory, accountability" system[210] and through alternative accountability models based on a more "dynamic experimentalist vision of benchmarking, borrowing, innovating, monitoring and mutual learning."[211]

Human rights and development are inextricably interwoven, but their governing frameworks and regimes have remained largely separate. A growing, but as yet uneven, integration of human rights into development regimes is occurring, and there is some evidence of growing recognition of the relevance of human rights treaty obligations in development regimes. This trend signals—despite the prevailing distinctions, fragmentation, and potential conflict—evidence of the possibility for strategic links between human rights and development regimes and the political will to forge them. The trend also augurs well for the possibility of mutually beneficial norm definition through regime interaction at the formal legal level in ways that both avoid harm and do good.

---

210 Kingsbury et al., *supra* note 139, at 58, drawing on Grant & Keohane, *Accountability and Abuses of Power in World Politics*, IILJ Working Paper 2004/7, at 14.

211 Kingsbury et al., *supra* note 139, at 58, drawing on Grant & Keohane, *supra* note 211.

Legal Transplantation and Legal Development in Transitional China

CHENGUANG WANG

China claims that its legal system and the rule of law it intends to build have strong Chinese characteristics distinct from those in the Western world and closely associated with the Chinese socialist political system and social environment.[1] There is no doubt that China's legal system and its commitment to building a rule of law have had a great effect on the nation's social and economic development; the Chinese economic boom could not have been achieved without a functional legal system compatible with international and foreign legal practices. In this regard, legal transplantation was a useful tool in the establishment of the Chinese legal system.[2] This chapter does not examine the credibility of China's legal system, but rather proposes that the Chinese legal system has borrowed elements from other legal systems in order to promote its unique market economy reform and social transition in the context of globalization.

Legal Transplantation Is a Typical Aspect of Legal Development

A function of comparative law is to better understand and improve national legislative work through comparison with foreign and internal legal systems.[3] Comparison of different legal systems and the adoption of foreign law on the basis of such comparison or military occupation are established practices in

---

The author is grateful for Dr. Ju Chengwei's assistance in collecting materials and offering valuable comments on the draft and also for Mr. Hassane Cissé's insightful comments on the paper.

1 Wu Bangguo, chairman of the National People's Congress of China, has emphasized that the Chinese legal system embodies Chinese socialist characteristics. In 2011, he announced that "China has established a legal system with Chinese characteristics" and that "we do not use the legal systems in some Western countries as models to cast China's legal system with Chinese characteristics." He further indicated that "we are not going to make those laws which exist in foreign systems but do not fit into the Chinese social environment and reality." Wu Bangguo, *Annual Report of the National People's Congress' Work of 2011*, available at http://english.gov.cn/2008-03/15/content_921044.htm.

2 Wu Bangguo has said that "we should also learn from foreign experiences in the law making process and adopt those experiences useful to us." *Id.*

3 Shen Zongling, *On Comparative Law* 50–51 (Peking U. Press 1998); Konrad Zweigert & Kein Kötz, *Introduction to Comparative Law* 17 (Oxford U. Press 1998); Alan Watson, *Society & Legal Change* 141 (Scottish Academic Press 1977); Rudolf B. Schlesinger, Hans W. Baade, Peter E. Herzog, & Mirjan R. Damaska, *Comparative Law: Cases-Text-Materials* 9 (5th ed., West Press 1998).

history. Legal transplantation—the movement of laws and legal institutions from one state to another—is central to the study of comparative and international law.[4] In the midst of globalization, legal transplantation has become more frequent and common. The purposes of legal transplantation are not confined to better understanding and improving national legal systems; legal transplantation also promotes the convergence, at least in some fields of law, of different national laws in the global arena. Legal transplantation can be used to improve a national legal system and to promote a uniform global legal framework in the areas of international trade, environmental protection, antiterrorism, international peace, and the protection of human rights.

The concept of legal transplantation is an ancient one. Solon of Athens studied laws of other Greek city-states as a basis for social reform. Aristotle studied more than 150 constitutions of other cities to compose *Politics*. It is said that the XII Tables, the first Roman code, incorporated references to ancient Greek city-states.[5] While the Roman Empire declined, the conquering German tribes retained the Roman legal tradition.[6] During the Renaissance and the Industrial Revolution, the use of comparative law became increasingly significant in the rising nation-states. Even the "original" Western legal systems were affected by foreign law: French and German legal systems are based on the Roman legal tradition;[7] Anglo-American law is also influenced by civil law.[8] In the 19th and early 20th centuries, the emergence of the global market and colonization brought these legal systems to Africa, Asia, and Latin America.[9] After World War II, globalization engulfed the world. The US model of law and development introduced "ideal" legal models to the newly independent states.[10] Despite the failure of the first law and development movement,

---

4 Jonathan M. Miller, *A Typology of Legal Transplants: Using Sociology, Legal History and Argentine Examples to Explain the Transplant Process*, 51 Am. J. Comp. L. 839 (2003).

5 René David & John E. C. Brierley, *Major Legal Systems in the World Today: An Introduction to the Comparative Study of Law* 1–2 (2d ed., Stevens & Sons, 1978); Andrew Borkowski, *Textbook on Roman Law* 26 (Blackstone Press Limited 1994).

6 Alan Watson, *The Evolution of Law* 77–92 (Johns Hopkins U. Press 1985); M. H. Hoeflich, *Law, Society and Reception: The Vision of Alan Watson* 85 Mich. L. Rev. 1086 (1987).

7 John Henry Merryman, *The Civil Law Tradition: An Introduction to the Legal Systems of Western Europe and Latin America* 10 (2d ed., Stanford U. Press 1985).

8 Watson demonstrates that *Commentaries on the Laws of England*, by William Blackstone, the founder of English law, was based on a reference to Dutch scholar Dionysius Gothofredus's (1549–1622) interpretation of the *Institutes* of Justinian. English and American conflicts of law referred to *Praelectines Iuris Vivilis et Hodienrni* by Ulrich Huber, a Dutch scholar. *See* Alan Watson, *Legal Transplants: An Approach to Comparative Law* 94, 109–110 (U. Georgia Press 1993). Jerome Frank points out that "[c]ivil law tradition has many impacts on common law." He expounds on the far-reaching but often neglected impacts of civil law tradition on American common law in the areas of the constitution, conflicts of law, legal interpretation, and judicial procedure: "The influences of civil law on common law are legion. Many of them doubtlessly can't be detected." Jerome Frank, *Civil Law Influences on the Common Law: Some Reflections on "Comparative" and "Contrastive" Law*, 104 U. Penn. L. Rev. 888 (1956).

9 David & Brierley, *supra* note 5, at 69–73; and Shen, *supra* note 3, at 75–77.

10 Daniel Berkowitz, Katharina Pistor, & Jean-Francois Richard, *The Transplant Effect*, 51 Am. J. Comp. L. 163 (2003).

subsequent movements emerged with different theoretical foundations and strategic emphases.[11] The collapse of the former Soviet Union and the socialist bloc encouraged the transplantation of the European and American legal model to East European and former Soviet Union countries as they tried to restructure their legal systems.[12] In today's world, no national legal system can be separated entirely from foreign and international law.

Many comparative law scholars emphasize the importance of legal transplantation in legal and social development. Orucu states that "the movement of legal institutions and ideas is trans-border and such transmigration is a natural phase in legal development. This is both a historical and present fact and the future will see more of it."[13] He further asserts, "It is a truism that the amount of innovation in law is small and borrowing and imitation is of central importance in understanding the course of legal change."[14] Sacco holds that "borrowing and imitation is therefore of central importance to understanding the course of legal change."[15] Watson points out that direct transplants of legal systems have proliferated in human history and constitute the most important forces for legal development.[16] Watson questions Savigny's *volksgeist* (popular consciousness), the Marxist theory of economic determinacy, and Jhering's and Pound's theory of the sociology of law. He contends that the relation between law and society is more remote than people think and that legal rules are not designed for the particular society in which they operate.[17]

Not all scholars recognize the important role of legal transplantation in legal development. Montesquieu asserts that "the political and civil laws of each nation ought to be only the particular cases in which this human reason is applied. They should be adapted in such a manner to the people for whom they are framed that it should be a great chance if those of one nation

---

11 David M. Trubek, *Law and Development in a Time of Multiple Visions: The Challenge of the New Developmental State,* presentation at Renmin University Law School, available at http://www.law.ruc.edu.cn/Article/ShowAritcle.asp?ArticleID=11151. Trubek states, "In the first moment, law was seen as a strong tool to be used by the state to shape and guide behavior. In the second it was promoted as a shield against state intervention and a framework for private transactions." The third moment is a new type of law and development in developing countries, exemplified by China and Brazil, which show "signs of wanting to move beyond neo-liberalism without simply trying to return to the developmental state of the 1950s and 1960s. . . . The new theories stress the idea that policies must be constructed through experimentation and public-private collaboration and tailored to the needs of specific industries and regions, . . . [and] suggest the need for variation within each nation as well as among them."

12 Daniel Berkowitz, Katharina Pistor, & Jean-Francois Richard, *Economic Development, Legality and the Transplant Effect,* 47 European Eco. Rev. 166 (2003).

13 Esin Orucu, *Law as Transposition,* 51 Intl. Comp. L. Q. 205 (Apr. 2002).

14 *Id.,* at 206.

15 Rodolfo Sacco, *Legal Formants: A Dynamic Approach to Comparative Law,* 39 Am. J. Comp. L. 394 (1991).

16 Watson, *supra* note 3, at 95.

17 Watson, *supra* note 6 at 8.

suit another."[18] Savigny advocates *volksgeist* and theoretically rules out the feasibility of legal transplantation. In the contemporary field of comparative law, Kahn-Freund and Legrand represent the opposite theory, which objects to the possibility of legal transplantation. They hold that transplantation is impossible due to ingrained differences in the systems involved—transplantation does not occur at all: the product of moving a rule elsewhere is always something else, "not the same rule."[19]

In recent years,

> both these absolutist visions have long collapsed into a middle ground, densely populated by authors who reject both the sunny aspects of Watson's world of ever-flourishing transplants and Legrand's rejection of that vision. Much of the study has followed a culturalist path, under which outmoded legal formalism was replaced by realist, socio-politico-cultural theories that consider law as a living social construct. Here, legal culture was offered as a key determinant of the viability of transplantation; complete isolationism and hermeneutical closeness were replaced by a vision of law as rooted in its cultural/social frameworks, but also amenable to various influences, among them foreign ones.[20]

Even those who assert that legal transplantation is the normal path of legal development, such as Watson, cannot refute the effects of national spirit, domestic economic and social foundations, and distinct culture, religion, and political factors on legal development. Watson quotes Engels' statement that "in a modern state, law must not only correspond to the general economic position and be its expression, but must also be an expression which is *consistent in itself*, and which does not, owing to inner contradictions, look glaringly inconsistent."[21] Watson believes that these social factors are the cause of the transplantation of various forms of legal rules.[22]

In the post–Cold War world, ideological barriers for legal transplantation may seem insignificant and legal transplantation may appear to be a common phenomenon. But legal systems are based on the foundation of democracy, human rights, and a market economy and have enforced the impulse for exportation or transportation. Developing and transitional countries with newly developed market economies have introduced foreign laws in response to the pressures of economic development, democratization, and globalization. "To be in line with international conventions" is the accepted practice in the process of globalization, which encourages convergence or harmonization of legal systems in the areas of economic transactions, cultural exchanges, en-

---

18 Baron de Montesquieu, *The Spirit of Laws* vol.1, 6 (Cosimo Inc. 2007).

19 Margit Cohn, *Legal Transplant Chronicles: The Evolution of Unreasonableness and Proportionality Review of the Administration in the United Kingdom*, 58 Am. J. Comp. L. 586 (2010).

20 *Id.*, at 587–88.

21 Watson, supra note 3.

22 Watson, *supra* note 6, at 97.

vironmental protection, international peace, and some public law fields. The formation of a common market and the wide acceptance of universal values provide a solid foundation for legal convergence and harmonization. The World Bank, the Asian Development Bank, and various foundations that support economic and social development in developing and transitional countries often require the reform of legal systems and the establishment of the rule of law as prerequisites for providing funds and other assistance. This obligation further promotes legal transplants from developed countries to developing countries. "However, the economic development, democratization, and globalization have today so sharply increased the number of legal transplants that at least in developing countries, most major legislation now has a foreign component."[23] The common trajectory of legal transplants is from developed and international legal regimes to developing countries.

Thus, from both historical and practical perspectives, legal transplants are a common form of legal development. With the irresistible trend of globalization, the role of legal transplantation becomes ever more significant.

Typology of Legal Transplants

The transplantation debate continues, on issues of form, basic conditions, effects, function, compatibility, and implementation. There is little true consensus on the typology of and basic conditions for legal transplantation.

In practice, governments of different countries adopt different approaches toward legal transplantation because of practical concerns about national sovereignty, culture, history, ideology, and social system. Support or disapproval, toleration or rejection, wholesale or selective acceptance, uncritical or flexible adoption of different types of law—legal transplantation takes diversified and multidimensional forms. Moreover, the social, economic, and institutional contexts often differ remarkably between the countries of origin and of transplant, creating fundamentally different conditions for effectuating the imported legal order in the latter. Transplant countries therefore are likely to suffer from the transplant effect, that is, the mismatch between preexisting conditions and institutions and transplanted law, which weakens the effectiveness of the imported legal order.[24] Although Su Li's concept of "indigenous legal resources" explains the mismatch problems from the Chinese perspective,[25] an examination of the typology of and basic conditions for legal transplantation is in order.

Watson divides voluntary legal transplantation into different types:

- The transplantation of original law into an uncivilized area by massive immigration

23 Miller, *supra* note 4.

24 Berkowitz, Pistor, & Richard, *supra* note 10, at 171.

25 Su Li, *The Rule of Law and Its Indigenous Resources* (China U. of Political Science & Law Press 2004).

- The transplantation of original law into a civilized area
- The voluntary acceptance of another nation's law by the native people

In addition, there are other types, such as imposed acceptance, selective adoption, intrusion, filtration, and tacit acceptance. Watson believes that both the type and scale of transplantation vary and that, without specific study of individual cases, categorization has little value and cannot bring new ideas to comparative study.[26] Although legal transplantation is a normal form of legal development, it is by no means the only form. A particular social environment and country-specific factors are the major determinants of the development of a legal system. The necessity for and inevitability of revision, adaption, and naturalization of transplanted rules by the recipient country cannot be overlooked.

Miller uses motives of legal transplantation to categorize its types. This categorization helps explain the internal impetus for legal transplantation in China. Miller believes that there are four types of legal transplantation:

- The cost-saving transplant
- The externally dictated transplant
- The entrepreneurial transplant
- The legitimacy-generating transplant[27]

This typology shifts the focus of transplantation from the donor's perspective to the recipient's perspective. In practice, "many transplants are a mix of the four types, and one rarely encounters a type in pure form."[28]

The Cost-Saving Transplant

Implemented to save time and costly experimentation, a cost-saving transplantation "involves a drafter who when confronted with a new problem pulls a solution from elsewhere off the shelf of the library to save having to think up an original solution."[29] This type of transplantation has the benefit of speed, convenience, and direct application. However, it must be supplemented by a functional and systematic approach that is "the starting point and basis of all comparative law and that different legal systems can be compared only if they solve the same factual problem, satisfying the requirement in adequate legal regulation."[30] In the cost-saving approach, the prospective laws and mechanics to be transplanted are analyzed and selected after it has been determined

---

26 Watson, *supra* note 6, at 29–30.

27 Miller, *supra* note 4, at 842.

28 *Id.*

29 Miller, *supra* note 4, at 845.

30 Zweigert & Kötz, *supra* note 3, at 34; *see* also Jeffrey L. Dunoff & Joel P. Trachtman, *Ruling the World? Constitutionalism, International Law, and Global Governance*, in *Constitutionalism, International Law and Global Governance* 9 (Jeffrey Dunoff ed., Cambridge U. Press 2009); Djalil Kiekbaev, *Comparative Law: Method, Science or Educational Discipline?* 7.3 Electronic J. Comp. L. (Sep. 2003), available at http://www.ejcl.org/73/art73-2.html.

that both the donor and the recipient face similar social problems capable of being solved by the transplanted rules, and that the transplanted rules and mechanics will function in the same manner in both countries. Basing the decision purely on function is not sufficient because social environments may differ substantially, rendering the transplant a failure. This approach poses difficulties that make a complete checklist for comprehensive analysis of function and social factors unrealistic.[31]

China adopted this approach. It "pays attention to draw 'international experience' in the process [of] drafting important laws and regulations, namely, comparing with the relevant foreign and international laws."[32] For example, in the initial stage of "opening to the outside," China had no experience in the area of foreign investment. To attract foreign investment and cooperation, the Chinese legislature reviewed laws relating to joint ventures and foreign investment from more than 20 countries. It borrowed directly from foreign and international experience in drafting its first law, the Sino-Foreign Equity Joint Venture Law, and thus laid the legal foundation for attracting foreign investment.[33] To meet the needs of the increasing volume of foreign trade, the legislature has applied the United Nations Convention on Contracts for the International Sale of Goods to cases of international trade involving Chinese parties. In the areas relating to market formation and transaction, such as property, intellectual property rights, securities, companies, and bankruptcy, the legislature has also borrowed from foreign experience. This practice has become a conventional and regular step in China's legislative process—the legislature sends staff and experts to other countries for field study or to collect similar laws for further research and adoption.[34] By using this cost-saving transplant model, China has implemented laws based on foreign and international laws and mechanics to foster economic development.

The Externally Dictated Transplant

"Externally dictated transplants have become ubiquitous, particularly in developing countries. This kind of transplantation may involve a foreign individual, entity, or government that indicates the adoption of a legal model as a condition for doing business or for allowing the country a measure of political autonomy."[35] In the era of colonialism, a typical way to effect legal

---

31 Dunoff & Trachtman, *id.*

32 Shen, *supra* note 3, at 52.

33 Zhao Xin & Zhang Li, *Deng Xiaoping on Sino-Foreign Equity Joint Venture Laws: A Political Declaration*, Procuratorial Daily (Sep. 9, 2009).

34 Li Lin, *Thirty Years of Reform & Open Policy and China's Legislative Development*, 7(2) Beijing Union U. Rev.—Social Science, 8–10 (2009). *See* also the civil law section of *Comparison of Articles of Contract Law of the PRC with Relevant Foreign Contract Rules* (Legislative Affairs Commission of the National People's Congress ed., Law Press 1999). This detailed comparison indicates clearly that, in the process of drafting this statute, the legislative body conducted systematic and detailed comparisons and borrowed from successful foreign practices.

35 Miller, *supra* note 4, at 847.

transplantation was to dictate acceptance of foreign law. In the contemporary world, adoption dictated by military occupation or colonization is rare, although adoption in developing counties dictated by other means, such as economic or diplomatic pressure, is not uncommon. China accepted certain unfavorable rules and conditions imposed by powerful trading partners in the process of negotiating for its membership in international organizations.[36] Facing an established international market and regulatory regimes, China had to comply with externally imposed requirements and standards, including inspections and reviews by foreign agencies. To participate in the global market and export China-made products, China had little choice. Because of the pressure of this model, a recipient country often becomes the victim of economic, political, ideological, and diplomatic confrontation while reflecting the intrinsic demand for globalization and harmonization of the international legal framework; this type of legal transplantation is very common.

The Entrepreneurial Transplant

This model refers to individuals and groups who reap benefits from investing in, learning about, and encouraging local adoption of a foreign legal system. Its success depends on an exporter willing to provide capital and an importer interested in the import, each side guided by what it might gain domestically by operating internationally.[37] In tandem with China's opening to the outside and economic development, economic entities ranging from large state-owned enterprises to small private companies want to participate in international investment and trade, resulting in direct contact with foreign companies and acceptance of foreign rules. For example, all Chinese companies (both state owned and private) must follow foreign rules when they intend to participate in a foreign securities market. Some enterprises directly apply foreign commodity standards or labor standards in order to export their products to particular countries. Products with quality below the standards of the importing country have no chance of entering the market; labor safety standards (such as safety protection and work environment) below a legal requirement in the importing country may result in the blockade and boycott of the exported products. Some scholars claim that legal transplantation through private actors, by borrowing law through private contracting, has formed another type of transplantation. Through the channel of contracting, private transactors "smuggle" law across borders.[38] As a large export-oriented trading country,

---

36 Pitman B. Potter, *Globalization and Economic Regulation in China: Selective Adaptation of Globalized Norms and Practices,* 2 Wash. U. Global Studies L. Rev. 121–25 (2003). Potter analyzes the demands for China to adopt the principles of transparency, uniformity, national treatment, nondiscrimination, and compatibility with WTO rules, as well as the demands for certain rules and mechanics in the areas of trade, service, intellectual property rights, foreign exchanges, customs, independent courts, and dispute settlement.

37 Miller, *supra* note 4, at 849–50.

38 Li-Wen Lin, *Legal Transplants through Private Contracting: Codes of Vendor Conduct in Global Supply Chains as an Example,* 57 Am. J. Comp. L. 713–14 (2009).

China has implemented this model of legal transplantation through private economic and cultural exchanges.

The Legitimacy-Generating Transplant

This model refers to the process of consciously emulating the most prestigious foreign legal systems. Developing countries tend to regard the legal orders in developed countries as models to be copied. The wide acceptance in developing countries of the doctrine and mechanics of the separation of powers and an independent judiciary, which are deemed as legitimate legal orders by the people just coming out of dictatorship, is an example.[39]

Different legal systems have their respective levels of prestige. "A country's legal family is a significant determinant of the effectiveness of its legal system. Countries belonging to the English common law family have the most investor-friendly laws, French and German civil law countries have the least investor-friendly laws, and the Scandinavian countries fall somewhere between."[40] The US securities market is widely regarded as a prestigious legal regime because of its efficiency, flexibility, and security. In the process of drafting its securities laws and building its securities market, China turned to the US model. Similar borrowing and acceptance occurred in the areas of companies, insurance, antitrust, banking, and accounting. Despite the fact that the US securities market was hit hard by the worldwide financial crisis, because of its critical role and function in the international securities market, its legal regime is still regarded by many countries as the most prestigious legal model, even though this model may harbor potential risks, such as financial bubbles and speculation.

These four models focus on the motives and purposes of legal transplantation. A pure form of any one model is rare in practice, and a mix of the four is common.[41] This mix will take different forms. For example, although China employs all these transplantation models, its incremental approach, the stability required by social transition, the national independence asserted by China in the international community, and its unique historical and social backgrounds constitute a unique Chinese environment of legal development that is distinct from those in other transitional and developing countries.

Legal transplantation in China may have created a new model, positioned within a legal framework underpinned by socialism, based on the Chinese social environment, and developed to explore the possibilities of a Chinese socialist market economy and the Chinese socialist rule of law. Legal transplantation is an effective instrument to promote a legal system with Chinese characteristics that mixes transplantation models based on rational and active selection.

---

39 *Id.*

40 Berkowitz, Pistor, & Richard, *supra* note 10, at 166.

41 Miller, *supra* note 4, at 842.

Conditions for a Successful Legal Transplant

Simply establishing a typology of transplantation does not, of course, guarantee the success of legal transplantation. No matter what type of transplantation is employed, the process may end in failure or with setbacks. The failure of the first law-and-development movement triggered reexamination of the concept. Trubek and Galanter offered the first critique. In 1974, they asserted that the movement was dead because of excessive dependence on the governments of newly independent states and the one-sided intention of American scholars and lawyers to bring the legal order of developed countries to new states without considering the social conditions of the recipient countries.[42] The second wave of the law-and-development movement was initiated by neoliberalism and the free market doctrine espoused by Ronald Reagan and Margaret Thatcher. This new round took the rule of law as its banner; democracy, free market doctrine, and liberalism as its theoretical foundation; and the Washington Consensus as its guiding principle. The collapse of the socialist bloc headed by the Soviet Union cleared the way for the introduction of American and European legal systems into Russia and East European countries. But to a great extent, the results have not been satisfactory. The global financial crisis delivered a heavy blow to the theory and strategy of law and development. As a result, scholars question the credibility of the legal transplants in this mode and wonder how to guarantee the success of a legal transplantation, and how to use legal transplantation to achieve positive social effects.

The success of a legal transplant does not depend exclusively on the choices of laws to transplant, on the system selected as the model, or on the faithful introduction of an entire system. No less important to success are the conditions for transplants in the recipient country. These conditions may already exist or may have to be created to ensure that a transplant is accepted. These conditions include internal demand for the transplant and the local environment, such as relevant institutions, procedures, and social factors that promote and implement the transplanted laws and systems.[43] A friendly environment for transplanted laws is one in which social and popular attitudes favor acceptance of the transplant, and in which there exists the capacity to absorb the transplant and the ability to resolve possible conflicts between the transplanted law and indigenous law and customs.[44] If these conditions are absent or incomplete, no matter how magnificent the intention behind the transplant or how well designed it is, its final result will be disappointing.

In the past 30 years, as China has faced numerous challenges in the transition from a planned economy to a market economy, it has experienced an astonishing economic boom and rapid changes in its social structure. The

---

42 David Trubek & Marc Galanter, *Scholars in Self-Estrangement: Some Reflections on the Crisis in Law and Development Studies in the United States*, 14 Wis. L. Rev. 1062 (1974).

43 Berkowitz, Pistor, & Richard, *supra* note 10, at 179.

44 Zhang Jianyuan, *Symptoms and Diagnosis of Legal Transplantation—Taking HIV Legal Policy as a Case for Study*, 4 Ideological Front (2010).

decisive factor for such change has been the strong desire, embraced by the populace, the government, and the party in power, to build a "strong modernized country" and to elevate living standards. The Cultural Revolution brought the Chinese economy to the edge of bankruptcy; under the planned economy commodities were in short supply and living standards remained at a very low level. The populace concluded that in the wake of the Cultural Revolution there was a need to "shift the working focus to socialist modernization and economic construction"[45] and to improve living standards. Based on a strong consensus, the policy and practice of borrowing, introducing, and transplanting foreign and international law and legal systems triumphed. Despite different views regarding choices and modes of transplantation, consensus to borrow foreign and international laws was achieved and maintained. By rationally borrowing and transplanting foreign laws to constitute a new legal system that pushes social reform and maintains the open-door policy, China has turned onto a new road.

In regard to basic conditions for a successful transplant, China faces a complicated situation. First, as to the institutions and mechanisms that could facilitate transplantation, the existing apparatus, such as law enforcement agencies and judicial organs, has traditional ways of operating that are rife with defects and loopholes and often incompatible with newly transplanted law or mechanisms. When China introduced contracts as a means for market transactions, for example, organs such as the State Administration for Industry and Commerce still had the mind-set of a planned economy and exercised their control over business contracts by requiring them to be registered with the administration. Second, legal consciousness in China may still lag behind the laws that are being introduced. Although China has made an effort to build a legal system and promote the rule of law, the law is not regarded as the predominant norm in Chinese society, and the legal system and apparatus are not considered the primary means for constructing a new social structure or solving social problems. The Communist Party and state policies (or even the decisions of individual leaders) continue to play more significant roles than the law. In the areas of rural economic reform and state-owned enterprise reform, policy is more effective and timely than law.[46] Law is often used to enforce or institutionalize policy. In this regard, social and legal conditions are not sufficient for newly introduced laws that cannot have immediate legal effects without policy support. Finally, an inadequate legal consciousness creates hurdles to acceptance and implementation of introduced laws and mechanisms.

---

45 The Communiqué of the Third Plenary Session of the Eleventh Central Committee of the Communist Party of China (Dec. 22, 1978).

46 The Chinese Communist Party's policy is usually carried out in party documents. For example, to promote rural reform in China, every year's first party document states major rural reform policies from 1982 to 1986 and from 2004 to 2012. Thus, the "first party document" is the nickname of rural reform policy. These policies often introduce new reform measures that do not have sound legal grounds and will push law in new directions.

China is in the long process of learning how to march to the rule of law. There are bound to be defects, problems, and loopholes in the legal system and in society as this process unfolds. For example, after drafting securities laws and regulations based on foreign models (introducing foreign law), listed companies with state assets are habitually interfered with by the state organs exercising power over them as state-owned enterprises. Based on these kinds of conditions, securities law and regulations operate differently than does the original model and their functions are very much restricted.

Traits and Effects of Legal Transplantation in China

At this point, China has a relatively comprehensive legal system. Although the legal system needs to be developed and perfected, its role in promoting economic and social development and constructing a new legal and social structure is widely recognized. The system has borrowed and transplanted many foreign laws and legal mechanisms that have been integrated into the system and play a significant role in providing readily gained experience and shortening the process of lawmaking. Why have these transplants been successfully integrated into the Chinese system?

Integration of Transplanted and Aboriginal Concepts

The modern Chinese legal system is built on Western legal patterns that have been transplanted on a grand scale. The traditional Chinese legal system (such as the Tang and Qing royal codes and legal apparatus) no longer exists in China. Nevertheless, the legal system has maintained certain traits, including strong nationalist and socialist characteristics.

The traditional Chinese legal system, which lasted for more than 2,000 years, is an aboriginal legal system. The system was fundamentally transformed due to the formation of international markets and the effects of globalization. Although the legal culture and ideology of the system maintain a strong influence (both positive and negative), the Chinese structure and system have been entirely taken over. This transformation took place in the late Qing dynasty and early Nationalist Republic, when the royal "ancestor's law and the traditional legal system" were abandoned and replaced by the Western legal system. Transplantation has since become a significant feature of the Chinese legal system.[47] After the establishment of the People's Republic of China in 1949, the new government of China abandoned the Western legal pattern and introduced the legal system of the Soviet Union. This massive process of transplantation ended in the early 1960s, when China broke away from the Soviet Union. During the disaster of the Cultural Revolution, the legal system modeled on the Soviet example was dismantled. With the ending of the Cultural Revolution, the Chinese government led by Deng Xiaoping

---

47 Zhou Shaoyuan, *Chinese Legal Changes and Legal Transplantation in the 20th Century*, 2 Chinese and Foreign Legal Science (1999).

decided to initiate structural reforms and open China's door to the world. A policy of strengthening the legal system was begun to rebuild the ruined legal system. Since then, China has borrowed and introduced many foreign and international laws and mechanisms. Nevertheless, the dominant ideas in the process of transplantation are either "insisting on Chinese learning as the foundation and Western learning for practical use," as introduced in the late Qing period, or "Chinese characteristics" (socialism under Chinese conditions), used currently, in which the transplanted laws and mechanisms are organically combined with traditional Chinese culture, popular ideology, and local environments. Therefore, China's legal development is unlike that in Asia, Africa, and Latin America during the law-and-development movement of the 1960s, when foreign experts espoused the wholesale transplantation of the Western legal system.

In the process of transplantation, China has emphasized the following concepts:

- An insistence on the nationalistic and socialist nature of legal development, by which China tries to integrate transplanted laws and mechanisms into the framework of the legal regime embedded in Chinese culture, particularly ideology and the dominant political doctrine.
- An insistence on facing and solving real Chinese problems, by which China adopts a functional approach to set up clear targets for the transplanted laws and mechanisms in order to combine the transplanted laws with Chinese social reality.
- An insistence on national sovereignty and the principle of "taking facts as basis,"[48] by which China's legislative, administrative, and judicial agencies, after carefully analyzing the Chinese social environment and international needs, have maintained their authority of initiation and renovation and never blindly borrowed.
- An insistence on integration within the national legal system, in which transplanting goes through careful study and adaptation in order to make individual transplants compatible with other laws and mechanisms.

This type of transplantation might be described as "selective transplantation"—China has built its legal system with its own needs and purposes in mind. Although there are debates over the concepts of "Chinese characteristics" and socialism, and these concepts do need further explanation and substantiation, the concepts emphasized by China have the de facto effect of guaranteeing the independence of the Chinese legal system and maintaining its distinctive traits, and therefore integrating the introduced laws and mechanics into the social environment and the existing Chinese legal framework. The unique approach taken by China to incorporating foreign elements into

---

48 Gu Ang'ran, *Significance of Contract Law Legislation*, in *Legislative Materials on Contract Law of China*, 37 (Law Publishing House 1999). *See* also Li Peichuan, *Theory and Practice of Chinese Socialist Legislation* 31–34 (China Legality Press 1991).

its legal system represents a major innovation and has directly advanced the country's economic development. As a result, China has been successful in avoiding an unhappy marriage of the transplanted and aboriginal systems as evidenced in other developing countries. This particular way of integration has also avoided the result of "rejection reaction"[49] and guaranteed the naturalization of transplanted laws while maintaining their vitality. If legal transplants have played an important role in promoting social transition and reform in China, the above-mentioned general approaches, unique models, and tactics of legal transplantations were preconditions for success.

Selective Transplantation

"Selective adoption is the process of interplay by and mixing of the international rules and local cultural norms."[50] This concept, proposed by Potter, relates to the application of international rules and foreign laws in different countries, particularly in developing countries in today's environment of globalization. China's legal transplantation is by no means a blind or wholesale form of transplantation; to a great extent, it is a transplantation based on "self-need." It requires that recipients scrutinize the target laws to be transplanted, the problems to be solved by transplanted laws, the possible social effects of transplantation, and the differences and similarities of the social environments of exporting and importing countries in order to come up with an active, purposeful, and selective legal transplant.

In the current development wave, international institutions such as the World Bank and the International Monetary Fund often make the rule of law a prerequisite of financial support and ask recipient countries to implement overall or fundamental legal reform. Facing such requirements, many recipient countries have no other recourse but to accept. There is nothing wrong with such requests, but they often overlook the internal environment of the recipient countries, making the countries passive in the process of reform and transplantation. Therefore, the transplanted laws often appear aimless or mismatched to local needs or environments.

In contrast, China, in its social transition and legal development, has adopted selective borrowing and transplantation rather than wholesale absorption.[51] In economic law, China adopted a series of foreign investment and trade laws and regulations when it opened the door to attract foreign

---

49 Wang Chenguang, *Inter Borrowing and Absorption of Legal Systems of Different Countries—An Important Topic in Comparative Law*, 4 China Legal Science (1992).

50 Pitman Potter, *Selective Adoption and Institutional Capacity Building: Methods of Applying International Rules under the Impacts of Globalization*, in *The Hypothesis of "Selective Application" and China's Legal Practice* 2 (Pitman Potter & Gu Xiaorong ed., Shanghai Academy of Social Sciences Press 2009).

51 Pitman Potter, *Selective Adaptation of Economic Governance Norms in China: Transparency and Autonomy in Local Context*, in Pitman & Gu Xiaorong, *id.*, at 30. Chen Yun, *On the Approaches of China's Rule of Law Resources*, in *Legal Transplantation and Legal Naturalization* 298 (He Qinhua ed., Law Publishing House 2001).

investors and businesses. At the same time, China made a number of rules in the areas of foreign currency exchange, choices of laws, and management of joint ventures in order to maintain autonomy in conducting foreign trade. In the political field, China emphasizes its socialist nature and the Communist Party's leading role and rejects the doctrine of separation of powers while it explores efficient means of restricting power, actively borrows and introduces foreign laws of legal supervision and control of governmental power, and sets up anticorruption bureaus in the procuratorial organs. In the process of judicial reform, China has pushed for adjudicative reform based on the adversarial model of common law while hesitating to adopt fully the principle of judicial independence; it introduced the reform of evidence rules based on the foreign evidence structure; and it actively promoted China's guiding case system, based on the pattern of case law.[52] These selective and adapted transplants play effective and practical roles with clear purposes in the incremental process of reform.

Openness and Tolerance for Transplanted Laws

Chinese reform has another characteristic: to allow a "bold charge" (*da dan chuang*),[53] even new methods may be incompatible with the current rules. Generally speaking, Chinese reform adopts an incremental approach and follows a piecemeal path, but it also encourages bold experiments and tolerates failures,[54] including in the process of legal transplantation.

In the aspects of structure and legal framework, particularly in the area of reforming concrete rules and institutes, the bold introduction and transplantation of foreign effective laws and mechanisms have been a regular practice in pushing legal reform. Theoretically, there is a consensus that "borrowing and absorbing foreign laws cannot take the distinction of capitalism and socialism as a standard for borrowing and absorbing, but take the functional approach as standards to test whether the borrowing and absorbing is conducive to social reform and economic development or not."[55]

Transplants of concrete rules and mechanisms have affected many areas of the law. In the field of civil law, transplants have included the right to privacy, spiritual damages, and the principle of changing situations; in the criminal field, presumption of innocence, exclusion of illegal evidence, and evidence rules; in the administrative law field, administrative litigation, administrative permission, and protection of private information; and in the

---

52 Detailed reform is demonstrated in Supreme People's Court, *The Third Five-Year Reform Program of the People's Courts* (Mar. 2009). *See* also Xia Jinwen, *Contemporary Chinese Judicial Reform: Achievements, Problems and Future—An Analysis of People's Courts,* 1 China Legal Science (2010); Huang Zaizai, *On Legal Transplantation and Establishment of China's Case Law System,* 4 Shanghai Carders Management College of Pol. & L. Rev. (2002).

53 The phrase "bold charge" was used by Deng Xiaoping when he made his famous visit to Shenzhen and encouraged further reforms in 1991.

54 Cao Ying & Hu Liguo ed., *Xiaoping's Centenary* 551–52 (Jinghua Press 2004).

55 Wang, *supra* note 49.

commercial and economic law field, company law, anti-unfair competition, protection of consumer rights, intellectual property rights, and the stock market. In the social protection field, a social security and social insurance system is garnering attention.[56]

The Chinese model of legal transplantation has had significant impacts on social transition and economic development. It facilitates the integration of the existing system with the transplanted system by reducing the conflicts between them; at the same time, it exerts enormous momentum for social transition. A good example is in the field of foreign investment: China has successfully introduced many foreign laws and at the same time kept transplanted laws compatible with society. Thus, the transplanted laws and mechanisms maintain their vitality and effectiveness in the Chinese environment while promoting the transformation of the old legal and social systems. This model creates a vital framework that is capable of accommodating the contradictions of innovation and status quo and of reform and stability.

The Chinese model promotes a mixed legal system. China's current legal system is an open system that has absorbed positive experience from many foreign and international systems. It is based on a continental legal tradition and actively borrows from the common law tradition, for example, in the fields of commercial law and banking law. This mode of transplantation implements the cost-effective formation of a modern legal system in line with international practice and development in other countries. Legal transplantation has the advantage of providing legal rules more advanced than existing ones in developing countries. Rather than following the conventional method of going through all the developmental stages, legal transplantation may help a developing country effectively and efficiently upgrade its old-fashioned system. When China started to foster social reform and economic development, it could not wait for slow autogenous development but looked at more advanced systems with experience in the market economy; nor could it accept the wholesale transplantation of foreign legal systems. By using this new innovative method of legal transplantation, China adopted market rules and mechanisms that have proved successful in other countries and successfully built a new market system and developed new market behavior patterns.

The Chinese model pushes social reform and development. Chinese legal transplantation is never made without a clear purpose; therefore, legal transplantation is always directed toward tackling particular problems or issues. This problem-oriented approach is based on social reality and effectively

---

56 *See* Chen Xiaojun, *On Contract Law Evolution in China*, 6 Commercial L. Research (1999); Yu Guohua, *On Comparative Study of China's Contract Law*, 2 Exploration (2000); Li Xiaoming, *On the Presumption of Innocence Principle and Its Legislation*, 6 China Prosecutor (2005); Wu Weishan, *Calling for Legislative Efforts for Presumption of Innocence*, 7 People's Forum (2005); Wei Zong, *Major Points of Administrative Litigation Law*, 6 China Legal Science (1988); Ren Erxin, *Economic Analysis of Commercial Legislation in China*, 2 Gansu College of Pol. & L. Rev. (2001); Chen Yadong, *Several Important Issues in Social Insurance Law Making*, 6 Social Protection Research (2009).

plants the transplanted rules in Chinese soil. The function and potential effect of facilitating social development are embedded at the beginning of any process of transplantation.

Conclusion

Although some scholars claim that "the amount of innovation in law is small and borrowing and imitation is of central importance in understanding the course of legal change,"[57] China's experience shows that legal transplantation as a means of legal reform and development requires innovation: innovation in the methods and ways of transplantation, and innovation in the content of transplanted laws and mechanisms to ensure that they fit into the recipient legal system. Legal transplantation is conducted not for the transplantation per se but for social development. The Chinese approach toward legal transplantation and the selective strategy of transplantation constitute an innovative model that enables the recipient legal system to be reformed and revitalized, which in return empowers society to accept successful experience from other countries and to rise to the challenges of social transition, modernization, and globalization.

57 Orucu, *supra* note 13.

Rule of Law as a Watermark

China's Legal and Judicial Challenges

Stéphanie Balme

Because the law and legal systems are crucial in promoting business interactions in the course of globalization, one might well ask, what is the status of the law and the legal system in China, the world's second-biggest economy?[1]

This chapter answers that question by examining the major turning points in Chinese legal theory and legal practices since the 1990s, when China became a global economic and political actor. It covers some of the major accomplishments of the People's Republic of China (PRC) since the end of the Mao era and the beginning of Deng Xiaoping's "open door policy" in 1978 and after China's accession to the World Trade Organization (WTO) in 2001. Under Deng Xiaoping, law reforms legitimized the process of economic change. The legal framework affected business growth, while China's wealth helped build a modern court system. Generally, access to justice for ordinary citizens is better today than ever before in Chinese history.

After three decades, reform objectives have evolved from quantitative reforms to more qualitative reforms. This chapter explores some of the key constraints and challenges facing China today in terms of legal and judicial practices. The lack of guarantee to a fair trial is a recurring concern. One might well ask if Chinese law is inherently unfair because it denies due process or because of deficient enforcement mechanisms. Reform of China's legal and judicial systems relies on a balance among the country's ruling party and various legal groups with diverging opinions and standards. Supremacy of the constitution, the law in action rather than in statutes, and legal certainty are fundamental challenges in building a rule of law in China. *Legal certainty* refers to clarity, predictability, and fairness in the implementation of legal rules. New to China's legal tradition, this Western standard has been translated into Chinese (*falü quedingxing*) even though it does not yet have a legal recognition.

The author wishes to thank Professor Wang Chenguang (Tsinghua University), Ms. Marina Lou, and M. Can Zhao (Sciences Po Paris) for their comments on an earlier version of this chapter. The author is entirely responsible for its final content.

1 World Bank, *Doing Business* (World Bank 2004).

From Laws of Power to the Power of the Law?

The difficulty in establishing a genuine and innovative rule of law in China can be explained by the fact that, at the conceptual level, traditional law has been repeatedly rejected by China's own lawmakers. The modern law that exists is a combination of a system influenced by Western legality,[2] the Maoist legacy (a combination of Stalinist theories with Chinese characteristics), and traditional legal reasoning as well as modern court practices.

After the establishment of the PRC in October 1949 by Mao Zedong, a Soviet-style revolutionary regime of criminal justice was implemented. The new government regarded the existing system of law as a straitjacket that aided criminal suspects and in turn restricted its own prosecutorial powers. The anti-rightist movement in 1957, which witnessed the persecution of hundreds of thousands of people, further marginalized the role of law in society. In 1959, the Ministry of Justice was abolished. During the Cultural Revolution, from 1966 to 1976, the poorly shaped legal system, which lacked fundamental statutes such as criminal law, civil law, and administrative law, was almost entirely abolished. Only after the disastrous Cultural Revolution did reformist leader Deng Xiaoping use law to promote his policies: legal changes in China in 1978 were a technical response as well as a political answer to the fragmentation of the state under Mao. This is the point at which China began to take the role of law seriously and to embark on the current process of legal construction.[3]

In assessing China's main achievements in terms of legal and judicial developments since 1978, this chapter focuses on two areas: the legislative arena and access to justice. Compared to the anarchical and rigorous charismatic rule of the Maoist period, modern law has become, at least in theory, a legitimate instrument of public action both for authorities and for civil society. To use Max Weber's typology, China has moved from a charismatic type of authority to a more rational-legal authority where legitimacy derives from the existence of a legal order. However, as shown in this chapter, the rhetoric of the rule of law is often confined to a formula of legal positivism, or pure theory.

Important New Regulatory Policies

The development of China's current legal system dates to the late 1970s. The founding text is a speech given by Deng Xiaoping on December 13, 1978, announcing the "policy of opening up," as well as the official communiqué of December 22, 1978, published at the end of the third plenary session of the 11th Central Committee of the Chinese Communist Party (CCP). This communiqué formally abolished the dominant party policy of class struggle and

---

2 Philip C. Huang, *Chinese Civil Justice: Past and Present* (Rowman & Littlefield 2010).

3 See Wang Zhenmin & Li Zhenghui, *The Rule of Law History, Theory and Criticism*, 80(6) L. & Phil. Lib. 647–70 (2007).

the orthodox Marxist conception of law, according to which law is an instrument of bourgeois or proletarian dictatorship.

The period between 1978 and 1982 marked a transition in terms of the Chinese legal system. The CCP clearly controlled the legal reform agenda. With the trial of the Gang of Four (November 1980 to January 1981), the new regime demonstrated its willingness to use legal instruments for dispute resolution (despite clear flaws in the trial, such as insufficient legal representation, evidence errors, and political instruction to the special court). The work carried out since then has been considerable: restoration of the Ministry of Justice, rehabilitation of victims of the Cultural Revolution and the antirightist movement, and enactment of a new constitution, followed by a decade referred to by some Western academics as "legal bulimia."

The Struggle between Two Philosophies: Rule by Law and Rule of Law

The idea of "rule by law" gradually emerged as the nation transformed from a planned economy to a state market economy. The fifth National People's Congress (NPC) adopted the current constitution of the PRC on December 4, 1982. Comprising 138 articles, the constitution reflects a major change that shifts the primary task of the state from a class struggle to economic development and social reform. It stipulates the objectives of the state, the fundamental political and economic systems of the country, a list of basic citizens' rights, and the structure and power of the political regime.

In June 1985, the first of a series of educational campaigns on the "popularization of the law" (*pufa*) was launched with the idea of creating a Chinese "society governed by law" (*fazhi shehui*) and not "rule by men" (*renzhi*). The main slogan was a call to "reinforce the legal system and improve legislative quality" (*jianquan de lifa zhidu yu hao de lifa zhiliang*). In the 1990s, China adapted many international economic and trade laws with a view to the country's accession to the WTO. Over a period of more than 20 years, a genuine system of economic and trade laws was thus instituted. Until 2004, constitutional amendments were concerned almost exclusively with changing the orthodoxy of economic matters: namely, the diversification of property rights (1988), the establishment of a socialist market economy (1993), the acceptance or recognition of the individual and semiprivate economy (1999), and the recognition of private property rights (2004).[4]

Moreover, based on previously existing contract laws, the 1999 economic contract law (symbolically promulgated on October 1, the date of the founding of the PRC) further validated the principles of autonomy, freedom, and equality of contracting parties. The law is voluminous (more than 400 articles) and was rapidly disseminated in consideration of investors, particularly

---

4 *See* also Donald Clarke, Peter Murrell, & Susan Whiting, *The Role of Law in China's Economic Development*, available at http://econweb.umd.edu/~murrell/articles/ChinaInstitutions.pdf.

foreigners.[5] Contract law is now involved in almost every commercial transaction in China. Article 26 gives contracting parties the right to request adjustment or even rescission of a valid contract but also sets up strict precedents. It aims to bring more certainty to an uncertain economic situation, stating:

> After a contract is legally formed, in view of objective circumstances not anticipated by the parties when the contract was formed, caused neither by force majeure nor commercial risks, and significant changes occur such that continuing the performance of the contract is unfair and inequitable to one party or the objective of the contract cannot be fulfilled, then a party or both parties may request the People's Court to modify or rescind this contract.

Ten years later, in the aftermath of the international economic crisis, the Supreme People's Court (SPC) issued a judicial interpretation of the 1999 economic contract law to provide guidance on the right to rescind or modify a contract when a "fundamental change of circumstances" has occurred.

A New Objective: "An Administration Based on Law"

Between the mid-1980s and China's entry into the WTO in December 2001, the government focused on enhancing the administrative law system to control governmental authority, which had previously been unlimited, and on adapting the legal system to comply with international norms. This period saw the re-emergence of administrative law and use of the slogan "an administration based on law" (*yifa xingzheng*). By the mid-1990s, theories on administrative law were said to be "exploding,"[6] with the appointment of more administrative law professors and the founding of the National School of Administration (now called the Chinese Academy of Governance).

In April 1989, a new administrative litigation law allowed citizens and all legal persons to bring legal challenges against "specific administrative actions." Through the mid-2000s, various regulations were passed to allow administrative sanctions, such as the Regulations on Public Security Management and Sanctions (*Zhi'an guanli chufa tiaoli*), and to restrict the power of administrative organs. Passed in the mid-1990s, the State Compensation Law (Article 2) states:

> Where State organs or State functionaries, in violation of the law, abuse their functions and powers infringing upon the lawful rights and interests of the citizens, legal persons and other organizations, thereby causing damage to them, the victims shall have the right to State compensation in accordance with this Law.[7]

---

5 Available at http://www.law-lib.com/law/.

6 *See* Zhang Li, *Le contrôle juridictionnel de la légalité des actes administratifs en Chine: Eléments d'analyse comparée des contentieux administratifs chinois et français* (Bruylant 2010).

7 http://en.chinacourt.org/public/detail.php?id=109.

Other notable laws were the Law on Administrative Punishments (1996), the Law on Administrative Supervision (1997), the Implementation Regulations (2004), and the Administrative Licensing Law (2004).[8]

In ancient China, people beat a drum outside the government offices (*yamen*) to start litigation, to petition a visiting imperial envoy, or "to appeal to the emperor" (*gao yu zhuang*). As recently as a few decades ago, the petition system had not been standardized. Under Mao, the government developed a comprehensive network of agencies, the *xinfang* (letters and visits) offices, throughout the county, as well as a petition system (*shangfang*). These mechanisms were "to petition the government for a redress of grievances by means of letters (*xin*) or visits (*fang*)," according to Isabelle Thireau and Hua Linshan.[9]

The *xinfang* system today looks different. Under Mao, only people defined as "legitimate" could express grievances. Nowadays, the *xinfang* offices must, in principle, allow anyone to exercise his or her constitutional rights. Also, under Mao, the petition system mostly involved the denunciation of enemies and counterrevolutionaries. Now, it aims to maintain social stability by compensating people and solving people's problems. In May 2005, a principle of "solving problems at the grassroots level" (*ba xinfang wenti jiejue zai jiceng*) was adopted. For the first time, an individual or organization could not retaliate against petitioners; if it did, it would face legal action. Although there has been an increase in the number of petitioners (12.72 million letters, calls, or visits in 2003, for example) and a growing number of visits, the success rate (in terms of petitioners' cases being accepted) for these visits has always been low, less than 1 percent, according to unofficial statements.

In the wake of *Li Maorun v. Langzhong Police Station* in 2001, citizens can sue local governments for actions in violation of their rights, including administrative punishments, administrative coercive measures, interference with the operation of enterprises, refusal to take action or perform an obligation, unlawful demands for performance of duties, and violations of individual rights or property rights. Cases commonly involve encroachment by the government on the interests and rights of ordinary citizens, inadequate compensation for land appropriation, illegal land seizures, and expropriation or house demolition. Since the mid-2000s, administrative litigation and landmark cases involving the government have increased as citizens become more comfortable using legal measures to protect their property from government violation.

The relationship between the *xinfang* system and the judicial system remains unclear. In 2011, it is still difficult for the judiciary to give transparent and consistent judgments or efficient enforcement. Judicial review of government action is not permitted in situations of "national defense," a loosely interpreted concept, or foreign affairs. In addition, judicial review is not permitted for

8 *See* Chen Jianfu, *Chinese Law: Context and Transformation* 207–60 (Martinus Nijhoff, Brill Academic 2008).

9 Isabelle Thireau & Hua Linshan, *Les ruses de la démocratie: Protester en Chine* (Le Seuil 2010).

"abstract administrative action," which refers to rule and policy-making activities. The relationship between the state and citizens in public administration is still problematic in terms of not being regulated by due process.

A Growing Recognition of Labor and Economic Rights

By the late 1990s, restructuring of state-owned enterprises (SOEs) had led to the closure, merger, or privatization of underperforming SOEs and the laying off of more than 30 million workers (*xiagang zhigong*). Although various arrangements were made for the laid-off workers (for example, buying out employment, reducing salaries, and providing assistance for self-employment), the smashing of the "iron rice bowl" (i.e., job security and guaranteed benefits) triggered massive labor disputes and unrest.

Scholars and think tanks developed a five-year program (1996–2001) for the government with the objective of developing labor protection laws in the new market situation. The Labor Law of 1999 (*Laodong Fa*) states that it will "protect the legitimate rights and interests of laborers, re-adjust labor relationship, establish and safeguard the labor system compatible to the socialist market economy, and promote economic development and social progress" (Article 1). It further states that

> laborers have the right to equal treatment, choose occupations, obtain remunerations, take rests, have holidays and leaves, receive labor safety and sanitation protection, get training in professional skills, enjoy social insurance and welfare treatment, and submit applications for settlement of labor disputes, and other labor rights stipulated by law. (Article 3)

China's Labor Law of January 1, 2008, requires that labor contracts be in writing and limits the use of term contracts and probationary periods for employees. Their length of probationary periods is limited based on the terms of the employment contract, with a maximum of six months. "Virtually every violation of the law gives the employee the right to sue the employer for penalties and damages in the local employment arbitration bureau or in the local courts," explains lawyer Steve Dickinson.[10]

In March 2001, China ratified the International Covenant on Economic, Social, and Cultural Rights, but it still places a reservation on obligations regarding Article 8, which guarantees trade union rights and the right to freedom of association. Legislative activity in this area developed rapidly as the workers' movement intensified in 2007 and 2008. Four important laws were adopted to face this new legal challenge: the Law on Prevention and Treatment of Occupational Diseases, the Employment Promotion Law, the Law on Labor Dispute Mediation and Arbitration, and the Social Insurance Law.

---

10 Steve Dickinson, *China's New Labor Law: Power to the People,* China International Business Magazine (2007), available at http://www.chinalawblog.com.

Legal Empowerment at the Local Level

According to Zhu Jingwen's quantitative measure of rule of law reforms in China, in 1979, there were 15 laws, 68 administrative regulations, and 72 local regulations. In 2006, there were 36 laws, 164 national administrative regulations, and 14,124 local regulations.[11] Thus, between 1979 and 2006, the average annual growth of national laws and national administrative regulations was around 11 percent, compared with more than 30 percent for local regulations. These figures reveal that there was a massive legislative effort over 30 years, particularly at the local level. This situation contributed to a growing deficit of legal visibility and accessibility of regulations and laws in China.

With China's integration into the international economy through the WTO and the increasing development of the Internet, the decade of 2000–2010 was characterized by new and multiple interactions between authorities and civil society in defining the legal reform agenda. The Law on Legislation (*Lifa Fa*), enacted in March 2000, was designed to rationalize the system and regulate legislative processes. It also set up procedures for public participation, such as publication of legislative drafts and public hearings (*tingzheng*).

In March 2008, the chairman of the Standing Committee of the National People's Congress, Wu Bangguo, controversially announced that a socialist legal system with Chinese characteristics had been fundamentally accomplished. "There are laws to cover basically every area of economic, political, cultural and social activities in the country," he stated in a report on China's Assembly.[12]

Table 1. Number of Laws and Regulations in China, 1979-2005

Year	Law	Administrative Regulation	Local Regulation	Amount
1979	15	68	72	404
1982	21	145	485	1055
1989	15	111	1,508	3,339
1991	27	111	1,601	3,879
1996	40	118	3,475	6,349
2000	31	171	5,628	8,846
2005	36	164	14,124	18,121
Average Annual Rate of Growth	11.8%	10.7%	33.1%	21.3%

Source: Zhu Jingwen, *Report on China Law Development: Database and Indicators* (RUC Press 2007).

Translation S. Balme.

11 Zhu Jingwen, *Report on China Law Development: Database and Indicators* (RUC Press 2007).

12 *Id.*

Toward Better Access to Justice

China's judicial system resumed in 1979, after the chaotic events of the Cultural Revolution. The reform of the judiciary must be assessed through the lens of judicial transformation under the Maoist regime. During successive Maoist campaigns, particularly in 1950–53, 1957–58, 1967–71, and 1975–76, the number of cases registered as criminal cases exceeded the number of civil cases. Post-Mao China's legal and judicial reforms were characterized by stop-and-go cycles. For example, the last historical period, after Mao's death, when the number of criminal cases almost reached the number of civil cases was during the 1983 "strike hard" (*yanda*) campaign against criminal suspects.

In 1981, Deng Xiaoping used the trial of the Gang of Four to display the regime's intentions to govern with reference to the law instead of by individual political decisions. Since then, ordinary, daily justice has been largely depoliticized and professionalized. According to Professor Zhu Jingwen, the percentage of judgments made through formal procedures increased from 16.5 percent to 35.7 percent between the mid-1990s and the mid-2000s.[13] According to the China National Bureau of Statistics, recent growth in the number of civil disputes has been irregular: from 5,346,986 in 2008 to 6,458,573 in 2009 and 4,980,721 in 2010. Altogether, between 2008 and 2010, Chinese jurisdictions received and adjudicated 16,786,280 cases. The number of marriage and heritage disputes (1,286,437 cases in 2008; 1,423,180 cases in 2010) and the number of contract disputes (2,905,603 cases in 2008; 3,222,555 cases in 2010) also increased during this period.[14]

In 30 years, successive reform plans have evolved from quantitative reforms (reestablishing a judiciary, building courts, hiring judges, and training lawyers) to more qualitative reforms such as enhancing the quality of judicial training, improving access to justice, and creating alternative dispute-resolution techniques. For litigants who have access to the Internet, judicial services are increasingly available in China, and, according to author Bi Shaofeng, legal aid services are more developed than in the past in coastal areas and in remote places.[15] However, few legal aid offices or legal clinics (*falü yuanzhusuo, falü zhensuo*) exist in rural areas or for nonprivileged categories of the population such as the migrant workers or disabled persons.

An Emerging Country with an Emerging Judiciary

China is a centralized state with a decentralized judicial administration that is largely funded and supervised by local governments. All civil servants in the judicial organs are appointed by local people's congresses. The SPC, not the Ministry of Justice, supervises the judiciary at various levels through a hierar-

---

13 Zhu Jingwen, *Judicial Transformation and Legal Sociology in China* (2008).

14 http://www.stats.gov.cn.

15 Bi Shaofeng, *Rural Legal Clinics: An Educational Handbook* (China Law Press 2010).

chical system of more than 3,000 courts. Politics and law committees (*Zhengfa wei*) of the CCP at various levels are in charge of the direction and cooperation of courts, procuratorates, and police. The committees ensure the CCP's leadership over judicial issues in every tribunal. The public security organs (*gong'an jiguan*) represent the principal police authority, which is responsible for conducting criminal investigations and, with the authorization of procuratorates (except under certain circumstances), arresting suspects. The committee also ensures the CCP's leadership over judicial issues in every tribunal. Lawyers are kept under control by both the legislative and the judicial branches.

Since 2002, anyone with a university degree can take the Unified Judicial Exam (*Tongyi sifa kaoshi*), which is common to all legal professions, including lawyers, judges, and prosecutors. Every year, approximately 300,000 candidates (50 percent of whom are from 11 provinces, although the largest portion are from Beijing and Guangdong) take this competitive exam. Since 2010, the passing rate has been slightly above 20 percent. Among the 90 percent of undergraduates who take the exam, only a minority are law students who specialize in law. However, overall, the number of graduates from law schools or legal institutes in China increased from around 8,000 in 1996 to more than 135,000 in 2010. There are more than 640 "real" law schools around the country, and the legal education market is booming.

In 2002, among the 360,000 candidates who registered to take the exam in order to obtain a Certificate of Legal Practice, the success rate was 8 percent, including a very small proportion of candidates from the remote western regions.

In 1980, the Provisional Law on Lawyering in the PRC defined lawyers as "state legal workers" and law offices as "legal counseling services" (*falü guwenchu*). In 1986, the Chinese National Lawyer's Association was established in Beijing, with branches throughout the country. By 2012, a lawyer was defined as "a professional who legally obtains a lawyer's certificate and provides the society with legal services." The Lawyers Law (*Lüshi fa*), as amended in October 2007, recognized the specificity of the lawyers as a legal profession. However, judges and prosecutors still greatly outnumber lawyers.

Except in the biggest cities and along the coastal provinces, the total number of lawyers per habitant in China is very low. In addition, the distribution of lawyers in China is uneven. In 1996, 100,198 people were "employed as attorneys" (this number refers to all categories of personnel working in a law firm; *lüshi gongzuo renyuan*); in 2011, this number was 204,000.[16] This category can be divided between full-time attorneys (47,879; *zhuanzhi lüshi*), part-time attorneys (20,243; *jianzhi lüshi*), and legal workers (*falü gongzuozhe*). From 1998 to 2006, the number of people employed as "lawyers" increased from 101,220 to 164,516. The number of full-time attorneys increased dramatically (from 51,008 to 122,242), while the number of so-called nonprofessional lawyers (not employed on a full-time basis) decreased from 17,958 to 8,068. In 2002, after

---

16 http://www.stats.gov.cn.

introduction of the Unified Judicial Exam for the professions of lawyers, judges, and procuratorates, the number of nonprofessional lawyers (or legal workers) decreased considerably. A majority of lawyers are now on full-time status and are supposedly fully qualified.

According to Sida Liu and Ethan Michelson's studies on the development of the legal profession in China, the economic and institutional "vulnerabilities" of Chinese lawyers constitute a difficult issue. Lawyers in medium-size cities often have to rely on state judicial agencies to find business and guarantee the annual renewal of their license. Lawyers have to contend with "deadbeat clients who fail to pay their legal fees, exploitative employers who fail to support their professional work and to protect their social security," and institutional actors "who interfere with and obstruct [the lawyers'] work."[17] This situation weakens the role of lawyers in courts and constrains their capacity to represent clients.

China's Judges Law (*Faguan fa*) was adopted in 1997 and amended in 2001 after the establishment of the Unified Judicial Exam. Theoretically and legally, all judges in China have passed the exam. Their status is somewhat ambiguous: they are called "judge" (*faguan*) in everyday life and "adjudicator" (*shenpanyuan*) in court. Article 2 of the Judges Law states that "judges are the judicial personnel who exercise the judicial authority of the State." They shall "faithfully implement the constitution and laws, and serve the people whole-heartedly" (Article 3). The functions and duties of judges in China are different from those of their counterparts in the West; Chinese judges must "take part in a trial as a member of a collegial panel or try a case alone according to law" as well as perform all other functions and duties as provided by law (Article 5). In addition, they must accept legal supervision and "supervision by the masses" (Article 7).

In 1999, the SPC published its first guiding instrument for enhancing the judiciary: the Five-Year Reform Program for People's Courts. This document aimed to enhance the efficiency and fairness of adjudication by reforming the courts' "inquisitorial" trial pattern to a more "adversarial" trial pattern. Since then, the main slogan of the SPC has been "judicial efficiency and judicial fairness" (*sifa xiaolü yu sifa gongzheng*). In 2004, *Measures on the Management of the Publication of Judgment Documents* and *Several Opinions of the Supreme People's Court on Strengthening the Work on Judicial Openness in People's Courts* were published, completing the transition.

A second Five-Year Reform Program for People's Courts (2004–08) stressed the importance of bringing greater professionalism and integrity to the judiciary. The reform program called for courts to begin "exploring within a certain geographic area the implementation of a system of uniform recruitment and

---

17 *See* Ethan Michelson & Sida Liu, *What Do Chinese Lawyers Want? Political Values and Legal Practice* (Brookings Institution 2010), available at http://www.indiana.edu/~emsoc/Publications/Chapter14_Michelson_Liu.pdf. *See* also local reports such as those found at http://www.fabang.com/a/20111207/460510.html.

uniform assignment of judges for duties in the basic-level courts." The SPC also explored the establishment of guaranteed national funding for local courts by inserting provisions in central and provincial government budgets. Conflict of governance (budget, nomination, management, and judicial independence) between central and local judicial authorities remains a subject of concern for some judicial authorities.

A network of modern courts, inspired by Western architectural styles (Greek temple or US Supreme Court–style), affects citizens' and litigants' perception of the judiciary. To that end, the SPC developed a policy of erecting new court buildings and investing in hardware and access to justice. Many older court buildings have been demolished. In 2007, the litigation fees' management system was reformed, separating the collection of litigation fees from courts' expenditures. Litigation fees are no longer directly handed to courts but are paid instead by litigants through designated banks that are often directly located within the courts. In April 2007, a regulation from the State Council (the Chinese government) unified charging standards and promoted lower litigation fees for civil and administrative disputes.

This regulation to reduce litigation fees "to diminish ordinary people's burden and facilitate access to justice" had a direct and immediate impact on the Chinese courts' source of income.[18] In September 2007, an article in the *Legal Daily* explained that courts lost an average of 53.55 percent of their revenues due to this change. Consequently, 2.4 billion renminbi was allocated to compensate local tribunals for the losses in budgets. In 2008 and 2009, the situation improved. Most courts have received partial or total compensation for losses and have implemented the regulation forbidding arbitrary fees.

In March 2009, the SPC promulgated a third Five-Year Program for the Reform of People's Courts (2009–13), initiating a new round of court modernization. This program was formulated with a view to maintaining social fairness and justice and satisfying the new demands and new expectations of the general public regarding the judiciary. Much attention was paid to aspects of "judicial efficiency" such as the cost and speed of judicial procedures as well as the enforcement of judicial decisions. These qualities are crucial in the effort to build trust and confidence among litigants.

Since the mid-2000s, mediation has been given great significance by the Chinese Communist Party and therefore by all judicial organs. In 2009, the SPC, in its annual *Report on the Work of People's Courts*, put forward the policy of mediation first, followed by a combination of mediation and adjudication. The same year, the SPC promulgated the *Opinion on the Establishment*

---

18 *See* also the *Report on the Implementation of the Central and Local Budgets for 2006 and on the Draft Central and Local Budgets for 2007*, 9 (Ministry of Finance 2007), which states that in 2006, the central authorities supported the strengthening of government authority at the county and township levels. Funds were set aside in the central budget in 2006 to help lower-level procuratorial, judicial, and public security departments to improve conditions for processing cases. Available at http://www.chinaview.cn.

and Improvement of Dispute-Settlement Mechanisms with Coordination between Litigious and Non-Litigious Means. This opinion was a major step in the promotion of the development of multiple dispute-settlement mechanisms, including arbitration and administrative and civil mediation, to avoid the danger of forced, or imposed mediation.

In June 2012, the SPC revealed a detailed *Working Guide to Improve Judicial Efficiency* (*Tigaosifa xiaolu gongzuo zhinan*). The guide's emphasis is on the quality and the effectiveness of justice to enhance judicial efficiency, which refers to a sense of providing accessible, professional, and fair dispute-settlement services. This implies incentive mechanisms for judges, the simplification of complicated dispute settlement procedures, the professionalization of the judicial management system, and the reinforcement of a variety of dispute resolution mechanisms, including some alternative or nonlitigation procedures. The guide is the product of an innovative international collaboration with the European Union, the UN Development Programme (UNDP), and the Supreme People's Court. It will provide a benchmark for local courts to use to evaluate their efficiency.[19]

China has stated its intention to undertake certain reforms, such as promoting open, publicly accessible courtroom proceedings, more media interaction and public outreach, and more public access to written judgments including judges' rationale.

Thus far, these reforms have been uneven and limited in terms of both their substance and their geographic scope. Although several reforms have been designed to strengthen the professionalism of the judiciary and to address judicial corruption and build public confidence, such as the passage of an ethics code for judges, they still need to be institutionalized and fairly, uniformly, and effectively enforced.

The improvement of the "hardware" of the legal and judicial systems has largely benefited plaintiffs and citizens in China. Civil justice in China has been overhauled. A broad range of reforms have been adopted, covering institutional as well as procedural aspects. Although the general context is different, the global aim of the reforms has been much the same as elsewhere in Europe where civil justice is being reformed: to ensure fair justice with greater efficiency in terms of both time and costs, in response to an increasing demand from the public at large.

The Status of Human Rights vs Human Rights in Action

In the late 1980s, the term *fazhi* (legal system) was gradually abandoned in favor of its homonym *fazhi* (rule of law), which implies the necessity of the establishment of a formal system to guarantee people's rights and to check governmental power. In December 1999, a notion similar to the concept of

---

19 *See* Stéphanie Balme, *Review of Efforts to Improve Judicial Efficiency and Costs* (Governance for Equitable Development Aug. 2012).

rule of law but not yet due process was incorporated into China's constitution. Article 5 states:

> No law or administrative or local rule and regulation shall contravene the constitution. All state organs, the armed forces, all political parties and public organizations and all enterprises and undertakings must abide by the constitution and the law. All acts in violation of the constitution and the law must be investigated. No organization or individual may enjoy the privilege of being above the constitution and the law.

Another major step toward reforming the post-Mao state is the progressive integration of human rights into Chinese law.

Until the 1980s, human rights discourses were ignored or attacked. Today, Marxist critics of human rights still exist among some CCP leaders who continue to advocate historical materialism, deny the notion of *jus naturalism*, emphasize collective rights over individual rights, advocate equality rather than liberty, and prefer "real rights" (the right of subsistence, for example) over so-called formal rights, such as freedom of expression.

However, Beijing has signed—if not ratified—most of the existing international treaties or conventions related to human rights, including the International Convention on the Elimination of All Forms of Racial Discrimination (March 1966), the Convention on the Elimination of All Forms of Discrimination against Women (December 1979), the International Convention against Torture and Other Cruel, Inhuman or Degrading Treatment or Punishment (of December 1984; although China does not yet recognize the competence of the committee against torture); the Convention on the Rights of the Child (November 1989), the International Covenant on Economic, Social, and Cultural Rights (ICESC; 1997) and the International Covenant on Civil and Political Rights (ICCPR; 1998).

In 1991, the Chinese government published its first white paper on human rights. In 2009, a national action plan on human rights was officially launched, demonstrating a general yet genuine recognition of the morality of human rights as described by Michael Perry: "each and every born human being has inherent dignity which is inviolable."[20]

The 1996 Criminal Procedure Law (CPL) recognizes the "principle of presumption of innocence" (*wuzui tuiding)* of innocence without adopting the actual words, which are similar to those found in Article 11 of the Universal Declaration of Human Rights.[21] Article 162(3) of the 1996 CPL states that, "if

---

20 Michael J. Perry, *Toward a Theory of Human Rights* (Cambridge U. Press 2006).

21 According to the law, everyone charged with a penal offense has the right to be presumed innocent until proved guilty in a public trial at which he or she has had all the guarantees necessary for his or her defense. Stéphanie Balme, *La justice pénale en Chine: Son évolution et son avenir; Analyse du projet 2011 de réformes de la Loi de procédure pénale* (Institut des Hautes Etudes sur la Justice 2012); available at http://www.ihej.org/la-justice-penale-en-chine-son-evolution-et-son-avenir/.

the evidence is insufficient and thus the defendant cannot be found guilty, he/she shall be pronounced innocent accordingly on account of the fact that the evidence is insufficient and the accusation unfounded."

The right to life and the protection against cruel, inhuman, and degrading punishments (International Covenant on Civil and Political Rights, Article 6, paragraph 1) restricts the use of the death penalty to the most serious crimes. China's Criminal Law, Article 40, stipulates: "the death penalty should only be applied to criminals who have committed extremely serious crimes and be restricted and excluded for juveniles, pregnant women, mothers and the insane." A penalty of death must be based on clear and convincing evidence, leaving no room for other explanations of the facts.

The maximum term for concurrently applied sentences was raised from 20 to 25 years (Article 69), and individuals originally sentenced to life imprisonment will be obliged to serve longer prison terms before they can be released through sentence reduction (Article 81). The most serious offenders will not be offered sentence reduction. However, the law requires lenient treatment of offenders aged 75 and older, and judges have been given more specific instructions about how "lenient punishment" should be applied in sentencing (Articles 17 and 49). Additionally, in 2010, 13 crimes (among a total of 68) were removed from death penalty eligibility under criminal law.

The official contestation, in the 1990s—following the Tiananmen Square incident—of the principle of the universality of human rights came not so much from a supposed Confucian tradition, but rather from a Marxist critique. Human rights still are sometimes considered a threat to the political status quo. Finally, this contestation is paradoxically growing at a time when a new generation of human rights (e.g., animal rights and rights to reputation) are emerging in China. Both a developing country and an emerging power, Chinese authorities question the path of contemporary developed societies on human rights and the rule of law. However, it seems that China's authorities also do not want their performance to be subjected to international scrutiny.

The diversity of voices in China makes the judicial and legal systems more difficult to change now than immediately after the Cultural Revolution. Open debates, the vitality of public opinion, reflections on publicized trials, and judicial cases are also assets as China's rule of law faces new challenges.

Rule of Law in China: Current Challenges and Future Perspectives

Although the framework of law that has evolved since the end of the Cultural Revolution provides a foundation for rule of law, a more determined and sustained effort is necessary to reform China's legal regime in depth.

Experts observed a significant regression of the rule of law in the 2000s, under the guise of preserving social harmony. Wang Shengjun, the president of the SPC, publicly advocated the policy of the "three supremes": first, the supremacy of the party, then of the people, and finally of the constitution and the law. The many legal and judicial challenges faced by China can be summarized by the increasingly urgent need to create a systematic legal framework and a hierarchy of norms respectful of both collective and individual rights. Areas of potential reform include legal sources, legal writing and reasoning, due process, the stability of legal institutions, the predictability of the judicial process, and legal certainty.

Chinese judges are civil servants with no real power. The Ministry of Public Security, the principal police authority, holds the power to conduct investigations and arrest suspects in criminal cases; a Politics and Law Committee (*Zhengfa wei*) is in charge of the direction and cooperation of people's courts, people's procuratorates, and the police. The committee also ensures the CCP's leadership over judicial issues in every tribunal. Lawyers are kept under strict control by both the legislative and the executive branches.

Conflicts of Norms

After more than three decades of reforms, China's legal developments are not immune from defects; some are serious, such as a lack of hierarchy of norms and inconsistency among rules, the absence of a transparent and comprehensive constitutional review system (*weixian shencha*), and a lack of harmonization of law and judgments. Also, the CCP charter and regulations are de facto full-fledged laws. What, then, is China's *grundnorm*?

To show the complexity of the situation in China, this section focuses on the evolution of three domains of law: criminal procedure, property, and antidiscrimination. In criminal procedure and property law, abuses and legal uncertainty are mainly a consequence of unlawful behaviors, which are facilitated by the vagueness and ambiguities of the law. In antidiscrimination regulations, legal discrimination leads to behavioral abuses against the basic principles of rule of law.

The Criminal Procedure Law (CPL; 1996) and its amendments (2012) typify how the inconsistencies among laws at different levels generate an opposition to judicial discretion and foster a sense of arbitrariness. Ambiguities of and inconsistences among legal norms affect their credibility and reveal that the court system, which is not even charged with interpreting the law, is not a powerful institution. Chinese courts play very few roles in supervising the police during criminal investigations. Another example: the system of rehabilitation through labor (RTL) (*laojiao*) is an administrative sanction taken by the police and the RTL committee without interference from the procuratorate or the tribunal. Under the RTL system, a person can be deprived of liberty without having interacted with any judicial authority.

Although the CPL was revised in 2012, many ambiguities remain both with and within the Lawyers Law. Amended in October 2007, the Lawyers Law allows lawyers to meet with clients without the presence of police officers. Lawyers have an obligation of confidentiality but are limited by the fact that theycannot keep certain information secret (Article 38 of the Lawyers Law). In addition, a lawyer can be condemned if he or she influences a client not to confess to a crime (Article 38 of the CPL). In China, the absence of a guarantee to the right to a fair trial is a serious issue, especially because the right to remain silent is not clearly established.

The CPL stipulates that evidence obtained through torture cannot be used as grounds for a verdict. However, the law emphasizes that accused persons must give "truthful answers" (*rushi huida*) and that "resistance to answer will be treated severely" (*kangju congya*). The March 2012 revision of the CPL exhibits a punitive philosophy, mainly based on the traditional Marxist notion of crime, and the goal of maintaining public order. (There are more than 60 references to the terms "raison d'Etat" or "state secrets" in the revision.) A lack of empowerment by the judges within the judicial system, in contradistinction to the role played by the public security forces, emphasizes the effectiveness of exceptional police procedures on ordinary judicial procedures.

Legal guarantee of ownership rights is a fundamental characteristic of a state that has rule of law. China's legal system does not provide legal certainty in this regard for the following reasons: the system of ownership is extremely complex in China and public ownership often trumps private ownership; the lack of legal quality (precise rules) leads to legal uncertainty; and the judicial system does not have a strong authority to regulate chaotic legal norms.

In 1949, civil codes enacted under the previous, Nationalist, regime were abolished. Land reform policies in 1950 resulted in massive and violent land expropriations and the abolishment of the notion of private property and ownership rights. The land collectivization that took place during the Maoist period led to the replacement of the notion of property rights (*suoyou quan*) with "a system of property" (*suoyou zhi*). After the Cultural Revolution, the abolition of the people's communes allowed a growing recognition of the notion of "real rights," espoused by administrative regulations specifying rules of transfer and the attribution of rights. In 1986, the General Principles of Civil Law (*Minfa tongze*) defined, for the first time since the Kuomintang's codes, the notion of property rights.

The Rural Land Contracting Law of 2002 (*Nongcun tudi chengbao Fa*) clarified the rights and obligations of the rural household and the agricultural collective based on a contractual system (*chengbao zhi*). In 2007, after a decade of consultations and debates, a Property Law was adopted by 96.9 percent of the 2,889 legislators of the NPC, with 53 delegates opposing and 37 abstaining.

In 2004, a constitutional amendment specified that "the lawful private property of citizens is inviolable" (Article 13). Yet, according to the Property Law of 2007, "the state may in the public interest [*gonggong liyi*] expropriate or take over land for its use in accordance with the law and provide compatible compensation [*xiangying buchang*]" (Article 10, paragraph 3). Because the notion of public interest is vague and the judiciary has almost no independent authority, the law does not provide protection or legal certainty to the people whose land is being expropriated.

The legal system has improved in recent years in that access to property rights is now guaranteed. Still, because urban lands belong to the state and rural lands belong to collective organizations, owners' rights are limited when expropriations are deemed justified by public authorities. For rural lands, each farmer must be allocated a land parcel based on a contractual system of 30 to 70 years, depending on the status of the land (cultivated land, forest land, etc.). As for nonrural lands, rights are delegated by the state, which can transfer, use, and exchange the land (the notion of *sûreté* in European systems).

To fight against the many abusive expropriations that took place in China between 1990 and 2010, new local and administrative regulations have been passed, creating a chaotic legal structure. This lack of legal quality has led to increasing legal uncertainty. For example, a Law on Planification of urban and rural zones (Articles 22–26) was enacted in 2007, as was a resolution amending the Land Management Law (*Tudi guanli Fa*). These texts present two major amendments to the existing system: "According to the needs of public interest, the state can expropriate [*zhengshou*] or requisition [*zhengyong*] land and provide adequate compensation." In other words, the state can expropriate collectively owned land for the purposes of national projects such as dams, railroads, and highways through a transfer of land from collective ownership to state ownership, and requisition does not entail a change in ownership. The state can also temporarily lease land from a collective for public benefit, but in theory, it must return the land once the lease is over. These provisions include the rights to use and profit from contracted land, to profit from the transmission of the land's management authority, and to organize and manage one's own production.

Judges review disputes on compensation for expropriated land based on the 2007 Administrative Law on Urban Land and Real Estate Property. According to Article 45 of that law, only the central government (sometimes in coordination with provincial governments) can expropriate lands with the precondition of obtaining a "demolishing license."[22] Lands can be expropriated only for public service construction, not for commercial use, and transformation of farmlands into "industrial land" is limited. However, the distinction is primarily administrative, and courts seldom take expropriation cases. In most cases, local governments decide expropriations.

Persistence of Legal Discrimination

When he was working as a consultant to the World Bank on China's labor legislation in the late 1990s, Ronald Brown noticed a job advertisement that

---

22 Li Bin, *Droit de la Propriété et Expropriation en Droit Chinois* (Université Paris I 2010).

read, "Seeking an office clerk. Female, decent height and appearance. 'All five facial organs must be in the right place' [*wu guan duanzheng*]."[23] In China, discrimination based on physical appearance is common.[24] Although general antidiscrimination provisions are included in various laws, administrative regulations and local regulations remain discriminatory.[25]

The 1982 constitution recognizes that "all citizens are equal before the law" (Article 33). Women enjoy equal rights with men in all spheres of life—political, economic, cultural, and social—including family life (guaranteed by Article 48 of the constitution and the 2005 Law on the Protection of the Rights and Interests of Women). The Labor Law of 1995 states that employees must not be discriminated against on the basis of nationality, gender, or religious belief (Article 12). The 1991 Disabled Persons Protection Law, amended in 2008, protects "the lawful rights and interests of people with disabilities."

Professor Li Dun, a scholar at the Chinese Academy of Social Sciences, showed that the Civil Servants Recruitment Health Check-Up Standard (*Gongwuyuan pinyong tijian biaozhun*) issued by the Ministry of Health and the Ministry of Human Resources and Social Security was unconstitutional.[26] This "standard" prevents people with various physical conditions, including HIV/AIDS, from taking civil service jobs. It also violates many norms that have superior legal authority, including the Employment Promotion Law and the International Labor Organization Convention on Nondiscrimination in Employment.

Although the number of lawsuits against discrimination is increasing, there is little sanction for violations. The first landmark case was that of Zhang Xianzhu in 2002. Zhang was a 25-year-old college graduate who received the highest score on the Wuhu city (Anhui Province) civil service qualification exam but was rejected by the civil service because he tested positive for the hepatitis B virus (HBV). Zhang filed an administrative suit against the local personnel bureau alleging that the rejection of HBV carriers was a discriminatory practice, which violated his fundamental constitutional rights. On April 2, 2003, the Wuhu court issued its judgment, affirming the validity of the government regulation while ruling that the decision by the defendant to refuse to

---

23 Ronald Brown, *China's Employment Discrimination Laws during Economic Transition*, 19 Columbia J. Asian L. 361 (Spring 2006).

24 *Investigation Report on Hepatitis B Discrimination in China's Higher Education System* (Oct. 2008) by the Yirenping Center (a Chinese NGO operating in Beijing), and *Investigation Report on Hepatitis B Discrimination in Multinational Corporations Based in China* (Feb. 2009).

25 For further information, *see Legal Protection against Employment Discrimination Handbook* (Sep. 2007), and *Investigation Report on Employment Discrimination in Shenzhen* (May 2010). *See* also Lin Yanling ed., *Report on Non-discrimination in Employment: Legal Systems and Practices in Asia* (Social Sciences Academic Press 2010).

26 Professor Li Dun was invited by the Ministry of Health to participate in the drafting of *The Regulations on HIV Prevention and Treatment*. Interview with the author.

hire the plaintiff based on his HBV status lacked sufficient evidence. The court refused to grant Zhang's request to enter the civil service on the ground that the recruitment period was over. However, the court failed to invalidate the discriminatory government regulation on constitutional grounds. A decade later, the judicial decision has not been enforced, but the trend in recent regulations regarding public hiring and university admission has mandated that physical tests for employment screening not include testing for HBV.

A Weak Constitutional System

In China, the lack of respect for the constitution is explained by the de facto absence of a hierarchy of norms (despite a clear theoretical definition of the "sources of the law" [*fa yuan*]), resulting in confusion both in the organization and in the legal texts, administrative regulations, and decrees. It can also be explained by the lack of a clear conception of the position of the constitution in the hierarchy of the normative system, despite unambiguous terms used to designate it, such as the "fundamental law" (*genben dafa*) or the "mother of all laws" *(mufa)*. The constitution in truth is an abstract political document remote from people's daily life and social operation.

The government and the CCP have a long history of using policy rather than law to steer social development. Every change or amendment of the constitution is initiated by CCP policy changes. This practice results in paying lip service to the constitution and marginalizing its legal function. The constitution then serves as a footnote to party policy and governmental practice. There are numerous examples of liberties taken with the text of the constitution and of legal deadlock arising from social complexity and confusion of the legal system due to the absense of consensus on the effective sources of the law.

The lack of respect for the constitution testifies to the historical lack of respect for the hierarchy of norms in general, due to their nonexistence in both practical and conceptual terms. However, since the Law on Legislation in 2000 established a principle of unity of the legislative system and initiated a hierarchy of norms, the constitution is theoretically at its highest position. The next challenge lies in the political courage of the government and the CCP to respect the constitution not only in words but in action.[27] Another means is to entrust the Supreme People's Court with a role that is neither recognized in the political system as a whole nor compatible with its present organization, given that the existing system is one of an a posteriori and legislative review of the constitution through the work of the National People's Congress.

While debate on constitutionalism is very rich, it has not yet been followed by any official call for open debate or adoption. Probably in May 2004, the Law and Regulation Filing Office (*Fagui shencha bei'an shi*) was created

27 *See* Cai Dingjian & Wang Chenguang, *China's Journey toward the Rule of Law: Legal Reform, 1978–2008* (Brill 2010).

within the Commission for Legal Affairs (*Fazhi gongzuo weiyuanhui*) of the Standing Committee of the NPC. Constitutional experts have been critical of this new body whose activities and structure have remained secret.

Chinese scholars hold the view that a legal apparatus is a common good through which citizens and organizations may achieve justice. They also believe in the theoretical supremacy of the constitution as a means to effectively check and control governmental and political power by establishing a constitutional review system. The Western concept of constitutionalism is accepted academically but the political conception of a constitution as a substantive legal norm is not.

Indeed, in Western rule of law democracies, the constitutionality of the law is intended to give rise to precise and rigorous examination. The constitutionality of the law is a matter of legal certainty and judicial consistency, of the practical reliability of legislative arrangements, and of democratic guarantees.

Addressing the Role of Judges within the Judicial System

Since 2010, judicial reform in China has been more piecemeal than systemic. It also has been oriented more toward access to justice for citizens than toward reform of the system and its actors. As in the rest of the world, litigants in China ask for much better legal services and have higher expectations than in the past. Litigants, via social networks, demand that their disputes be handled with greater transparency and uniformity in applying substantive and procedure law. The growing call in China that alternative dispute resolutions and mediation be viewed as intertwined with formal litigation procedures expresses a movement toward "informalizing" legal institutions.

In this context, the legal profession faces many challenges in China. One is uneven geographical distribution: in 2011, there were more lawyers in Shanghai than in the whole of Shaanxi Province, and more lawyers in the city of Shenzhen than in Fujian Province. In 2010, there were 23,000 lawyers in Beijing, out of a total estimated 140,000 lawyers nationwide.[28] Other problems include an uneven level of professionalization and an accompanying lack of specialization (the number of defense lawyers trained every year in the country is low); an absence of legal recognition of the unique capacity of lawyers to act as agents *ad litem*; and an inadequate representation of lawyers in courts compared to the number of judges and procuratorates. Also, lawyers' fees remain far too high for most litigants.

Many non-lawyer legal experts act as agents *ad litem* in litigation procedures and lawsuits in China. Experts have shown that in China, lawyers face competition from a variety of alternative legal service providers, includ-

---

28 Beijing Bar Association, interviews with the author in January and May 2012.

ing legal workers at grassroots levels and other practitioners, presenting a challenge to the government on how to regulate these competing groups.[29]

Lack of trust and credibility regarding the court system are among the most pressing issues the government faces. It is important to build trust among judges and all the actors involved in courts' management; to remain flexible with planned new reforms; and to create mechanisms for institutionalizing changes and build the conditions for achieving sustainable reforms within the judiciary.[30]

One of the main weaknesses of the Chinese judiciary system is the extremely decentralized administration of a centralized legal system where national laws tend to be abstract and local specificities are given short shrift.

The role of people's courts in the harmonization and convergence (if not unification) of legal practices must be encouraged. The main goal is to create better cooperation between and consistency of the lawmaking and judicial-making process to achieve a greater uniformity in the application of law and to protect citizens. People's courts should ensure that rules are interpreted consistently throughout the country. This interpretation can be achieved only if courts are given real power and a specific status and specific tasks within the judicial system.

Both legal harmonization and consistency of law enforcement require that the judicial body play both legal and moral roles. Reforms need to be oriented toward the reform of the judges' status.

Conclusion

During recent decades, the Chinese legal system has undergone a fascinating transformation from barely any law to a relatively comprehensive and complicated network of laws and norms. The foundations of the legal-rational state are undergoing rapid change. The law has been not only an instrument of post-socialist transition, social control, and governance but also a means of social transition and market reform in China. The concept of law is perceived as a modern means of regulation, a tool in the service of this objective.

In 30 years, the rule of law rhetoric in China has moved from a concept focused on economic considerations (the Deng Xiaoping era) to one focused on maintaining stability within society and the control of the CCP (during the Hu Jintao–Wen Jiabao era). Yet, the rapid legal development cannot hide the defects in China's legal system. Besides those mentioned above, the biggest

---

29 *See* Terence Halliday, Ethan Michelson, & Sida Liu, *China's Emerging Middle Class: Beyond Economic Transformation*, ch. 14 (Cheng Li ed., Brookings Institution Press 2010).

30 *See* Randall Peerenboom, *Economic and Social Rights: The Role of Courts in China* (Oct. 17, 2010), available at http://ssrn.com/abstract=http://papers.ssrn.com/sol3/papers.cfm?abstract_id=1693613.

problem is that the notion of due process of law is underdeveloped because of the lack of constitutional review and the low predictability of legal outcomes.

Despite ideological transformations, social changes, and radical economic reforms, the world's second-biggest economy is not yet governed by the rule of law. Many observers in and outside China question whether rule of law is necessary for a rich, emerging country such as China. The lack of legal certainty affects leadership succession processes as well as governance on a large scale and confidence in business. Demands for rule of law changes by public and legal professionals have been unprecedented.

What China can achieve depends on how the legal system develops and whether the concept of the rule of law can be translated into judicial practices. What China can achieve depends largely on what China wants.

Achieving Development through Innovative Constitutionalism

A China Story

ZHENMIN WANG AND YUAN TAO

Constitutions are created to balance political powers, to regulate the behavior of political institutions and individuals, and to protect citizens' rights. The interplay between constitutionalism and reality constantly changes, with the evolution of a constitution the most obvious proof of that transformation. Traditionally, constitutionalism has been correlated with separation of powers, limited government, and democracy. Today, however, a constitution is no longer seen as a purely political and legal document; it is also viewed as a document incorporating guiding economic principles, and growing attention is being given to the economic functions of a constitution and how constitutions might be used to promote economic development. Most transitional and developing nations face the challenge of proper allocation of available economic and financial resources as well as the compatibility of economic decisions with the constitutional framework and the limitations created by that framework. The economic function of the constitution can be used to narrow the gap between practical enforcement of the economic, social, and political rights granted by the constitution and the economic policy, budget legislation, and administrative policies conducted by the national government.

Constitutions in the 18th and 19th centuries were purely political documents. They had little to do with economy. The first constitution to introduce economic provisions was the 1918 Weimar Constitution of Germany. As constitutions have evolved, some are more focused on citizens' rights vis-à-vis the government and private property ownership, while others provide for both political and economic affairs in a comprehensive fashion. A key challenge for modern constitutionalists, especially in developing countries, is how to use constitutional provisions to facilitate economic advancement and the development of a market economy.

If a constitution can be defined as a framework of fundamental rules and principles according to which a state is governed, the locus of constitutionalism lies at the intersection of law and politics. Every theory of constitutionalism must take both law and policy into account and apply them in a way that is open to country-specific variations. The purpose of a constitution should be multifold: the balanced and rational allocation of governmental powers among various branches and levels; the assurance that government behavior is subject to supervision and constraints; the obligation that government agencies or executive officials, whether appointed or elected, be bound by the constitution, abstain from abuse of power and corruption, and be held accountable to the people; and the protection of basic human rights and freedom.

Based on this definition of a constitution, economic constitutionalism encompasses and addresses several issues: first, what economic freedoms and rights can the constitution provide for the people; second, to what extent may the government intervene in economic affairs; and third, where does the boundary lie for government intervention in the economic arena—in other words, how does the government redistribute resources and social wealth among members of the society.

The evolution of China's constitution is an example of the changing and multifaceted nature of economic constitutionalism. The first National People's Congress (NPC) adopted China's first constitution in 1954. In 1975, the constitution was completely revised to become the second constitution. Three years later, it was rewritten and adopted as the 1978 constitution. In 1980, the Chinese authorities established the high-profile Constitution Revising Committee with the mandate to thoroughly review the 1978 constitution and make a new one. After two years' consultation and deliberation, the new constitution was passed by the fifth NPC in 1982. The 1982 constitution has been amended four times: in 1988, 1993, 1999, and 2004. Most of the amendments are related to economic freedoms, especially the constitutional and legal status of private economy. As such, not only is the 1982 constitution, and its amendments, a document for legal and political affairs, but it also provides a foundation for economic development and economic justice.

The 1982 constitution was adopted shortly after Deng Xiaoping took power and initiated China's "opening and reform" policy. Law played a vital role in Deng's administration as he sought to provide greater institutional order to support China's development. The 1982 constitution puts the constitution above all organizations in the country, including the Communist Party of China (CPC). Post-Deng leaders have modified the constitution through amendment, rather than replacement, preserving the continuity of economic reform ideology ushered in by Deng. Amendments have been used to constitutionalize ideological landmarks of unfolding economic developments. For example, the constitution was revised in 1988 to make reference to a private sector to complement the "socialist public economy." The 1993 amendments added the phrase "socialism with Chinese characteristics" to the preamble and introduced the "socialist market economy," thus incorporating Deng's economic theory into the document. A reference to the recently deceased Deng was added to the preamble in 1999. The constitution was amended in 2004 to guarantee private property rights and provide for compensation for expropriated land, an important signal for both foreign investors and China's own business sector. In addition, in keeping with the tradition of each Chinese leader leaving his imprint on the constitution, President Jiang Zemin introduced his theory of the "three represents" into the preamble. This provided ideological coverage for inclusion of the business class ("bourgeoisie").

China has been the fastest-growing major economy in the world for 30 years, with an average annual growth rate above 10 percent. By 2012, as the second-largest economy in the world, China could claim that per capita income had grown at an average annual rate of more than 8 percent over the previous three decades, increasing from 379 yuan, or US$44.6, in 1978 to about US$5,184 (US$8,394 purchasing power parity, or PPP) in 2011, according to the International Monetary Fund (IMF).[1] According to the World Bank, China's economic growth fueled a decline in the poverty rate from 85 percent in 1981 to 16 percent in 2005 (poverty being defined in 2005 as the number of people living on less than US$1.25 per day).[2]

There are many reasons for such an economic achievement, and the constitution and its amendments have played a crucial role in this development. This chapter examines how a developing country such as China made such remarkable progress by enacting a new constitutional system, in particular, a new economic constitutionalism. This chapter shows how China's economy exemplifies the development of a more traditional constitution into one that reflects many of the advantages of economic constitutionalism. The following pages trace China's constitutional history to show this development, noting major changes that reflect innovative policies in China's particular historical context.

The Basic Economic System Established by the 1982 Constitution

The political revolution that aimed to build China into a socialist country resulted in the founding of the People's Republic of China in 1949. However, the 1954 constitution characterized the country as "neodemocratic" because private ownership and property rights were allowed to exist and were in fact protected. But the 1954 constitution was short-lived—it was cast aside for years, including during the 10-year "Cultural Revolution" (1966–76).

Although socialist reform was completed in the late 1950s, the constitution remained unchanged until 1975. Reflecting the ultra-leftist ideology of the Cultural Revolution, the 1975 constitution declared that China was a "pure socialist country." The constitutional protection of private economy that appeared in the 1954 constitution was abolished. The 1975 constitution incorporates the protection of public ownership, eliminating all elements of private economy.

As a result of the paradigm shift that took place after the Cultural Revolution, during the 1982 constitution-making process, a main consideration was how to build an economy-friendly constitutional system and establish a rational economic system. In its preamble, the 1982 constitution stipulates "the basic task of the nation in the years to come is to concentrate its effort on [socialist] modernization."

---

1 http://en.wikipedia.org/wiki/Economy_of_the_People%27s_Republic_of_China.

2 Shauna Chen & Martin Ravallion, *"The Developing World Is Poorer than We Thought, but No Less Successful in the Fight against Poverty* (World Bank Aug. 2008).

Public Ownership of the Means of Production and Distribution Principles

Article 6 of the 1982 constitution stipulates that "the basis of the socialist economic system of the People's Republic of China is socialist public ownership of the means of production, namely, ownership by the whole people and collective ownership by the working people."

Article 6 also provides for distribution principles: the system of socialist public ownership supersedes the system of exploitation of person by person; it applies the principles of "from each according to his ability" and "to each according to his work."

There are two forms of socialist public ownership mandated in the 1982 constitution. First, ownership by the whole people: Article 7 states that "the state economy is the sector of socialist economy under ownership by the whole people; it is the leading force in the national economy. The state ensures the consolidation and growth of the state economy." Second, collective ownership by the "working people": Article 8 provides that

> rural people's communes, agricultural producers' co-operatives, and other forms of cooperative economy such as producers' supply and marketing, credit and consumers co-operatives, belong to the sector of socialist economy under collective ownership by the working people. Working people who are members of rural economic collectives have the right, within the limits prescribed by law, to farm private plots of cropland and hilly land, engage in household sideline production and raise privately owned livestock. The various forms of co-operative economy in cities and towns, such as those in the handicraft, industrial, building, transport, commercial and service trades, all belong to the sector of socialist economy under collective ownership by the working people. The State protects the lawful rights and interests of the urban and rural economic collectives and encourages, guides and helps the growth of the collective economy.

The 1982 constitution allows for the individual economy of urban and rural working people, but only as a complement to the socialist public economy. The official policy toward individual economy is that the state protects the lawful rights and interests of the individual economy. The state guides, helps, and supervises individual economy through administrative control. These provisions stem from the then-prevailing ideology that emphasized "socialist ownership" and tended to marginalize private ownership.

Although the 1982 constitution does not permit Chinese citizens to run private companies, it does permit foreign enterprises, other foreign economic organizations, and individual foreigners to invest in China and to enter into various forms of economic cooperation with Chinese enterprises and other economic organizations in accordance with Chinese law. All foreign enterprises and foreign economic organizations in China, as well as joint ventures with Chinese and foreign investment located in China, must abide by the laws of China. Their lawful rights and interests are protected by the law (Article 18).

Property Rights

According to Article 9 of the 1982 constitution, mineral resources, waters, forests, mountains, grassland, unreclaimed land, beaches, and other natural resources are owned by the state, that is, by the whole people, with the exception of the forests, mountains, grassland, unreclaimed land, and beaches that are owned by collectives in accordance with the law. The state ensures the rational use of natural resources and protects rare animals and plants. The appropriation or damage of natural resources by any organization or individual by whatever means is prohibited. This provision is important for the state to maintain economic stability.

Urban land is owned by the state. Land in rural and suburban areas is owned by collectives, except for those portions that belong to the state in accordance with the law. House sites and private plots of cropland and hilly land are owned by collectives. The state may in the public interest take land over for its use in accordance with the law. No organization or individual may appropriate, buy, sell, or lease land or unlawfully transfer land in other ways. All organizations and individuals who use land must make rational use of the land (Article 10).

The 1982 constitution emphasizes that socialist public property is sacred and inviolable (Article 12). The state protects socialist public property. Appropriation or damage of state or collective property by any organization or individual by whatever means is strictly prohibited.

As for private ownership, Article 13 stipulates that "the state protects the right of citizens to own lawfully earned income, savings, houses, and other lawful property. The state protects by law the right of citizens to inherit private property." Therefore, the 1982 constitution seems to suggest that citizens cannot have large-scale property such as factories or companies.

Management of Economic Affairs

According to the 1982 constitution, China practices economic planning on the basis of socialist public ownership, with a view to a proportionate and coordinated growth of the national economy by balancing economic planning and market regulation. Disruption of the state economic plan by any organization or individual is legally prohibited.

Constitutions in many countries do not stipulate how to manage the economy. Yet, China's constitution has very detailed provisions on economic affairs. For example, Article 14 states that the

> state continuously raises labor productivity, improves economic results and develops the productive forces by enhancing the enthusiasm of the working people, raising the level of their technical skill, disseminating advanced science and technology, improving the systems of economic administration and enterprise operation and management, instituting the socialist system of responsibility in various forms, and improving organization of work. The state practices strict

> economy and combats waste. The state properly apportions accumulation and consumption, pays attention to the interests of the collective and the individual as well as of the state, and, on the basis of expanded production, gradually improves the material and cultural life of the people.

The constitution also provides that state-owned enterprises have decision-making power in operation and management within the limits prescribed by law, on the condition that they respect the centralized leadership of the state and fulfill all their obligations under the state plan. State-owned enterprises practice democratic management through congresses of workers and staff.

Collective economic organizations also enjoy decision-making power in conducting independent economic activities, on the condition that they accept the guidance of the state plan and abide by the relevant laws. Collective economic organizations practice democratic management in accordance with the law, with the entire body of their members electing or removing management and deciding on major issues concerning the operations and management of their community.

Economic Freedoms and Rights

The 1982 constitution provides for a wide range of freedoms and rights related to economic affairs. All citizens are equal before the law. Every citizen enjoys these rights and at the same time must perform the duties prescribed by the constitution and the law (Article 33).

The 1982 constitution also recognizes that the freedom of individual citizens is inviolable. No citizen may be arrested except with the approval or by decision of a people's procuratorate or by decision of a people's court, and arrests must be made by a public security organ. Unlawful deprivation or restriction of a citizen's freedom by detention or other means is prohibited; unlawful search of the person of citizens is also prohibited (Article 37). The individual dignity of citizens is inviolable. Insult, libel, false charge, or frame-up directed against citizens by any means is prohibited (Article 38). The home of a citizen is inviolable. Unlawful search of, or intrusion into, a citizen's home is prohibited (Article 39). The freedom and privacy of correspondence of citizens are protected by law (Article 40).

In addition to the above political rights, citizens have the right as well as the duty to work. Using various channels, the state creates conditions for employment, strengthens labor protection, improves working conditions, and, on the basis of expanded production, increases remuneration for work and social benefits. Work is a duty of every able-bodied citizen. The state provides necessary vocational training to citizens before they are employed (Article 42). Working people have the right to rest (Article 43).

Social security is provided for under the 1982 constitution. The state prescribes the system of retirement for workers and staff in enterprises and undertakings and for functionaries of organs of the state. The livelihood of retired personnel is ensured by the state and society (Article 44). Citizens have the right to material assistance from the state and society when they are old, ill, or disabled (Article 45). Citizens have the duty as well as the right to receive education (Article 46).

Citizens have the freedom to engage in scientific research, literary and artistic creation, and other cultural pursuits. The state encourages and assists creative endeavors conducive to the engagement in education, science, technology, literature, art, and other cultural activities (Article 47).

The exercise by citizens of their freedoms and rights may not infringe upon the interests of the state, society, or the collective, or upon the lawful freedoms and rights of other citizens (Article 51).

Economic Reforms and Constitutional Amendments in 1988, 1993, and 1999

When the constitution was enacted in 1982, China was embarking on large-scale and wide-ranging economic reform. During the pilot phase of the reform, various restrictions were placed on economic autonomy. For example, the original 1982 constitution did not permit citizens to own and run private companies, although it did permit foreign citizens to do so in China. A significant portion of China's economy was still based on the state plan. The restrictions imposed by the constitution became obstacles to economic reform. Since 1988, China has amended the constitution four times, all in the interest of further liberalizing its economy and promoting greater economic freedom.

1988 Constitutional Amendments

On April 12, 1988, the seventh NPC made two constitutional amendments. One concerns private economy. It reads:

> The state permits the private sector of the economy to exist and develop within the limits prescribed by law. The private sector of the economy is a complement to the socialist public economy. The state protects the lawful rights and interests of the private sector of the economy, and exercises guidance, supervision and control over the private sector of the economy.

Thus, owning and operating private businesses is legitimized, whereas some citizens were penalized before 1988 simply for owning a factory that employed seven or more employees. If a private business owner employed six or fewer helpers under the original 1982 constitution, it could fall under the "individual economy," or sole proprietorship, which was protected by Article 11. Therefore, this amendment, which decriminalized private economy, opened the door for the development of a market economy.

The other amendment also relates to economic development. Article 10 was amended from "no organization or individual may appropriate, buy, sell, or lease land or otherwise engage in the transfer of land by unlawful means" to "no organization or individual may appropriate, buy, sell, or otherwise engage in the transfer of land by unlawful means. The right to the use of land may be transferred according to law." This amendment laid out a constitutional foundation for the development of the real estate industry.

1993 Constitutional Amendments

On March 29, 1993, the eighth NPC made more amendments to the 1982 constitution.

One amendment states that "China is at the primary stage of socialism" and introduces "the theory of building socialism with Chinese characteristics." This amendment provides a rationale for promoting a private and market-oriented economy.

A more fundamental change was introduced with another amendment. Article 15 was amended from

> The state practices economic planning on the basis of socialist public ownership. It ensures the proportionate and coordinated growth of the national economy through overall balancing by economic planning and the supplementary role of regulation by the market. Disturbance of the orderly functioning of the social economy or disruption of the State economic plan by any organization or individual is prohibited

to

> the state has put into practice a socialist market economy. The state strengthens formulating economic laws, improves macro adjustment and control and forbids according to law any units or individuals from interfering with the social economic order.

According to this amendment, the economy in China is no longer a planned economy but a market-oriented one, even though many Western countries still do not recognize the market economy status of China.

1999 Constitutional Amendments

On March 15, 1999, China again proposed a sweeping set of constitutional amendments. Seven amendments were passed altogether. Important changes to the economic system include the following.

- Deng Xiaoping theory was incorporated into the constitution as state guidance, in addition to Marxism-Leninism and Mao Zedong thought.
- It was acknowledged that "China will stay in the primary stage of socialism for a long period of time."
- Rule of law was officially introduced for the first time. Article 5 was added: "The People's Republic of China practices ruling the country in accordance with the law and building a socialist country under rule of law."

- Article 6, which covers the economic system, was amended from

> The basis of the socialist economic system of the People's Republic of China is socialist public ownership of the means of production, namely, ownership by the whole people and collective ownership by the working people. . . . The system of socialist public ownership supersedes the system of exploitation of man by man; it applies the principle of "from each according to his ability, to each according to his work."

to

> The basis of the socialist economic system of the People's Republic of China is socialist public ownership of the means of production, namely, ownership by the whole people and collective ownership by the working people. The system of socialist public ownership supersedes the system of exploitation of man by man; it applies the principle of "from each according to his ability, to each according to his work."
>
> . . .
>
> During the primary stage of socialism, the state adheres to the basic economic system with the public ownership remaining dominant and diverse sectors of the economy developing side by side, and to the distribution system with the distribution according to work remaining dominant and the coexistence of a variety of modes of distribution.

- Article 11, on private economy, was amended from

> The individual economy of urban and rural working people, operating within the limits prescribed by law, is a complement to the socialist public economy. The state protects the lawful rights and interests of the individual economy. . . The state guides, helps and supervises the individual economy by exercising administrative control. . . . The state permits the private economy to exist and develop within the limits prescribed by law. The private economy is a complement to the socialist public economy. The state protects the lawful rights and interests of the private economy, and guides, supervises and administers the private economy.

to

> Individual, private, and other nonpublic economies that exist within the limits prescribed by law are major components of the socialist market economy. . . . The state protects the lawful rights and interests of individual and private economies, and guides, supervises, and administers individual and private economies.

Thus, the status of the nonpublic economy was endorsed by official constitutional amendments.

2004 Constitutional Amendments

The 2004 constitutional amendments are significant.

From "Socialism with Chinese Characteristics" to "Chinese-Style Socialism"

In the preamble, "along the road of building socialism with Chinese characteristics" was revised to "along the road of Chinese-style socialism." This seemingly editorial change means that the socialism in China is "made in China," not imported from another country or copied from textbooks. This change has been widely interpreted to mean that the development model in China is unique in nature, neither capitalist nor conventionally socialist. Both capitalist and traditional socialist models have their merits and demerits. In this amendment, China recognizes the value of both systems. How China develops its own model will be based on Chinese circumstances and the current world situation, rather than on transplanting economic systems from other countries.

The Three Represents

In the preamble, "under the guidance of Marxism-Leninism, Mao Zedong thought, and Deng Xiaoping theory" was revised to "under the guidance of Marxism-Leninism, Mao Zedong thought, Deng Xiaoping theory, and the important thought of 'three represents.' "

This change is more than merely political window dressing. Since 1988, when a constitutional amendment first green-lighted private economy, the private sector has undergone substantial development. By 2004, the private sector dominated the local economy in many coastal provinces. Historically, however, according to the constitution, China was a country for workers and farmers, not the bourgeoisie. The Chinese government constitutionally did not represent nonpublic sectors. The "three represents" means that the party and the state (government) must always represent the development trend of China's advanced productive forces, the orientation of China's advanced culture, and the fundamental interests of the majority of the Chinese people. Thus, the Chinese Communist Party and the government also represent the private sector and the business class. According to this amendment, China is not only a country for workers and farmers but also a country for the emerging private sector. This ideology will guide the party and the government for years.

State Compensation for Land Expropriated or Requisitioned

Article 10 was amended from "The state may, in the public interest, requisition land for its use in accordance with the law" to "The state may, in the public interest and in accordance with the provisions of law, expropriate or requisition land for its use and shall make compensation for the land expropriated or requisitioned."

Protection of Lawful Rights and Interests of the Nonpublic Sectors

Article 11 was amended from "the state protects the lawful rights and interests of the individual and private sectors of the economy, and exercises guidance, supervision, and control over individual and the private sectors of the economy" to

> The state protects the lawful rights and interests of the nonpublic sectors of the economy such as the individual and private sectors of the economy. The state encourages, supports, and guides the development of the nonpublic sectors of the economy and, in accordance with law, exercises supervision and control over the nonpublic sectors of the economy.

Citizens' Lawful Private Property Is Inviolable

Article 13 was amended from "The state protects the right of citizens to own lawfully earned income, savings, houses, and other lawful property" and "The state protects according to law the right of citizens to inherit private property" to "Citizens' lawful private property is inviolable"; "The state, in accordance with law, protects the rights of citizens to private property and to its inheritance"; and "The state may, in the public interest and in accordance with law, expropriate or requisition private property for its use and shall make compensation for the private property expropriated or requisitioned."

For the first time, a socialist constitution explicitly provides for the protection of private property.

Social Security System

In 2004, China added to Article 14: "The state establishes a sound social security system compatible with the level of economic development."

Human Rights

China added Article 33: "The state respects and preserves human rights." This is the first time that the Chinese constitution has formally recognized the value of human rights.

Conclusion

The multifarious nature of constitutionalism has inspired different understandings of the meaning of "constitutionalism." Adding to this confusion is the inevitable disparity between what is contained in the text of a constitution and how those provisions are implemented. By all accounts, however, progressive economic constitutionalism has contributed to China's change in one generation from a poverty-stricken country to one of the world's largest economies. While China has been learning from the rest of the world, it has established its own way of development based on its unique circumstances.

China's experience shows that constitutional changes and economic reforms are intertwined and that they should be coordinated in a gradual and pragmatic manner. It took many years for China to recognize and accept concepts such as private economy, market economy, private property rights, human rights, and rule of law. There is no statically ideal constitution in any dynamically changing society; constitutionalism does not mean that there must be a perfect constitution before its practice. Perhaps there is no perfect constitution—constitutional development is a never-ending process.

Ultimately, a constitution resides in the particular historical and circumstantial settings of its country. One country can draw experiences from other countries, but it is impossible to transplant a constitutional system completely.

To achieve national modernization, democracy alone is not adequate; it must be governed by constitutionalism and rule of law. The presence or absence of constitutionalism and rule of law is crucial to the success or failure of democracy. The development of democracy and constitutionalism can be categorized into two models: the success of the British-American model lies in the establishment of constitutionalism and rule of law in the first place, followed by democracy under a ready and stable constitutional and legal framework; while the French model aimed to introduce full democracy first and establish constitutionalism and rule of law later. Either way, to emphasize constitutionalism does not mean to ignore the development of democracy, or vice versa. A synergetic coordination of constitutionalism and rule of law is the ultimate goal for China.

The past and current financial crises have proved that a free market economy is not omnipotent. Government involvement and redistribution of resources and social wealth are not always counterproductive. Early constitutions in Western countries established a completely free market economy system, which was suspicious and hostile toward government intervention. As the recent crisis has shown, however, a modern constitution should give the government reasonable powers to regulate the market economy and allocate social resources. This has nothing to do with ideology—it is a matter of distributive justice and social administration.

Daniel Webster wrote, "One country, one constitution, one destiny."[3] To a great extent, the nature of a country's constitution determines the destiny of the country. From the Chinese legal perspective, a constitution not only reflects the country's economic base but also contributes to the economic base. As such, the constitution in China is not only the supreme law of the state but also an active social, economic, and political program for social transformation and development.

---

3 From a speech of March 15, 1837; reported in Edward Everett ed., *The Works of Daniel Webster* 349 (Little, Brown 1853).

The Role of Laws and Institutions in Expanding Women's Voice, Agency, and Empowerment

JENI KLUGMAN AND SARAH TWIGG

"Voice, agency, and empowerment" refers to the ability of individuals and groups to make effective choices. Across all countries, the ability of women and men to exercise voice and agency differs—and women are usually at a disadvantage. The *World Development Report 2012: Gender Equality and Development* (WDR 2012)[1] highlights the vital importance of women's voice and agency in both the household and society in general. This report—a landmark for the World Bank because it recognizes both the intrinsic and instrumental values of women's voice, agency, and empowerment—identifies shrinking gender differences in voice and agency as a policy priority for future action.

Voice, agency, and empowerment have intrinsic value for women's individual well-being and quality of life; they are valuable ends in their own right. This concept is in line with Amartya Sen's view of development as the process of enlarging a person's "functionings and capabilities to function, the range of things that a person could do and be in her life."[2] But the WDR 2012 also shows that these goals are instrumental in achieving sustainable social and economic development. When women and men have equal voice and participation in public life, significant societal benefits result. For example, public health spending in the United States increased dramatically in the early 1920s after women won the right to vote. Women's participation in politics led to an intensive scaling up of hygiene campaigns and a sharp decline in child mortality. It is estimated that roughly 20,000 child deaths were averted every year because women won the right to vote, which explains about 10 percent of the reduction in child mortality in the United States between 1900 and 1930.[3]

What roles do laws play in fostering women's voice, agency, and empowerment? Laws formalize individual and collective rights and provide the framework within which people are empowered to exercise their voice and agency. Laws and their effective implementation and enforcement can be especially

---

The views expressed in this article are solely those of the authors and do not reflect those of the World Bank or its Executive Directors. The authors are grateful to Humay Gulyieva for assistance and Tazeen Hasan for comments.

1 World Bank, *World Development Report 2012: Gender Equality and Development* (World Bank 2012) (hereinafter, WDR 2012).

2 A. Sen, *Development as Capability Expansion*, 17 J. of Dev. Planning 41–58 (1989).

3 Grant Miller, *Women's Suffrage, Political Responsiveness, and Child Survival in American History* (Stanford Medical School & NBER 2007).

important for disadvantaged individuals and groups as they try to overcome underlying discrimination and structural inequalities—although laws sometimes serve to further entrench disadvantage and existing inequalities.

The interaction between laws on the one hand and voice and agency on the other is mutually reinforcing. Changes in agency, patriarchal attitudes, and social norms can be important triggers for changes in laws, as evidenced by the significant role played by women's collective movements since 1975 in promoting more egalitarian family laws in 70 countries around the world.[4] At the same time, the very act of bestowing the stamp of legality, or illegality, has been a catalyst for increasing agency and transforming attitudes when introduced as part of a multisectoral package. As Martin Luther King declared, "It may be true that the law cannot make a man love me. . . . But if it keeps him from lynching me, I think that's pretty important also."[5]

There has been some progress in recognizing women's equality and women's rights at the international level. The Convention to Eliminate All Forms of Discrimination Against Women (CEDAW), agreed upon in Mexico in 1975, has been a pioneering instrument of human rights for women. It addressed for the first time discrimination in the private sphere, including the extension of protection to women against family violence, and sought to tackle substantive inequalities. To this end, CEDAW recognized the centrality of eliminating all forms of discrimination in order to achieve equality for women; it articulated the need to eliminate prejudices, customary practices, social norms, and stereotyped roles for men and women; and it focused on achieving equality of outcomes, that is, equality in real terms.[6] There are many examples of CEDAW helping to win tangible gains for girls and women, as in India, where the Supreme Court in 1997 relied on CEDAW to draw up a set of guidelines and norms for the processing of sexual harassment complaints.[7]

This chapter, building on the evidence and insights presented in the WDR 2012, reviews the potential power of laws to expand women's voice and agency. The analysis follows the framework set out in the WDR 2012, which finds that limited progress in women's agency is explained by mutually reinforcing constraints in markets, formal institutions, and informal institutions (see figure 1). This points to the need to systematically analyze the interplay of these sectors. The focus of this chapter is confined to the role of formal and informal laws.

---

4 Mala Htun and S. Laurel Weldon, *Communism, Colonialism and Clerical Power: Historical Legacies and Feminist Activism in the Struggle over Family Law* (Harvard U. 2011).

5 Dr. Martin Luther King, Jr. *Towards Freedom*, speech given at Dartmouth College (May 23, 1962).

6 For broader discussion of the significance of CEDAW for women's rights and gender equality see Richard Jolly, Louis Emmerij, & Thomas G. Weiss, *UN Ideas That Changed the World* (United Nations 2009).

7 *Vishaka and others v. State of Rajasthan and others* (AIR 1997 SUPREME COURT 3011) J.S. Verma C.J.I., Mrs. Sujata V. Manohar, & B.N. Kirpal, JJ.

Figure 1. Limited Progress in Women's Agency Is Explained by Mutually Reinforcing Constraints in Markets, Formal Institutions, and Informal Institutions

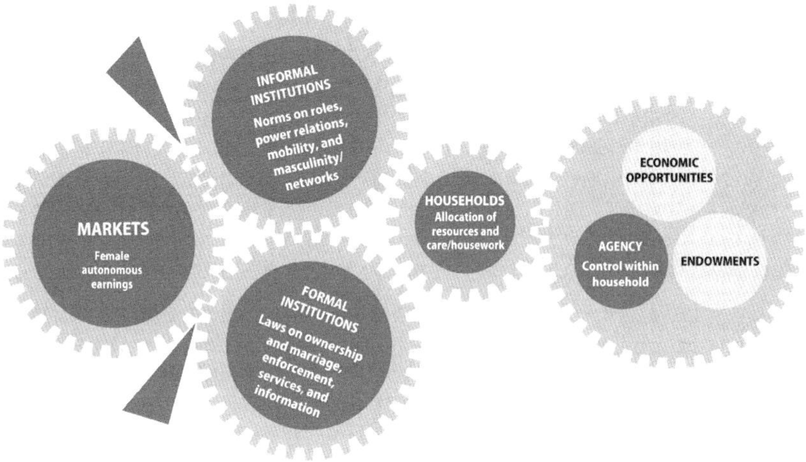

Source: WDR 2012, 153.

The chapter begins by outlining the pathways through which laws affect women's empowerment and their ability to exercise voice and agency, followed by a review of the role of plural legal systems and customary and religious laws. It then investigates the reality of laws in practice, which includes looking at issues such as access to justice and enforcement of laws, and closes with a discussion of the role of social norms in shaping or constraining the application of laws.

Pathways through Which Laws Enhance Women's Ability to Exercise Voice and Agency

Laws formalize individual and collective rights and provide the framework within which people exercise agency. Progress has been made globally in reforming legislative and constitutional frameworks to advance gender equality and women's rights. A nondiscrimination clause covering gender now appears in the constitutions of 97 countries, and 132 countries have constitutional guarantees of equality before the law.

Yet many countries still have legal provisions that overtly discriminate against women in both statutory and customary law, sometimes in the constitution and sometimes despite what the constitution requires. Indeed, in 47 of the countries with constitutional equality provisions, legislation on access to institutions means women are less able than men to interact with public authorities and the private sector. This includes restrictions on a woman's ability to get a job, sign a contract, register a business, open a bank account, be the head of the household, or choose where to live.[8] According to *Women, Business, and the Law,* of the 53 countries studied that formally recognize customary or religious law as valid sources of law under the constitution, more than half exempt such laws from constitutional provisions on nondiscrimination or equality.[9] This discrepancy reveals a disconnect between constitutionally protected rights and statutory and customary law, which affects what plays out in practice. In the Democratic Republic of Congo, for example, the constitution expressly prohibits discrimination on the basis of gender and provides for equality before the law; yet married women cannot get a job, sign a contract, register a business, or be the head of a household in the same way as men. The constitution does not invalidate customary law that is discriminatory or in conflict with constitutional provisions of equality.

Family laws, laws related to gender-based violence, and laws related to economic opportunities are among the domains of law most likely to limit women's empowerment; these are discussed briefly below. In some countries, women's citizenship rights are limited—a woman cannot confer citizenship on a foreign spouse in the same way as a man in 35 countries, and in 20 of those, women cannot confer citizenship on their children.[10]

Restrictions can limit women's mobility and access to work. Countries such as the Islamic Republic of Iran, Saudi Arabia, Sudan, and the Republic of Yemen, where married women are required to have male permission to travel or to work outside the home, show how the law itself can restrict women's agency. One result of this restriction is very low rates of female labor force participation—ranging from as low as 20 percent (Yemen) to 32 percent (Iran)—compared with male labor force participation of 73 percent (Iran) to 80 percent (Saudi Arabia).

Legal disparities can reduce women's ability to participate on an equal footing with men in the economy. *Women, Business, and the Law* finds that greater lack of legal gender parity in business and institutional laws is associated with lower labor force participation by women (both in absolute terms and relative to men) and lower levels of women's entrepreneurship. This is supported by a study in Africa that found that gender gaps in legal capacity and property rights limited women's roles as entrepreneurs. The gap between the share of women and men who are employers is 30 percent higher in countries where there are larger gender disparities in economic rights.[11]

---

8 World Bank, *Women, Business, and the Law 2012: Removing Barriers to Economic Inclusion* (International Bank for Reconstruction and Development/The World Bank 2012) (hereinafter, WBL).

9 Twenty-seven countries do not consider customary or personal law as invalid if the law violates constitutional provisions on nondiscrimination or equality; *id.*

10 WBL, *supra* note 8.

11 M. Hallward-Driemeier & T. Hasan, *Empowering Women: Legal Rights and Opportunities in Africa,* World Bank Africa Development Forum Series (2012).

Women's collective voice in society is a critical component of the full exercise of empowerment and agency. There are many examples of women's groups at the local level and movements at the national and global level enabling voice and affecting change. Perhaps one of the better-known examples is the Self-Employed Women's Association in India (SEWA), which represents the interests of a large number of informal sector workers and entrepreneurs. SEWA provides information, support, and training services to its members; offers a platform for voicing concerns; and has created space for public action through which women workers have actively challenged their employers and the state.[12] A major campaign in 2003 in support of better wages for incense stick rollers resulted in around half of all workers (10,000 women) receiving an increase in pay; another 2,000 were able to restart working after having received training in new techniques.[13] In situations like this, the legal framework is key—in Ethiopia, where the framework for civil society has been tightened since 2009, civil society organizations are unable to receive foreign funding if they engage in any work pertaining to human rights. The Ethiopian Women Lawyers Association (EWLA) is one civil society organization whose work has been affected. EWLA provided free legal aid to more than 17,000 women in 2008 and supported other activities that tens of thousands of participants benefited from. As a result of the legislation passed in 2009, EWLA cut back services, which now are restricted to limited legal aid for women provided by volunteers.[14]

For their voices to be transformative, women need to be present when and where decisions are made—in parliament, legal institutions, formal professional institutions, and local and state governments. Yet, women make up only 19 percent of parliamentarians worldwide, and in some regions their presence is even lower. In the Middle East and North Africa, women are only 1 in 10 parliamentarians, and in Papua New Guinea there is only 1 female parliamentarian.[15]

Quotas, while sometimes controversial, can be an effective means of improving women's representation. More than half of the countries in the world have implemented some type of political quota, in the form of voluntary quotas by parties on electoral lists, reservation of a certain share of candidate positions for women, or reservation of a share of legislative slots. The use of such quotas has led to a dramatic increase in female leaders across the globe. Voluntary party quotas, for example, currently in place in 51 countries, can both reflect and fuel changes in public attitudes and signify a commitment

---

12 WDR 2012, *supra* note 1.

13 J. Blaxall, *India's Self-Employed Women's Association (SEWA). Empowerment through Mobilization of Poor Women on a Large Scale: A Case Study from Reducing Poverty, Sustaining Growth; What Works, What Doesn't, and Why: A Global Exchange for Scaling Up Success* (World Bank 2012).

14 Amnesty International (Mar. 11, 2012), available at http://www.amnestyusa.org/news/news-item/ethiopia-human-rights-work-crippled-by-restrictive-law.

15 Inter Parliamentary Union, available at http://www.ipu.org/wmn-e/world.htm.

to gender equality, which also contributes to higher levels of female participation. Mandatory quotas in the form of reserved legislative seats have had positive results for women's representation and participation in South Asia and parts of Africa. In Rwanda, where the constitution stipulates a 30 percent quota for women members of parliament, this number has been far exceeded: women now make up 56 percent of the lower house and 39 percent of the upper house.[16] This change has translated into legislative gains for women in the form of revised family and inheritance laws, for example, and women report increased respect from family and community members, enhanced capacity to speak and be heard in public forums, greater autonomy in decision making in the family, and increased access to education.[17]

The same is true in the private sector. Women have low representation on the boards of large firms (around 12 percent in Europe, 10 percent in the Americas, 7 percent in Asia and the Pacific, and 3 percent in the Middle East and North Africa). Quotas can be one way to tackle that representation. Norway was the first country to introduce legislated corporate quotas in 2003, prior to which female representation had increased slowly. Female board representation jumped rapidly from around 16 percent in 2004 to the mandated 40 percent in 2008. In Australia, the prospect of reform had a positive effect on women's participation. In 2011, the Australian Stock Exchange (ASX) Corporate Governance Council implemented a diversity policy requiring all publicly listed companies in Australia to set gender-diversity targets. Anticipation of the reforms had a positive impact on women in ASX leadership—which saw a 600 percent increase in new women board appointees between 2009 and 2010 (increasing from 5 percent to 27 percent).[18]

Yet there have been some unexpected negative consequences of quotas. Reports from Rwanda suggest there has been some withdrawal of men from politics, increased marital discord, and a perception that marriage as an institution has been disrupted by the upheaval of gender roles.[19] In Pakistan, quotas that violated strong social norms have been associated with increased discrimination of women.[20]

We now turn to look more closely at three key domains of law that affect women's voice and agency: family law, which is an underlying building block; laws regulating domestic and gender-based violence; and laws regulating women's economic rights.

---

16 International Parliamentary Union, available at http://www.ipu.org/wmn-e/classif.htm.

17 J. Burnet, *Women Have Found Respect: Gender Quotas, Symbolic Representation and Female Empowerment in Rwanda,* 7(3) Politics and Gender 303–34 (2011).

18 Australian Human Rights Commission, available at http://www.hreoc.gov.au/sex_discrimination/programs/women_leadership.html.

19 Burnet, *supra* note 17.

20 Mona Lina Krook, *The Diffusion of Electoral Reform: Gender Quotas in Global Perspective,* paper presented at the European Consortium for Political Research, Lisbon (2009).

Family Law

Laws that regulate relations within the household play a significant role in fostering or restricting women's empowerment and agency. Legislation directed at domestic relations between men and women can lead the way in changing social attitudes. But change on this front has been slow. According to the WDR 2012, progress in law reform has been the slowest in areas that regulate household relations (family laws). Major inequalities still exist in inheritance rights; 26 countries have statutory inheritance laws that differentiate between women and men.[21] These inequalities have serious negative consequences for women's empowerment because inheritance is often a key way to accumulate assets. They can also have serious consequences in terms of impoverishment of widows.[22]

Land laws and laws around land titling are important for access to assets, especially for female farmers and entrepreneurs. Joint ownership in marriage, for example, increases women's ability to use land in accessing economic opportunities, while mandatory joint land titling has the added benefit of protecting a wife's rights to land in the event of her husband's death. Evaluations are under way to help document how much difference these policies make in practice.

In many countries, women and girls still have fewer inheritance rights than men and boys. All Organization for Economic Cooperation and Development (OECD) countries, the former Soviet Union, and Latin America reformed their inheritance laws more than 50 years ago to reflect more equal distribution, while in other regions the picture is mixed. All 14 countries from the Middle East and North Africa included in *Women, Business, and the Law* have differential inheritance rights for women as compared to men, as well as 7 in Sub-Saharan Africa, 3 in South Asia, and 2 in East Asia and the Pacific. In majority-Muslim countries, important doctrinal differences affect the extent to which females and males inherit equally. In Turkey, for example, inheritance rights for girls and boys have long been equal in law and in practice, while in Bangladesh, the law provides for unequal inheritance rights, albeit with the option for families to agree on more equal distribution.

Law reform to improve women's inheritance rights could provide an effective means to reduce gender discrimination and improve a wide range of socioeconomic outcomes for women. There are some solid examples of reform. In Rwanda, following reforms to inheritance laws in 1999 that provided for women's equal inheritance rights with men, land tenure reform was passed in 2004 to ensure that Rwandan men and women have secure title for

---

21 Countries included in *Women, Business, and the Law* with gender-unequal inheritance laws are Bangladesh, Burundi, the Arab Republic of Egypt, Guinea, Indonesia, the Islamic Republic of Iran, Kuwait, Lebanon, Malaysia, Mali, Mauritania, Morocco, Nepal, Oman, Pakistan, Saudi Arabia, Senegal, Sudan, the Syrian Arab Republic, Tanzania, Tunisia, the United Arab Emirates, West Bank and Gaza, and the Republic of Yemen. *See* WBL, *supra* note 8.

22 *See* D. van de Walle, *Welfare Effects of Widowhood in a Poor Country* (World Bank 2011).

their land. The law provides that new land titles for couples include the names of both the husband and the wife and that girls are able to inherit land from their parents in the same way as boys.[23] In India, law reforms at the state level that eliminated gender discrimination in inheritance rights resulted in delays in the age of marriage for girls and improvements in girls' education—girls' mean years of schooling increased by between 11 and 25 percent following the reforms in 1994.[24]

UN Women's 2011–2012 Progress of the World's Women Report notes that, historically, legal jurisdiction was divided between public and private matters, leaving the private sphere of the family and intimate relationships outside formal justice systems. The seeming resistance by governments to step into the private sphere to regulate personal relations is reflected in the reservations demonstrated by many countries in signing on to CEDAW. Out of the 187 countries that have ratified CEDAW, 29 have registered reservations to Article 16, which calls for the elimination of all forms of discrimination in all matters relating to family and marriage relations. In many cases, reservations exist because family laws are subject to discriminatory plural legal provisions—an issue discussed in greater detail below.

In a number of countries, the act of marriage weakens a woman's legal and property rights—married women cannot legally choose where to live in 23 countries, married women do not have the same legal ownership rights to movable and immovable property as men (or unmarried women) in 7 countries, and married women cannot apply for a passport in the same way as men (or unmarried women) in 20 countries.[25]

Marital property regimes that allow a woman to leave a marriage with a significant or equal share of household assets can increase her bargaining power, even if she never exercises that right.[26] Conversely, laws restricting a woman's options for exiting a marriage, such as those that leave her financially insecure in cases of divorce, can limit her agency and bargaining power within the family. Changing these laws can have a dramatic impact, as seen in the United States: domestic violence fell about 30 percent between 1970 and 1990 after equitable divorce laws were introduced.[27] Laws that constrain a woman's mobility limit options for extended social and support networks and restrict her ability to leave in the case of disagreement, violence, or abuse. In 20 countries covered by *Women, Business, and the Law*, married women cannot apply for a passport in the same way as a man; and in 4 countries, a married

---

23 OECD, *Women's Economic Empowerment Issues* (DAC Network on Gender Equality 2011).

24 Klaus Deininger, Aparajita Goyal, & Hari Naharajan, *Inheritance Law Reform and Women's Access to Capital: Evidence from India's Hindu Succession Act*, Policy Research Working Paper No. 5338 (World Bank 2010).

25 WBL, *supra* note 8.

26 WDR 2012, *supra* note 1.

27 Betsey Stevenson & Justin Wolfers, *Bargaining in the Shadow of the Law: Divorce Laws and Family Distress*, 121 Quarterly Journal of Economics 267–88 (Feb. 2006).

woman legally cannot travel outside her home or outside the country in the same way as a man. Yet, these numbers capture only formal statutory restrictions; the numbers are much larger when one considers customary laws.

Laws that set a minimum age for marriage are important. Yet in 50 countries, the minimum legal age of marriage is lower for females than for males[28]—as low as 14 years in Mexico, Mozambique, and Venezuela.[29] Early marriage exposes girls to early pregnancy and childbirth, increases their risk of contracting HIV/AIDS, and can limit opportunities for education.[30] For example, only 2 percent of married girls between the ages of 15 and 19 in Nigeria attend school, compared with 69 percent of their unmarried female peers.[31]

Figure 2. Discrimination in Social Institutions Impedes Women's Education and Literacy

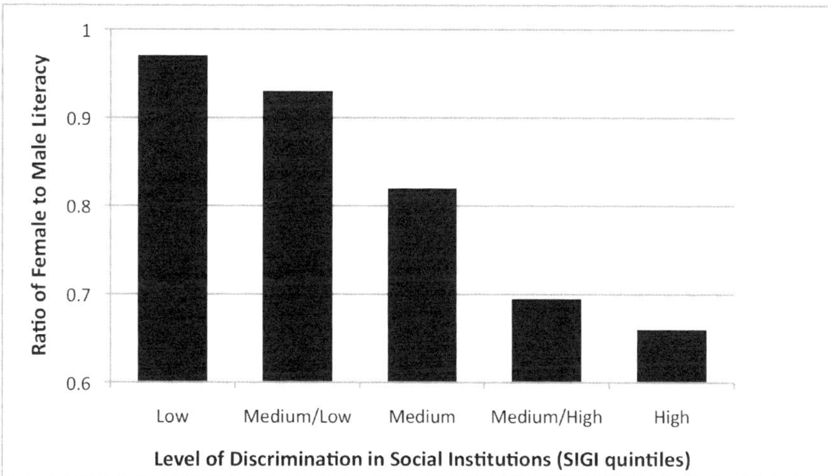

Source: OECD SIGI, 2009.

The OECD's Social Institutions and Gender Index (SIGI) captures critical societal norms and institutions that affect how women fare—using family code, physical integrity, son preference, civil liberties, and ownership rights—and is applied to 102 developing countries. Figure 2 shows that countries with high levels of discrimination in social institutions have a lower ratio of

---

28 UN Statistics Division (2010), "UNdata," http://data.un.org, as cited in *UN Women (2011–2012)*.

29 http://data.un.org/Data.aspx?d=GenderStat&f=inID:19 (accessed Apr. 30, 2012).

30 S. Clark, *Protecting Young Women from HIV/AIDS: The Case against Child and Adolescent Marriage* (International Family Planning Perspectives Jun. 2006).

31 Gordon and Sarah Brown Foundation, *Out of Wedlock into School: A Review by Gordon Brown* (Office of Gordon and Sarah Brown 2012).

female to male literacy rates; that is, women are less literate compared to men in countries with high levels of social institutional discrimination, while those countries where discrimination is lower are closer to parity in education.[32] The causality can run in both directions. Evidence from Turkey shows that extending compulsory education age by three years reduced the proportion of 16-year-old girls who were married by 44 percent, and those who had given birth by age 17 by 36 percent.[33]

Yet, even when countries reform their laws toward more equal treatment of men and women, differences can persist. The amendment of inheritance law reform in India resulted in a range of benefits for girls, as noted above, but it did not fully eliminate the underlying inequality in girls' access to inherited land.[34] This discrepancy may be due in part to a lack of dissemination of information on the changed legal provisions. Laws are also sometimes ignored or weakly enforced, or they may be circumvented.

Laws Regulating Domestic and Gender-Based Violence

Gender-based violence both reflects and reinforces inequities between men and women and damages the health, dignity, security, and autonomy of its victims. It is inextricably linked to gender inequality and perpetuates male power and control, in particular when it takes place within the home. Paragraph 12 of the Beijing Declaration and Platform for Action codifies this message, stating: "Violence against women both violates and impairs or nullifies the enjoyment by women of their human rights and fundamental freedoms."

Violence against women, much of which occurs in the private domain, has not been widely legislated against until recently. But significant progress has been made—as of April 2011, 125 countries had passed legislation on domestic violence, and almost two-thirds of countries, in efforts to make workplaces and public spaces safer for women, had passed laws on sexual harassment.[35] The Protocol to the African Charter on Human and Peoples' Rights on the Rights of Women in Africa reflects progress in this area. The protocol states that "parties shall prohibit and condemn all forms of harmful practices which negatively affect the human rights of women and which are contrary to recognized international standards."[36]

---

32 The SIGI is calculated based on the following indicators: early marriage, polygamy, parental authority, inheritance, female genital mutilation, violence against women, freedom of movement, freedom of dress, access to land, access to credit, and access to property other than land.

33 Murat G. Kirdar, Meltem Dayıoğlu Tayfur, & İsmet Koç, *The Effect of Compulsory Schooling Laws on Teenage Marriage and Births in Turkey*, Institute for the Study of Labor Discussion Paper No. 5887 (July 2011).

34 Deininger, Goyal, & Naharajan, *supra* note 24.

35 *UN Women (2011–2012)*, *supra* note 28, at Annex 4.

36 African Union, Protocol to the African Charter on Human and People's Rights on the Rights of Women in Africa, paragraph 5 (2003).

World Bank Efforts to Improve Women's Land Rights Foster Empowerment and Agency

In recognition of the importance of property rights in fostering women's empowerment and agency, the World Bank has been working with local authorities in some areas to facilitate more equal property ownership.

In Aceh, Indonesia, where the 2004 tsunami affected 800 kilometers of coastline and destroyed close to 53,800 parcels of land, the Bank integrated gender into its post-tsunami reconstruction efforts. The land administration system sustained significant damage—documentation of land ownership was washed away, one-third of the National Land Agency's staff were killed, and physical boundary markers disappeared. The impact on women was particularly grave, because the tsunami deprived them of the safety nets offered by families, especially spouses and parents. In Aceh, land issues are traditionally considered to be the "natural" dominion of men, and this norm is reinforced by the lack of female representation on local committees and the absence of gender-disaggregated data.

The Reconstruction of Aceh Land Administration System (RALAS) project integrated a well-functioning and gender-informed approach to land and property rights by introducing joint titling and recording gender in the official register. Neither of these practices existed before. Considering that more than 275,000 land parcels have been registered during RALAS, the recording of gender is a significant step forward.

In addition, RALAS has been engaged in the promotion of women's land rights by advocacy and policy dissemination with the study *Gender Impacts of Land Titling in Aceh*. The experience in Aceh has informed the work of reconstruction teams in Haiti, who recognize that taking gender-related factors into account in land administration can diffuse tensions over identity, status, and power that may threaten peace and security in postconflict situations.

Yet, many penal and civil law codes fail to criminalize certain kinds of physical, sexual, or emotional violence. As a result, domestic violence statistics around the world are horrifying: at least 1 of every 10 ever-partnered women is physically or sexually assaulted by an intimate partner or someone she knows at some point in her life.[37] Progress in legislating to prevent violence against women has been uneven across regions. The Middle East and North Africa in particular lag behind in legislating against all forms of violence against women—no country in the region has legislation criminalizing marital rape, less than 20 percent of the region has legislation against domestic violence, and just over 20 percent of countries have legislation against sexual harassment. Other regions are more varied—less than 40 percent of countries in East Asia and the Pacific have legislation against sexual harassment, and

37 WDR 2012, *supra* note 1.

just over 40 percent of countries in South Asia and Sub-Saharan Africa have legislation against domestic violence.[38]

Violence against women and girls perpetrated by family members also remains largely outside the law. Rape within marriage is illegal in only one-third of all countries.[39] Even where legislation exists, societal norms may result in persistently high rates of domestic violence. These norms may be widely shared by women and men. In too many countries—including Burkina Faso, Ethiopia, Guinea, Mali, Morocco, and Sierra Leone—more than half of women think it is acceptable for a man to beat his wife when they argue.[40]

Laws Regulating Women's Participation in the Economy

Women make up only 41 percent of the total workforce in the formal sector and tend to be concentrated in lower-paid and lower-status jobs.[41] Evidence suggests that laws explain part of this disparity. Laws can restrict a woman's participation in the economy, including restrictions on working hours, the sectors in which a woman can work, and mandates requiring lower retirement ages for women. *Women, Business, and the Law* documents 44 countries that restrict the working hours of women and 71 that limit the industries in which women can work relative to men. These restrictions are evident across all income levels and all regions of the world—this is not just a developing-country phenomenon.

Statutory provision for child care and maternity leave and benefits, alongside the recognition of flexi-time or part-time work, can improve women's participation in the labor force. In Latin America, 19 of the 20 countries included in *Women, Business, and the Law* legally require the state to provide or subsidize child care. These mandates can translate into available and affordable child care, as in Colombia, where the government's Hogares Comunitarios program pays women a small fee to take care of other women's children and provides the caregiver food to feed the children three times a day.[42] Yet, in Guatemala and Mexico, notwithstanding the legal obligation of the state to provide or subsidize child care, the lack of available care often pushes women into informal employment, and in Peru, 40 percent of working mothers take their children to work.[43]

The availability of part-time or flexible work can increase women's participation in the labor force, particularly women with young children. In Argen-

---

38 *UN Women (2011–2012)*, *supra* note 28, at Annex 4.

39 WDR 2012, *supra* note 1.

40 WDR 2012, *supra* note 1.

41 WBL, *supra* note 8.

42 Orazio Attanasio and Marcos Vera-Hernandez, *Medium and Long-Run Effects of Nutrition and Child Care: Evaluation of a Community Nursery Programme in Rural Colombia* (Centre for the Evaluation of Development Policies, Institute for Fiscal Studies EWP04/06 2006).

43 WDR 2012, *supra* note 1.

tina, as a result of the availability of part-time employment contracts, participation by married women with children in formal employment increased 9 percent and self-employment was reduced by 7 percent as compared to that by married women without children.[44] In 41 countries, employees with children who are minors have additional legal rights to flexible or part-time work schedules, whereas in many countries, part-time work is not legally recognized at all.[45]

There has been progress toward equal rights in the workplace, at least on the statutory side. More than 100 countries now have laws on nondiscrimination in hiring, and 128 have laws requiring equal pay for equal work. Laws against sexual harassment in the workplace are lagging, however, with only 75 countries having formal sexual harassment laws in place. This may be a reflection of underlying social norms that permit such behavior, as touched on above and discussed further below.

Legal Pluralism and Its Impact on Women's Agency

Many countries have plural legal systems that formally recognize religious or customary laws alongside statutes. Today, 52 countries recognize customary and religious law as valid sources of law under constitutions. This is most common in Sub-Saharan Africa, where 25 countries formally recognize at least one religious or customary law, followed by the Middle East and North Africa, where 11 countries constitutionally recognize alternative sources of law.[46] The recognition of legal pluralism is generally welcome—reflecting the right of all communities to their own cultures and for indigenous communities the right to determine their own systems of law and justice.[47]

Plural legal systems are not inherently good or bad for women's agency; the value depends on the extent to which such systems (both statutory and customary) are nondiscriminatory.[48] In practice, as documented below, plural legal systems can create barriers for women's rights and access to justice. The plurality may affect both the content of the law—in Indonesia, there are six official religions and the state recognizes different provisions regulating marriage and divorce for each—and the process—in the United Kingdom, the 1996 Arbitration Act allows for private religious arbitration by Jewish and Muslim organizations on some disputes between spouses.[49]

---

44 WDR 2012, *supra* note 1.

45 WBL, *supra* note 8.

46 WBL, *supra* note 8.

47 UN General Assembly, United Nations Declaration on the Rights of Indigenous Peoples, UN GA Res. 61/295 (2007).

48 Sandra Fredman, *Anti-discrimination Laws and Work in the Developing World: A Thematic Overview* (forthcoming).

49 *UN Women (2011–2012)*, *supra* note 28.

Legal pluralism matters for the exercise of women's agency because the scope of customary or religious laws often pertains to marriage, divorce, assets and land ownership, inheritance, or other "personal" laws. Legal pluralism can give rise to gender discrimination in family laws, gender-based violence, and procedural bias.

In at least 28 countries, parallel legal systems are exempt from meeting constitutional standards, such as nondiscrimination or equal protection provisions. Among these countries, 20 differentiate between men and women in areas covering access to institutions and 15 differentiate between men's and women's legal capacity to own, manage, control, and inherit property.[50]

Formal and informal customary and religious laws sometimes contradict constitutional or statutory gender parity. The constitution of Botswana expressly exempts laws pertaining to divorce, adoption, marriage, and devolution of property and other personal and customary laws from the constitutional equality guarantee. This exemption has permitted continuing discrimination against women in customary law and practice, including early marriage, polygamy, and the continued practice of legal guardianship by men of unmarried women.[51] In the Philippines, despite the constitutional guarantee of equality before the law, the Code of Muslim Personal Laws permits polygamy and the marriage of girls under 18. Forced marriages are also still tolerated under this system.[52]

In other countries, including Kenya[53] and South Africa, the constitution overrides such laws in cases of inconsistency, subordinating them to the overriding principle of equality. In South Africa, the bill of rights has enabled women to challenge discriminatory elements of customary law on the basis of their unconstitutionality.[54]

Plural legal systems can create barriers to women accessing justice. Multiple systems can lead to a complex web of overlapping systems, which can in turn generate gaps and exacerbate the challenges women already face in realizing their legal rights. Multiple legal systems can mean that issues such as domestic violence are dealt with by alternative dispute-resolution mechanisms, often with the effect of decriminalizing the offense or allowing scope for the male perpetrator or his family to influence the victim. In Brazil, special criminal courts were set up as a form of alternative dispute resolution mechanisms for minor offenses. In practice, 60 to 80 percent of plaintiffs were women, mainly bringing complaints of physical abuse and threats. Reportedly,

---

50 WBL, *supra* note 8.

51 S.15, Constitution of Botswana, as discussed in Fredman, *supra* note 48.

52 Fredman, *supra* note 48.

53 There is a limited exception for the Khadis courts, applying Muslim law; *see* WBL, *supra* note 8. Apart from that, no other customary or personal-status law is exempt, as made explicit in Article 2(4) and Article 60(1)(f) of the Constitution of Kenya.

54 South Africa Constitution, Section 39(3).

90 percent of domestic violence cases ended at the first stage of conciliation, either because of intimidation by the accused or because the judge pressed for the case to be closed. Recognizing the negative impact of the trivialization of these crimes, Brazil passed a new law on domestic and family violence in 2006, ending the practice.[55]

Laws in Practice—Barriers to Access and Enforcement

The expansion of economic opportunities, the adoption of progressive laws, and the evolution of legal systems are all critical to—indeed, necessary for—translating women's rights into the true exercise of agency, but they are not sufficient on their own. Lack of access to justice for women in many parts of the world persists. This can be explained in part by the unaffordable costs of justice or the lack of awareness of rights. Women can be more adversely affected by lack of access due to lower incomes, lower literacy, less mobility, and more restricted social networks. Lack of mobility and time, as well as social stigma and psychological trauma involved in bringing claims, often impedes women from seeking justice. When combined with rigid social norms, these factors can prevent women from seeking and receiving justice according to the rights they already have.

The vast majority of countries formally grant equal access to the court system for men and women. However, in 11 countries (the Islamic Republic of Iran, Kuwait, Malaysia, Oman, Pakistan, Saudi Arabia, Sudan, the Syrian Arab Republic, the United Arab Emirates, the West Bank and Gaza, and the Republic of Yemen), the testimony of a woman carries less evidentiary weight than that of a man in family law cases. In the Democratic Republic of Congo, married women need the permission of their husbands to initiate legal proceedings in court.[56]

Women face a range of social barriers to accessing the justice system. These can include a lack of knowledge about legal rights, dependence on male relatives, and restriction of mobility, as well as the threat of social stigma outlined above. In Uganda, statutory land reform resulted in more ownership rights for women than traditional practices had accorded them, yet many women were unaware of these new rights or were precluded in practice due to the high cost of legal procedures and/or loyalty to customary practices.[57]

In some communities, social norms dictate that women cannot approach the justice system without the assistance of a male relative. This is the case in Timor-Leste, where 58 percent of Timorese, both men and women, disapproved

---

55 *See UN Women (2011–2012)*, *supra* note 28, for discussion.

56 WBL, *supra* note 8.

57 Debbie Budlender & Eileen Alma, *In Focus: Women and Land, Securing Rights for Better Lives* (International Development Research Centre 2011).

of women speaking on their own behalf in local disputes.[58] A lack of voice in household decisionmaking can also impede women from being sufficiently empowered to bring a claim before the justice system. A woman's limited control over household property and assets can make her less likely to bring a claim of domestic violence, for example, because the case is likely to be taken against a family member upon whom she may be financially reliant. Social stigma in the case of sexual and domestic violence is a significant barrier in both developed and developing countries. In Haiti, fear of social stigmatization and retribution, as well as distrust in the ability of the judicial system to protect them, causes many female victims of sexual violence to remain silent. It may also prevent victims from seeking medical attention.[59]

Institutional barriers pose a significant challenge. Courtrooms may be distant and costs may be unaffordable. In Kenya, a formal claim for land in an inheritance case can involve up to 17 different legal steps, which translates into legal fees of as much as US$780. Service providers, including police, lawyers, and court officials, may not be versed in or responsive to women's needs. Data on sexual violence and robbery demonstrate that underreporting of offenses by women results from the interaction of these various factors. Across 57 countries, 10 percent of women say they have experienced sexual assault, but among those victims, only 11 percent reported the assault.[60] And where women lack access to or control over financial resources or independent income, the financial costs of pursuing legal recourse in the absence of free legal aid can be prohibitive.

Police, court staff, and even judges often reflect the discriminatory attitudes of wider society, and in some cases they may not be fully aware of the rights pertaining to women. This situation provides an additional barrier to women's access to justice and results in women facing hostility or push-back from the very people who are supposed to uphold their rights. The first step in overcoming this barrier is better representation of women in the organizations charged with implementing and enforcing the law. Quotas have been used in Ethiopia, where one member on each land committee must be a woman. The benefits of this representation have been twofold—it has helped raise awareness about land issues among local women, and it has increased their participation in the land registration process.[61]

The CEDAW committee expressed concern about bias in judicial decisionmaking that stemmed from a complaint lodged by a rape survivor in the Philippines, which alleged that societal misconceptions about rape—such as the idea that rape victims are timid or easily cowed and that when a woman

---

58 Asia Foundation (2008), as reported in *UN Women (2011–2012)*, *supra* note 28.

59 Lisa Davis & Blaine Bookey, *Respecting the Right to Health of Haitian Women and Girls*, 13(1) Health & Hum. Rights (2011).

60 Lovett & Kelly (2009), as reported in *UN Women (2011–2012)*, *supra* note 28.

61 N. Kumar & A. Quisumbing, *Policy Reform towards Gender Equality in Ethiopia: Little by Little the Egg Begins to Walk* (Institute for Food Policy Research 2010).

knows her attacker, consent is implied—were relied on by the judge in acquitting her alleged rapist.[62] A 2004 report of the World Bank Workshop on the Development Implications of Gender-Based Violence demonstrates that women's access to justice in the context of gender-based violence needs to be improved. In particular, the report notes that many judges and other legal professionals lack the necessary knowledge about gender-based violence to apply international conventions on women's rights, and that empowering ministries for women's affairs is essential because they can play a central role in creating the political space needed for this issue to be included more frequently in policy dialogue.[63]

There are some promising cases of reform in this area. Women in Indonesia identified high court fees as an obstacle to obtaining divorce certificates, which are required to access social assistance programs such as free health care, cash transfers, and subsidized rice. In response, the World Bank, in collaboration with PEKKA—an Indonesian NGO that works with more than 12,000 female heads of household across 330 villages to raise awareness of women's legal rights and to improve women's access to justice through formal legal processes—encouraged the Supreme Court to waive court fees for poor women and to hold circuit courts in rural areas. This quadrupled the number of people in remote areas who have been able to access the courts for family law matters. The Bank also worked with PEKKA to provide training for village paralegals on issues related to family law and domestic violence.

To promote greater understanding among government officials, a World Bank project in Kosovo is working with Municipal Cadastre Offices (land management offices) to implement more accurate procedures for registering land transactions, in part by ensuring that their practices are fully following the law, including the Gender Equity and Family Law, in all areas related to inheritance, purchasing, or the sale of property and mortgages. The goal is to help ensure that women receive their inheritance rights, that married women's rights are properly registered, and that married women actually agree to the transactions made by their husbands.[64]

World Bank Projects Have Unintended, yet Positive, Effects on Increasing Women's Agency through Access to Justice

A project in Jordan aimed to enhance community-driven legal aid services to the poor. The project was housed within offices of an NGO providing social welfare services, which allowed women to seek advice without attracting attention or hostility from their community. During a two-year period between

62 *UN Women (2011–2012), supra* note 28.

63 World Bank, *Report on the Outcomes of the Workshop: The Development Implications of Gender-Based Violence* (Gender and Development Group, PREM 2004).

64 World Bank, *Mainstreaming Methods to Improve Property Rights in the Kosovo Real Estate Cadastre and Registration Project* (World Bank 2012).

2009 and 2011, it provided free or reduced-cost legal counseling for 700 people; more than 70 percent of its clients were women. Inspired by the example, the Jordan Center for Legal Aid, with the Jordan Bar Association, created the first pro bono lawyers' association. The association provides a system of "one-stop shops" for legal aid and counseling and improves access to and quality of service. The Ministry of Social Welfare agreed to refer poor women in need of assistance to the Justice Center for Legal Aid.

In Vietnam, the World Bank has provided ongoing support to the government to foster effective implementation of the 2007 Law on Gender Equality and the National Strategy on Gender Equality. The National Strategy on Gender Equality set out 5 objectives and 20 quantitative targets to eliminate discrimination and ensure women's equal rights in the fields of labor employment, education, and health care; to improve the quality of women's participation in economic, political, and social fields; and to enhance the capacity of national machinery for the advancement of women. To further these goals, the World Bank supported awareness raising and capacity building within relevant ministries, and worked with these ministries to build systems of accountability, including through a series of development policy loans.

Social and Cultural Norms Interact with Laws

The persistence of patriarchal attitudes and deep-rooted gender stereotypes in relation to women's roles and responsibilities perpetuates gender inequality and limits the extent to which formally recognized women's rights can be realized in practice. As eloquently noted by Devaki Jain in her review of the United Nations' 60-year quest for equality and justice, "Many cultural traditions have embargoes on many dimensions of women's concerns and freedom. It is here that culture clashes with women's access to the universality of human rights; often traditions and religious practices hurt and discriminate."[65] In this sense, disequalizing social norms and values can prevent laws from removing constraints to agency.

A stark example of the impact norms can have on women's empowerment, voice, and agency is the restriction on women's mobility. Legal restrictions on mobility are present in certain countries: 4 of the 141 countries included in *Women, Business, and the Law* legally restrict married women from leaving the home in the same way as a man; 16 countries restrict married women from getting a job in the same way as a man; and in 22 countries, married women cannot apply for a passport in the same way as a man. Social norms in many more countries dictate what is acceptable behavior for women. In all 19 countries included in the WDR 2012 qualitative study on gender and economic choice, for example, social norms were the most frequently cited constraint on women's physical mobility. In Malawi, social norms deterred

65 Devaki Jain, *Women, Development and the UN: A Sixty-Year Quest for Equality and Justice*, United Nations Intellectual History Project (Indiana U. Press 2005).

pregnant women from using a bicycle ambulance that was set up to improve emergency obstetric care.[66]

Social norms can interact with formal laws to dictate the extent to which women's higher personal incomes translate into greater voice and bargaining power within the household. About 20 percent of the participants in the WDR 2012 qualitative study said that husbands have complete control over their wives' income. Participants also reported that when women do not retain control over their earnings, the potential empowering role of those earnings is limited.

High rates of domestic or gender-based violence can be traced to prevailing norms. Several countries with serious problems of violence against women have passed legislation relating to domestic and other violence—Bangladesh, Brazil, Nepal, the Philippines, and Zambia—yet patterns of violence continue. A World Health Organization multicountry study revealed that 13 to 61 percent of women experience physical violence in their lifetime,[67] while more than 60 percent of women in Bangladesh experience some form of domestic abuse during their lifetime.[68] Thus, although legislation protecting against such behavior is critical, so is the effective implementation of laws and revised cultural perspectives about the acceptability of violence.

Because prevailing social norms in a number of areas can limit the effect of laws to the detriment of gender equality, concerted efforts on this front are needed. Gender norms can be persistent and resilient to change. This is particularly true when an increase in women's empowerment and agency threatens the balance of power within households and communities. The good news is that change is possible. In India, increased female leadership influenced adolescent girls' career aspirations and educational attainment. Following a 1993 law that reserved female leadership positions for women in randomly selected village councils, the gender gap in career aspirations closed by 25 percent in villages that were assigned a female leader for two election cycles, and the gender gap in adolescent educational attainment was erased completely, with girls spending less time on household chores.[69]

---

66 K. Lungu et al., *Are Bicycle Ambulances and Community Transport Plans Effective in Strengthening Obstetric Referral Systems in Southern Mali?* 13(2) Malawi Med. J. 16–18 (2001).

67 World Health Organization, *WHO Multi-country Study on Women's Health and Domestic Violence against Women* (WHO 2005).

68 L. M. Bates et al., *Socioeconomic Factors and Processes Associated with Domestic Violence in Rural Bangladesh,* 30(4) Intl. Family Planning Perspectives 190–99 (2004).

69 Lori Beaman et al., *Female Leadership Raises Aspirations and Educational Attainment for Girls: A Policy Experiment in India* (2012), available at http://www.sciencexpress.org/12 January 2012/Page 1/10.1126/science.1212382.

Conclusions

This chapter has considered how laws can enhance or limit women's voice and agency. There are several highlights. First, discrimination persists in many formal statutory legal systems, especially for married women. Second, many countries have plural systems of law related to marriage, divorce, succession, or other "personal" issues that limit rights that may exist. Third, the enforcement of rights and the ability for women to seek redress are critical if rights are to encourage the exercise of voice and agency. Finally, and also related to enforceability, social and cultural norms interact with laws to limit or enhance their effectiveness.

Although there has been much progress on the front of enhancing women's voice, agency, and empowerment, the challenges that remain are significant. The dearth of gender-disaggregated data is also a limiting factor, impeding the policy and advocacy work necessary to reform laws.

The priorities now are twofold: legal reform is critical. But legal reform alone is insufficient. It must be combined with changes in accessibility and enforceability of laws and changes in social norms around gender roles and women's abilities. Such norms can limit the effect of laws, services, or incomes to the detriment of women's voice, agency, and empowerment. By employing innovative approaches, legal structures have the potential to significantly increase women's agency. The World Bank has a strong track record in working in partnership to promote women's voice, agency, and empowerment through financing, innovation and learning, and investing in data and knowledge to help better understand and address the underlying inequalities.

"We Want What the Ok Tedi Women Have!"

Guidance from Papua New Guinea on Women's Engagement in Mining Deals

NICHOLAS MENZIES AND GEORGIA HARLEY

Despite global gender equality gains in education, life expectancy, and labor force participation, two areas of persistent inequality remain: asset gaps and women's agency.[1] In many developing countries, including Papua New Guinea (PNG), natural resources are citizens' key asset. Women's agency over these assets—their ability to make choices and transform those choices into actions and outcomes (or more simply, the ability to define goals and act on them)—is commonly weak. This is especially so when the resources are accessed for capital-intensive development. Empowering women to exercise agency and control over natural resources and the revenues that flow from them is thus an important contemporary focus for engagements related to gender equality and economic development.

The mining regulatory regime in PNG provides a relatively strong position for communities. Agreements between the state, companies, and impacted communities commonly include significant community benefits, such as a share of royalties and an equity stake in the mine. However, significant gender inequality, both locally and at the national level, means that women's voices are rarely represented in agreement making.[2] Women end up with control of

---

The authors would like to thank Belden Dasa, Musje Werror, Nigel Parker, Ian Middleton, Jamila Abassi, Almah Tararia, Patricia Kassman, Nicole Haley, Adriana Eftimie, Waafas Ofosu-Amaah, Lwanzo Amani, Sakuntala Akmeemana, Laura Bailey, and Phillipa Carr, who were closely involved in the design, implementation, and write-up of this work. Even so, errors of fact and interpretation are those of the authors, as are the views expressed in this paper, which should not be attributed to the World Bank, its executive directors, or the countries they represent.

1 World Bank, *World Development Report 2012 Gender Equality and Development*. Strengthening the role of women in household and community decision making has been shown to have positive development impacts, as women tend to prioritize productive expenditures for their families and communities (including for food, health, and education) over unproductive consumption (such as of alcohol, cigarettes, and gambling).

2 Prior to the 2012 election, when three women were elected at once, only three women had ever been elected in the 37-year history of PNG's parliament. Moreover, roughly two-thirds of women experience gender-based violence in their lifetimes, and maternal mortality rates are some of the highest in the region.

few, if any, benefits, while bearing a disproportionate burden of the social and environmental costs of mining.[3]

The Ok Tedi mine, located in the northern corner of PNG's Western Province, is an exception, albeit qualified, to this general state of affairs. The province receives a significant share of mining revenues, yet service delivery in the area remains weak. On top of provincial government revenues, impacted communities have received benefits totaling more than 2 billion PNG kina (US$980 million) over the past decade.[4] Revised compensation agreements at the Ok Tedi mine, called Community Mine Continuation Agreements (CMCAs), concluded in 2007 are an encouraging innovation.[5] Women had a seat at the negotiating table and secured an agreement giving them 10 percent of all benefits, 50 percent of all scholarships, cash payments into family bank accounts (to which women are cosignatories), and mandated seats on the governing bodies implementing the agreement (including future reviews of the agreement). Women's entitlements are elevated to legally enforceable rights at the heart of the mining company's license to operate. Such an arrangement is unprecedented anywhere in the world.

At the 2010 Women in Mining conference in the town of Madang,[6] women from mining communities across PNG exclaimed, "We want what the Ok Tedi women have!" This chapter is based on research in the North Fly (one of three areas impacted by the 2007 agreement).[7] It explores the process of negotiation and progress in implementation of the agreement, examining how the agreement came about, assessing whether its promise is being realized in practice,

---

3 *See*, for example, M. Macintyre, *Modernity, Gender and Mining: Experiences from Papua New Guinea*, in *Gendering the Field: Towards Sustainable Livelihoods for Mining Communities* (ANU E-Press 2011). *See* also M. Macintyre, *Petztorme Women: Responding to Change in Lihir, Papua New Guinea, Women's Groups and Everyday Modernity in Melanesia*, 74 (1–2) Oceania (Special Issue) 120–33 (2003). The experience of some indigenous communities in Australia and Canada provides examples of women playing key roles. *See* C. O'Faircheallaigh, *Women's Absence, Women's Power: Indigenous Women and Negotiations with Mining Companies in Australia and Canada*, Ethnic and Racial Studies 1–19 (2012).

4 Mine operator, Ok Tedi Mining Limited (OTML) data.

5 The five main benefit streams under the CMCAs are cash (the mine operator disburses cash into a mix of family and some clan bank accounts with an annual payment per person); village projects (each village submits applications for small-scale projects and goods, such as water tanks, outboard motors, and animal husbandry); investments (the foundation invests funds in projects to earn an ongoing return, such as passenger and cargo vessels on the Fly River, housing in Kiunga, and passenger planes); school scholarships (primary, secondary, and tertiary); and the Women and Children's Fund (10 percent of all benefits are set aside for women, whose use is to be decided upon by women's groups).

6 The third in a series of meetings focused on communities and women in mine-affected areas, sponsored by GoPNG and the World Bank as part of the ongoing sectoral program of technical assistance financed by the Bank in PNG.

7 Villages visited for this research were mine villages (Finalbin); river villages (Atkamba, Moian, and Yogi); and road villages (Ningerum, where people came from other road villages to participate in focus group discussions). All villages were in North Fly District (except for Moian, which is in Middle Fly). Impacts and conditions in Middle and South Fly districts are known to be different and are not covered in this study.

and providing guidance for mining and gender practitioners hoping to use mining agreements to improve development outcomes for women, both in PNG and farther afield.

Underpinning the approach to assessing the implementation of the agreement are two widely held tenets of contemporary development practice:

- Community-driven development (CDD) has played an increasingly important role in fragile institutional contexts. Rather than treating poor and marginalized people as the target of poverty-reduction efforts, CDD gives control over planning decisions and investment of resources to community groups and local governments—it operates on principles of empowerment, community ownership, participatory governance, greater downward accountability, and enhanced local capacity.[8] Complexity often undermines accountability and transparency, and thus key principles, such as clear and simple rules of the game and access to information, are crucial to the premise of CDD.
- A political economy approach to delivering development programs is one that is designed to mitigate some key risks (such as elite capture and leakage) through a better understanding of existing power structures and patronage systems and by working actively to overcome constraints. Implementation is an ongoing process of measuring progress against articulated development objectives and adjusting delivery of the program accordingly.

Background of the Ok Tedi Mining Negotiations

The history, ownership structure, and importance of Ok Tedi to PNG's economy have been critical in shaping the negotiation process and outcomes.

The mine and affected communities have been engaged in long-running disputes that primarily concern significant environmental damage from the disposal of tailings and mine waste into the Ok Tedi and Fly river systems.[9] The disputes occur in the historical context of tension over the impacts of the Panguna mine on Bougainville, which led to conflict and the creation of an autonomous region with a pathway to independence from PNG. Issues of concern regarding the Ok Tedi mine include loss of fish stocks and water sources, increased flooding leading to the destruction of forests and food gardens, and increased mosquito-borne diseases. Residents along the road between the

8 Experience has shown that given clear rules of the game, access to information, and appropriate capacity and financial support, poor men and women can effectively organize in order to address local problems by working in partnership with other state and nonstate development actors.

9 Ok Tedi website, http://www.oktedi.com/community-and-environment/the-environment/impacts-of-mining. The original project design included a tailings dam, but the dam's foundations were washed away in a landslide early in construction in 1984 and were not rebuilt. The national government and OTML agreed to allow the tailings to discharge directly into the river.

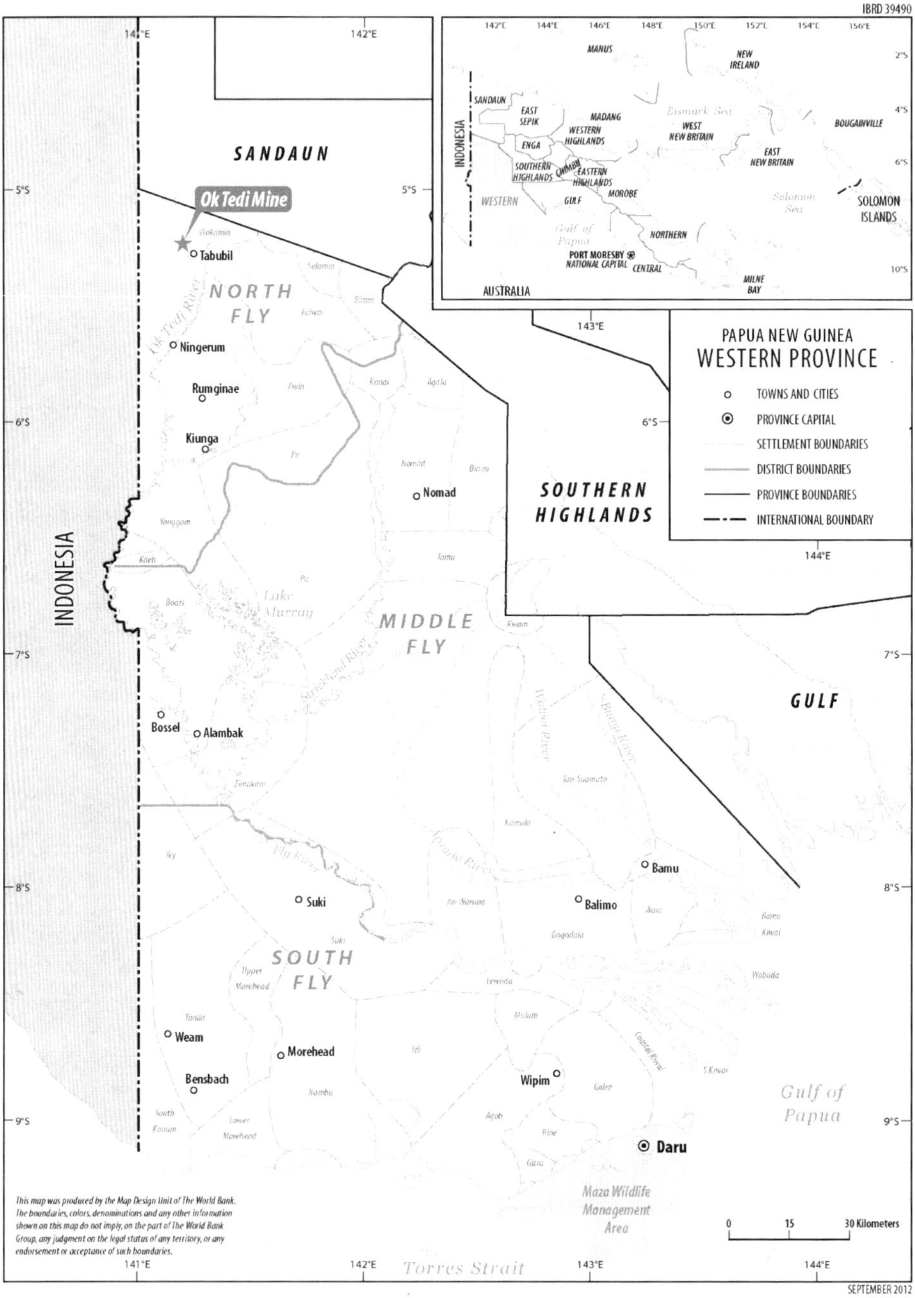

Figure 1. Map of Western Province, PNG

Source: World Bank.

mine and the river port in Kiunga also complain about dust from passing convoys. According to an independent environment expert, the riverine impacts are likely to be felt for "several hundred years" and are borne more heavily by women, who are traditionally responsible for crop production, than by men.[10] In 1994, affected communities mounted a class action lawsuit against the mine's then major shareholder, BHP Pty Ltd, in the Supreme Court of Victoria, Australia, (where BHP is registered). The case was settled with a US$500 million payout and a commitment to contain tailings and mine waste disposal.[11] The case drew international interest at the time for its use of tort law to secure the accountability of a multinational company for environmental damages.[12]

In 2000, due to community complaints about the mine's continued use of riverine tailings disposal and the mine's concern about ongoing environmental liability, BHP queried whether the mine should close.[13] The mine is the single largest contributor to the PNG economy,[14] and thus the state had, and still has, a strong interest in its continued operation.

To allow operations to continue, the mine's majority shareholding was divested to a development trust, the PNG Sustainable Development Program Limited (PNGSDP), beneficially owned by the people of PNG and registered in Singapore to ensure relative independence from day-to-day politics.[15] The

---

10 Alan Tingay, *Letter of Endorsement from the Independent Scientist Appointed to the CMCA 2006/7 Review Process* (Apr. 16, 2007) (Attachment B to CMCAs).

11 G. Banks & C. Ballard, *The Ok Tedi Settlement: Issues, Outcomes, and Implications* (Asia Pacific Press 1997).

12 Since the Ok Tedi case, class actions have become increasingly prevalent, including actions taken against Freeport-McMoRan's Grasberg mine in West Papua, Indonesia; Exxon-Mobil's natural gas installation in Aceh, Indonesia; Unocal's oil pipeline in Burma; Shell's petroleum operations in the Nigerian delta; Rio Tinto's copper mine on Bougainville; Texaco's petroleum operations in the Ecuadorian Amazon; and Thor Chemical's use of mercury-based chemicals in South Africa. *See* Banks & Ballard, *supra* note 11. *See* also Peter Newell, *Access to Environmental Justice? Litigation against TNCs in the South* 32(1) R. Crook and P. Houtzager, *Making Law Matter: Rules, Rights and Security in the Lives of the Poor*, IDS Bulletin 83–93 (2001); Halina Ward, *Securing Transnational Corporate Accountability through National Courts: Implications and Policy Options*, 24 Hastings Int. & Comp. L. Rev. 451–74 (2001).

13 BHP reported that, even if mining stopped immediately, downstream environmental impacts would continue to increase and would likely persist for at least 50 years. Parametrix, Inc. and URS Greiner Woodward Clyde, *Draft Executive Summary: Assessment of Human Health and Ecological Risks for Proposed Mine Waste Mitigation Options at the Ok Tedi Mine, Papua New Guinea; Screening Level Risk Assessment*, prepared for Ok Tedi Mining, Ltd., 1–13 (Aug. 13, 1999), available at http://www.oktedi.com.

14 In 2010, export earnings represented 18 percent of the country's GDP, and taxes and dividends to the national government represented 18 percent of tax revenue and 17 percent of government domestic revenue.

15 The PNGSDP comprises a long-term fund and a development fund. The long-term fund invests two-thirds of the net income received from OTML in low-risk investments for the future benefit of the people of PNG after the mine's closure. It has a balance of more than US$1.2 billion. The development fund invests one-third of net income received from OTML in sustainable development projects. Two-thirds of those projects are national and one-third are focused in Western Province. For a full description of BHP's exit strategy and the PNGSDP, *see* http://www-wds.worldbank.org/external/default/WDSContentServer/WDSP/IB/20

PNGSDP invests significant amounts in Western Province, including in communities affected by the Ok Tedi mine, which, with other mine-related and government sources, creates a complex web of real and potential benefits for communities.[16] The mine was required under law to enter into legally enforceable consent agreements with affected landowners and users. These became known as Community Mine Continuation Agreements (CMCAs). In 2001, the first CMCAs were negotiated. In accordance with a five-year review period, a revised set of CMCAs was negotiated in 2006 and 2007. The revised set of CMCAs now covers more than 90,000 people in 156 villages stretching from the villages in the Highlands around the mine site near Tabubil, along the Ok Tedi and Fly Rivers, to the mouth of the Fly (see figure 1).[17]

Negotiation of the Agreement

Negotiations between mining companies, the state, and landowners are invariably subject to extreme asymmetries of information and power. These characteristics reduce the likelihood of equitable agreements and limit the potential of mining investment to contribute to development outcomes. Over time, entrenched asymmetries can build tension between the parties and undermine the durability of mining investment. The CMCA review process at the Ok Tedi mine addressed these challenges to some extent.

For the CMCAs, the experience with Bougainville's Panguna mine; the long history of dispute, litigation, and engagement around Ok Tedi; the mine's beneficial ownership; and the advanced stage of the mine's life were key factors resulting in a more positive consultation process being established. For the 2006–07 review, with over 20 years of experience in the area and production ongoing during negotiations, the mine operator suffered fewer of the time pressures that mining companies often face when negotiating agreements prior to the commencement of operations. Mine management also responded to the international pressure (from NGOs and multilateral organizations) that the environmental damage and litigation had brought, with a desire to leave an improved legacy.

Although not without its challenges, the 2006–07 CMCA review process was in many ways a model one, and the quality of the process was important to women's ability to secure the deal they did. The broadly consultative process, significant time taken, and independent facilitation and advice all helped to ameliorate asymmetries and build trust. The review process lasted

---

11/06/14/000333037_20110614052552/Rendered/PDF/624980NWP0P1160ns00trusts0and0funds.pdf.

16 In addition to five main sources under the CMCAs, other sources of local projects include the Alice River Trust (set up after the class action suit), mine charitable projects, mine-implemented tax-credit projects, member-of-parliament-controlled constituency development fund projects, and local government projects.

17 The number of villages has increased over time because some communities that were originally opposed to the agreements have since joined.

18 months and cost K7 million (US$3.4 million), paid for by the mine. See the box below for a summary of the negotiating process.

CMCA Negotiations: An Innovation

Independent international (the Keystone Center) and local (the Tanorama Network) facilitators were selected jointly by the mine and CMCA community leaders to design, support, and guide the process. Independent legal, environmental, and accounting advice was engaged for communities at no cost to them. Prominent former chief justice of the PNG Supreme Court, Sir Arnold Amet, was appointed as the independent legal observer; he became an adviser to the affected communities. The top-level negotiations were held in Tabubil, the township at the base of the mine. Regional-level meetings were held in each of three impacted subregions, and village meetings in almost all the impacted villages. Delegates to regional meetings were directly elected by their village constituencies, and the representatives at the top-level negotiating table in Tabubil were elected from the regional meetings.

Women's Engagement in the Negotiations

The quality of the overall process provided a positive environment for women to exercise agency. Yet initially, women were not included at all. In the negotiation's early stages, all community representatives were men. In deference to their understanding of local custom, the independent facilitators did not challenge this situation. As one facilitator noted, "we had to be very careful not to be perceived as undermining local authority or customs." Instead, facilitators asked the male representatives to ensure that they represented the views of their entire group, including women and children. The on-site nature of the discussions meant that, at least for the regional meetings, some women were able to sit outside the negotiations and listen, even though they were not seated at the negotiating table.

As negotiations continued, it became apparent that women's views were not being represented. The mining company's management understood that the CMCAs would be more likely to achieve development outcomes if women were involved. One senior company representative reflected that "there would be a payout at the end, and there was some concern that the men may drink that away, or buy jeeps, cigarettes etc." A delegate noted that "the women were so involved in health and education, they would end up being responsible for implementing social projects in the region." Improved development outcomes could foster community support in favor of the mine and reduce the chances of mining-related complaints. And so it was recognized that women's voices should be heard in the negotiations. The combined support of the company and independent facilitators was critical in convincing the male beneficiaries and the state that women should have a seat at the main negotiating table. With negotiations at midpoint, a women's delegation was established. As one facilitator noted, "the women were so happy that they had a seat at the table—they felt they had won something already."

Women's involvement was structured around a single delegate at the central negotiating table and a separate women's caucus that gathered outside of the main meeting to formulate negotiating positions. There were also consultations with women in impacted villages. The facilitators worked closely with the mine's gender desk, which had received prior support from a national-level Women in Mining project[18] and had assessed women's development needs.

Ume Wainetti was identified as the women's delegate. Mrs. Wainetti is from the impacted region yet also has a national profile as former chair of the National Council of Women and current convener of the national Family and Sexual Violence Action Committee. In negotiations, Wainetti used cultural cues and tactics, describing herself to other delegates as a "sister and aunty." Coming from the impacted area, Wainetti could both be more assertive and employ a range of emotions with the male village representatives more freely than an outsider. Wainetti ensured that she sat next to the mining company managing director at key moments. Presentations of health statistics for women and children, combined with emotive personal stories, helped to influence the men at the table. One facilitator observed that Wainetti was "one of the best negotiators at the table." Her competence in this regard likely stemmed from a combination of tertiary education (when most of the other delegates had only primary level), a combination of national status and local roots, and substantial leadership and negotiation skills acquired in national and international settings.

In support of Wainetti as the women's delegate, a caucus of about 20 women constituted an important forum for both education and developing an informed negotiating position that Wainetti would take to the main negotiating table. The caucus brought together at least two women from each of nine impacted areas, along with the provincial government's women's officer and female facilitators. A side workshop held over several days included information sessions from mine staff and independent experts about the overall mining operation, environmental impacts, and the benefit envelope. Wainetti, the facilitators, and the mine outreach team also visited women in mine-affected villages, exchanging views and developing a shared negotiating position. As one facilitator put it, "they [the women's caucus] were great because they were great leaders, great negotiators, not just because they were women."

18 Launched in 2003, the Women in Mining and Petroleum project (funded by the World Bank–managed Japan Social Development Fund) has included the drafting of women in mining action plans for affected communities, three national conferences leading to a cabinet-endorsed five-year national action plan, and capacity building (including in basic literacy, numeracy, and economic development skills) to allow women to manage and benefit from the resources that accrue as a result of extractives industries.

Initially, the women's key proposal was that a minimum of 5 percent of all funds be specifically set aside (that is, ring-fenced) for the benefit of women and children. Wainetti described how women "wanted a separate pot to make sure that women and kids were not forgotten as usual." The proposal was not intended to exclude women from the remainder of the benefits, nor was it intended to be a maximum amount that women would receive—rather, it was to be a separate minimum amount prioritized for specific initiatives for women and children. Drawing on personal relationships and networks, the women's caucus approached influential players out of session to seek their support for the proposal. One such participant was Sir Arnold Amet, a well-respected statesman. He was supportive, and suggested that they raise the figure. The delegation also secured the support of the mine's senior management. The figure of 10 percent was ultimately chosen on the basis that the male beneficiaries would be unlikely to accept more and that 10 percent might fly "under the radar" at the negotiating table.

In tabling the proposal at the main negotiating session, the women's delegate emphasized the complementary roles of women and men in the community and stressed that "we are not asking for much, only 10 percent." Following a silence, Amet spoke in support of the proposal, followed by the mining company representative. One facilitator described how "the backing of prestigious people was critical to the proposal being supported in the room." No questions or concerns were raised, and the proposal was adopted unanimously.

The women secured additional provisions on an ad hoc basis throughout the negotiation, including

- Cash compensation payments deposited into family bank accounts, to which women were encouraged by the mine to be signatories. (Previously, cash was transferred to clan accounts, which were controlled by men and subject to persistent concerns regarding misuse and leakage.)
- Fifty percent of all educational scholarships awarded to women and girls, and women would make up half of the membership of the scholarship selection panels.
- Women represented in the CMCA's key local governance bodies, village planning committees.[19] Each committee would include two women representatives out of the five members (or three women representatives out of a maximum of eight members).
- Women represented on each of nine regional trusts and on the board of directors of the Ok Tedi Fly River Development Program, the foundation responsible for the agreement's implementation.

---

19 Village planning committees engage in a participatory process to identify, plan, and allocate village-level CMCA projects. Committee members are elected every three years in a process supervised by the foundation.

To address what was seen by communities as poor implementation up to that point, key tenets of the 2007 agreement were new structures to ensure "a high level of ownership and decision-making power over resources, programs, and projects" by impacted communities.

The agreement provides more explicit entitlements for women than any other mining agreement in PNG or, as far as can be discerned, globally. It thus represents an innovation in efforts to empower women to exercise agency over natural resources. However, the deal alone is not necessarily a success for women. Ring-fencing can be seen as "both a victory for women and a failure."[20] On the one hand, it promises to improve the status of women by offering control over a specific allocation of funds. Indeed, effects could be even greater if the women taking up decision-making roles over the ring-fenced funds are able to generate positive spillover effects for women in other areas, such as stronger household decision making, greater participation in political life, and economic empowerment.[21] On the other hand, it is hard to argue on its face that control of 10 percent of all benefits for more than two-thirds of the population (once children are included) is fair. Further, if ring-fencing entrenches norms that women are somehow undeserving of equal participation and equal benefit sharing and excludes women from the remaining 90 percent of benefits, then its effectiveness should be questioned. Some of these issues can be addressed only in the context of implementation.

Implementation of the Agreement

The novelty of the deal secured for women in the 2007 agreement raised high expectations; experience during implementation has been mixed.

Informed Awareness of the Women's Deal Is Low

Research reveals that in many villages, a wide cross-section of women and men had heard about "the women's 10 percent," but no beneficiaries were able to explain how much money was available, the process by which projects were selected, or what had been approved to date. Several women complained that they have not received guidance or training on how to access the benefits. "How do we get the money? . . . It is very hard. . . . Since the launching, nobody knows what has happened with the 10 percent. There are no courses on how to apply for the money. Mothers are in a complete blackout." More positively, male residents did not express any resentment or complaints about the women's 10 percent other than a critique that the women weren't using their

---

20 *See* B. Sharp, *Renegotiating a Papua New Guinea Compensation Agreement: Applying an Informed Consensus Approach,* 69 Resource Management in the Asia Pacific, Working Paper No. 69 (2008).

21 *See,* for example, the impact of reserved seats for women in Indian village councils on attitudes toward women, investment priorities, and reporting of crimes against women. For a summary of the results and links to the literature, *see* http://blogs.worldbank.org/impactevaluations/when-women-are-in-charge.

money. This may suggest a "normalization" of women having control over some portion of resources.

This lack of understanding of the women's 10 percent echoes broader confusion among communities about the CMCAs in general, *mipela no clia* ("We don't understand/we're not clear") being the most common refrain when asked about the agreement. Few people (beyond those serving on the village planning committees), could explain the process for CMCA project approval. Even members of the committees did not appear to understand how much money was available for CMCA projects in their village or region. Beneficiaries repeatedly expressed a desire for written information—"in black and white"—to dispel misinformation, build awareness, and foster accountability.

Representatives of the foundation note the information problem but state that "we can't get information to 90,000 people": indeed, the geographical challenges are considerable. The foundation relies on village planning committee chairs to be conduits to the rest of their committee and the village at large. Minutes of meetings, notices, and verbal updates are sent to the chairs for dissemination. One mine representative explained low levels of beneficiary awareness as a function of community "backwardness," perhaps reflecting an assumption that communities with little exposure to sophisticated financial topics are not able to understand the arrangements. This conclusion—that awareness is inherently and permanently constrained by the exotic novelty of trust funds and financial flows—is not uncommon on the part of community development technocrats and resource company staff. But global experience shows that targeted and skillful discussions at the community level can indeed empower village people to understand and engage effectively quite quickly.

The Ring-Fenced Women's Fund Is Operational, but Impacts Are Not Widely Felt

In accordance with the agreement, a separate process was established to make decisions about the women's ring-fenced benefits, governed by all-women groups elected by women from the beneficiary villages. From 2007 to 2010, K69.8 million (US$34 million) was set aside for the women and children's fund.[22] As of 2012, the major spending decision was to invest in three learning centers. This decision is in line with the intent of the CMCA, which foreshadowed initial investments in capacity building to allow women to actively engage in development processes—including the informed use of their funds. One learning center is open, and construction of the remaining two centers is yet to commence. Of the money that has been allocated, it is likely that much of it remains unspent. In one region (covering 18 villages), approximately US$20 million of general funds (that is, not the 10 percent women and children's fund) remained unspent as of September 2011, and figures show up to half

22 This comprises K21.2 million from OTML, K8.6 million from the PNGSDP, and K40 million from the state. The payment from OTML has been made regularly, and PNGSDP funds have been forthcoming for women's projects. State funding has been more difficult to access.

of individual village funds have not been spent. One trustee attributed the underspending to the failure of villagers to submit project proposals. Underspending seems unlikely to be a consequence of lack of need for community improvements in the face of basic service failures and profound development challenges. A targeted effort to improve, simplify, and streamline the proposal process could yield results.

In the villages, however, very few women have heard of the training centers, and neither women nor men report feeling any benefits from the 10 percent deal. Women in the villages often express concern that they are not being faithfully represented in the women's bodies to decide on use of the 10 percent. Many of the women in these groups are the wives of local ward councilors or village planning committee chairmen, suggesting that elite divides may compound existing gender inequality. In one village, women complained that their representative on the regional women's group had moved and was no longer resident in the village and did not provide feedback from meetings. Such an impression is reflected more broadly in the functioning of village planning committees, which appear beset by challenges related to information, coordination, and representation. Communities report that committees do not faithfully represent community interests, "hoarding information and keeping benefits" for personal or family gain. Committee chairs are frequently reported to no longer reside in the village they represent (having moved into towns), limiting their ability to identify community needs, convey information, and be held accountable for decisions made.

Family Bank Accounts Show Promise

The introduction of family bank accounts for disbursing the cash compensation component of the agreement appears to be having a positive impact, improving access to resources by both women and youth.[23] Unlike with the project component, there is general understanding of the entitlements and the timing of the payments, including among women and youth. In most of the villages visited for this research, male and female beneficiaries reported that women are cosignatories to bank accounts.[24] Women reported much greater access to money than under the previous system of clan accounts. They also claim to spend more productively than men, though this has not been independently verified. Some youth also reported receiving their entitlements in cash from their parents.

---

23 The compensation amount varies per village but is in the order of K400 (US$200) per person per year, including for children.

24 The exception to this was reported by communities in and around Ningerum. Prior to 2007, most families did not have bank accounts, so the mine and foundation undertook a process to provide bank accounts through two operators, BSP and PNG Microcredit. Bank representatives traveled to each of the CMCA villages with the requisite paperwork and opened accounts for most families. The mine and foundation encouraged male and female cosignatories to the accounts.

Even so, villagers face high transaction costs in accessing the cash compensation. As in many parts of PNG, access to banking facilities in the CMCA area is extremely limited. Beneficiaries must travel to one of three bank locations, and travel costs are high. In one example, the cost of return boat-and-bus travel from Atkamba village, on the lower Ok Tedi, to the nearest branch in Kiunga is K120 (US$57). For two parents (as account cosignatories) to access funds for a family of five, the cost of transport alone would be more than 15 percent of the annual compensation payment. Initial plans to provide banking in boats along the river were shelved due to security concerns of traveling with large amounts of cash. Mobile phone-facilitated payments have yet to reach the CMCA area, although the rollout of mobile towers offers promise in this regard.

Family bank accounts appear not to have increased family savings. The foundation, mine, and villagers report that beneficiaries routinely withdraw the annual cash compensation amount in full. Monthly account-keeping fees of K7 (US$3.40) reduce the incentive for families to save money through the banking system. The full withdrawal of funds also poses administrative burdens because this action automatically closes the account, which needs to be reopened to receive the following year's payment.

Implementation of the Scholarship Scheme Has Been Partially Successful

The implementation of the scholarship program has occurred in accordance with the CMCA. Women currently make up half of the members on the scholarship selection panel. However, the selection process requires little discretion—in practice, supply exceeds demand and the money set aside for scholarships each year exceeds the money demanded from all applicants.[25] The selection panel simply identifies whether an applicant is from a CMCA village. Scholarships have been awarded for primary, secondary, and tertiary education in PNG. Full scholarships are awarded to younger students; for older students, the amount is dependent on the student's scholastic achievement the previous year. This rubric is widely understood by beneficiaries and supported.

In practice, fewer than 50 percent of the scholarships are awarded to girls because fewer girls apply. Boys are often preferred for educational opportunities, because a girl's productive capacity and eventual bride price payment regularly factor into the decision on whether to send her long-distance for formal education.[26] Furthermore, few schools have boarding facilities, and parents have expressed a reluctance to send young girls to stay with relatives for long periods in light of security and financial concerns.

---

25 For example, according to personal communications from the foundation, the Highway (Tutuwe Trust) has allocated from K1 million to K1.5 million per year; Ok Tedi region (Waitri Trust), K500,000; and Nupmo Trust (Ningerum), K200,000 per year.

26 Thanks to a peer reviewer for these insights.

More broadly, villagers expressed concern about the lack of economic opportunities in the region for scholarship recipients (and others) after graduation. Few graduates return to the CMCA area, raising concern for future local economic development.

Decision-Making Structures Do Not Reflect the Levels of Women's Representation Mandated by the Agreement

In all the villages visited for this research, the village planning committee included only one woman, rather than the two or three required under the agreement. In most cases, the women's representative is the wife or a family member of a ward councilor, village planning committee chairman, or other elite male. No committee chairs were women. In the villages visited, few women reported being aware of what the village planning committee does and few women participate in planning for CMCA village projects.

Three women have not been appointed to the board of the overarching foundation as required by the agreement. Indeed, there are no voting beneficiary representatives—male or female—on the board. The overarching foundation continues to be controlled by the mine, which continues to hold 75 percent of the foundation's shares. The mine is assisting the impacted communities to set up an association (Ok Tedi Mine Impact Area Association) that could then take a shareholding in the foundation. The mine reports that it has taken longer than planned to build the capacity of the association and its members, and the foundation is working with the executive of the association to achieve this. Yet, two out of four seats on the foundation's board are reserved for mine company representatives, and the mine's managing director chairs the board. Furthermore, the CMCA requirement for the mine to transfer equity in the mine to the foundation (for the benefit of the impacted communities) has not occurred. These missed opportunities mean that the foundation has not yet been able to make the transition to a "high level of community ownership," as called for in the agreement.

Lack of Community Ownership Affects Development Outcomes

The failure to transfer ownership and control to beneficiaries affects the development approach adopted by the foundation and ultimately development outcomes. There is a sharp divergence between the views of those implementing the agreement (primarily mine and foundation representatives) and the beneficiaries (the villagers) regarding the success of implementation. This is perhaps not surprising, not least because it is difficult for the foundation to visit every village frequently.[27] Implementation could benefit from a structured mechanism through which valuable information about community needs, implementation challenges, and grievances—direct from beneficiaries—is fed back to the foundation to facilitate continuous improvement. The reliance on

---

27 The service standard for 2011 was one visit to each village each year; for 2012, it was an overnight stay.

village planning committee representatives overlooks intracommunity equity issues that often arise in community development.

It is hard for mining companies to "do" community driven development. The ethos of mining companies tends to be technocratic, linear, output focused, grounded in the scientific method, and focused on engineering solutions in often-difficult physical environments. Community development, on the other hand, routinely revolves around political dynamics, privileging process as much as outcomes and balancing competing interests and versions of the truth. Although the forms for inclusive community development have been put in place by the agreement, their function currently falls short of community-driven development.

This observation is exemplified in Moian village, where the mine arrived to install a water pump. Mine technicians selected a site easily accessible from the village health clinic, but 15–20 meters away from the village's customary burial grounds. Residents expressed concern that the site was too close to their burial site and suggested an alternative location for the well farther away from the village, with a pipe to bring the water in. The technicians explained to the villagers that this would be more costly and the pipe would be likely to break—thus limiting the villagers' access to water. They built the pump in the originally proposed location, which was a logical technical choice. The villagers do not use the well, which is an equally logical sociocultural choice. The result is an unsatisfying development outcome.

The foundation is taking some steps to improve the participation of villagers in project implementation. A skills census has been undertaken in each village to identify resident capacity to assist with projects. However, a focus on local labor is unlikely to result in greater community empowerment in the absence of specific actions that embed community ownership and control. The lack of community ownership is also demonstrated by another situation in Moian village, where neatly erected house poles dot the village. The poles were erected as part of a housing scheme decided on for all villages in the Middle Fly area. Each village received poles (cemented into place) and zinc roofing to connect to water tanks (delivered to the villages). The villages were asked to supply "local content" in the form of bush material for the floors and walls of houses. In addition to the poles and roofing, Moian also received a saw for villagers to cut the bush material. The saw reportedly broke. Landowners were unwilling to allow a broader group of villagers to cut trees for timber. The sets of poles remain unused, as does most of the zinc. Lopsided tanks dot the village collecting stagnant water.

The Broader Impacts of the Deal Have Not Yet Accrued

The strong leadership demonstrated by women during the early negotiation phase has not been present in the implementation phase. After a change in women's leadership, there is no identifiable cadre of women who demonstrate a similar rigor and collective agency in implementation—a challenge given the dispersed nature of the population and poor communication. There are a few positive spillovers for women from the CMCAs, with representatives of the mine and foundation reporting increased attendance and assertiveness of women in community consultations. However, village women report few changes in their own material circumstances, and there are few, if any, signs of greater entrepreneurship, participation in broader political life, or increased bargaining power for women. The anticipated empowerment gains appear not to have accrued.

This lack of spillovers is reflected in overall implementation of the agreement. Since the original agreements were reached in 2001, more than K1 billion (almost US$500 million at today's rates) has accrued to CMCA communities (with another K1 billion to the six villages immediately surrounding the mine site).[28] Regional coordinators for the foundation report being "treated like the MP" given the amounts of money they oversee.[29] Despite the significant financial flows associated with the mine, there are few visible projects in CMCA villages, basic infrastructure and service delivery are severely limited, rates of poverty are high, and health and education indicators are poor—with women tending to be worse off than men.[30] Some reasons for the lack of development include slow rollout of the foundation and underspending, intravillage divisions, poor village-level decision making, and elite capture. There are, however, very few observable projects funded from other sources, such as local government or from MP-controlled constituency development funds. The topographical and institutional landscape makes this an extremely challenging development context. The largely parallel CMCA governance structures are not linked to government: village planning committees do not coordinate with ward development committees, and relations between the mine, the foundation, the PNGSDP, and the provincial government are a topic of continuing concern.[31]

Looking Ahead: Guidance for Strengthening Women's Engagement in Mining Agreements

The PNG government is considering changes to policy and law to apply the basic tenets of the Ok Tedi Agreements to mining contexts across PNG. From the government's perspective, the agreement is an innovation worth modeling. Such policy reform is widely popular among women in other impacted communities, even though the details and shortcomings of the Ok Tedi deal

28 Over the next two years of the mine's current phase, another K292 million is projected to be received, and further extension of the mine's life is being considered.

29 As chair of a joint district planning and budget priorities committee for each constituency, MPs have significant control over sizable resources (K6 million in 2008; K4 million in 2009), which provides the potential for strong visibility and influence of MPs at the village level.

30 *2007 CMCA Census Report Appendix: Basic Statistical Tables*. *See* also D. Cammack, *Chronic Poverty in Papua New Guinea* (Chronic Poverty Research Center 2009).

31 There are efforts to address this through a project matrix that captures all the government, foundation, and PNGSDP projects to guide decisions on implementation and funding.

are not well understood. Acknowledging the unique history and context of the mine, the CMCA process provides insights for other PNG resource projects as well as for stakeholders in other resource-rich countries that have "wealth" in the form of resources but suffer regular elite capture of rents, severe gender inequality, collective action problems, and chronic development challenges.

With a view to informing future policy and practice in both PNG and elsewhere and to improving empowerment outcomes for women, the following broad guidance is provided to mining and gender practitioners engaging in these kinds of deals.

Guidance for the Negotiation Phase of Mining Agreements

- Mine operators can be powerful allies for women vis-à-vis male beneficiaries if the *business case for women's inclusion is made*.[32] In mining areas, stronger roles for women—including as mine employees—may be associated with reduced risk of conflict and increased stability of production. Women should focus on highlighting how their participation increases efficiency in the use of funds and fosters opportunities to generate positive development outcomes while also reducing the risks of complaint, conflict, and disruption of production.
- The characteristics of the individual women who participate in negotiations can make a real difference to the negotiated outcome. *Representatives who combine both local ties with national or international skills* and experience can be particularly effective.
- *Separate caucusing sessions for women*, alongside the primary negotiating stream, allow information to be shared, capacity to be built, and negotiating strategy to be developed.
- *Independent facilitators and advisers* (environmental, legal, financial) help overcome asymmetries of information and power, build trust, and ultimately construct more equitable and thus durable deals. This is of benefit for all stakeholders, but a transparent, open, and informed process also provides space for capable women. The PNG Mineral Resources Authority has an officer (who was involved in the CMCA negotiations) who now advises women in negotiation processes across the country. Although this is a step forward, it cannot be the only mechanism, because the state is also a party to these agreements and thus faces possible conflicts of interest. Similar tensions can arise for staff of mine gender desks, thus highlighting the importance of independent advice in improving negotiated outcomes.
- *A complex web of benefit streams undermines accountability*, making it difficult for beneficiaries to understand their entitlements and know who is responsible for delivering what, let alone demanding performance if it

32 *Why Gender Matters: A Resource Guide for Integrating Gender Considerations into Communities Work at Rio Tinto* (Rio Tinto 2010), available at http://www.riotinto.com/documents/ReportsPublications/Rio_Tinto_gender_guide.pdf (accessed Feb. 28 2012).

is not delivered. Complexity provides space for a small elite to exploit community benefits for personal gain; over time, confusion and capture can breed tension and conflict. It is better to deliver resources through a small number of channels that are easy for beneficiaries to understand and transparent in their delivery. This also enhances accountability while minimizing administrative overheads.

Guidance for the Implementation of Mining Agreements

- *Family bank accounts (with women as cosignatories) enhance women's control* of cash compensation payments. Mobile banking could further enhance accessibility of funds in remote areas and strengthen women's control over funds. Opportunities exist to incentivize savings, for instance, by lowering account-keeping fees, providing returns on investments, and instituting a "bonus" compensation payment or matching grant to accounts that retain an operating balance. In countries like PNG that have an increasingly interested banking sector keen to exploit rapidly increasing teledensity and a regulator focused on financial inclusion (the PNG Central Bank), the potential for pilot programs that address the constraints outlined here is significant.
- Setting aside scholarships for girls, and having women on scholarship selection panels, may not be enough to overcome cultural and logistical barriers. *Further incentives could be built in to enhance gender equality of educational opportunities,* such as a requirement that boys' scholarships are conditional on a matching number of girls' scholarships, and supplementary financing for special provisions for girls' safety and security while attending school away from home.
- *Public written information reinforces accountability,* even in communities with low literacy. Basic information about benefit procedures, amounts, dates, and feedback/grievance channels should be posted in public places, such as community halls, health clinics, schools, and churches, and posters and pamphlets should be distributed widely, summarizing information in lay terms. Mobile phones can also be used to convey information.
- The responsiveness and accountability of village representatives to beneficiary communities are undermined when representatives do not live in the village—often moving away using the fruits of their newfound status. Consideration should be given to instituting a *residency requirement for village representatives in the village they represent.*
- *Structured feedback and grievance processes increase accountability* and ensure that those responsible for project implementation have better information on activity performance and challenges and increase accountability. These procedures should allow beneficiaries to bypass their local representatives, who may be the subject of complaints, and to register mobile numbers to receive periodic texts asking for feedback on local issues.

Conclusion

The 2006–07 Ok Tedi negotiation process and the resulting CMCA agreements are innovative in that they secured enhanced rights for women in legally enforceable mining agreements, even in the context of severe gender inequality. However, legal rights are not sufficient in and of themselves to produce better development outcomes. Implementation has faced many of the challenges facing other development efforts in PNG: logistical constraints, low administrative capacity, and elite capture. Nevertheless, the prevailing gender asset gaps in the context of the current global extractives boom highlight the need to engage women more proactively in mining agreements and support them in exercising greater agency over those resources. More attention to the principles and experiences of community-driven development, as well as more local political analysis, will likely benefit women's engagement and outcomes. The particular guidance for enhancing women's agency—in both the negotiation and the implementation phases—laid out above offers further opportunities to promote women's equality and, through this, to achieve better development outcomes.

Innovation in Asset Recovery

The Swiss Perspective

RITA ADAM

Recent international studies have strikingly illustrated the enormous challenges that corruption and similar crimes pose to developing and emerging economies. The World Bank has played a vital role in bringing these problems to light. According to World Bank estimates, developing countries lose between US$20 billion and US$40 billion each year through bribery, misappropriation of funds, and other corrupt practices. This amount represents 20 percent to 40 percent of the total international development aid received by these countries. Against this backdrop, the importance of efficiently recovering assets illicitly acquired by politically exposed persons (PEP) has been increasingly recognized.

Over the course of 25 years, Switzerland has become a world leader in the field of recovery of illegal assets held by former heads of state and other PEP. The expansion of expertise in and commitment to asset recovery issues was prompted by the events that followed the overthrow of Philippine dictator Ferdinand Marcos in 1986. The Swiss government reacted to the news within hours by invoking emergency constitutional powers to freeze all assets held by members of the Marcos regime with Swiss financial intermediaries. This immediate and determined action laid the foundation for the subsequent restitution, via official mutual assistance channels, of more than US$600 million to the new and democratically elected Philippine authorities.

In Switzerland today, there is broad political consensus about determined and proactive action on the part of the authorities against illicit assets held by former heads of state and other PEPs. Switzerland has no interest in its financial sector being abused to conceal assets of dubious provenance that should be used to benefit local populations in the form of state-run programs and projects. Questions of reputation and integrity have become key factors in the global competition among financial centers. Switzerland has proven its commitment to tackling the underlying problems not only by its active participation in international initiatives but also in the number of cases that have been resolved worldwide. Over the past 25 years, Switzerland has returned to their countries of origin a total of US$1.7 billion in assets acquired unlawfully by PEPs. The World Bank puts the total value of PEP assets returned during the same time period at US$4–5 billion. As the world's seventh-largest financial center, Switzerland is thus well ahead of other countries in terms of the restitution of unlawfully acquired assets.

The Swiss authorities have acquired a great deal of experience in the restitution of PEP assets since 1986. One of the main lessons learned is the importance of creativity and innovation in resolving cases successfully. No two asset recovery cases are exactly alike. As the example of the former Nigerian head of state Sani Abacha underscores—at US$800 million, the largest sum of money ever returned worldwide—such cases are extremely complex because a large number of banks, countries, and third parties are usually involved. Because mutual legal assistance (MLA) procedures often stretch over periods of many years, the interaction between internal and international instruments in each specific case is of the utmost importance.

Following a brief general overview of the Swiss legal framework for asset recovery, this chapter highlights two specific areas that have seen considerable progress and developments in recent years. First, the chapter addresses the creation of new legal provisions tailored specifically to cases in which the state structures in the country of origin are so weak that the restitution of unlawfully acquired assets by international MLA channels is impossible. Second, the chapter turns to the Arab Spring and Switzerland's initial findings on implications for asset recovery.

Overview of the Swiss Institutional and Legal Framework to Combat and Return Assets Illicitly Acquired by PEP

Switzerland has a comprehensive range of legal instruments and measures in place for turning away assets of criminal origin and for identifying, blocking, and returning them if they nonetheless find their way into the local financial center. Swiss banking secrecy law does not apply to assets of criminal origin and therefore does not impede existing protective and preventive measures in any way.[1]

The Swiss legal framework rests on five pillars comparable to the provisions familiar in many other states. The various elements are outlined below.

Prevention of Corruption

The first pillar aims to prevent high-ranking foreign officials from illegally enriching themselves in the first place. Promoting good governance and tackling the root causes of corruption rate highly in Switzerland's foreign policy. In its development cooperation, Switzerland gives priority to combining measures at the governmental level through institutional reforms and activities involving civil society, such as awareness raising, participative approaches, social audits, and investigative journalism.

Due Diligence/Know Your Customer

Another pillar is due diligence; Switzerland takes the necessary measures to prevent illicit assets of PEPs from being transferred to Switzerland or laun-

---

1 For more information, *see* http://www.eda.admin.ch/eda/en/home/topics/finec/intcr/poexp.html.

dered via the Swiss banking system and thus being brought into legal economic circulation. Switzerland does not want to function as a safe haven for illicit assets of PEPs. Stringent "know your customer" rules oblige providers of financial services in Switzerland to identify their clients and ascertain the origin of their assets. To comply with these rules, financial intermediaries are required to identify the beneficial owner of assets. When dealing with PEPs, Switzerland's legislation also stipulates, in conformity with internationally recognized standards, special clarification requirements (enhanced due diligence) and requires that business relations with PEPs be considered as involving increased risks.

Obligation to Report

All financial intermediaries operating in Switzerland are subject to a legal reporting obligation if they become aware, or have reasonable grounds to suspect, that the assets involved in a given business relationship are, or may be, associated with money laundering or terrorism financing, originate from criminal activities, or are connected with a criminal organization. In such cases, financial intermediaries are required to block assets immediately and to notify the Swiss financial intelligence unit, the Money Laundering Reporting Office Switzerland (MROS), without delay. If there is reason to believe that this may be a case of corruption, MROS will alert the criminal prosecution authorities, who will conduct a preliminary inquiry into the origin of the assets. If suspicions persist, the competent authorities will initiate criminal proceedings for money laundering.

International Mutual Legal Assistance

Under international standards, the unlawful acquisition of the assets in question must be proven in judicial proceedings before they can be returned. International MLA in criminal matters is a central instrument in this examination.

The Swiss Federal Act on International Mutual Assistance in Criminal Matters entered into effect on January 1, 1983. It empowers Switzerland to grant legal assistance to countries with which it has not concluded a bilateral agreement. Swiss authorities take care, wherever possible, to apply the provisions of the law with the flexibility needed to respond to the specific circumstances of individual asset recovery cases and to develop creative approaches to resolving them. This approach makes it possible to actively support states that have encountered difficulties in their recovery efforts. This support may be necessary when the state in question is unable to provide all the evidence required or to comply with the formalities necessary in the context of MLA. In such cases, Switzerland can help the state complete the request for international MLA and might even pay for the translation of such a request so that it can be submitted to the competent Swiss authorities in one of the national languages, as required by the act. In some cases, Switzerland has exceptionally paid lawyers' fees to enable requesting states to benefit from counseling, thus increasing their chances of recovering embezzled funds.

In parallel with the establishment of international MLA where there are sufficient suspicions to justify it, Swiss authorities will instigate criminal investigations into money laundering, organized crime, or similar offenses. The primary channel for any restitution of assets nonetheless remains the international MLA process, in combination with the associated criminal proceedings in the state of origin, because it is there that the evidence can generally be found that will determine whether the assets were acquired as the result of a criminal act. If the unlawful origin of the assets is evident, Switzerland may under certain conditions return the assets without any legally enforceable forfeiture order from the state concerned, as in the Abacha case, mentioned above.

Restitution

Switzerland has made it a priority to return unlawfully acquired PEP assets rapidly and in full to their country of origin. As soon as it is established that assets located and frozen in Switzerland originate from a criminal act, authorities will determine which form of restitution best takes into account the circumstances of the individual case. Experience over 25 years shows that there is no one-size-fits-all solution. Hence, Switzerland finds an ad hoc solution to ensure that the assets in question will indeed benefit the population of the country of origin. Furthermore, restitution can be a delicate matter if corruption is endemic in the country of origin of the assets. In such cases, finding a way to ensure that the assets in question will not simply be recycled into criminal activities is crucial. Possible approaches in such cases include setting up an independent monitoring mechanism, returning assets via an international organization that runs projects and programs in the country of origin, or cooperation with NGOs.

In the Sharing Act (the Federal Act Pertaining to the Sharing of Confiscated Assets), Switzerland has a legal foundation on which it can enter into international asset-sharing agreements in cases of organized crime and money laundering. The act provides for the waiver of any share of assets forfeited in Switzerland so that the entire amount is repaid to the country of origin. It is a standing policy of Switzerland to return in their entirety to the state concerned any confiscated illicit assets of PEPs originating from bribery or misappropriation of funds, without insisting on asset sharing.

Lessons Learned from the Mobutu and Duvalier Cases

The Federal Act on the Restitution of Assets of Politically Exposed Persons Obtained by Unlawful Means (Restitution of Illicit Assets Act, or RIAA) is a significant enhancement to Switzerland's legal arsenal in the field of asset recovery.[2] The RIAA, in force since 2011, contains legal provisions tailored

---

2 *See* http://www.admin.ch/ch/e/rs/c196_1.html; for more information, *see* also http://www.eda.admin.ch/eda/en/home/topics/finec/intcr/poexp/faqria.html.

specifically to cases in which the state structures in the country of origin are so weak that the restitution of kleptocrat funds via international MLA channels faces insurmountable barriers. The drafting of the act was prompted basically by Switzerland's experiences in the cases of Mobutu (the Democratic Republic of the Congo, DRC) and Duvalier (Haiti).

In the first case, the Swiss government made use of its emergency powers anchored in the Swiss Federal Constitution to freeze any Mobutu assets located in Switzerland immediately after the fall of the dictator in 1997.[3] In doing so, the Federal Council intended to make it possible for the new government, headed by Laurent Kabila, to submit a request for international MLA within the necessary time frame. Unfortunately, due to the inactivity of the Congolese authorities, who failed to supply the information required and to initiate proceedings against Mobutu, the first international MLA procedure had to be stopped in 2003. The Federal Council, confronted with the imminent risk that the frozen assets would become available again to the members of the Mobutu family, felt it was necessary to act. Indeed, in view of Mobutu's universally acknowledged kleptocracy, the return of this money to the Mobutu family was as unacceptable to Switzerland as it was to the DRC. The Federal Council mandated the Swiss Federal Department of Foreign Affairs to make contact with the Congolese authorities in an effort to find a solution that would allow restitution of the assets. This collaboration made it possible, after several years of negotiations, to obtain the agreement of the DRC authorities to allow a Geneva lawyer, paid for by the Swiss Confederation, to begin criminal proceedings in an effort to recover these assets. A lawsuit filed in Switzerland against the Mobutu family on behalf of the DRC alleging the establishment of a criminal organization was not pursued by the Swiss Attorney General's Office. It decided not to commence investigations because the statute of limitations on the alleged acts had already expired. Unfortunately, the Congolese government instructed its lawyer not to contest the decision of the Attorney General's Office and, in doing so, destroyed all hope that the frozen assets would be returned to the Congolese people. Hence, the procedure was terminated, and Switzerland had no other choice but to unfreeze the Mobutu assets after twelve years of relentless efforts to avoid exactly that.

Switzerland regards such an outcome as extremely unsatisfactory. It is all the more objectionable that a despot continues to profit from the result of his poor governance even after he has been overthrown—it is precisely his years or decades of dictatorship that weakened state structures to the point that renders the new authorities incapable of successfully conducting MLA proceedings with a partner state. The result is that assets that are frozen in foreign financial centers, such as Switzerland, are ultimately unfrozen and placed back in the hands of the overthrown dictator.

---

3 *See* discussion in the section of this chapter entitled "The Arab Spring and Its Implications for Asset Recovery."

It seemed that the Duvalier case would have a similar outcome. Beginning in 1986, the Duvalier case went through a period involving MLA. Following the difficulties of Haiti to sufficiently substantiate their MLA request, this procedure was terminated in 2002. Again, the Federal Council decided to intervene, given the manifestly illicit nature of the assets in question. After an asset freeze was ordered on the basis of Swiss constitutional powers, negotiations for a settlement were conducted with the government of Haiti, and with the Duvalier family, but without results until 2007. President René Préval indicated his desire to combat the impunity of the Duvalier family and to take possession of the assets with the help of another MLA procedure, which made its way to the Swiss Federal Supreme Court. In early 2010, the court ruled that restitution in accordance with current Swiss law was no longer possible due to the statute of limitations. At the same time, however, the court confirmed that the assets were of illicit origin. While regretting the need to apply the statute of limitations, the court expressed its view that the conditions imposed by the Federal Act on International Mutual Assistance in Criminal Matters "seem too strict for this type of affair." In making this observation, the court invited Swiss lawmakers to take into consideration the nature of fragile states and to try to increase their chances of benefiting from the restitution of assets.

Fortunately the authorities—prompted by experience gained in the Mobutu case—had already embarked on the corresponding legislative work. In an effort to safeguard the Duvalier assets, the government decided to freeze them while awaiting completion of the parliamentary procedure. Work on new draft legislation was driven forward with the highest priority. The Federal Act on the Restitution of Assets of Politically Exposed Persons Obtained by Unlawful Means (Restitution of Illicit Assets Act, RIAA) entered into force in February 2011, just one year after the Supreme Court's ruling. It makes Switzerland the first nation in the world to have a law enabling the state to overcome the difficulties involved when dealing with another state that is no longer able to meet the requirements of an MLA procedure due to the collapse of all or a substantial part of its judicial apparatus or judicial dysfunction. The RIAA's innovative approach attracted worldwide attention. Stuart Levey, the former undersecretary for terrorism and financial intelligence at the US Department of the Treasury, described the RIAA as "arguably the world's toughest law for repatriating the ill-gotten gains of corrupt politicians."[4]

The RIAA came into existence as a result of the difficulties encountered by the Swiss authorities in returning assets frozen in Switzerland to such states following the failure of the international MLA process to produce a satisfactory result. The aim of the act is to prevent such situations from recurring and to resolve cases of assets that have been frozen on the orders of the Federal Council's constitutional powers. The RIAA is a subsidiary solution to the Federal Act on International Mutual Assistance in Criminal Matters. In contrast

---

4 *See* Stuart Levey, *Fighting Corruption after the Arab Spring*, Foreign Affairs (online edition, June 16, 2011), http://www.foreignaffairs.com/articles/67895/stuart-levey/corruption-and-the-arab-spring.

to criminal law, the RIAA makes the distinction between the conduct of PEPs and the unlawful origin of their assets. In this way, it provides for a different approach to the criminal prosecution of the PEP concerned and enables the forfeiture of assets that clearly have been obtained by unlawful means without the need for a criminal conviction against the PEP in question.

There are three stages to the repatriation of misappropriated assets under the terms of the RIAA:

- To prevent an outflow of suspicious assets, the Federal Council may, under the conditions outlined in the RIAA, take the first step of ordering that assets be frozen to secure them.
- This is followed by the forfeiture of the assets in proceedings under administrative law. Here, the state appears as plaintiff against the holder of the disputed assets.
- Once a forfeiture ruling has attained legal effect, the assets are repatriated to their state of origin in a transparent process.

A major innovation of the RIAA is the reversal of the burden of proof in respect to the unlawful origin of frozen PEP assets. With the Mobutu and Duvalier cases in mind, the law provides for a reversal of the burden of proof with regard to the assets' illicit origin. In other words, forfeiture is justified under the RIAA if the current owner of these assets is unable to prove that the assets are, in all probability, of lawful origin. This concept rests on the assumption that if a notoriously corrupt PEP or associates hold powers of disposal over an amount of assets that are out of proportion to the PEP's official salary, these assets are, in all probability, unlawful in origin.

The RIAA stipulates that the unlawful origin of assets may be presumed if both of the following two conditions are met:

- The wealth of the person who has powers of disposal over the assets has been subject to an extraordinary increase during the PEP's period of office. This provision is intended to cover two cases: one in which PEPs hold powers of disposal, and one in which the person who holds powers of disposal is not the same person who exercised a public office but is one of their associates. An "extraordinary increase" means that there is a significant discrepancy between the income derived from the public office and that generated by the assets concerned that cannot be explained by normal empirical patterns and the country's overall situation. A similar provision exists in the UN Convention against Corruption, which talks of a significant increase in the assets of a public official that he or she cannot reasonably explain in relation to his or her lawful income. Concrete evidence, to be introduced by the Swiss authorities as plaintiff, must prove that the concerned assets have increased extraordinarily over the relevant period. This would be true, for example, of a minister who became a millionaire while in office, despite not previously having had any wealth. Another example is a person associated with a PEP whose construction or service company generated very high profits from public contracts in connection with the office in question. The extraordinary increase condition does not, however, apply to assets that have grown as a result of skilled portfolio management on the part of the bank with which the assets are lodged.

- There is a notoriously high level of corruption of the state or PEP in question during the PEP's period of office. Whether or not the level of corruption is "notoriously high" is determined in a status analysis based on reports from organizations, such as the World Bank or Transparency International, that conduct research work and analyses on corruption issues. Typical cases include those of Suharto, Mobutu, and Duvalier. During their periods in office, the level of corruption was recognized as high in respect to the persons themselves and the country as a whole. Criminal acts that are not necessarily classified as corruption under Swiss law but that constitute the improper conduct of a public official in other respects (for example, misappropriation of funds, embezzlement, or another unlawful use of funds) must also be taken into account in this evaluation.

The persons concerned can invalidate the presumption of unlawful origin of the assets by presenting a convincing case for their lawful enrichment. In other words, the presumption ceases to apply if it can be demonstrated that, in all probability, the assets were acquired by lawful means, specifically by presenting suitable evidence and explaining suspicious transactions.

The Swiss authorities are confident that the innovative approach of the RIAA is a significant enhancement to the legal framework for asset recovery. The first case of application of the RIAA is pending: the planned forfeiture order for the Duvalier assets. The corresponding legal action was brought before the competent Federal Administrative Court by the Swiss authorities in April 2011, just two months after the RIAA went into effect.

The Arab Spring and Its Implications for Asset Recovery

General Remarks

The upheavals in the Arab world in 2011 brought the discussion on the freezing and recovery of illicit assets attributed to PEPs to the forefront.[5] In view of the historic dimension of the events taking place, the Swiss government decided to act very swiftly. Only a few days after the overthrow of presidents Zine el Abidine Ben Ali (Tunisia) and Hosni Mubarak (Egypt), the Federal Council invoked its emergency constitutional powers to make Switzerland the first country in the world to freeze all the assets held with its financial intermediaries by Ben Ali, Mubarak, and their associates. The Federal Council's aims were twofold. First, it wished to avoid the movement of any unlawfully acquired assets to other financial centers, thereby evading justice—at least in

---

5 For more information, *see* http://www.eda.admin.ch/eda/en/home/topics/finec/intcr/poexp/sperr.html.

the short term. Second, its swift action sent a clear signal to the states of origin that Switzerland was willing to accept requests for international MLA so that misappropriated assets could be returned in full as quickly as possible. There were soon signs that this signal had been understood. Just a few weeks after the freeze was imposed, Switzerland received the first requests for MLA from Tunisia and Egypt. A further unilateral freeze on the assets of Muammar Gaddafi (Libya) and his associates was replaced by a regime of sanctions following the adoption of the corresponding UN sanctions in March 2011. In parallel with the efforts moving through international MLA channels, the Swiss criminal prosecution authorities began their own investigations into associates of Ben Ali and Mubarak on suspicion of money laundering and membership in a criminal organization.

The legal foundation for the preventive freezing of assets is given by a specific provision in the federal constitution. Article 184, paragraph 3, reads, "Where safeguarding the interests of the country so require, the Federal Council may issue ordinances and rulings. Ordinances must be of limited duration." The Swiss government has made use of this option in several exceptional cases, starting with the Marcos funds in 1986, to freeze assets. This tactic is a Swiss specialty: no other country practices such "constitutional freezing." Three months after the freezes with regard to Tunisia and Egypt were ordered, the government conducted an initial review of its action and decided to create a legal basis for the freezing of PEP assets for the purpose of securing them. This resolution represents a clear commitment to maintaining the practice developed over more than 25 years, that is, that Switzerland is willing to freeze assets as a preventive step in extraordinary cases to prevent their flight elsewhere and to create the best possible conditions for successful international MLA proceedings for the state of origin. The planned legal basis is intended to set out the conditions for a freeze in greater detail and to determine the basic parameters for its implementation. As a next step following the RIAA, it will complete the Swiss legal framework on asset recovery.

The successful restitution of unlawfully acquired assets via international MLA channels is a complex undertaking that demands political will, persistence, and creativity. Switzerland knows from experience that a close partnership between the requesting and the requested states is a key factor. Indeed, as the term "mutual" implies, MLA procedures cannot be successfully achieved by the requesting or the requested state alone. Furthermore, effective implementation of existing norms can sometimes be challenging. MLA proceedings are by nature rather static. Hence, in order to successfully address asset recovery, one of the main questions is how best to make dynamic use of the legal framework. This means, for example, that requests for MLA that do not satisfy all the formal requirements are not simply returned without comment or even ignored by the requested state. It is preferable in such situations actively to seek dialogue with the authorities of the requesting state to resolve possible problems such as those that might arise in connection with expert-level meetings. It can also be helpful for the requested state to make an expert in MLA and asset-tracing issues available to the authorities of the requesting state to provide targeted support and address any outstanding questions. To date, Switzerland's experience with this approach—which was applied to the requests for international MLA from Tunisia and Egypt—has been positive. To take the Tunisian example, the local prosecutorial authorities are professional and competent, but they have handled few corruption cases in Tunisia, for obvious reasons. However, thanks to Switzerland's providing an expert in MLA and asset tracing, by the end of 2011 the Tunisian authorities were able to submit several formally complete requests for MLA to Switzerland. These were passed directly on to the Swiss judicial authorities for a substantive review.

Possibilities for Future Action

Complex asset recovery proceedings generally involve several jurisdictions. To resolve the issues that this causes, a close partnership between the requesting and the requested state is required, as is intensive communication between the various states to which requests for international MLA have been addressed when it is suspected that unlawfully acquired assets are being held within their financial sectors. Therefore, since 2001, the Lausanne Seminars have provided a forum in which experts from requesting and requested states, as well as those from international organizations (including the World Bank) are able, at Switzerland's invitation, to discuss the practical problems of asset recovery.

One year after the beginning of the Arab Spring, the purpose of the sixth edition of the seminar, held in January 2012, was to take stock of progress made and to identify challenges with a view to examining possibilities for future action. Centered on the experiences of requesting and requested states in the wake of the events in North Africa, representatives from Egypt, Libya, and Tunisia voiced their observations and concerns, followed by remarks from requesting states and third actors, such as the World Bank, the UN Office on Drugs and Crime (UNODC), the European Commission, and the International Centre for Asset Recovery, and an in-depth discussion. While acknowledging the existence and possible added value of domestic criminal investigations conducted in requested states, participants agreed that international cooperation through MLA is the prime vehicle for achieving the recovery of such assets. They identified the following key actions for accelerating pending procedures:

- Build and deepen effective MLA partnerships based on dialogue and trust between requesting and requested states through the following actions:
    - Strengthen trust and mutual understanding by developing personal contacts between the competent authorities and persons in charge in requesting and requested states.
    - Increase dialogue through institutionalized communication channels, for example, regular meetings between experts from both sides, to address issues directly and to ensure consistent follow-up to pending procedures.

    - Ensure continuity with the competent authorities and persons in charge by avoiding "wandering files."
    - Improve the quality of communication; for example, no MLA request remains unanswered. If not all formal requirements are met or other problems exist from the point of view of the requested state, the requesting state is rapidly informed.
    - Deepen the partnership between requesting and requested states through the joint determination of possible fields for technical cooperation, for example, by dispatching MLA experts from the requested state.
- Improve coordination mechanisms, at both international and domestic levels, with a view to making relevant information more rapidly and effectively available through the following actions:
    - Improve coordination at the domestic level by, for example, creating focal points and/or task forces in charge of pending asset recovery cases, with clearly attributed responsibilities for each task force member.
    - Use existing international practitioners' networks more consistently, for example, in the framework of Interpol, Eurojust, Egmont, and the like, to increase the flow of information.
    - Create, if needed, new, tailor-made networks and communication platforms or international task forces to share information more effectively.
    - Explore ways to increase cooperation with financial intelligence units (FIUs) with a view to exploiting more effectively the information and intelligence available in FIU networks.
    - Collect facts on the ongoing measures of financial centers to support requesting states; for example, develop a matrix of assets frozen, seized, and finally repatriated by (and for) each state in question.
- Customize the approach that best fits a specific case, with particular attention to creativity and complementarity, through the following actions:
    - Combine the available instruments, such as MLA proceedings, domestic criminal proceedings (for example, for money laundering or for participation in a criminal organization), and civil forfeiture.
    - Within the existing legal framework, make use of one's own MLA requests to substantiate partner states' MLA requests by providing relevant information.
    - Increase cooperation with third actors such as the World Bank/StAR, UNODC, and nongovernmental service providers such as the International Centre for Asset Recovery, bearing in mind the important role they can play in capacity building, as well as with "matchmakers" to bridge information gaps.

- Explore the possibility of establishing international standard practices in MLA proceedings and asset recovery as a blueprint for action in current and upcoming cases (typical sequencing, main legal challenges to be addressed, and the like).
- Actively search for innovative and creative solutions, bearing in mind that in asset recovery, there are no one-size-fits-all solutions.

Participants concluded their discussions by expressing the wish for a follow-up to take stock of progress and to keep the momentum developed at the seminar.

Conclusions

Experience has shown that asset recovery cases raise complex legal issues across several jurisdictions. Resolving these issues demands close and unwavering partnerships between the states involved, including the states of origin, as well as a considerable degree of tenacity and perseverance. The dynamic application of the existing legal framework can go a long way toward simplifying efforts via international mutual assistance channels and speeding up restitution. In most cases, innovation and creativity play a decisive role in asset recovery. By its very definition, however, innovation is a process. Each case that is resolved offers new insights that allow the authorities concerned to review their procedures, amend them as necessary, and develop new approaches for the future.

Switzerland has a fundamental interest in ensuring that its financial sector is not used as a hiding place for assets of unlawful origin. Since the Marcos case in 1986, Switzerland has gathered a great deal of experience in the field of asset recovery and has refined its national legal framework accordingly. Regular contact with the competent authorities of partner states has been an important part of this development. Switzerland plans to continue this dialogue through knowledge and experience sharing and will maintain its commitment in this area.

International Asset Sharing

A Multipurpose Tool for Development

Karyn Kenny

The ability of governments across the globe to work effectively together to identify, seize, and forfeit illicit gains and combat the money laundering and the corruption that stem from these illicit gains is a critical component of international development. "Taking the profit out of crime" is an important goal within the international asset forfeiture (AF) and anti-money-laundering (AML) community. The need to strengthen AF/AML cooperation on a global level is even more important. As the US Attorney General pointed out in March 2012, "[i]n an era where crime is not limited by physical boundaries, our international partnerships are more critical than ever in the work of bringing criminals to justice."[1] One such tool for development that strengthens international cooperation, builds domestic capacity, and combats transnational economic crime is international asset-sharing programs (IASPs). IASPs are agreements that permit the sharing country to recognize case-related assistance received from other countries during a domestically prosecuted forfeiture and/or money-laundering case.

This chapter outlines the components of an IASP and examines IASPs as a mechanism to aid economic and legal development. The chapter first examines the topic of international asset sharing from the perspective of an international organization, specifically, the United Nations (UN). The analysis then turns to a discussion of countries participating in asset-sharing agreements, such as The Bahamas and Canada. Then it explores the US Department of Justice's (DOJ) IASP program in detail, focusing first on the US legislative framework regarding forfeiture and the DOJ's management model for forfeited property and funds and then on the manner in which DOJ international sharing agreements are structured. The chapter concludes with an overview of the benefits of implementing a transparent and accountable IASP.

Interwoven throughout the discussion are the developmental benefits that can be realized by implementing an IASP. Tangible benefits include building international cooperation among justice and financial agencies (for example,

---

Any opinions expressed in the chapter are the author's own and do not, in any way, reflect the official position or views of the US DOJ. The author would like to thank Hassane Cissé, Thomas Dougherty, Agustin Flah, Jenifer Preston, Matthew Moorhead, Milena Sanchez de Boado, and Linda Samuel for their support.

1 Remarks by the Attorney General of the United States Eric J. Holder, Jr. (Mar. 26, 2012), available at http://www.gsnmagazine.com/node/25953 (accessed Mar. 28, 2012). Mark Rockwell, *U. S., Mexico to Split Millions in Seized Assets to Cripple Drug Gangs, Government Security News* (Mar. 27, 2012).

financial intelligence units and prosecution and law enforcement agencies), building capacity in domestic AF/AML sectors, and taking money out of the pockets of criminals.

UN Support for Asset Sharing

Support for international asset sharing can be found in a number of UN conventions, including the UN Convention against Illicit Traffic in Narcotic Drugs and Psychotropic Substances of 1988[2] (commonly referred to as the Vienna Convention), the UN Convention against Transnational Organized Crime[3] (commonly referred to as the Palermo Convention), and the International Convention for the Suppression of the Financing of Terrorism.[4]

Pursuant to UN Resolution 2004/24,

> the Economic and Social Council, determined to strengthen international cooperation in the confiscation and disposal of the proceeds of crime covered by the Organized Crime Convention and the United Nations Convention against Illicit Traffic in Narcotic Drugs and Psychotropic Substances of 1988, and recognizing that a model bilateral agreement on sharing confiscated proceeds of crime could facilitate greater international cooperation in that matter, requested the Secretary-General to convene an open-ended intergovernmental expert group to prepare such a draft model bilateral agreement. The group met from 26 to 28 January 2005.[5]

As a result of these meetings, the UN Office on Drugs and Crime successfully developed a model agreement on international asset sharing. The UN Crime Commission endorsed this agreement in May 2005, and the UN General Assembly endorsed it in December 2005. The model provides a useful framework for countries needing an asset-sharing agreement to facilitate international forfeiture cooperation.

---

2 Article 5(a) provides that "proceeds or property confiscated by a Party . . . shall be disposed of by that Party according to its domestic law and administrative procedures." Article 5(b)(ii) encourages the sharing of such confiscated assets with other parties "on a regular or case-by-case basis" in accordance with domestic law or any applicable bilateral or multilateral agreements." Available at http://www.unodc.org/pdf/convention_1988_en.pdf (accessed Mar. 3, 2012).

3 Article 14 calls for forfeited assets to be disposed of pursuant to domestic law, but "if so requested" the country should "give priority consideration to returning the confiscated proceeds of crime or property to the requesting State Party so that it can give compensation to the victims of the crime or return such proceeds of crime or property to their legitimate owners." *See* http://www.unodc.org/unodc/en/treaties/CTOC (accessed Mar. 3, 2012).

4 This convention recommends, but does not mandate, sharing. *See* http://www.un.org/law/cod/finterr.htm (accessed Mar. 3, 2012).

5 *See* Eleventh United Nations Congress on Crime Prevention and Criminal Justice, Bangkok 6 (Apr. 2005). *See* also http://www.un.org/events/11thcongress/docs/programme.pdf (accessed Mar. 12, 2012).

In addition to the UN conventions, recommendation 38 of the Financial Action Task Force (FATF)[6] advocates international asset sharing. Specifically, this recommendation states that

> [t]here should be authority to take expeditious action in response to requests by foreign countries to identify, freeze, seize and confiscate property laundered, proceeds from money laundering or predicate offences, instrumentalities used in or intended for use in the commission of these offences, or property of corresponding value. There should also be arrangements for co-ordinating seizure and confiscation proceedings, which may include the sharing of confiscated assets.[7]

In addition to UN support for international asset-sharing agreements, many nations, recognizing the benefits of such agreements, have established their own IASPs. The US Attorney General states, "It is the policy of the United States to encourage international asset sharing and to recognize all foreign assistance that facilitates US forfeitures so far as consistent with US law."[8] This chapter examines in detail the components of one such IASP—that of the DOJ.[9]

Bermuda and Canada—International Asset-Sharing Agreements

Bermuda and Canada are two countries that have entered into formal asset-sharing agreements. In March 2009, officials from the Bahamian and Canadian governments signed an asset-sharing agreement that reinforced their shared commitment to confiscate the proceeds of drug trafficking and money laundering, among other criminal acts. Prior to the agreement, The Bahamas and Canada had relied primarily on the 1990 Mutual Legal Assistance in Criminal Matters Treaty to exchange information and confiscate illegal assets.

A mutual legal assistance treaty

> facilitates the gathering of evidence and intelligence in the investigation and prosecution of criminal offences. It also enhances the capabilities in the confiscation of the proceeds of crime. Mutual legal assistance treaties are concluded between two countries for the pur-

6 "The Financial Action Task Force (FATF) is an inter-governmental body established in 1989 by the Ministers of its Member jurisdictions. The objectives of the FATF are to set standards and promote effective implementation of legal, regulatory and operational measures for combating money laundering, terrorist financing and other related threats to the integrity of the international financial system. The FATF is therefore a 'policy-making body' which works to generate the necessary political will to bring about national legislative and regulatory reforms in these areas." *See* http://www.fatf-gafi.org/pages/aboutus/ (accessed Mar. 10, 2012).

7 *See* http://www.fatf-gafi.org/media/fatf/documents/40%20Recommendations.pdf, at 13 (accessed Mar. 24, 2012).

8 *US Attorneys Manual, Chapter 9-116.000, Equitable Sharing and Federal Adoption, 9-116.400, International Sharing of Forfeited Assets* (2011).

9 The US Department of Treasury maintains its own IASP for cases handled by the agencies that fall within the Treasury's domain, such as the Internal Revenue Service.

> pose of gathering and exchanging information in an effort to enforce criminal laws and confiscate the ill-gotten gains of criminal activity.[10]

Then, in 2000, "[p]ursuant to the 1988 United Nations Convention against the Illicit Traffic in Narcotic Drugs and Psychotropic Substances, the Government of The Bahamas implemented the Proceeds of Crime Act 2000 (Act), where Sections 52 and 53 provide[d] for the establishment and administration of the Confiscated Assets Fund."[11] Following the passage of the act, the government of the Bahamas expressed a desire to formalize their existing cooperation efforts with the government of Canada. In 2001, both countries participated in negotiations that resulted in an agreement to enter into a formal asset-sharing agreement. In 2009, officials representing the governments signed an asset-sharing agreement. With this agreement, Bahamian and Canadian officials were able to strengthen their mutual cooperation efforts in combating international money-laundering offenders while facilitating bilateral confiscation of illicitly obtained assets.

Asset Forfeiture Framework—US Federal Statutes

The fundamental building block for any IASP is a strong and comprehensive legal framework. The statutory authority that enables the DOJ to enter into international asset-sharing agreements is found in Statute 18 US Code (USC) Section 981(i), Statute 21 USC Section 882(e)(1)(E), and Statute 31 USC Section 9703(h)(2).[12] Statute 18 USC Section 981(i) sets forth the conditions under

---

10 *See* http://www.thebahamasweekly.com/publish/bis-newsupdates/Bahamas_and_Canada_Sign_Asset_ Sharing_Agreement 5788.shtml (accessed Jul. 19, 2012).

11 *Id.*

12 Statute 18 USC Section 981—Civil Forfeiture, Section (i), reads, in part: "(1) Whenever property is civilly or criminally forfeited under this chapter, the Attorney General or the Secretary of the Treasury, as the case may be, may transfer the forfeited personal property or the proceeds of the sale of any forfeited personal or real property to any foreign country which participated directly or indirectly in the seizure or forfeiture of the property, if such a transfer (A) has been agreed to by the Secretary of State; (B) is authorized in an international agreement between the United States and the foreign country; and (C) is made to a country which, if applicable, has been certified under Section 481(h) [4] of the Foreign Assistance Act of 1961. A decision by the Attorney General or the Secretary of the Treasury pursuant to this paragraph shall not be subject to review. The foreign country shall, in the event of a transfer of property or proceeds of sale of property under this subsection, bear all expenses incurred by the United States in the seizure, maintenance, inventory, storage, forfeiture, and disposition of the property, and all transfer costs. The payment of all such expenses, and the transfer of assets pursuant to this paragraph, shall be upon such terms and conditions as the Attorney General or the Secretary of the Treasury may, in his discretion, set. (2) The provisions of this section shall not be construed as limiting or superseding any other authority of the United States to provide assistance to a foreign country in obtaining property related to a crime committed in the foreign country, including property which is sought as evidence of a crime committed in the foreign country. (3) A certified order or judgment of forfeiture by a court of competent jurisdiction of a foreign country concerning property which is the subject of forfeiture under this section and was determined by such court to be the type of property described in subsection (a)(1)(B) of this section, and any certified recordings or transcripts of testimony taken in a foreign judicial proceeding concerning such order or judgment of forfeiture, shall be admissible in evidence in a proceeding brought pursuant to this section.

which the US Attorney General may transfer personal property, or the proceeds from the sale of any personal or real property, that has been civilly or criminally forfeited to a foreign country. The critical component of this statute is that it grants the attorney general discretionary authority regarding sharing agreements.

Forfeiture Statutes

Forfeiture is the taking, by the government, of property derived from a crime, involved in a crime, or that facilitates a crime, without compensating the owner. Many countries have enacted forfeiture laws in both their civil and their criminal codes. In the US federal system, there are two types of forfeiture: administrative and judicial. Judicial forfeiture, which requires a prosecutor to start a case in court, is further subdivided into criminal and civil forfeiture. Each of these types of forfeiture is briefly discussed below.

Administrative Forfeiture

Administrative forfeiture is a nonjudicial matter handled by a law enforcement agency; the majority of all forfeitures are administrative. In this process, the seizing agency declares the property forfeited without a judicial proceeding; this status is reserved for uncontested cases. An administrative forfeiture typically begins with a law enforcement agent making a seizure based on probable cause.[13] Each step of the administrative forfeiture process includes procedural and constitutional protections for owners.

Following the initial seizure, the law enforcement agency commences the administrative forfeiture process by sending a notice to the party informing it of its right to file a claim for the return of the seized property within a certain period of time. After the period of time has lapsed, and if no claim is filed, the property may be declared forfeited by the federal agency. However, if a claim is filed, the case is referred to a prosecutor for judicial forfeiture, a process in which the party may challenge the forfeiture.

Pursuant to US federal law, the seizing or adopting[14] law enforcement agency may proceed to administratively forfeit a defined category of items. For example, the following may be forfeited: monetary instruments, such as cash, checks, stocks, and bonds; or conveyances, such as vehicles, vessels,

---

Such certified order or judgment of forfeiture."

13 "[P]robable cause is a flexible, common-sense standard. It merely requires that the facts available to the officer would 'warrant a man of reasonable caution in the belief,' *Carroll v. United States*, 267 U.S. 132, 162 [45 S.Ct. 280, 288, 69 L.Ed. 543] (1925), that certain items may be contraband or stolen property or useful as evidence of a crime; it does not demand any showing that such a belief be correct or more likely true than false." *United States v. Dunn*, 946 F.2d 615, 619 (9th Cir. 1991), *cert. denied*, 502 U.S. 950 (1991).

14 Under US federal law, a state or local law enforcement agency may request that a federal agency "adopt" a seizure if certain conditions are met, including if the underlying act supporting the seizure was a violation of US federal law.

and/or aircraft that have been used to commit or facilitate a crime. In regard to other property, such as bank accounts and jewelry, only items valued at US$500,000 or less may be seized. Although most property can be forfeited administratively, an important exception is real property.[15]

Judicial Forfeiture

Judicial forfeiture "is the process by which property is declared forfeited to the United States by a court. This status is required for any property other than monetary instruments and hauling conveyances if the value of the other property exceeds US$500,000; a valid, timely claim has been filed in an administrative forfeiture; or if the property is real estate."[16]

Once a property claim enters into a judicial forfeiture procedure, it will proceed as either a criminal or a civil case, depending on the circumstances regarding the seizure.

Criminal Forfeiture

Because it is *in personam*, that is, forfeiture against the person, only property that the defendant in a criminal case has an interest in, and that does not belong to a third party, can be forfeited in a criminal case. In criminal forfeitures, the forfeiture allegation is contained within the criminal indictment.[17] If the defendant is convicted, the jury or court hears additional evidence and/or argument on the forfeiture matter. If applicable, the court may also hold a post-trial ancillary hearing to address any third-party interests.

Civil Forfeiture

Civil forfeiture, also referred to as non-conviction-based forfeiture, is a civil action in-rem, that is, against the property itself, and forfeiture is limited to specific property involved in the crime.[18] In this type of forfeiture action, the government must prove that the property, not the person, was derived from, or was used to, commit a crime. In a civil judicial forfeiture case, the case moves through a civil discovery process, with motions practice and trial stages.

In terms of burden of proof, the government bears the initial burden of establishing the forfeitability of the property by a preponderance of the

---

15 US Department of Justice, Criminal Division, *Guide to Equitable Sharing for State and Local Law Enforcement Agencies* (Apr. 2010).

16 *Id.*

17 Criminal indictment is defined by the *Merriam-Webster Dictionary* as a formal written statement framed by a prosecuting authority and found by a jury (as a grand jury) charging a person with an offense.

18 In *The Recovery of "Criminal" Assets in New Zealand, Ireland and England*, 41 Victoria U. of Wellington L. Rev. 26 (2010), Liz Campbell observes that "[i]n the same way that a civil action for misappropriation of property seeks to restore the injured party to the position he was in prior to the commission of the tort, it is arguable that civil forfeiture also seeks to return the state of affairs to that before the alleged criminal offence."

evidence,[19] and the innocent owner defense may be asserted. If forfeitability is proved and the innocent owner defense fails, the court will order judgment for the government.

Countries that have incorporated forfeiture laws into their legal framework often have a version of the types of forfeiture discussed above. Regardless of the approach, the key is a strong legal framework to support the government's ability to seize and forfeit property in accordance with constitutional and due process rights. In the United States, pursuant to Statute 28 USC Section 1355(b)(2), regardless of where the assets are physically located, the government may bring a civil forfeiture action before a federal court. However, a "US court's jurisdiction over international property is a legal fiction without the cooperation of the foreign country where the property is located. If the foreign country does not agree to enforce a US district court's civil forfeiture order, the US government would be unable to seize the property."[20]

In addition to a strong statutory-based framework, an effective IASP requires the establishment of an agency or office that is tasked with an oversight role regarding the maintenance and accountability of seized and forfeited property and any resulting funds. In the US federal system, these responsibilities fall under the DOJ's Asset Forfeiture Program.

The DOJ's Asset Forfeiture Program

The need to efficiently preserve, manage, and (if the forfeiture process is finalized) dispose of forfeited assets is an important component of any successful IASP[21] and requires the presence of an agency or a specialized division. Such an agency can work to ensure that seized assets are properly maintained, which guarantees that their value is retained during the pendency of the seizure process—an important responsibility—regardless of whether the assets are returned to the original owner or ultimately forfeited to the government.

In the United States, this function is carried out for the DOJ by the US Marshals Service.[22] The US Marshals Service "has primary responsibility for holding and maintaining real and tangible personal property seized by

---

19 "A preponderance of evidence is described as just enough evidence to make it more likely than not that the fact the claimant seeks to prove is true . . . the definition serves as a helpful guide to judges and juries in determining whether a claimant has carried his or her burden of proof." *See* http://legal-dictionary.thefreedictionary.com.

20 Jorene Soto, *Show Me the Money Part II*, 13–14 Oregon Review of Intl. L. 141, 152 (2011), quoting, in part, "See, *US v. Meza*, 856 F. Supp. 759 (E.D.N.Y/ 1994, *aff'd*, 63 F.3d 148 (2nd. Cir. 1995)."

21 Agencies participating in the Asset Forfeiture Program must also ensure that data in the property and financial management systems of the program are updated in a timely manner.

22 "The [US] Attorney General is authorized to use the Assets Forfeiture Fund to pay any necessary expenses associated with forfeiture operations such as property seizure, detention, management, forfeiture, and disposal. The Fund may also be used to finance certain general investigative expenses. These authorized uses are enumerated in 28 USC. Section 524(c)."

participating agencies for disposition. Seized property can be either returned to the owner or forfeited to the Government. Forfeited property is subsequently sold, placed into official use, destroyed, or transferred to another agency."[23] Moreover, funds that are forfeited to the government must also be managed in a transparent, accountable, and efficient manner.

In cases where the seizing agency participates in the DOJ's IASP, the responsibility for oversight of the funds and program management falls under the power of the DOJ's Asset Forfeiture Program:

> The Comprehensive Crime Control Act of 1984 established the Department of Justice's Assets Forfeiture Fund to receive the proceeds of forfeiture and to pay the costs associated with such forfeitures, including the costs of managing and disposing of property, satisfying valid liens, mortgages, and other innocent owner claims, and costs associated with accomplishing the legal forfeiture of the property.[24]

The Asset Forfeiture Program operates at the federal level and manages the individual DOJ components that are "charged with lawfully, effectively, and efficiently supporting law enforcement authorities in the application of specified forfeiture statutes."[25] The program was designed to support law enforcement initiatives across the United States and around the globe to "remove the tools of crime from criminal organizations, deprive wrongdoers of the proceeds of their crimes, recover property that may be used to compensate victims, and deter crime."[26]

The DOJ's Asset Forfeiture Program comprises two financial funds.[27] Funds involving seized and forfeited property are managed in the United States by the Assets Forfeiture Fund (AFF), which works in conjunction with the Seized Asset Deposit Fund (SADF) to create a single financial reporting entity for the DOJ. These funds include the "specified funds, property seized for forfeiture, and the transactions and program activities of the DOJ forfeiture program components and other participating agencies."[28]

---

23 *See Assets Forfeiture Fund and Seized Asset Deposit Fund Annual Financial Statements Fiscal Year 2011*, available at http://www.justice.gov/oig/reports/2012/a1212.pdf (accessed Mar. 21, 2012).

24 Statute 28 USC Section 524(c). *See* http://www.justice.gov/jmd/afp/02fundreport/02_2.html (accessed Feb. 18, 2012).

25 *See Assets Forfeiture Fund and Seized Asset Deposit Fund Annual Financial Statements Fiscal Year 2011*, available at http://www.justice.gov/oig/reports/2012/a1212.pdf (accessed Mar. 2, 2012).

26 US DOJ, Criminal Division, *Guide to Equitable Sharing for State and Local Law Enforcement Agencies* (Apr. 2010).

27 *See Assets Forfeiture Fund and Seized Asset Deposit Fund Annual Financial Statements Fiscal Year 2011*, at 3, available at http://www.justice.gov/oig/reports/2012/a1212.pdf (accessed Apr. 1, 2012).

28 *Id.*

The Asset Forfeiture Program invests cash balances from both the AFF and the SADF in government securities. "All amounts earned from the investment of AFF and SADF balances are deposited into the AFF. The interest earned on the AFF balances is the property of the United States Government."[29] The AFF and SADF accounts are maintained at the US Federal Reserve Bank in New York.

In accord with statutory requirements, the AFF managers must file an annual report with the US Congress detailing areas such as the total net deposits to the fund and the total expenses paid from the fund by category of expense, including equitable-sharing payments. The statute also sets forth the limitations governing use of the AFF, and the statutory authority is further controlled by policy guidelines.[30]

In total assets, the AFF

> (which present as of a specific time the amounts of future economic benefits owned or managed by the AFF/SADF), increased in FY 2011 . . . 71.7 percent . . . [s]pecifically, in FY 2011, ten major fraud cases resulted in extraordinary forfeiture income of $733.6 million compared to the nine FY 2010 fraud cases that resulted in extraordinary forfeiture income of $630.3 million. The term extraordinary is considered nonrecurring forfeiture income greater than $25 million.[31]

The management and disbursement of forfeited funds must be carried out in a transparent manner. This transparency is necessary not only to preserve the viability of the IASP itself but also to ensure public and global trust in international asset sharing as an effective and accountable tool for reaching development goals.

The DOJ's International Sharing Program

The DOJ's international sharing program[32] is "guided by standing international sharing agreements or [by] the subject of a future case-specific forfeiture sharing arrangement to be negotiated by AFMLS [Asset Forfeiture and Money Laundering Section of the US Department of Justice] and approved by the

---

29 *See Assets Forfeiture Fund and Seized Asset Deposit Fund Annual Financial Statements Fiscal Year 2011*, available at http://www.justice.gov/oig/reports/2012/a1212.pdf (accessed Mar. 21, 2012).

30 *See Attorney General's Guidelines on Seized and Forfeited Property* (Jul. 1990).

31 *See Assets Forfeiture Fund and Seized Asset Deposit Fund Annual Financial Statements Fiscal Year 2011*, at 5, available at http://www.justice.gov/oig/reports/2012/a1212.pdf (accessed Mar. 21, 2012).

32 Although not the focus of this chapter, the DOJ also maintains a domestic equitable-sharing program, which as of 2009, had "shared over $4.5 billion in forfeited assets with more than 8,000 state and local law enforcement agencies." *See* US Department of Justice, Criminal Division, *Guide to Equitable Sharing for State and Local Law Enforcement Agencies* (Apr. 2010).

Department of State."[33] When entering into sharing agreements, the DOJ and the recipient country must agree that the funds will be used to strengthen important development goals, such as building capacity in the recipient's AF/AML sector. The preference is for shared funds to be used to support AF/AML reform and development; however, with some exceptions, shared funds can be used to support a wide variety of domestic development needs. Regardless of the ultimate manner in which the funds are spent, each case-specific forfeiture-sharing arrangement is negotiated in a manner designed to ensure that it meets the needs of the recipient country.

Between 1992 and 2011, the DOJ, through its international asset-sharing program, shared more than US$234,949,197 with more than 39 countries.

Case-Specific Sharing Agreements

Countries can enter into case-specific sharing agreements (CSSAs). A CSSA is used when forfeited funds are shared as a result of a specific case.[34] Typically, a CSSA is an official written agreement, entered into between two or more countries after a series of negotiations. The CSSA sets forth the percentage of total seized proceeds to be shared, memorializes the mutual understanding of how those proceeds will be used by the recipient country (preferably to enhance its AF/AML regimes), and addresses accountability and transparency issues regarding expenditures.

The DOJ's AFMLS negotiates the terms of the CSSA, with the US Department of Treasury's concurrence and the US Department of State's authorization. Through this process, the DOJ, often viewed as a domestically focused agency, can exercise a degree of assistance in the international development process.

The Process for Requesting a CSSA

An assisting country may request a CSSA for DOJ sharing in the following ways:

- A request pursuant to a treaty between the United States and the assisting country
- A request made within the diplomatic arena
- The submission of an official, signed letter by a country's appropriate representative addressed to the US law enforcement agency that the country assisted in the investigation

---

33 *US Attorneys Manual, Chapter 9-116.000, Equitable Sharing and Federal Adoption, 9-116.400, International Sharing of Forfeited Assets* (2011).

34 In addition to CSSAs, related tools for international asset-sharing agreements are global asset-sharing agreements, which serve the same function as CSSAs, but the terms of which apply to all sharing between two countries, and agreements not limited to a single case agreement (as is a CSSA).

The Reviewing Process

Once the initial request has been received, the appropriate agency in the DOJ will begin the first in a series of reviews to determine if an international asset-sharing agreement is an appropriate action. The review process normally includes the prosecution office(s) and law enforcement agency (or agencies) that received the foreign assistance and additional divisions within the DOJ. During the review process, the following factors are considered:

- Whether the foreign country directly or indirectly participated in the seizure or the forfeiture of property
- Whether the transfer is authorized in an international agreement (that is, a mutual legal assistance treaty or an asset-sharing agreement) between the United States and the recipient country
- Whether the underlying forfeiture has been finalized
- Whether the country has been certified under section 481(h) of the US Foreign Assistance Act[35]

The decision regarding whether to enter into negotiations for a CSSA is not reviewable.[36] However, if the above factors have all been satisfied, the process continues, with additional factors reviewed:

- Whether the country provided the information that led to the seizure(s) of property that was ultimately forfeited
- Whether the country provided unique and indispensable assistance during the investigation and prosecution of the case by the DOJ
- Whether the country initially identified the assets for seizure
- Whether the country seized one or more assets that were forfeited in nonfederal proceedings during the same investigation
- Whether the country could have pursued forfeiture under domestic law but instead joined forces with the United States to conduct a more effective investigation or prosecution[37]

Because individual factors may vary, the review process attempts to take into account the totality of circumstances regarding the underlying case, including recognizing any unique challenges that were present in the investigation and prosecution.

---

35 Chapter 8, section 481(h) of the Foreign Assistance Act, known as the Certification Law, serves as a link between foreign aid and positive drug-control performance. *See* http://www.usaid.gov/policy/ads/faa.pdf (accessed Apr. 3, 2012).

36 The DOJ also shares forfeited proceeds domestically, among US federal, state, and local agencies. As with the global CSSA approach, domestically and pursuant to the Equitable Sharing Program conditions, the percentage of shared funds is based on participation and assistance in the underlying case.

37 US DOJ, Criminal Division, *Guide to Equitable Sharing for State and Local Law Enforcement Agencies* (Apr. 2010).

How Is the Percentage of Shared Funds Determined?

If the DOJ determines that the case is appropriate for international sharing, the next stage is the determination of what percentage of the total amount of forfeited funds will be shared with the assisting country. This determination is at the discretion of the DOJ and typically reflects the degree of assistance provided by the foreign country, which falls into one of three categories: essential assistance (EA), major assistance (MA), and facilitating assistance (FA).

Essential Assistance

The highest level of sharing funds is EA. Cases falling into this category may enter into CSSAs in which 50 to 100 percent of the total forfeited funds can be shared. In deciding what cases fall in the EA category, the DOJ examines factors such as whether the case involved victims or if the assisting country was the victim.

In addition, the DOJ considers additional factors such as whether the assisting country waived its own forfeiture actions and provided all necessary evidence to US authorities and whether the country initiated defending litigation or agreed to repatriate funds without an account signatory letter. In essence, the greater the amount of bilateral cooperation in a case, the greater the percentage of funds shared.

Major Assistance

In cases deemed to be MA, sharing percentages typically involve 40 to 50 percent of the total forfeited amount. In determining whether a case falls into the MA category, the DOJ considers several factors, such as whether the assisting country enforced a final forfeiture order from a US court or assisted in repatriating the assets to the United States. Other factors include whether the assisting country aided the US case by freezing or lifting a freeze over assets, whether the assisting country repatriated defendants via an extradition request, or whether their law enforcement agents were put at physical risk by assisting in the case. Equally important is whether the assisting country expended substantial prosecutorial and law enforcement resources on the case. A recent example of MA sharing is the March 2012 signing of a letter of intent between the United States and the government of Mexico to share 70 percent, approximately US$6 million. According to a DOJ press release:

> On March 26, 2012, U.S. Attorney General Eric Holder and Mexican Attorney General Marisela Morales Ibáñez signed a letter of intent for the United States to share approximately $6 million in forfeited funds with the Office of the Attorney General of the Republic of Mexico (PGR) to support Mexican efforts to combat the financial infrastructure of organized criminal groups and to enhance bilateral cooperation between the two countries in forfeiture matters.
>
> The letter of intent and anticipated fund sharing recognized the PGR's valuable cooperation in the investigation and resolution of the US government's case against the Sigue Corporation for viola-

tions of the Bank Secrecy Act. In January 2008, Sigue entered into a deferred prosecution agreement with the Department of Justice on charges of failing to maintain an effective anti-money laundering program. As a result, Sigue forfeited $15 million to the United States and agreed to commit an additional $9.7 million to improving its anti-money laundering program.[38]

Facilitating Assistance

In FA cases, up to 40 percent of the total forfeited funds may be shared. Cases are categorized as FA when the assisting country provided critical information regarding an investigative lead, assisted the United States by obtaining and sharing extensive bank documentation, provided other financial records, and/or assisted in ensuring that foreign banks repatriated assets. Once the decision regarding the percentage to be shared has been determined, the process continues to the negotiation stage.

Negotiation of CSSA Terms

No other US government officer or agency may bind the DOJ to terms of a CSSA, which are negotiated by the AFMLS of the DOJ. For the assisting country, negotiations are typically handled by the corresponding attorney general, minister of justice, or minster of foreign affairs or a representative. The negotiation process includes a series of meetings to discuss how the shared funds will be targeted and addresses mechanisms to ensure accountability and transparency regarding the shared funds. These decisions are arrived at via a process of mutual agreement, and discretion is granted to the assisting country depending on individual circumstances.

In discussing areas in which shared funds may be targeted, the domestic AF/AML sector will receive particular attention. The preference is for shared funds to target AF/AML issues; examples include

- Support for establishing an AF/AML division with the recipient country's prosecution office
- Funding of joint investigations, programs to identify emerging trends in domestic and regional economic crime sectors, and to strengthen the overall anti-money-laundering mission of the assisting country
- Funding to explore ways to strengthen financial data mining and analysis capacity and to improve the tracking of suspicious bank transactions
- Funding initiatives to increase bilateral asset forfeiture cases

Typically, the target areas are written into the terms of the CSSA. Although there are some notable exceptions in which shared funds should not be targeted (such as paying for salaries for prosecutors), the process allows for a great deal of flexibility in determining how funds should be expended.

---

38 US Department of Justice press release (March 26, 2012).

IASPs as a Tool for Development

Development has been defined as "the process which facilitates for every human and all persons the enjoyment of economic, social, cultural and political development."[39] This definition includes the critical need to ensure that citizens around the globe have both access to and faith in a functioning and transparent justice sector. The primary question posed here is exactly how does the adoption and implementation of an IASP contribute to international development? The answer lies in the ability of the IASP to, if properly implemented, act as a mechanism to support domestic capacity building in a number of different areas, including the AF/AML sector, to foster international cooperation, and to provide a means to combat transnational crime.

In Resolution 2004/29, the United Nations recognized that

> the laundering of the proceeds of crime ha[s] spread internationally and ha[s] become a worldwide threat to the stability and security of financial and commercial systems [and] urged Member States that had not yet done so to strengthen their capacity to prevent, control, investigate and suppress serious crimes related to money-laundering, including money-laundering related to the financing of terrorism.[40]

An IASP can adapt and respond to the specific needs of both the recipient and the sharing country in various ways.

First, an IASP can address development needs often encountered in fragile or weak states. The ability to target shared funds to specific areas of need can assist fragile states transitioning from postconflict to stable societies. For example, a transparent IASP can assist in the design and implementation of development projects in fragile states by using the shared funds to target key economic and justice sector reforms. It can also effectively address identified constraints that businesses and officials in weak states cite as limitations to growth, such as weak banking and court sectors.[41] In these cases, shared monies can provide funding for the establishment of a strong financial intelligence unit, an anticorruption office, or prosecutor and judicial training academies.

Second, an effective IASP can provide fragile states with the opportunity to establish or strengthen their AF/AML sectors while also developing key partnerships that enable future capacity-building programs.

Third, IASPs can be an effective tool in addressing unique challenges in justice sector growth—such as the absorption challenges that new member

---

39 Article 1 of the Declaration on the Right to Development (adopted by General Assembly Resolution 41/128 of Dec. 4, 1986), as quoted in A. H. Qureshi & A. R. Ziegler, *International Economic Law* 494 (2nd ed., Thomson/Sweet & Maxwell 2007). *See* also http://labspace.open.ac.uk/course/view.php?name=PUB_46_1.2 (accessed Feb. 26, 2012).

40 *See* 11th United Nations Congress on Crime Prevention and Criminal Justice, Bangkok, 13 (Apr. 2005) (A/CONF.203/1). *See* also http://www.un.org/events/11thcongress/docs/programme.pdf (accessed Mar. 12, 2012).

41 *See* http://www.cgdev.org/content/publications/detail/1426232 (accessed Jul. 18, 2012).

states of the European Union must confront. For example, shared funds can be focused on assisting new member states in their efforts to address economic, institutional, and justice sector absorption challenges, such as the need to improve fiscal management practices and to strengthen anticorruption capacities. In these areas, an IASP can act as a mechanism to assist new member states in overcoming obstacles while continuing to foster key partnerships and encourage innovative planning initiatives.

Fourth, IASPs can serve overall global development goals by strengthening international cooperation efforts among countries, regardless of the economic or legal differences that may separate them. By serving as a mechanism that encourages countries to work together, IASPs create global partnerships to prevent, control, investigate, and suppress transnational economic crime.

Finally, an accountable and transparent IASP demonstrates, at a very public and visible level, the ability of governments to work globally to take profits away from criminals and redirect them back to the very agencies and offices tasked with combating economic crimes. In a related manner, the successful completion of a bilateral CSSA represents an opportunity to share, domestically and internationally, the message that international cooperation in fighting economic crime not only occurs but, more important, succeeds.

Conclusion

The ever-increasing globalization of transnational criminal groups not only endangers global economic systems but also undermines rule of law and good governance practices. Encouraged by the United Nations and domestic governments alike, asset sharing at an international level is an effective and powerful tool for development. It can assist in disrupting and dismantling transnational criminal organizations while strengthening international cooperation on AF/AML issues.[42] The ability of countries to cooperate on a bilateral scale and enter into mutually beneficial asset-sharing agreements serves a number of goals, including "taking the profit out of crime."

---

42 DOJ equitable sharing applies only to sharing of assets that were seized by the DOJ and that were "forfeited judicially or administratively to the United States by the United States Attorney's Offices or Forfeiture Program Participants." The participants include the Asset Forfeiture and Money Laundering Section, Criminal Division (AFMLS); Organized Crime Drug Enforcement Task Force (OCDETF); Asset Forfeiture Management Staff, Justice Management Division (AFMS); Bureau of Alcohol, Tobacco, Firearms and Explosives (ATF); Defense Criminal Investigative Service (DCIS); Drug Enforcement Administration (DEA); Bureau of Diplomatic Security, Department of State (DS); Executive Office for United States Attorneys (EOUSA); Federal Bureau of Investigation (FBI); Food and Drug Administration (FDA), United States Department of Agriculture (USDA); United States Marshals Service (USMS); and United States Postal Service (USPS). *See* US DOJ, Criminal Division, *Guide to Equitable Sharing for State and Local Law Enforcement Agencies* (Apr. 2010).

Toward a New Law and Development

New State Activism in Brazil and the Challenge for Legal Institutions

David M. Trubek, Diogo R. Coutinho, and Mario G. Schapiro

At the intersection of law, economics, and the practices of states and development agencies, the field of law and development undergoes continuous realignment.[1] As economic policies, legal theories, and institutional practices change, the salient issues in law and development change as well.[2] The 21st century has ushered in a new era. Development theories are being challenged and new practices are emerging. Law and development scholars need to understand the new trends and explore their implications for legal studies and practice.

In the past couple of decades, development policy and practice have shifted in many regions, but nowhere more clearly than in Latin America. After a long period when neoliberal policies prevailed and the state's role in the economy was curtailed, many countries in the region have begun to explore new forms of state activism. Brazil has been a leader in the formation of new development policies and in the creation of a new development discourse. Starting with the election of Lula da Silva in 2002 and gaining momentum during Lula's second term in 2006, Brazil has instituted new forms of industrial and social policy, experienced a surge in growth, and seen a reduction in economic inequality.

This trend has led scholars to begin to talk about a "new developmentalism" and speculate about the emergence of a new kind of developmental state in which the government plays an active role in mobilizing resources, stimulating investment, and promoting innovation but does not command or

---

1 This article draws on David M. Trubek, Diogo R. Coutinho, and Mario G. Schapiro, *New State Activism in Brazil and the Challenge for Law*, in *Law and the New Developmental State: The Brazilian Experience in Latin American Context* (David M. Trubek et al. ed., Cambridge U. Press, forthcoming) (hereinafter, Trubek et. al). An earlier version of the article was discussed at the 2012 IGLP Workshop at Harvard Law School and the Conference on Global Governance: Critical Legal Perspectives at the European University Institute (July, 2012). The authors are grateful to Peter Houtzager, Willy Forbath, Alvaro Santos, David Kennedy, Duncan Kennedy, Helena Alviar, Jeremy Perelman, Lucie White, Mushtaq Kahn, Shunko Rojas, and Yves Dezalay for comments and suggestions. The authors also received useful comments from Professor Wang Chenguang of the Tsinghua University School of Law.

2 For a discussion of the history of law and development, *see* David M. Trubek and Alvaro Santos, *The New Law and Economic Development: A Critical Appraisal* (Cambridge U. Press 2006).

control the economy. In this approach, the state employs an open-economy industrial policy to restructure production and increase international competiveness while simultaneously using an active social policy to eliminate poverty, reduce inequality, and stimulate domestic demand. Unlike the old paradigm, in this new model, such a state seeks to benefit from participation in the global economy while avoiding the dangers of free trade fundamentalism, and it tries to stimulate, not replace, the private sector.[3]

This chapter explores shifts in government policy in Brazil since 2000, showing how these changes are influencing developments in the law. After a limited experience with neoliberalism, the country has embraced new forms of state engagement in the economy and social relations. Because these changes are recent and have not yet been fully consolidated, the resulting constellation can be viewed as *new state activism* (NSA),[4] a term that suggests neither a return to the past nor a clearly consolidated alternative "model." The chapter covers the emergence of NSA; identifies its salient features, noting how it differs from prior forms of state intervention; explores some of the forces that have shaped this new form of state action; and provides a preliminary assessment of the significance and challenge of these developments for the law.

Introduction: From the "Long 1990s" (1988-2004) to NSA

The evolution of NSA in Brazil was preceded by a series of policy changes that dismantled some of the institutions of the old developmental state and embraced some aspects of the Washington Consensus. Like several other developing Latin American countries, Brazil had a classic developmentalist phase in the twentieth century: from 1930 until the end of the 1980s, economic policies consisted of state-led initiatives to promote import substitution industrialization, and growth through state-owned enterprises, economic planning, price control, regulatory and administrative authorities in key sectors, and the use of tax and financial incentives.

---

3 For a discussion of new developmentalism and the idea of a new development state, *see* David M. Trubek, *Law, State and the New Developmentalism: An Introduction*, in Trubek et. al, *supra* note 1.

4 *See* Glauco Arbix & Scott B. Martin, *Beyond Developmentalism and Market Fundamentalism in Brazil: Inclusionary State Activism without Statism*, paper presented at the workshop on "States, Development, and Global Governance," Global Legal Studies Center and the Center for World Affairs and the Global Economy (WAGE), University of Wisconsin, 2010, available at http://www.law.wisc.edu/gls/documents/paper_arbix.pdf (accessed Jul. 15, 2012); and Renato Boschi, *Estado Desenvolvimentista no Brasil: Continuidades e incertidumbres* (2010), 2 Ponto de Vista, available at http://neic.iesp.uerj.br/pontodevista/pdf/Ponto_de_Vista_01fev2010.pdf (accessed Oct. 10, 2010). For an account of "new developmentalism" in Brazil, *see* Luiz Carlos Bresser-Pereira, *From Old to New Developmentalism in Latin America*, in *Textos para Discussão–Escola de Economia de São Paulo* 193 (2009). *See* also Eli Diniz, *É possível um Novo Modelo de Estado Desenvolvimentista no Brasil?* 2 IPEA – Boletim de Análise Político-Instiutional 17 (2012).

Between 1988 and 2004, known as the "long 1990s," Brazil partially dismantled these structures and policies and shifted to more market-oriented approaches. In 1988, after 24 years of military dictatorship and in a context of a threat of hyperinflation,[5] Brazil passed a new constitution that has influenced and shaped policy ever since. The 1988 constitution is a social democratic document that created a vibrant democratic polity and includes civil, political, and social rights and a number of policy goals such as building a free, just, and socially integrated society; fostering national development; acquiring technological autonomy; eradicating poverty and marginalization; and reducing economic and social inequalities. Many of the constitution's provisions have had a direct effect on government policy and budgetary allocations.

President Collor de Mello was elected in 1989, immediately after the new constitution came into force. Stressing the need for "modernization," Collor de Mello rapidly liberalized the economy using drastic tariff reductions, privatization, and flawed attempts to control inflation. Under Itamar Franco, who replaced Collor de Mello after he was impeached, a stabilization plan (the Plano Real) was successfully adopted and inflation was controlled.[6] New legislation on social assistance and welfare for the poor was also passed.

Franco's minister of finance, Fernando Henrique Cardoso (known as FHC), became the next president in 1994. During Cardoso's eight years in office, Brazil continued to move away from the *dirigiste* policies of the developmentalist period, embracing many of the neoliberal prescriptions favored by the Washington Consensus.[7] In the Cardoso period, state owned-enterprises were privatized, direct subsidies for certain industries were scaled back, areas of the economy were deregulated, import barriers were reduced, competition was fostered and enforced, intellectual property rights were tightened, bilateral investment treaties protecting foreign investors were signed, and fiscal responsibility was enhanced. Also, the currency (the real) was constantly kept overvalued as monetary stability was pursued and attained.[8]

Under Cardoso, the bureaucracy was partially modernized, regulatory agencies were created, public-private partnerships were designed, and new

---

5 In January 1990, inflation in Brazil reached 56 percent per month, raising to 73 percent in February and peaking at 84 percent in March; *see* Luiz Carlos Bresser-Pereira and Yoshiaki Nakano, *Hiperinflação e estabilização no Brasil: O Primeiro Plano Collor,* Revista de Economia Política 4 (1991). During the same period, economic inequality reached its worse level since it had been measured (the Gini coefficient peaked at 0.647, according to the Brazilian Office of Statistics).

6 "Despite that, a period of strong deterioration of the Balance of Payments began, which led the current-account deficit to achieve 4.0% of the GDP in 1998." Antonio Barros de Castro, *From Semi-Stagnation to Growth in a Sino-Centric Market,* 28 Brazilian J. of Pol. Eco. 3–27 (2008).

7 Cardoso has always rejected the neoliberal label and claimed that his goal simply was to modernize the economy.

8 "[T]he goal of price stability has remained sacrosanct and the instruments for achieving this goal have been in line with the latest international fashions: central bank independence and inflation targeting." Cornel Ban, *Brazil's Liberal Neo-Developmentalism: New Paradigm or Edited Orthodoxy?* Rev. Intl. of Pol. Eco. (forthcoming).

social policies were adopted. To carry out privatization and encourage foreign investment, Congress made several changes in the constitution. But although the country adopted some ideas from the Washington Consensus, it did not wholeheartedly embrace neoliberalism. Privatizations were limited; Banco do Brasil, BNDES (the Brazilian Development Bank), and Petrobrás, three major state-owned enterprises, remained under government control. None of the bilateral investment treaties signed in the 1990s was ratified.

Institutional and Political Background: The New Democratic Constitution of 1988 and the Cardoso Administration

Political parties and social movements had been repressed during military rule (1964–85). When the constitution-making process started in the late 1980s, an eruption of social-political demands had to be accommodated. Not surprisingly, the resulting constitution was nicknamed "the citizen's constitution." Not only did it create democratic institutions, it also included an extensive charter of civil-political and social rights and reframed public-private relationships. The constitution incorporates provisions guaranteeing the rule of law, protecting individual rights, and guarding against arbitrary state action. It also created positive—and justiciable—rights that could impose policy obligations. The 1988 constitution includes rights to health, education, housing, social protection, and pensions. These guarantees have shaped a new and complex welfare system, including a massive universal public health system and a system of universal pensions. The new system in turn has had a major impact on the role of the state and on patterns of government spending.[9] Instead of cutting back on social spending as many countries did during the 1990s, Brazil increased the percentage of GDP devoted to social protection during that period.[10]

Besides facilitating political mobilization and participation, instituting social rights and shaping social policies, the new constitution facilitated modernization of the state apparatus and reframed public-private relationships with consequences for the business environment. The 1988 constitution initiated a slow process of professionalizing state administration. Until the 1930s, public employees were hired through the "spoils system" of political appointments. A partial reform under Getulio Vargas had instituted meritocratic selection for some key agencies such as BNDES and the Foreign Ministry, but left most government jobs subject to political appointment.[11] The 1988 constitution carried

---

9 *See* Jorge Abrahão de Castro & José Celso Cardoso Jr., *Políticas Sociais no Brasil: Gasto Social do Governo Federal de 1988 a 2002*, in *Questão Social e Políticas Sociais no Brasil Contemporâneo* (Luciana Jacoud et. al. ed., IPEA 2005).

10 *See* Kleber Pacheco de Castro & José Roberto Afonso, *Gasto Social no Brasil Pós 1988: Uma Análise sob a Ótica da Descentralização Fiscal*, 1 Revista de Política, Planejamento e Gestão da Saúde 34–56 (2009).

11 The first initiative to reform the public sector to create a more professional public staff was under taken by President Getulio Vargas (1930–45), whose government created the Department

the reform further, requiring that all public employees be selected through meritocratic processes and capping state salaries.

The constitution significantly affected relations between the state and business. It required competitive bidding for all state purchases and made the process more transparent. The special federal prosecutors (Ministério Público) were authorized to combat corruption and enforce laws protecting consumers and the environment. The constitution also protected individuals and businesses against regulatory takings and expropriation without compensation.

Although the new constitution embraced social-democratic values and norms and some developmentalist ideas, during the 1990s, Brazil flirted with neoliberal policies. In 1994, President Itamar Franco and Minister of Finance Fernando Henrique Cardoso launched the Plano Real, a macroeconomic stabilization effort that eventually managed to control inflation in Brazil.[12] One of Cardoso's first acts as president was to get Congress to remove some provisions in the 1988 constitution that enshrined "old developmentalist" policies such as state monopolies and restrictions on foreign investment.[13]

Under Cardoso, Brazil experienced a strong devaluation of the real as a result of a harsh international crisis (particularly in Mexico, Russia, and Asia). The government raised the interest rate to a very high level, which severely hindered growth. At the same time, the Cardoso government managed to embed Brazil in the world economy through trade liberalization. In 2000, it ensured fiscal austerity by passing a fiscal responsibility act, and it sought to modernize public administration by adopting tenets of a "new public administration" that allowed outsourcing of certain functions to the private sector.[14]

Under Cardoso, Brazil accelerated privatizations initiated by Collor and Itamar Franco:[15] in 1997, Vale do Rio Doce, a major state-owned mining and steelmaking company, and Sistema Telebrás, the public-owned telecommunication conglomerate, were sold. In the same year, several electricity and gas distribution companies, as well as some state-level banks, were transferred to private owners. During his eight years as president, Cardoso raised

---

of Public Service Management (DASP), a preliminary attempt at establishing a public career path in Brazil.

12 In 1999, Brazil officially adopted an inflation target system (the target in 2012 is 4.5 percent per year).

13 João Paulo M. Peixoto, *The Brazilian States since Vargas*, in *The Brazilian State: Debate and Agenda* (Mauricio Font & Laura Randall ed., Lexington Books, 2011).

14 The strategy segregated core activities that should be performed by politicians and senior officials, including conducting support activities that may be outsourced, separating policy formulation from policy execution, and granting more autonomy and accountability to services performed by the state, which would take the form of either "executive agencies" or of "social organizations" that are a special type of nonprofit. *See* Luiz Carlos Bresser-Pereira, *The 1995 Public Management Reform in Brazil: Reflections of a Reformer*, in *Reinventing Leviathan: The Politics of Administrative Reform in Developing Countries* (Ben Ross Schneider & Blanca Heredia, ed., North-South Center Press, 2003).

15 Franco privatized CNS, an important steel company, in 1995.

approximately US$79 billion through privatization. However, like Petrobrás, the Brazilian state oil and gas company, the three large federal banks—Banco do Brasil, Caixa Econômica Federal, and BNDES—were not privatized. Indeed, BNDES played an important role in facilitating privatization by offering credit to both domestic and international buyers. Table 1 lists the state-owned enterprises that were privatized in the 1990s.

Table 1. State-Owned Enterprises Privatized

USIMINAS	24.10.1991	CSN	02.04.1993
USIMEC	24.10.1991	FEM	02.04.1993
CELMA	01.11.1991	ULTRAFÉRTIL	24.06.1993
MAFERSA	11.11.1991	COSIPA	20.08.1993
COSINOR	14.11.1991	AÇOMINAS	10.09.1993
COSINOR DIST.	14.11.1991	EAC	07.12.1994
SNBP	14.01.1992	EAI	07.12.1994
AFP	14.02.1992	PQU	25.01.1994
PETROFLEX	10.04.1992	CARAÍBA	28.07.1994
COPESUL	15.05.1992	EMBRAER	07.12.1994
Can	15.07.1992	NEIVA	07.12.1994
ALCANORTE	15.07.1992	ESCELSA	11.07.1995
CST	23.07.1992	LIGHT	21.05.1996
FOSFÉRTIL	12.08.1992	VALE	06.05.1997
GOIASFÉRTIL	08.10.1992	MERIDIONAL	04.12.1997
ACESITA	23.10.1992	TELEBRÁS	29.07.1998
ENERGÉTICA	23.10.1992	GERASUL	15.09.1998
FASA	23.10.1992	DATAMEC	23.06.1999

Source: Ministério do Planejamento, Orçamento e Gestão (Brazil)

Brazil adapted the US model of regulatory agencies to supervise and enforce post-privatization rules and to introduce competition in natural monopolies. As a result, electrical distribution, fixed telecommunication networks, and transportation (railways, highways, waterways) were subject to a new legal and institutional framework that substantively changed the patterns of administrative law. New licensing and concession agreements were signed. For a list of areas subjected to regulation see table 2.

Table 2. Activity Regulated

Activity Regulated	Commission	Foundation	Law
Competition	CADE	1994	8.884/94
Electric power	ANEEL	1996	9.427/96
Oil & Gas	ANP	1997	9.478/97
Telecommunication	ANATEL	1997	9.472/97
Health Surveillance	ANVISA	1999	9.782/99
Health Insurance	ANS	2000	9.961/00
Water	ANA	2000	9.984/00
Water Transport	ANTAQ	2001	10.233/01
Land Transport	ANTT	2001	10.233/01
Aviation	ANAC	2005	11.182/05

The Cardoso administration rejected the idea of industrial policy, long a mainstay of Brazil's developmental state. Finance Minister Pedro Malan said that "the best industrial policy you can have is not to have one." BNDES, which for decades had provided financing to targeted sectors and supported many state-owned enterprises, shifted to support of privatization. Rather than trying to support priority sectors, the government focused on increasing the efficiency of government services and reforming credit markets. For example, starting with Cardoso and continuing into Lula's first term, the Central Bank sought to reduce the cost of credit. Among the microeconomic measures undertaken were improvements in bankruptcy procedures and debt collection.[16]

The Cardoso administration's opposition to industrial policy did not deter it from stimulating selected sectors in order to promote competiveness and innovation. Thus, in 1999, 16 new sectorial funds were charged with fostering innovation in strategic areas such as oil and gas, telecommunications, biotechnology, and agribusiness. The Cardoso period also saw important changes in social policy. Traditionally, the Brazilian welfare state has been regressive, clientelistic, and opaque. Between 1994 and 2002, the federal government took a number of measures aimed at transforming this system, including adding poverty-alleviation programs aimed at specific populations; introducing noncontributory social protection programs; decentralizing social policy implementation; and tackling some of the regressive features of the pension

16 According to Fabiani, during the 1999–2006 period, the law behind the government's microeconomic agenda was seen as an instrument to protect creditors and ultimately to promote economic efficiency. *See* Emerson Ribeiro Fabiani, *Direito e Crédito Bancário no Brasil* (Saraiva, FGV, 2011).

scheme.[17] The Cardoso government initiated the use of conditional cash transfers; for example, the Bolsa Escola program, implemented 2001, aimed to increase access to education, reduce poverty in the short term by transferring cash to impoverished households, reduce child labor, and serve as a social protection network.[18]

Another important development in this period was LOAS (the Social Assistance Act). Enacted under Itamar Franco and implemented by Cardoso, LOAS seeks to guarantee "minimum social standards." The noncontributory multilevel federal, state, and local program is designed to protect households, mothers, children, adolescents, and the elderly; to assist underprivileged children and adolescents; to promote labor market integration; and to train and rehabilitate persons with disabilities and promote their integration into community life.[19]

NSA Emerges

Luiz Inácio Lula da Silva was elected president in 2002. For two four-year terms, his government preserved some Cardoso policies such as inflation control and openness to foreign investment while changing others by adopting state-activist initiatives, including an active industrial policy and a massive poverty-fighting program. Dilma Roussef, elected president in 2010, has maintained Lula's priorities but expanded state activism in key areas.[20]

Lula's inauguration instigated a decade of experimentation. Developmentalist institutions have been reinvented, neoliberal policies were modified, new institutions were created, and a new form of state activism is emerging. Changes have occurred gradually.[21] Some of Cardoso's policies, such as

---

17 Almeida explains that during Cardoso's first term, some changes in universal social polices confronted the regressive feature of the Brazilian pension system (a constitutional amendment changed the minimum age and the period of contribution for retirement), although the problematic topic of public servants' pensions—a major source of inequality in the country—remained untouched. *See* Maria Hermínia Tavares de Almeida, *A Política Social no Governo Lula,* 70 Novos Estudos - CEBRAP 70 7–17 (2004).

18 Inspired by successful experiences at the local level, the federal Bolsa Escola program reached more than 5 million families. Other conditional cash transfer programs widened the scope of protection and helped build a multilevel public-private network of providers.

19 The federal government is assigned the task of coordinating and promoting LOAS and providing technical advice and financial incentives to states, cities, and welfare entities and organizations. States must transfer certain funds to municipalities, provide them with technical support, and stimulate the collective rendering of social services. Municipalities must, among other things, execute social assistance and poverty-fighting policies, which includes the possibility of establishing partnerships with civil society organizations.

20 *See* Alfredo Saad Filho, *Neo-Developmentalism and the Challenges of Economic Policy-Making under Dilma Rousseff,* 38 Critical Sociology (2012), available at http://crs.sagepub.com/content/early/2012/07/03/0896920512441635.abstract?rss=1 (accessed Oct. 5, 2012).

21 To win the election, Lula stated that debt agreements would be honored. Talking about the gradual manner through which changes would take place, Lula said in his "Letter to Brazilians" in 2002: "the premise of this transition will naturally be the respect to contracts

macroeconomic stabilization, have been preserved, and some of his social policy innovations have been improved and substantially expanded. Institutions like BNDES that survived from the period of state developmentalism have been reinvigorated and redirected. Other developmentalist institutions, such as industrial policy, that were rejected during the neoliberal period have been revived, albeit in different form. Finally, new institutions have been added to increase coordination between the public and private sectors.[22]

Macroeconomic Continuity

Scarred by decades of high and damaging inflation, Brazil adopted policies in the 1990s to preserve monetary stability. The Plano Real used various measures to control public spending and regulate the money supply. This has kept the inflation rate low (by Brazilian standards) for more than 15 years and enshrined monetary stability as a cornerstone of economic policy. During the first Lula administration, emphasis was placed on instituting, developing, and strengthening political and economic credibility using fiscally responsible macroeconomic policy, a floating exchange rate, and inflation targeting. In general terms, the Dilma administration has continued these policies. However, this emphasis has come at a price: the main tools of macroeconomic policy are restrictions on government spending and a relatively high interest rate, putting a brake on public investment and increasing the cost of credit, thus possibly hampering growth. To offset these effects, Lula introduced several growth-inducing microeconomic policies, including a new form of industrial policy and social policies that helped spur domestic growth while relieving poverty and reducing economic inequality.

Industrial Policy

In 2004, after a decade in which Brazil had explicitly rejected industrial policy,[23] the government introduced measures designed to foster selected industries. Lula's first try at industrial policy was limited and focused primarily on innovation. At the time, there was strong opposition to industrial policy in policy making circles and academic opinion. It was thought that governments were not able to strategically identify targets and that trying to do so would divert resources from horizontal structural measures such as tax reform and infrastructure investment that would benefit the entire economy.

However, some people were prepared to accept a limited role for government in overcoming market failures and reducing the coordination and systemic problems that hampered innovation; the Cardoso administration had taken modest steps in this direction. Lula's first foray into industrial policy

---

and obligations enforceable in the country." Available at http://www2.fpa.org.br/carta-ao-povo-brasileiro-por-luiz-inacio-lula-da-silva.

22 A notable example is the Public-Private Partnership Federal Act of 2004.

23 For a history of the rejection of industrial policy *see* Wilson Suzigan & A. V. Villela, *Industrial Policy in Brazil* (Editora da Unicamp 1997).

—called PITCE—stressed a combination of general measures to improve the business environment[24] and financial support in four sectors in which one could argue innovation was essential: semiconductors, software, capital goods, and medicines.

PITCE included substantial legislative activity, including the Innovation Law (designed to facilitate partnerships and synergy among universities, companies, and research institutes) and the Foundation Law (which facilitated government support for university research).[25] At the same time, the government started building institutions designed to improve coordination within government and between government and the private sector. These included the Council of Economic and Social Development (CDES), designed to help foster inclusive growth; the National Council of Industrial Development (CNDI), a public-private body charged with defining directives for industrial development; and the Brazilian Agency for Industrial Development (ABDI), which coordinates implementation of industrial policy by bringing together government, industry, labor, and universities. Arbix and Martin describe ABDI as a "networked institution, formally under the Ministry of Development, Industry, and Trade. ABDI has played an important role in seeking to develop an industrial policy and helps identify and guides investment decisions in technological research, innovation and industrial development."[26]

In 2008, during Lula's second term, the government launched the Program for Productive Development (PDP).[27] PDP replaced PITCE and was much more ambitious and complex. It included both horizontal measures designed to increase the overall efficiency of the economy and vertical programs for targeted sectors. Reflecting the scope and complexity of the Brazilian economy, PDP covered a wide range of industries. The program set goals, established a complex governance regime, and placed special emphasis on collaboration between the public and the private sectors. It called for industry-specific competiveness councils instituted by Cardoso and expanded under Lula. PDP relied on policy instruments such as financing, tax, public procurement, public-private alliances, coordination and consultation, and regulation.

Horizontal measures in PDP included improvements in infrastructure and education, increased investments in science, reductions in interest rates for investment, tax relief, and improvements in the legal environment, including

---

24 These include legal measures to improve incentives for innovation and to facilitate better relations between universities and business, as well as tax relief.

25 The Innovation Law allowed the government to invest directly in private companies as a minority shareholder in order to create new products and processes, and provides for sharing of any resulting intellectual property. The Foundation Law facilitated support from FINEP and the National Fund for Scientific and Technological Development for university-based research-support foundations.

26 Arbix & Martin, *supra* note 4.

27 The discussion in this section draws heavily on Luciano Coutinho et al., *"Industrial Policy and Economic Transformation,"* in *The Oxford Handbook of Latin American Political Economy,* 134–188 (Javier Santiso & Jeff Dayton-Johnson ed., Oxford U. Press, 2012).

modernizing the rules governing foreign trade. Vertical measures, which dealt with specific industries, were designed to meet three basic challenges. For each, there were different governance mechanisms and a different mix of policies and measures. Measures that might be employed included subsidized credit from BNDES and other public financial sources, tax incentives, technical assistance, advantages in public procurement rules, favorable trade policy, and supportive regulation.

The first challenge identified by PDP was to consolidate and expand leadership in sectors in which Brazil was deemed to have a competitive edge. The goal was to support Brazilian firms that could be world leaders or heavyweights in their industry. Sectors included aviation, mining, steel, cellulose, oil and gas/petrochemical, bioethanol, and meat. The second challenge was to foster and occasionally induce mergers and alliances (sometimes with BNDES holding a minority stake) to build up industries that had competitive potential but were not yet at the global frontier. These included capital goods, the automotive complex, wood and furniture, pharmaceutical, meatpacking, personal hygiene, perfumery and cosmetics, construction, various service industries, coastal and marine industry, leather, footwear and artifacts, the agro-industrial system, and plastics. The third challenge was to strengthen high-tech "vanguard" sectors that had both growth potential and whose growth could improve the technological capacity of the entire economy. These strategic areas included health, biotechnology, defense, nuclear energy, nanotechnology, and information and communication technology.

The governance of PDP was complex. A system of public management brings representatives of appropriate ministries and agencies together for each of the major tasks and links them to the private sector through a variety of coordination devices. Observers of PDP point to the importance of public-private coordination at every level, from setting overall priorities to working out packages of effective measures for each sector

PDP was overtaken by the global financial crisis before it got off the ground. But even if there had been no recession, a program like this, which envisions major structural changes, must be considered in a long-term context. Although the government can point to some real achievements, critics have questioned whether the plan truly shifted resources from traditional sectors to high-tech industries or if did enough for small and medium industry, which often is a major source of innovation.[28]

In 2011, the new administration, led by Dilma Rouseff, introduced an updated version of PDP called Brasil Maior (Greater Brazil) with the motto

---

28 According to information available from the BNDES, in 2008, out of the 179 beneficiary companies, 12 were listed in Bovespa (a Brazilian stock exchange). In 2009, out of the 156 beneficiary companies, 25 were listed in Bovespa. Available at http://www.bndes.gov.br/SiteBNDES/bndes/bndes_pt/Institucional/BNDES_Transparente/Consulta_as_operacoes_do_BNDES (accessed May 1, 2010).

"innovate to compete; compete to grow."[29] This plan continued many of the same objectives and policies of PDP. But reflecting rising concerns about "deindustrialization," the plan emphasizes efforts to protect domestic industries hit hard by global competition, an overvalued currency, and low-cost imports. Taxes on manufacturing have been reduced, attention is paid to antidumping measures, and substantial preferences for local producers in government procurement have been introduced. At the same time, funding from BNDES and FINEP, the Financiadora de Estudos e Projetos, were increased and efforts were made to channel more funding to innovative firms and sectors.

ABDI identifies three major strategic areas for development and explains how Brasil Maior addresses each area. To increase investment and spur innovation, Brasil Maior offers tax relief, increased financing for investment and innovation, and further improvements in the legal framework. To promote exports and protect domestic industry from unfair trade, the plan offers tax relief, export financing and guarantees, trade promotion, and enhanced defense thorough antidumping and other trade remedies. To protect hard-hit domestic firms, the plan includes exemptions from payroll tax for selected industries and a 25 percent margin of preference for local firms in government procurement.

An important part of the Brasil Maior plan is the system of public-private coordination that builds on structures created for PDP: the National Industrial Development Council (CNDI), sectorial executive committees, and sectorial competiveness councils. CNDI is a peak institution that includes ministers, the president of BNDES, and 18 representatives of industry, labor, and the public. Its role is to set strategic guidelines. The Brasil Maior plan identifies 20 priority sectors: petroleum, gas and marine construction, chemicals, health, renewable energy, furniture, automotive, mining, civil construction, defense, aviation and aerospace, agro-industry, capital goods, metallurgy, logistics services, electronics, personal hygiene, fragrances and cosmetics (HPPC), services, retail, shoes, textiles, candy and jewelry, cellulose and paper. There is an executive committee and a competiveness council for each sector. The executive committee consists of government officials charged with developing an action plan for the sector. These representatives meet with the sectorial competiveness councils to refine the action plans and explore implementation issues.

Social Policy

In addition to reviving industrial policy, the governments of Lula and Dilma have expanded Brazil's social protection system and antipoverty programs. The result is a significant decline in the poverty rate, a reduction in inequality, substantial growth of the middle class, and stimulus for the domestic market. Between 2001 and 2008, incomes of the wealthy grew at a moderate pace, while the income of the poor increased substantively. Approximately 28 million people moved out of poverty and a "new" middle class has emerged—between 2003 and 2011 approximately 10.5 million Brazilians became part of

29 Available at http://www.brasilmaior.mdic.gov.br/.

the middle class, which now includes 55 percent of the population.[30] The Brazilian social pyramid is now diamond shaped, with more citizens classified as middle class than as poor.

The distributive gains achieved in Brazil during the past decade are the result of a combination of economic and institutional reforms. These reforms include the reintroduction of previous efforts such as inflation control and changes in labor markets that include unemployment reduction and increases in the minimum wage, pensions, and social security improvements, as well as a new generation of social assistance policies, especially the Bolsa Família program (BFP), created in 2003 as a result of a consolidation of previously existing initiatives.[31] Health and education spending as a share of GDP has grown considerably in recent years, magnifying the impacts of institutional reforms instituted in the late 1990s. In another recent development, in 2011, the Brazilian Unified Social Assistance System (SUAS) was institutionalized and formalized by a federal statute.

In June 2011, President Dilma Rousseff launched the Brasil Sem Miséria program,[32] designed to rescue 16.2 million people from extreme poverty, 59 percent of whom live in the northeast region. Brasil Sem Miséria has been presented as a combination of complementary rural and urban sectorial actions—in the areas of income transfer, labor market integration, access to public services, education, health, social assistance, water, and sewage—and involves the creation of new initiatives and the reconceptualization of existing ones. This program aims to find and register extremely poor families and integrate them into different programs. Brasil Sem Miséria is also supposed to help those who graduate from BFP enter the labor market.[33]

The changes in social policy seem to be working: poverty has been cut drastically and income inequality has been reduced. Although Brazil still is one of the most economically unequal countries in the world,[34] the decline in poverty and the reduction of inequality in Brazil in recent years have been remarkable. Thanks to a wide range of policies—including universal, targeted, and decentralized programs—the Brazilian welfare state is becoming stronger.[35]

---

30 *See* Marcelo Nery, *A Nova Classe Média – o lado brilhante da base da pirâmide* 29 (Saraiva 2011).

31 Since its inception, BFP has reached more than 12 million families as beneficiaries. If one assumes that each family has four people on average, the total figure for individuals who have benefited from BFP reaches 48 million people, or approximately 25 percent of the Brazilian population. Half of its budget has been spent in the northeast part of Brazil, where millions of very poor families live. Considering its gigantic scale, the targeting of BFP (defined as the share of total benefits received by specific groups of the population) has been considered exemplary, outperforming other social assistance programs in both Brazil and internationally.

32 Translation: "Brazil without Indigence."

33 Brasil Sem Miséria also changed the number of children and adolescents who can obtain the BFP benefit—as of 2012, up to five (it used to be three).

34 The Brazilian Gini coefficient in 1960 was 0.5367; it was 0.6091 in 1990; and in 2010, it was still very high (0.5304). *See* Nery, *supra* note 30 at 27.

35 As put by Arbix & Martin, *supra* note 4: "while Brazil's 'welfare state' still has segmented

Brazil's NSA: Something New under the Sun?

The emerging profile of state activism differs from state action in both the developmentalist period and the neoliberal phase of the 1990s. In the developmentalist period, from the 1930s to the 1980s, the Brazilian government not only set priorities for industrialization in a top-down fashion, it also was a primary actor in industry. The state bureaucracy set goals; state-owned enterprises played a central role in many sectors, including steel, mining, aircraft, automobiles, and banking; and the state development bank provided funding for areas deemed priority by government planners. Emphasis was on "catching up" by building domestic industries. The new industries used imported technology and paid little or no attention to innovation.[36] The state created tariffs and multiple exchange rates to control imports. Social policy was not focused on redistribution or poverty reduction; social protection programs were elitist, designed to keep the industrial working class and the small middle class happy and managed in a clientelistic fashion.[37]

The 1990s saw a partial reversal of the developmentalist model with privatization, liberalization, dismantling of the instruments of industrial policy, and tentative steps toward poverty alleviation. But when it took office, the Lula government decided the state needed to resume a more active role in industrial development and to take more aggressive steps to relieve poverty and reduce inequality.

The Lula administration recognized that markets were necessary but not sufficient for inclusive growth. The state could do more to promote growth with equity, and it started to act more selectively and aggressively in the economy. This shift away from neoliberalism was as notable for what it did not do as for what it did. When Brazil began to develop new forms of state activism, it did not renationalize former state-owned enterprises, impose price controls, create a top-down development plan, discourage foreign investment, default on international obligations, engage in deficit spending, or close its markets to foreign goods. Rather, it sought to maintain and benefit from openness by ensuring the competiveness of the domestic industry. Efforts focused on

---

qualities, benefiting the better organized and remunerated in the formal and public sectors disproportionately, this segmentation is now much less acute than it has been for decades, and perhaps since the creation of the country's first social benefits many decades ago. In 2010 inequality in Brazil reached its lowest level since measurement started in 1960."

36 During the import substitution period, Brazil copied technology from developed countries. This was often manifested in the form of factories owned by foreign companies that located R&D and innovation outside Brazil with no obligations to transfer technology. That meant that Brazilian industry had a very low level of capacity for innovation. *See* Ignácio José Godinho Delgado, "*Desenvolvimento, empresariado e política industrial no Brasil,*" in *Estado, Empresariado e Desenvolvimento no Brasil: Novas Teorias, Novas Trajetórias,* 115–141 (M. A. Leopoldi, W. P. Mancuso, & W. Iglecias ed., Editora de Cultura, 2010).

37 Arbix & Martin, *supra* note 4 observe that "over the course of several decades, the statist model shifted resources from consumption to investment, limiting real wages and social spending and directing social spending in clientelistic fashion toward more organized segments of society with an eye toward political stability and control."

constructing new forms of industrial policy that emphasized innovation and partnership with industry. At the same time, an emphasis was placed on social policy and redistribution and the combination of social policy with industrial growth strategies.

The Rise and Shape of NSA

What explains NSA and why did it take the shape that it did in Brazil? What impelled the Lula government to reintroduce industrial policy? Why did it choose to emphasize innovation, engage with the private sector, and structure the program in a more bottom-up fashion? Why did NSA link industrial and social policy and refocus social policy toward poverty alleviation and reduction of inequality?

No one would claim that Brazil's new form of state activism was planned from the start or that a clear or completely stable model has emerged. No master plan ever emanated from a government think tank or planning ministry. These policies evolved in a piecemeal fashion and are still changing. The Brazilian government has been feeling the stones as it crosses the river—recalling Deng Xaoping's phrase—not following an existing blueprint. However, looking back over a decade of experimentation and policy evolution, one can see several factors that explain the decision to resume an active role for the state as well as the forces that affected the form this role would take. This section considers three of these factors: political opportunity, structural impediments to growth, and international and domestic constraints. Taken together, they exemplify the profile of what Arbix and Martin call "new state activism without dominance."

A Political Moment

When Lula was elected in 2002, growth had slowed and unemployment was very high. The effects of globalization and liberalization were being felt, and Brazilian companies were losing ground. It is not hard to understand why a government led by the Brazilian Workers Party (PT), predisposed to state activism, would want to increase the role of the state in the economy. But the PT was not alone—this view was shared by at least part of the wider business community. Business in general and many industrialists in particular wanted a more activist state and more voice in government policy.[38]

Although the PT was ideologically committed to state activism, the business community looked to the state as a force that could reignite growth. Dissatisfied by the effects of liberalization in the 1990s, powerful industrial groups (including the Federation of Industries of São Paulo, or FIESP) involved themselves in the electoral process in 2002 with the objective of "opening space for

---

38 Shunko Rojas suggests that changes in the leadership of the Federation of Industries in São Paulo led to FIESP support for an expanded state role well before the 2002 election. Private communication with the authors, Aug., 2012.

developmentalist ideas."[39] Industry had played an important role in the old development state, so at least some industrialists were comfortable with an increased role for the state as long as they had a voice in state policy.

Although Lula's first administration took cautious steps toward state activism, interest in a stronger role for the state grew during Lula's second term (2006–10). In this period, NSA gained appeal, importance, and political support from industrialists, unions, intellectuals, and academics. Brazilian economist Antonio Barros de Castro suggests that the Brazilian elite realized that it needed to "deal with China."[40] He notes that trade liberalization and the rise of China led much of Latin America to abandon industry and refocus on natural resources. Due to the large size and central importance of its industrial sector, Brazil could not and did not want to take this route. Despite the modernization of Brazil's industry that had made it globally competitive in some fields, once China came on the scene, Brazil was no longer as competitive. At the same time, Chinese demand for natural resources drove up the value of the real, thus further handicapping Brazilian industry by increasing the cost of exports and lowering the cost of imported manufactured goods. The situation worsened, leading to a slowdown in 2005 and a public outcry about the economic situation that generated calls for more action by the state.

The turning point came around 2006. As a result of a political scandal, Antonio Palocci, Lula's finance minister, was replaced by Guido Mantega, a heterodox economist and academic closely linked to Lula. Palocci was also closely linked to the PT, had maintained an orthodox approach to economic policy, and was closer to the financial sector than to industry. His replacement opened a window of opportunity for the industrialists represented by institutions such as the National Industry Confederation (CNI), FIESP, and the Economic Institute for Industrial Development (IEDI), a business think thank, to push for policies that would allow them to recover and protect industrial chains dismantled during the 1990s, foster international competitiveness, and channel more state funds into infrastructure investments. Business support for neoliberalism, never so robust, declined, and its acceptance of state activism increased. Jackson De Toni suggests that "Brazilian industrialists partly conceded in their unconditional defense of a minimalist agenda for the state in exchange for a political economy that would maintain the inherited stability and defend them against external competition, but would also revive public investments in infrastructure."[41]

---

39 They "correctly understood Lula's election as a mandate for a pro-growth strategy," says James Martin Cypher. *Brazil's Development Strategy: Maintaining the Industrial Base, Side Stepping the Staples Trap?* paper presented at at the 2012 Congress of the Latin American Studies Association, San Francisco, California, 8, 2012.

40 See de Castro, *supra* note 6.

41 Jackson de Toni, *Estado e empresários na política industrial brasileira recente: Processos de cooperação e mudança institucional*, paper presented at IPEA CODE (2011), available at http://www.ipea.gov.br/code/chamada2011/pdf/area10/area10-artigo2.pdf (accessed Jul. 21, 2012).

In this context, continues De Toni, the Lula government created some new "arenas" for public-private coordination (including councils such as CDES, CNDI, and the so-called competitiveness *fora*) and new agencies (such as ABDI) in an attempt to ensure legitimacy while controlling the increasing demands of industrial entrepreneurs. At the same time it launched the Growth Acceleration Program (PAC) in 2007. PAC was designed to restart investment using the strength of public companies like Petrobrás to lead the process.

Another factor that helped cement political support for state activism was the global financial crisis. The pervasive and worldwide failure of markets, which were deeply affected by financial disorganization, epitomized the crisis of deregulated capitalism and legitimized the adoption of alternative policies. This gave more support for the expansion of industrial policy and the growing role of BNDES. The government adopted a rhetoric that stressed that the crisis was an opportunity for Brazil to gain comparative advantages, requiring proactive state action.

When the financial crisis broke out in 2008, the Brazilian economy was seriously challenged by the lack of credit. Like many institutions in the United States and Europe, Brazilian financial institutions halted the supply of credit. This led to more pressure by the industrial coalition for action by the Brazilian state. As a result, BNDES was heavily capitalized so that it could play a countercyclical role in the economy. BNDES sharply raised its disbursements, thus galvanizing a national industrial sector already suffering from reduced competitiveness and an unfavorable exchange rate and now also buffeted by credit stringency. In general, because of the worldwide crisis, the Brazilian government was able to become more active in shaping the trajectory of economic development.

Structural Elements

What problems did policy makers face and respond to as they shaped NSA? Three structural features were important:

- Major market failures that impeded economic activity, including a low level of investment in infrastructure and a lack of innovation
- Long-standing Brazilian social concerns
- The international embeddedness of the Brazilian economy and its need to spur competitiveness

Market Failures: Innovation, Infrastructure, Financial Sector, and Competitiveness

Major domestic market failures forced policy makers to face the low level of innovation in Brazilian industry. By the early 2000s, they had recognized that Brazilian industry had slowed down and believed that markets alone could not restart the growth process and that state intervention was called for. The national economy had had its last impetus of vitality in the 1970s, during the apogee of "old" development state policies. In that decade, Brazil underwent a second industrial revolution, acquiring a diversified industrial base. But the economy started to stagnate due to external and internal factors, and beginning in the early 1980s, the economy endured a long period of stagnation, in which growth slowed and Brazil fell behind the rapidly growing Asian tigers.

One external factor was changing global capitalist accumulation patterns and the consolidation of a knowledge-based economy,[42] which made industrial innovation essential for economic competitiveness. The internal reasons included Brazil's failure to reshape the political economy and the legal-institutional structure that underpinned the old developmentalism based on an alliance among the state, foreign capital, and national capital.[43] The state provided infrastructure, organized key sectors of the economy through state-owned enterprises, generated savings that could be used for new investment, and created regulations and incentives to protect and promote the private sector. Foreign capital helped develop local industry using technology that had been created and perfected in advanced markets; sometimes this included bringing in equipment that had become obsolete at home.[44] One effect of this arrangement was that the Brazilian economy was largely insulated from international competition. This, in turn, reduced the pressure for national innovation and the development of new technology: Brazil was limited to buying externally-generated technology. This helped slow the pace of development. Suzigan and Villela conclude:

> It was necessary to change not only to correct these problems, but also because there was [an awareness] that the country had reached the zenith of a historical development process (which many erroneously described simply as import substitution). Once an ample and diversified industrial basis [had been built], it was necessary to make it efficient and competitive. It was also necessary to incorporate sectors and industries representing new technologies, particularly informatics and telecommunications, and to develop innovation ability, a crucial element in competition.[45]

During this time, Asian countries, noticeably South Korea and Taiwan, were on a brisk developmental pace, giving rise to a new round of growth based on knowledge, innovation, and reduction of poverty and inequality. Brazil and its Latin American counterparts lost vitality. One indicator is the

---

42 *See* Michael J. Piore & Charles F. Sabel, *The Second Industrial Divide: Possibilities for Prosperity* (Basic Books, 1984); and David Harvey, *The Condition of Postmodernity: An Enquiry into the Origins of Cultural Change* (Wiley-Blackwell, 1991).

43 Peter Evans, *Embedded Autonomy: States and Industrial Transformation* (Princeton U. Press, 1995).

44 *See* Lincoln Gordon & Englebert L. Grommers, *United States Manufacturing Investment in Brazil: The Impact of Brazilian Government Policies 1946–1960* (Division of Research, Graduate School of Business Administration, Harvard U., 1962).

45 Suzigan & Villela, *supra* note 23.

relative success in patenting: Asians far surpassed Latin Americans in patents issued in the United States.

Brazilian policy makers took steps to increase the rate of innovation in industrial activity. Modest efforts to stimulate innovation began as early as 1999, but with the reintroduction of industrial policy in 2004, substantial resources were devoted to improving the overall climate for innovation; supporting restructuring in targeted industries; and fostering the development of new areas of specialization considered relevant and potentially able to consolidate key industrial chains.

Another structural barrier to growth was the low level of investment in infrastructure. The private sector was unwilling to invest in needed infrastructure expansion, and the state had not compensated for this deficiency. Although Brazil has one of the highest tax burdens in the world, public sector investment was relatively low, even by Latin American standards.[46]

The private financial sector played a large role in the structural economic failure in Brazil. Although it had grown in size and importance, the private sector still funded industrial expansion in only limited amounts. State banks, which date to the developmental period, filled the gap. When the Lula government decided to implement a broader industrial policy, it looked to the state banks, especially to BNDES, to prove the capital and expertise needed for growth, innovation, and competiveness and to buffer the effects of the financial crises.[47] Unlike other developing countries, Brazil did not dismantle its development bank in the 1990s, so that institution was available when the government decided to intervene more actively in the economy. Today, the state bank is the main source of long-term financing in Brazil and a key actor in the conception and implementation of industrial policy.

The fourth structural problem that affected the emergence of state activism is the side effect of the Plano Real. Undeniably, the Plano Real achieved its goal of ending runaway inflation. Since 1994, when the plan was implemented, inflation has been kept in check at around 5 percent per year. The problem, however, is that this plan is anchored in the interplay of two

---

46 José Roberto Rodrigues Afonso, Erika Amorim Araújo, & Geraldo Biasoto Júnior, *Fiscal Space and Public Sector Investments in Infrastructure: A Brazilian Case-Study*, 1141 Textos Para Discussão IPEA (2005). Commenting on the infrastructure deficit in Brazil, Daniel Perrotti notes: "Although several factors were involved (such as high macroeconomic volatility, the lack of comprehensive policies and regulatory and financing issues), the effects of these physical constraints are obvious and seriously threaten future development." See *The Economic Infrastructure Gap in Latin America and the Caribbean*, 293 FAL Bulletin (2011), available at http://www.cepal.org/usi/noticias/bolfall/6/42926/FAL-293-WEB-ENG-2.pdf (accessed Jul., 20, 2012).

47 BNDES and the other major state banks have access to public (pension and treasury) funds, so their cost of capital is well below that of the private sector. BNDES also makes profits and raises funds in the capital market, besides offering substantial expertise; the bank has been financing the Brazilian industrial sector for 50 years and has developed detailed knowledge of many important sectors and close ties to industry that add to its advantages over the private sector.

macroeconomic variables: interest rate and exchange rate. Whereas the interest rate is the main control against inflation, the exchange rate is directly influenced by the interest rate: if the interest rate is high, it attracts foreign investment, which results in an appreciation of the exchange rate. This has two direct consequences. First, the regulation of inflation by management of the interest rate creates side effects in the financial markets, inasmuch as appreciation of the value of the currency encourages investors—including foreign investors—to buy government bonds. This means that less money is available for the private sector. Second, the resulting appreciation of the exchange rate affects domestic industry because it makes imports cheaper and exports less competitive. This situation put pressure on policy makers: industry pressed for solutions that would lower the cost of finance and guard against deindustrialization. Industrial policy seemed like a way to handle both concerns.

Social Concerns

Social concerns shaped the development of NSA in Brazil, in particular four issues: poverty, social inequality, unemployment; and the tendency of wages to lag behind productivity.

In 1981, 31 percent of the Brazilian population was living on less than US$2 per day. Other social indicators were negative: child mortality was high, life expectancy at birth was only 63 years, illiteracy was widespread, and many people had no regular access to sanitation and potable water.[48] Economic inequality was extreme. Brazil has been profoundly unequal and unjust for a long time: in 1990, the Gini coefficient was 0.6091. The degree of inequality is further aggravated when considering race and gender. Unemployment was also high: the rate of unemployment reached 10 percent in the early 1990s, and from the 1980s to 2000, unemployment was a crucial political issue.[49] Education was also a problem: the education system did not produce the number of skilled people needed by a growing and competitive economy. Industrial policies designed to spur technological upgrading were hampered by the lack of adequate human resources; people did not have the skills needed in a changing labor market. The government recognized the need for job creation and skills upgrading in connection with social and welfare initiatives.

Wage lag is another social issue in Brazil. Because of the large rural population in most Latin American countries including Brazil, a huge pool of underemployed workers depresses wage levels.[50] As a result, domestic demand does not grow as fast as domestic production, thus hindering growth of the

---

48 Data in this section is taken from Mauricio Font & Laura Randall, *The Brazilian State: Debate and Agenda* (Lexington Books, 2011).

49 *Id.* Some observers put the effective rate as high as 20 percent.

50 This is what W. Arthur Lewis called development with "unlimited supplies of labor."

domestic market. Economists stress the need for government action to offset this with an income policy that will bring wages up to optimal levels.[51]

International Embeddedness and the Need to Spur Competitiveness

A third structural feature affecting the emergence of NSA was Lula's decision to liberalize the economy and maintain openness. Although export promotion had been a development target since the 1960s, domestic industrialization dominated the governmental agenda until the 1990s. This situation changed with globalization and liberalization. In the 1990s, Brazil opened itself to international competition and began to actively pursue export markets, forcing the state to pay more attention to competitiveness.

When Lula's government took office, one of its first moves was to emphasize the need for state action to encourage the solutions needed to maintain competitiveness. This decision, brought about by the commitment to open economy policies, explains both the revival of industrial policy and the government emphasis on innovation. From PITCE through Brasil Maior, policies have focused on boosting the international competitiveness of Brazilian companies, including BNDES's support for the internationalization of Brazil's most competitive industries and various mechanisms to subsidize exports. Although the government has recognized the importance of competiveness and that maintaining openness to foreign goods is necessary to preserve competiveness, it has also taken measures to provide protection for domestic industries.

Structural Elements: Conditioning Factors

The stage was set for the government, led by the Brazilian Workers Party, to increase the role of the state in the economy. But why did Brazil's role as a development state take the shape that it did? Why did Brazil opt for an innovation-focused and collaborative public-private form of industrial policy rather than, say, renationalization as did Venezuela, Argentina, Ecuador, and Bolivia? Why was Brazil supportive of foreign investment in most sectors? This section discusses factors that influenced the choices Brazil has made in its search to help the economy regain dynamism and promote inclusive growth. Among these factors, four are especially important:

- Constitutional considerations
- The strength and scope of the private sector
- International economic law and policy
- Global financial markets

---

51 Bresser-Pereira, *supra* note 4 at 193.

Constitutional Considerations

The 1988 constitution influenced the choice of strategies and measures by making direct state control of industry both more expensive and less important than in the past. The new constitution protected property rights and regulatory commitments, thus making renationalization of privatized industries an expensive proposition. It reduced the possibilities for corruption and for private capture of state power, thus increasing the government's capacity to steer the private sector and provide control and accountability mechanisms for the public sector. This made state ownership seem less necessary. Finally, by creating an open and democratic political structure, the constitution enhanced the power and participation of civil society, including industry, vis-à-vis the state.

The Private Sector

The size, complexity, and sophistication of the private sector in Brazil influenced the path of collaborative innovation-oriented industrial policy. The Brazilian economy includes many well-developed sectors and a growing capital market. Many firms are either at the global competitive frontier or close to it. Others have incipient capabilities. Many sectors accept the need for restructuring and continuous improvement. Many firms have the kind of deep knowledge essential for effective innovation even though they may not be able fully to utilize this knowledge without public incentives and support.

It must have seemed much easier to create incentives for these firms to innovate and provide support for new private start-ups than to try to replace them with state-owned enterprises. At the same time, the size and scope of the private sector meant that once democracy was restored, the private sector gained an important voice in public affairs. The private sector was eager to support an expanded role for the state as long as this support was offered in collaboration with industry and was appropriate to resume growth. Thus, Cypher notes:

> given the many endemic macroeconomic problems that had made the 1990s a period of slow growth in spite of the restructuring of industry, powerful industrial groups (including the Federation of Industries of São Paulo) involved themselves in the electoral process in 2002 with the objective of "opening space for developmentalist ideas" (Delgado 2010: 125) . . . the business federations—the organizations representing the interests of Brazil's vast and diversified industrial base—correctly understood Lula's election as a mandate for a pro-growth strategy and as an indication that a structural change would occur opening-up channels of direct intermediation between the industrial sector and the new administration. . . . In short, there was a consensus between the PT and important fractions of industrial capital to reverse "the loss of the centrality of the State as an agent of accumulation."[52]

---

52 See *supra* note 39.

International Economic Law and Policy

World Trade Organization (WTO) law places restrictions on policies like export subsidies and weak enforcement of intellectual property that had been used by the East Asian states, so Brazil had to work around these restraints or find ways to defend them. The Lula administration did a little of both by defending some heterodox policies and modifying others.[53] Because it never ratified the Bilateral Investment Treaties (BITs) signed in the 1990s, Brazil did not encounter similar restrictions in international investment law. Nonetheless, because the government recognized that foreign investment was important for its innovation strategy and sought to encourage its own firms to invest in foreign markets, it followed many of the principles of the investment regime. Similarly, while Brazil's export surpluses and growing reserves have made it less dependent on international financial institutions, Brazil has been influenced by the World Bank and other international financial institutions that promote market solutions but accept industrial policy as long as it respects comparative advantage and focuses on innovation.

Global Financial Markets

The Lula government decided to rely on foreign investment to help it reach and maintain international competiveness. It realized that classic protectionism would threaten the availability of such investment, while an innovation-oriented and collaborative industrial policy offering selected benefits and incentives to both foreign and domestic firms would be acceptable to investors.

Other Influences on the Emergence of NSA

Several other factors help explain the profile of Brazil's NSA, including the increased professionalism of the state apparatus and bureaucracy, which made it possible to carry out industrial policy, and the rise of alternative economic theories that legitimized state activism. The macroinstitutional arrangement provided by the 1988 constitution contributed to upgrading state capacity and played an important role in NSA. In the past few decades, the Brazilian state has enhanced internal coordination, increased public-private collaboration, and learned how to better define policy mandates. Thus, NSA is partly the result of institutional learning, through which the Brazilian state progressively acquired greater administrative capacity and the expertise needed to implement complex and ambitious development policies.

Until recently, the vast majority of public employees was appointed politically, weakening the public service ethos necessary to build a professional bureaucracy staffed by people with technical expertise who can administer

---

53 *See* Alvaro Santos, *Carving out Policy Autonomy for Developing Countries in the World Trade Organization: The Experience of Brazil and Mexico;* and Michelle Ratton Sanchez Badin, *Developmental Responses to the International Trade Legal Game: Cases of Intellectual Property and Export Credit Law Reforms in Brazil,* in Trubek et al., *supra* note 1.

policies rationally and efficiently. There were some islands of excellence in public administration: some key institutions of developmental coordination, such as BNDES, Petrobrás, Embraer, Embrapa, IPEA, and the Central Bank, were professionalized. But these cases were in stark contrast to the rest of public administration, which compromised state capability. This lack of professionalism changed with the 1988 constitution, which mandated the recruitment of public employees through public and official exams (*concursos públicos*). As a result, there has been a substantial increase in the percentage of public employees selected meritocratically.

The constitution also regulates the ceiling of earnings, determining that the maximum wage should be no higher than that one received by members of the Supreme Court (Supremo Tribunal Federal). This rule was designed to limit public expense and curb discretionary distortions in the level of salaries. Although both meritocratic recruitment and wage policy face problems of enforcement, they represent an improvement in terms of governmental quality. When the Lula administration began to expand the state's role, it could count on a more professional workforce in government.

Other measures helped enhance state capacity, making it easier to carry out the direction called for by NSA. The constitutional framework established in 1988 gave rise to policy initiatives designed to "implement rights" and "modernize" the state. New ministries were created, several others were reorganized, subministerial entities were added, and councils and committees were formed to increase participation by business and labor. In addition, BNDES has played an increasingly important role in industrial policy.

Changes in the world of ideas also facilitated NSA. With the turn to a more robust role for the state in the economy, and its particular profile in Brazil, there have been corresponding changes on the intellectual scene. Internationally, more attention is paid to the positive role industrial policy might play, and the World Bank has endorsed certain types of industrial policy.[54] Similar developments are occurring within Brazil as Brazilian economists seek to explain and guide the evolving new configuration. Brazil has also attracted the attention of theorists around the world who hope to create a new political economy of development.[55]

The academic focus has resulted in analytical tools and offers intellectual justifications that can help sustain policy experimentation. Some observers have labeled the emerging set of ideas "new developmentalism." James Cypher describes this approach:

> On the one hand, New Developmentalism [rejects] prevailing ideas of neoclassical economics regarding a passive reliance on an export-

---

54 Justin Yifu Lin, *New Structural Economics: A Framework for Rethinking Development* (World Bank, 2012), available at http://siteresources.worldbank.org/INTVIETNAM/Resources/Jtin.pdf.

55 For a detailed discussion of Brazil and new developmentalism, *see* David M. Trubek, *Law, State, and the New Developmentalism: An Introduction*, in Trubek et al., *supra* note 1.

> led, resource-based economy [and agrees with]. . . . the original developmentalist economists such as Rosenstein-Rodan, Hirschman, and Nurkse, and their emphasis on the centrality of a developmentalist state. . . . On the other hand, New Developmentalism stresses a "growth with equity" approach along with an emphasis on industrial policy, highlighting public, growth-supporting, infrastructure spending, and a "neoschumpeterian" emphasis on building a national innovation system through deep public-private cooperative programs that will drive investment expenditures toward productivity-enhancing science and technology applications throughout the national industrial base of the economy.[56]

In Brazil, after the relative theoretical hegemony of liberal ideas associated with the Washington Consensus in the 1990s, a burgeoning literature has lent support for NSA. This can be seen in two different fields: economics (both macroeconomics and microeconomics) and political science. In economics, an important contribution has been research on the exchange rate and its effect on industrialization. According to the argument developed by Bresser-Pereira, there has been appreciation of the value of the real, leading to a "Dutch disease" effect that promotes deindustrialization.[57] Due to the floods of dollars that have been reaching the Brazilian economy, the currency has become overvalued, with a negative effect on national industry. By showing that free market policies can lead to these negative effects, Bresser-Pereira and his colleagues created a rationale for an aggressive industrial policy. This criticism was accompanied by microeconomic studies that challenge the market-oriented model. These studies include sectorial and market analyses and document specific and pervasive market failures that require active industrial policies.[58]

In addition, microeconomists and political scientists have been providing inputs to social policy. Studies have demonstrated how economic inequality itself is a problem, detaching this problem from poverty. This sort of consideration has given impulse to the formulation of two different sets of social measures: poverty alleviation measures and instruments intended to reduce economic inequality more generally.

---

56 Cypher, *supra* note 39, comments that "As yet, New Developmentalism has not been rigorously defined. Some find that trial and error rather than the adoption of a coherent 'model' such as 'new-developmentalism' better describes the current conjuncture," citing Arbix & Martin, *supra* note 4.

57 The "Dutch disease" refers to the effect of a commodities boom on industry. Increased demand for commodities leads to appreciation of the currency, which makes industrial exports less competitive. This occurred in the Netherlands with the discovery of natural gas. *See* Luiz Carlos Bresser-Pereira, *The Dutch Disease and Its Neutralization: A Ricardian Approach*, 28 Brazilian J. of Pol. Eco. 47–71 (2008).

58 Two issues have been highlighted: failures in the market for innovation and gaps in the industrial chain. Studies conducted by Arbix & Pacheco and the Institute for Economic Applied Research show the need for innovation policies, while Erber, Cassiolato, & Kupfer highlight gaps in supply chains that require government action.

Challenge for Law

What does the emergence of NSA mean for law, and vice versa? As the role of the state in the economy and social protection changes, there will be corresponding changes in law. And it seems possible that law will shape and channel the path for policy innovation, as well as providing room for adaptation. This section outlines some general considerations about NSA's challenges for law.

Although it is easy to say that law and NSA must in some way be mutually constitutive, it is another matter to say how NSA affects law and vice versa. Part of the problem derives from the complexity of the situation, and part from the paucity of empirical studies. Although abstract models of political economy such as neoliberalism and new developmentalism suggest clear delineations, in the real world, policies are a mix of the old and the new, layered on top of one another, and sometimes contradictory. This complexity and contradiction at the policy level carries over into the legal domain: key legal variables are difficult to define and causalities involving changes in the law and in policy outcomes are blurred. As a result, studies on relationships between the law and development policy present methodological challenges.

This section focuses on methods for understanding these relationships, outlines some functionalities that NSA seems to demand, and provides a few examples of how law has responded to these functional needs.

New Roles, New Frameworks of Analysis, New Functionalities

NSA will generate pressures for new laws and new roles for law. Much will be straightforward: statutes will change, procedures will be altered. This has been occurring in Brazil for years. Laws created ABDI, MDS, Cadastro Unico, and other institutions that are central to Brazil's NSA. Laws aiming at specific goals such as innovation and competiveness are also important. Although recognizing the importance of these legal changes, this section focuses on "new functionalities"—roles for law that have not been as important (or did not exist in Brazil) in the past and take on new importance with the emergence of NSA.

Three sources were used to identify new functionalities and legal responses: research done by the project on Law and the New Developmental State (LANDS), of which this study is a part;[59] other research on law and develop-

59 LANDS, the Project on Law and the New Developmental State, is coordinated by the Global Legal Studies Center at the University of Wisconsin, Madison with assistance from CEBRAP (the Brazilian Center for Analysis and Planning), and Los Andes University. Funding for LANDS was provided by the University of Wisconsin School of Law, the University of Wisconsin's Center for World Affairs and the Global Economy (WAGE), and the Ford Foundation.

ment polices conducted in Brazil;[60] and "reverse engineering."[61] Reverse engineering means starting with policies and programs, describing the functions associated with them, and seeing if law has contributed, or could contribute, to those functions.

For NSA to be successful and new development policies to work, the government must maintain flexibility, orchestrate the relations among public actors and between them and the private sector, create conditions that will maximize synergy between actors, and preserve legitimacy. These functional needs point to new roles for law: if one isolates the role law can play in these new functionalities, one can identify four roles the legal system could play in NSA in Brazil: safeguard flexibility, stimulate orchestration, frame synergy, and ensure legitimacy.

Safeguard flexibility means to use legal norms to allow room for experimentation, to promote innovation, and to facilitate feedback from experiments to policy. NSA demands legal regimes that permit learning by doing and that encourage path correction. Different from import substitution and neoliberalism, NSA requires the assurance of some degree of flexibility and learning to implement initiatives that in most cases do not resemble preexisting recipes or strategies; this is one reason why NSA employs "new governance" tools.[62]

Stimulate orchestration means to use law to structure state activities for effective industrial and social policy. This means facilitating coordination and articulation within the state—both horizontally (that is, between entities that belong to the same bureaucratic state level) and vertically (that is, between entities that are subject to hierarchies or belong to different state levels).

---

60 Diogo R. Coutinho & Paulo T. L. Mattos, *"Law and the New Developmental State: Brazil Pilot Project,"* paper presented at the workshop "Law and the New Developmental State: Latin America and Beyond," Global Legal Studies Center—Center for World Affairs and the Global Economy (WAGE), University of Wisconsin, Madison (2008); Fabiani, *supra* note 16; Roberto Pires, *Promoting Sustainable Compliance: Styles of Labour Inspection and Compliance Outcomes in Brazil*, 147 Intl. Lab. Rev. 199–229 (2008); Mariana Mota Prado & Ana Carolina da Matta Chasin, *How Innovative Was the Poupatempo Experience in Brazil? Institutional Bypass as a New Form of Institutional Change*, 1 Brazilian Pol. Sci. Rev. (2011); Mario Gomes Schapiro, *Development Bank, Law and Innovation Financing in a New Brazilian Economy*, 1045 L. & Dev. Rev.; Gregory C. Shaffer, Michelle Ratton Sanchez, & Barbara Rosenberg, *The Trials of Winning at the WTO: What Lies Behind Brazil's Success*, 41 Cornell Intl. J. 2 (2008).

61 The idea of reverse engineering appears in David Kennedy, *The Rule of Law, Political Choices, and Development Common Sense*, in *The New Law and Development—A Critical Appraisal* (David Trubek & Alvaro Santos ed., Cambridge U. Press 2006), in the context of a discussion of the postwar consensus (1945–70). Kennedy reckons that although there was a clear demand for instrumental law during this period, the legal theory was implicit. In order to reveal it, he proposes, "We need to reverse engineer the legal theory of mainstream development professionals from their economic and political projects, and from the attitudes toward law they manifested in managing developing policies within national administration. A great deal of law was required to translate the leading economic theories of development economic policy."

62 For a thorough account of new governance and its legal functions and tools, *see* Orly Lobel, *The Renew Deal: The Fall of Regulation and the Rise of Governance in Contemporary Legal Thought*, 89 Minn. L. Rev. (2004).

Orchestration can consist of norms and procedures that assign institutional tasks and foster cooperative (rather than competitive) governance regimes, including rules that encourage government to work with the private sector. Also, it can mean supporting policy networks that share tasks and interact in a complementary way to implement policies; this can include defining policy hubs. Finally, orchestration can mean using norms that harmonize new policies with preexisting ones to ensure coherence. Norms and processes playing these roles are crucial in NSA because it relies on the integration of different fields.

Frame synergy involves using the law to frame public-private partnerships and ensure that they are more effective than purely public or private solutions. Such modalities include collaborative governance regimes that create incentives for public-private cooperation (through incentive alignment and/or the use of private contracts by public entities), risk sharing,[63] and hybrid instances in which public and private players regularly meet to interact and exchange opinions on regulatory and contractual instruments that bring private expertise and public financial capacity together.

Ensure legitimacy means to keep government transparent and ensure adequate participation. NSA requires a regime in which it is easy for new ideas to percolate upward and be widely shared. This makes older authoritarian models obsolete and increases the importance of democracy. Legal regimes must ensure accountability, transparency, and participation in development policies, which requires norms for disclosure, frameworks for participation, methods to hold policy makers accountable for results, and ways to avoid industry capture of government at the same time public-private dialogue is fostered.

Developments in industrial and social policy illustrate how Brazil is dealing with these new needs and functionalities.

Flexibility and Synergy in Industrial Policy

The industrial policy promoted by NSA in Brazil is as much process as policy. It is part of a joint public-private discovery process, a collaboration through which partners experiment with different trajectories to identify products and processes that are optimal for individual firms and sectors as a whole. Efforts to encourage innovation through a full-scale partnership with the private sector move the state into new territory. For example, instead of traditional arms-length lending with well-defined goals set in advance, internationalization strategies for Brazilian companies and innovation financing call for substantial flexibility, risk sharing, and alliances—this requires legal innovation.

One area in which this is occurring is BNDES's program to foster innovation that replaced its traditional form of fixed obligation loan agreements with a variety of flexible devices that support collaboration and experimentation. The tools developed for this purpose represent a break in BNDES's

63 Coutinho & Mattos, *supra* note 60.

legal pattern: the bank relies on flexible legal structures that, formally or informally, support a financial relationship that permits changes of trajectory and adaptation of plans. These legal tools include partnerships with technological institutes and grants to promote the development of new products; relational loan contracts that include nonbinding performance criteria, staged disbursements, and constant BNDES monitoring through shared governance mechanisms; equity investments coupled with shared governance established through shareholder agreements that give BNDES a seat on the board and that subject certain corporate decisions to its approval; and arrangements by which BNDES participates on the investment committee of venture capital funds that it assists.[64]

Other new legal mechanisms connected with industrial policy include risk sharing with the private sector, soft law, and special public-private partnerships. Risk-sharing agreements are designed to encourage private investors to increase investments in technological research and innovation, expand industry capacity and exports, and acquire assets abroad in order to exploit comparative advantage in sectors where Brazil is a global leader. Soft law has also been used to induce investment. For example, governmental letters of intent communicate public investment strategies and serve as signals for the private sector, inducing private investment decisions. Other tools that create incentives for private companies to innovate include public-private partnership contracts, cooperation agreements between government and research centers, and flexible private law contracts (credit contracts, shareholder and investors agreements) between government and corporations.

Orchestration and Decentralization in Social Policy

Brazil has sought to strengthen its welfare state through cooperation among the several levels of government in the federation. It also brings together different types of social policies to deal with major problems. This requires a continuous orchestration of different levels and types of policies (universal and targeted, federal and local, contributive and noncontributive). Thus, the government has found new uses for old administrative law tools and created new instruments. This strategy can be seen in BFP, which uses a registry for all social programs (Cadastro Único) and a decentralized management index (IGD) to coordinate the work of several ministries, local administrators, and other public actors and to encourage policy innovation. BFP uses conditionalities—obligations of recipients for child education and health—that it enforces through revisable regulatory rules such as ordinances. It employs the Cadastro Único to gather data and reduce asymmetric information with the purpose of expanding education and health coverage. It also adopted a carrot-based

---

64 Mario Schapiro, *Rediscovering the Developmental Path? Development Bank, Law and Innovation Financing in the Brazilian Economy*, in Trubek et al., *supra* note 1. Although the bank's innovation funding clearly represents a new form of state activism and new approaches to law, Schapiro emphasizes that the program represents a tiny portion of the bank's total portfolio, and it is unclear whether this segment of the program will expand in the future.

federal arrangement through the use of financial incentives such as IGD to get municipalities to gather data on very poor families.

In addition, IGD aims to encourage Brazilian cities to deliver effective performance, employing funds to reward those who provide dependable and quality information, maintaining updated data in the Cadastro Único, and providing information on the effect of the health and education conditionalities. BFP uses contractual arrangements with cities to ensure that they set up local agencies of social control and participation. These agencies receive IGD funding to support the BFP management and develop activities with recipient households, including managing conditionalities and benefits, monitoring recipient households, registering new households, updating and reviewing data, implementing complementary programs for basic adult literacy, providing occupational training, creating jobs and income, stimulating regional development, and strengthening BFP's social control.

This system has led to a more collaborative (rather than imposed) and flexible (rather than based on rigid rules and sanctions) relationship between the federal and local levels.[65] Such an articulation fosters decentralization (with federal guidance, steering, and expertise) and is the result of a broader picture in which, although universal programs remain central, "targeting within universalism" has been fostering development outcomes.

Experimentation and Synergy in Labor Law

In a study of new approaches to the enforcement of labor laws in Brazil, Roberto Pires shows that labor inspectors using flexible and reflexive experimentalist governance approaches had more success than their peers who employed more traditional management tools.[66] The study compares two different styles of enforcement: one, drawn from the theories of the new public management stresses, specific targets and quotas[67]; the other, which draws more on the experimentalist governance literature, stresses public-private cooperation, dialogue, exploration of options for compliance, careful analysis of the causes of violations, and revision of goals and standards as mutual learning progresses. Pires shows that through a system of hybrid governance that employs experimentalist methods while keeping sanctions in the background, health and safety inspectors in Pernambuco are able to significantly reduce the incidence of industrial accidents.

The key to this success, Pires suggests, is creating institutions that allow interaction among government, business, and labor; encourage the search for

---

65 Diogo R. Coutinho, *Decentralization and Coordination in Social Law and Policy: The Bolsa Familia Program*, in Trubek et al., *supra* note 1.

66 Roberto Pires, *Promoting Sustainable Compliance: Styles of Labour Inspection and Compliance Outcomes in Brazil* 147(2–3) Intl. Lab. Rev. 199–229 (Jun./Sep. 2008).

67 New public management refers to the idea, and consequent policy prescriptions, that market-oriented management of the public sector will lead to greater cost efficiency for governments. It gained its momentum during the 1990s.

ways companies could revise their business plans to comply with the law and still prosper; and facilitate experimentation with new technologies that might reduce risks of accidents at low cost. He notes that because of the success of these methods, the experimentalist model has been scaled up to the federal level. Although Pires does not relate his study and the growth of experimentalism in governance directly to the new political economy of development or how the Brazilian government is redefining its role in that development, the affinity between the development literature and changes in public administration seems clear.

Building Legal Capacity for Development: Trade Law

In addition to adapting law to deal with functionalities demanded by NSA, Brazil has built the legal capacity needed to shield the new industrial and social policies from restrictions that might be imposed by international law and policy. Built into NSA are policies that challenge some orthodox prescriptions backed by international economic law, including restraints on export subsidies and stricter protection of intellectual property. The clearest example of this kind of legal response is in the field of trade law.[68]

When it initially joined the WTO in 1995, Brazil accepted the full package of WTO agreements without first determining to what extent they might clash with domestic policies and priorities. But as neoliberal enthusiasm waned, successive administrations protected domestic policy space by challenging restrictive interpretations of global trade rules. This growing willingness to challenge WTO-based restrictions is a result of changes in development policy and in the way trade policy is formulated in Brazil. As the state began to play a more robust role in the promotion of economic growth and social protection, trade policy making became more closely integrated with overall development policy, and Brazil invested in the legal and related skills needed for success in trade disputes. At the same time, the arena for discussion of trade policy expanded as more government agencies began to participate and the private sector and a flourishing civil society movement entered the debate. As a result, Brazil has been able to use trade law as a shield for policy innovation.

In the case of intellectual property, Brazil was able to carve out space within the regime for the Agreement on Trade-Related Aspects of Intellectual Property Rights (TRIPS) that allowed it to negotiate better prices for antiviral drugs. Although initially it seemed that TRIPS would preclude this kind of action, a number of changes in law, politics, and government organization at the domestic level, as well as action in the international arena, strengthened the Brazilian government's capacity to shape domestic health policy in the face of international constraints. The judiciary entered the arena to enforce a

---

68 *See* Alvaro Santos, *Carving out Policy Autonomy for Developing Countries in the World Trade Organization: The Experience of Brazil and Mexico;* and Michelle Ratton Sanchez Badin, *Developmental Responses to the International Trade Legal Game: Cases of Intellectual Property and Export Credit Law Reforms in Brazil,* in Trubek et al., *supra* note 1.

constitutional right to health, administrative changes were made that opened trade policy discussions to a range of interests, and the legislature was mobilized.

Specific legal changes at the domestic level included reforms of the legal system in order to eliminate TRIPS-plus provisions; authorization for use of flexibilities such as compulsory licenses; the approval of new mechanisms implicitly authorized by the international system that favor access to technology; and the creation of new government institutions that could serve as countervailing powers to industry interests in the patent approval process. Brazil and other developing countries carried on a campaign at the international level that led the WTO and the World Intellectual Property Organization (WIPO) to take a more supportive stance toward the use of policy in this field.

Brazil has been able to legally protect domestic trade policy from WTO restrictions. As part of its new industrial policy, Brazil sought to build Embraer into a national champion and facilitate efforts to develop market share in the global regional jet market. Government financing is an essential part of any deal for aircraft manufacturers, and Embraer had been hampered by the high cost of finance available to Brazilian companies. The government decided to provide a subsidy to the institutions that provided finance for Embraer sales. Canada's Bombardier challenged this practice as a violation of the WTO subsidies code. After a long and drawn out litigation, Brazil was forced to make changes in its subsidies. But through a partially successful campaign that drew on the growing capacity of government and industry working together in the trade law field, Brazil was able to preserve part of the subsidy program and shift the issue of aircraft financing terms into the Organization for Economic Cooperation and Development (OECD). By moving the issue to the OECD, Brazil gained a voice in the main forum affecting global rules for aircraft finance. This meant it has a say in the terms affecting its competitors and thus more bargaining leverage in the continuing dispute with Bombardier.

Conclusion: Assessing the Brazilian Experience in Development Policy and Law

The Brazilian foray into NSA is a work in progress. Policies are altered as domestic and international conditions change. Industrial policy seems to be working and is helping the country both weather the storms from the global financial crisis and resume economic dynamism. World markets have accepted this trend, and foreign investment has soared. Significant gains have been made in poverty alleviation and the reduction of economic inequality.

Yet questions remain. Is a coherent model of a new development state emerging, and is Brazil's new state activism likely to become consolidated? Does the government have the capacity to manage and implement the ambitious set of processes and policies that have been put in place? Can Brazilian institutions develop and sustain the new roles demanded by NSA? Finally, is the Brazilian experience unique to that country, or can it be replicated?

A New Development State?

Although the current situation in Brazil is described here as NSA, a discussion of a "new Brazil model" in the sense of a coherent and stable configuration of state, law, and political economy would be premature. Brazil is experimenting with a variety of new policies and procedures. Many of them have yet to stand the test of time. But the trends show continuous movement toward a set of policies that could cohere into a sustainable model. A new form of industrial policy stressing state assistance for innovation and competitiveness in the private and public sectors is in place and has been combined with a robust social policy. The commitment to NSA has lasted for more than a decade, through two presidential elections. President Dilma Rousseff has deepened the government's commitment to the new industrial and social policies.

Does Brazil Have the Capacity to Manage and Implement the New Policies?

NSA places great demands on the state, which must be able to assist the private sector without stifling it. It must make choices among sectors, industries, and firms in the public interest. Complicated decisions involving massive sums of money require both technical expertise and distance from special interests. Through a series of reforms, the Brazilian state bureaucracy is more professional today than it was in the past. But this is not true everywhere, and in many areas inefficiency, bureaucratic rigidity, or both, persist. Finally, the risk of corruption and capture is always present. Some measures have been taken to limit corruption; although new anticorruption laws and agencies have been created, corruption remains a problem in Brazil as elsewhere.

Can the Brazilian Legal System Meet the Needs of NSA?

Brazilian law can contribute to the operation of the new policies and procedures under NSA. In at least a few cases and a few areas, new legal tools are being created and old ones are being put to new use. The legal system has the capacity for innovation that new developmentalism demands. But it is not clear that this is happening—or will happen—in all the areas where change is needed. The cases that have been studied suggest it is possible, but they are too limited to warrant a conclusion. For that to happen, many rigidities and obstacles in the Brazil legal system must be overcome.

Is the Brazilian Experience Unique, or Can It Be Replicated?

There is no question that other nations can learn from the Brazilian experience in development policy. The approach to industrial policy that assists the private sector and fosters structural changes needed for competiveness can be followed in other countries. The potential for using a state development bank as an engine of innovation and growth also provides lessons that can be replicated. Brazil's successful merger of industrial policy and social policy is worth further study. The same can be said for the Brazilian experience in law and development. To the extent that countries adopt aspects of NSA, they will need to adapt their legal system to new functionalities and can learn from the way Brazil has developed legal institutions that address these needs.

That does not mean, however, that the Brazilian experience has resulted in a template that can be followed by everyone, everywhere. The account presented in this chapter has stressed the contextual features that explain Brazil's turn to NSA, such as a large, well-developed industrial sector, advanced research centers, a huge domestic market, a democratic constitution, a professionalized bureaucracy in key agencies, a long history of state involvement in the economy, and some transformative capacity in legal institutions. Because the development of NSA in Brazil is based on these contextual features, NSA in the Brazilian form will not be easily replicated in countries that lack any or all of these features.

The Role of the Public Ministry in the Defense of the Environment

Hydrogeographical Regions and Attitudes for Coping with Socioenvironmental Conflicts

LUCIANO BADINI AND LUCIANO ALVARENGA

The Brazilian Constitution of 1988, the first constitutional text since the fall of the Brazilian military dictatorship, devotes significant attention to the idea of democracy. The constitution entrusts the Public Ministry, a permanent institution that is crucial to the jurisdictional function of the state, with the defense of the legal order, the democratic regime, and so-called metaindividual interests and rights—rights belonging to society as a whole. The protection of the environment, claimed as a common possession for use by the people and recognized as essential to a healthy quality of life for current and future generations (Article 225), is a metaindividual right.

The defense of rights fits into the larger scope of implementing the essential principles of the Federative Republic of Brazil. As Marcelo Goulart reflects:

> The strategic goal of the Public Ministry is to defend the project of participative, economic and social democracy outlined in the 1988 Constitution through achievement of crucial objectives for the Republic, synthesized in Article 3, from Section I to IV (construction of a free, fair and solidary society in which cultural and socio-economic development should be directed towards the eradication of poverty and marginalization, thus reducing social and regional inequalities and promoting the welfare of all).

In order for the Public Ministry to fulfill this task, the Brazilian Constitution gives it legitimacy to adopt measures of civil and criminal liability against the violators of environmental rules.[1]

The authors would like to thank Mr. Matt Moorhead, the editors of this volume, Dr. Nigel Quinney, Gustavo Abreu, and Alessandra de Souza Santos, who collaborated on the technical revision and translation of this text.

1 M. Goulart, *Princípios institucionais do Ministério Público: A necessária revisão conceitual da unidade institucional e da independência funcional MPMG Jurídico*, 14 Belo Horizonte 13 (Oct./Dec. 2008).

The expansion of the power of the Public Ministry and other public agencies to protect the environment is vital in a country undergoing intense economic development. The use of law as a means of environmental protection is a way to compensate for the negative impacts of the increasing demand for natural resources. In this sense, the constitution of 1988 established "state activism" in regard to ecological matters in Brazil.[2]

According to the 1988 constitution, the Public Ministry's functions are to promote, on an exclusive basis, public criminal action and to institute civil investigations and public civil actions for the protection of the environment and other metaindividual interests. As the legitimate defender of these interests, the Public Ministry plays the role of "society's attorney" even against the state itself, because, in the Brazilian legal system, the Public Ministry is assured of operational independence. Thus, the Public Ministry is a public institution, attached to the state, but, as constitutional defender of society's interests, it is independent from the state. This feature guards against any forms of violation of metaindividual rights, including violations committed by agents of the state. Goulart notes that the operational independence of the Public Ministry "is a social guarantee because it was created to give people security of having a political agent which, while acting for the defense of social interests, can work independently, immune to the pressures of power."[3]

This chapter looks at the ways in which the Public Ministry, and especially the Public Ministry of the State of Minas Gerais, has used innovative legal mechanisms to address and resolve environmental and social conflicts. The chapter focuses in particular on a successful initiative to reorganize the ministry's environmental work so that it corresponds to natural, rather than administrative, boundaries.

The Problem-Solving Public Ministry: The Extrajudicial Activities of the Public Ministry

The Public Ministry has the power to resolve environmental conflicts without demanding the intervention of the judiciary. This power is exercised via two instruments:

- A recommendation, through which the Public Ministry sends the state guidelines to improve the provision of a service of public interest
- A "conduct adjustment," a type of out-of-court settlement through which a person or company that has put at risk or has caused damage to the public interest (for example, environmental quality) assumes obligations

---

2 This chapter is based on a draft of a chapter from a forthcoming book tentatively titled *Law, State, and Development: New State Activism in Brazil in Comparative Perspective* and edited by David Trubek, Helena Alviar, Diogo Coutinho, and Alvaro Santos.

3 Goulart, *supra* note 1, at 12.

to cease the illegal activity, to conform conduct to legislation, and to repair damage done

The out-of-court settlement, known as a term of conduct adjustment (TCA), has helped remove red tape from the processes of environmental conflict resolution, which are frequently complex, thereby avoiding court disputes that could drag on for years. The Public Ministry thus plays a problem-solving role: it offers quick responses consistent with the socioenvironmental demands of the society.

The Drainage Basin as a Territorial Unit for Analysis, Planning, and Action

An analysis of socioenvironmental processes and planning strategies cannot be isolated from the context of the natural systems in which they occur. In this context, the drainage basin is suitable for an investigation that aims to integrate physical, biotic, social, cultural, and economic aspects, providing an understanding of the ways in which different environmental aspects—such as vegetation cover, geology, and agricultural production systems—interact.[4] Drainage basins are multilevel systems that encompass political, economic, and cultural practices and as such are an important environmental and social area for analysis and planning. As Francisco Barbosa, João Antônio de Paula, and Roberto Monte-Mor comment:

> [A] "basin" has considerable merit as a physical and economic unit for analysis. Actions or policies external to the "basins" (pricing policies, for example) can have important effects within a system defined in them, and an economic analysis, even incorporating the issue of welfare, can capture only a part of the relevant interactions within the system. Appropriate management requires, therefore, that the basins be considered as "multilevel" systems that include water, soil, and sociopolitical components, internal and external. Thus, a typical "basin" would consist in the overlap of natural and social systems. The natural system would be defined on aquatic and terrestrial (fauna, flora, water resources, and minerals) bases. The social system would determine how these bases are used. Government policies as an extension of social and institutional organization influence local patterns of using natural resources.[5]

---

4 R. G. M. Botelho, *Planejamento ambiental em microbacia hidrográfica*, in *Erosão e conservação dos solos: Conceitos, temas e aplicações* 269–300 (A. J. T. Guerra, A. S. Silva, & R. G. M. Botelho ed., Bertrand Brasil 1999); and F. V. F. Castro, L. J. Alvarenga, & A. P. A. Magalhães Jr., *A Política Nacional de Recursos Hídricos e a gestão de conflitos em uma nova territorialidade*, 1(1) Geografias, Belo Horizonte 37–50 (2005).

5 F. A. R. Barbosa, J. A. Paula, & R. L. M. Monte-Mor, *A bacia hidrográfica como unidade de análise e realidade de integração disciplina*, in *Biodiversidade, população e economia: Uma região de Mata Atlântica* 258 (J. A. Paula coord., UFMG/Cedeplar/ECMXC/PADCT/CIAMB 1997).

Brazilian law recognizes the drainage basin as the territorial unit for environmental planning, management, and analysis. Law 8,171/1991, which concerns agricultural policy in Brazil, states, "The drainage basins constitute the basic units for planning [for] the use, conservation, and recovery of natural resources" (Article 20). Law 9,433/1997, known as the Water Law because it established the National Policy of Water Resources, also focuses on the drainage basin as the territorial unit (Article 1, Section V).

Although the Water Law presents several innovations, such as the adoption of socioenvironmental parameters, its application, like the application of environmental laws in general, has been marked by conflicts. Some of them derive from the coexistence of territorial units corresponding to the administrative units of Brazil's federation (union, member states, municipalities, and Federal District) with the natural divisions of drainage basins and ecosystems that they encompass. In other words, the geographic areas covered by the administrative units do not correspond to the geographic area of drainage basins. As Jorge Thierry Calasans et al. point out:

> [B]ecause the implementation of water resources management by basin does not coincide with the political-administrative division of the country, it creates a potential conflict between the entities that are part of SINGREH [National System of Hydric Resources Management]. The so-called water resources management agencies must now give up their administrative autonomy over the management of water resources in the state's territory to share their autonomy with the new deliberative body represented by the Basin Committees.[6]

Similar conflicts have been identified regarding the environmental protection provided by the Public Ministry. The Public Ministry is organized, like the judiciary, by counties, which creates several obstacles to prosecutors' work to protect environmental and water resources. These obstacles are identified by Antônio Herman Benjamin and include

- "County likeness," the concept that environmental and water resources can be safeguarded using the geographic and legal organization into counties, despite the fact that this method of organization is incompatible with the natural division of the natural systems.
- "Spontaneism," which prevents proactive and prospective action by the Public Ministry, whose work is reactive and retrospective. Thus, ministerial intervention is "always hostage to the degradation which has already occurred or is just about to occur, subjugating the institution to the *fait accompli* dictatorship."
- "Lack of specific techniques for the correct interpretation of environmental issues," which substantially restricts activities by the prosecution offices in defense of the environment. Lacking technical and scientific

---

6 J. T. Calasans et al., *A Política Nacional de Recursos Hídricos: Uma avaliação crítica*, in *Congresso Internacional de Direito Ambiental 7°*, *Anais* 585–602 (Imprensa Oficial 2003).

resources, the prosecution offices have problems identifying and measuring complex environmental problems.

- "Generalism," which hinders the expertise of prosecutors with regard to knowledge of environmental law, "hampering the implementation of environmental legislation and providing an inadequate service to our customers, the community, and the future generations."
- "Isolationism," which precludes the "efficient use of the institution's energies, leading to a shortsighted implementation, if not devoid of any real practical results, because it lacks the overall vision," that is, the view on the drainage basin to be protected as a whole.[7]

Benjamin is convinced that "environmental problems recognize neither the historic strength of the criterion of administration of the jurisdictional rules that guide the division of the state into counties, nor the political fragmentation of the territory."[8] Proposals for the territorial reorganization of the Public Ministry in the interest of environmental protection are gaining acceptance. The idea that ministerial action should have drainage basins as a basis—that action should be taken not on the basis of political units (counties) but on the basis of hydrogeographical regions (drainage basins)—would foster, in geographical and socioenvironmental terms, a more comprehensive view of ecological problems and their socioeconomic and cultural constraints and implications. It would also encourage the development of ecologically effective solutions that are socially appropriate.

The Public Ministry of Minas Gerais State (MPMG) pioneered the implementation of a drainage basin approach. In 2001, with the support of the federal government, MPMG created the Prosecution Office of the Rio Sao Francisco Drainage Basin and started planning and enforcing actions to protect natural and water resources associated with Rio Sao Francisco, considering the drainage basin as a whole. Before that, MPMG actions occurred in a fragmented way throughout the several counties (administrative geographical divisions, as opposed to natural ones) in the state. The Prosecution Office of Rio Sao Francisco is subdivided into five regions devoted to the preservation and restoration of natural and water resources from the drainage basin. In 2009, this working model was extended to all other basins and sub-basins within the territory of Minas Gerais state, effectively coordinating regional prosecution offices in their work to defend the environment. This reorganization of MPMG received social and institutional recognition in Brazil when it was awarded the Innovare Prize in 2010 in the Public Ministry Award category.

---

7 A. H. Benjamin, *Um novo modelo para o Ministério Público na proteção do meio ambiente,* 10 Revista de Direito Ambiental 7–13 (Apr./Jun. 1998). The quoted material is from page 11.

8 *Id.*, 10.

Conflict Resolution and the Promotion of Environmental Quality

Using the drainage basins of Minas Gerais as its basis and applying a problem-solving approach, the reorganized MPMG has been effective in resolving environmental conflicts in the state, as evidenced by a number of programs.

Between November 2008 and November 2011, prosecutors considered a total of 13,906 cases but submitted only 4,795 of them—that is, just 34 percent —to the courts. Conflict resolution through the formalization of out-of-court settlements, employing TCA, was used in 66 percent of cases (9,111 procedures). MPMG was involved in the defense of protected areas (53 percent of TCAs), the repair of environmental damage (22 percent), pollution control (8 percent), the protection of wildlife (3 percent), and the control of irregular mining (2 percent).

MPMG thus expanded its conflict-resolution role by implementing a set of extrajudicial techniques geared specifically toward the negotiation of environmental conflicts involving the protection of metaindividual and unavailable rights. In parallel, it instituted environmental damage valuation as a reference for the evaluation of "ecological compensation"—in other words, for an evaluation of procedures aimed at the improvement of environmental well-being according to the provisions of the Brazilian Constitution (Article 225, paragraph 1, Sections I, II, and VII) and the National Environmental Policy (Federal Law 6,938/1981, Article 2, Sections I, II, IV, VIII, and IX, and Article 4, Section VI).

It is difficult to translate into monetary terms the damage that environmental degradation can cause. Such degradation has multiple, cumulative, and synergistic impacts. Many valuation methods exist, but none can cope with the diversity and variety of the damage caused. The inability to predict the value of compensation for environmental degradation hinders the adoption of agreements.

For this reason, ecological compensation has become the most appropriate way to solve many socioenvironmental conflicts, especially in regard to the need to restore the damaged area. Ecological compensation also helps the company responsible for the damage to determine how to conduct its future activities so that it abides by the law, in the sense that by being held responsible for ecological damage, the company will be reeducated in environmentally friendly ideals.

Serra da Moeda

An example of the success of this approach can be seen in the Serra da Moeda (Mountain of Money) case. As a result of the decisions made in this case, a mining company whose activities could have caused serious damage to the environment stopped extracting ore in areas relevant to biological diversity conservation. These areas were turned into "conservation units"—that is, areas given special protection by environmental legislation.

In the Serra da Moeda, a mining company sought to carry out activities in an area believed to have high environmental value. The ensuing debate revolved around the question of how one can reconcile environmental preservation with the generation of jobs and income, considering the socioeconomic development of the region, in accordance with Federal Law 6,938/1981, Article 4, Section I.

MPMG defined the area that would be crucial to environmental preservation. No mining activities—indeed, no human activities that cause environmental damage—would henceforth be allowed in this area. Following careful studies, the company identified other areas in which it wanted to mine and presented an initial schedule for the extraction of ore. Subsequently, the company submitted to a regular environmental licensing process, carried out by Minas Gerais State, obtaining an authorization for mining in the areas defined as exploitable in the agreement signed by the Public Ministry.

Oasis

The Oasis project is another example of MPMG's role as a protector of the environment. This project was implemented through an agreement signed in 2011 by the Public Ministry and a mining company from the town of Brumadinho. In the course of a civil investigation, MPMG found evidence of environmental damage and quantified the environmental compensation. The compensation consisted of payments to 75 small producers around the mining venture whose farms included Permanent Preservation Areas (PPAs)—for example, river banks and hilltops—and Legal Reserve Areas—portions of property deemed necessary for the sustainable use of natural resources, biodiversity conservation, shelter, the protection of native flora and fauna, and the preservation of the quality, amount, and circulation of water resources in the environment.

In partnership with the Foundation O Boticario, MPMG developed a methodology to specify the monthly amount to be paid to each farmer, as well as an efficient system of inspection that demonstrated whether beneficiaries were afforded adequate funds to maintain the Legal Reserve and the PPAs. The partnership between MPMG and the foundation is innovative: this is one of the first projects in this state based on payment for environmental services (PES). It also contributes to social and environmental justice because it remunerates farmers who contribute to the implementation of environmental legislation.

Belo Horizonte

A third example of MPMG's expanded role involves the protection of the quality of life in the urban environment. In 2011, entrepreneurs from the real estate market in the southern section of the Minas Gerais capital, Belo Horizonte, signed a breakthrough agreement with MPMG. The civil building sector has a number of negative consequences with regard to the quality of urban environment, especially for urban mobility, and it increases demand for public services. Again, environmental compensation was the solution: 20 entrepreneurs committed themselves to a road construction project in the neighborhood, considered a priority by the associations of local residents. The agreement with MPMG was made with input from Minas Gerais State and the consent of the city of Belo Horizonte, representing the local community. Thus, there was a widespread effort to improve the quality of life in the urban environment.

Conclusion

The Public Ministry, notably in Minas Gerais State, has distinguished itself as an institutional defender of Brazil's environment. It enhances the effectiveness of the state's response to various types of socioenvironmental conflicts in two major ways: it prioritizes conflict-resolution work—that is, work that does not require the intervention of the courts; and it recognizes the need to reconfigure the territorial organization of institutions so that they are consistent with the organizational pattern of the natural systems. The Public Ministry has thus been able to expand access to justice and to implement the laws that protect natural and water resources in Brazil.

OHADA Nears the Twenty-Year Mark

An Assessment

RENAUD BEAUCHARD

On October 17, 1993, in Port Louis, Mauritius, 14 African heads of state signed a treaty creating the Organization for the Harmonization of Business Law in Africa, or Organisation pour l'Harmonisation en Afrique du Droit des Affaires (OHADA). The treaty came into force on September 18, 1995, and its signatories now number 17 member states.[1] Designed to modernize and harmonize business laws with the ultimate goal of increasing domestic and foreign trade and investment, OHADA constitutes a unique experiment involving the legal integration of states participating in different economic, trade, and monetary unions.[2] Almost two decades after the Port Louis treaty was signed, this chapter evaluates the initiative.[3]

That task is not made easier by the fact that little empirical evidence suggests that OHADA has had a beneficial effect on the economies of the member states, all of which are lower-tier countries crippled by structural problems and most of which have experienced numerous calamities since the creation of OHADA, including humanitarian crises, military coups, and the collapse of democratic governments.[4] The main issues analyzed here are whether any correlation can be identified between the good and bad fortunes of the OHADA member states and OHADA itself and whether OHADA can provide a workable basis for attracting investment in its member states.

OHADA was first conceived of during a meeting of finance ministers of the members of the Communauté Financière Africaine[5] held in Ouagadou-

---

1 In order of ratification, the OHADA member states are Guinea-Bissau (Jan. 15, 1994), Senegal (Jun. 14, 1994), Central African Republic (Jan. 13, 1995), Mali (Feb. 7, 1995), the Comoros (Feb. 20, 1995), Burkina Faso (Mar. 6, 1995), Benin (Mar. 8, 1995), Niger (Jun. 5, 1995), Côte d'Ivoire (Sep. 29, 1995), Cameroon (Oct. 20, 1995), Togo (Oct. 27, 1995), Chad (Apr. 13, 1996), the Republic of Congo (May 28, 1997), Gabon (Feb. 2, 1998), Equatorial Guinea (Apr. 16, 1999), Guinea (May 5, 2000), and Democratic Republic of Congo (July13, 2012). See http://www.ohada.org/etats-parties.html.

2 The Economic Community of West African States (ECOWAS), the West African Economic and Monetary Union (UEMOA), and the Monetary and Economic Community of Central Africa (CEMAC).

3 Parts of this chapter draw significantly on R. Beauchard & J. Kodo, *Can OHADA Increase Legal Certainty in Africa*, Justice and Development Working Paper No. 17/2011 (World Bank 2011), available at http://siteresources.worldbank.org/EXTLAWJUSTINST/Resources/17-2011CanOHADAIncrease.pdf?resourceurlname=17-2011CanOHADAIncrease.pdf.

4 Including the events in Guinea-Bissau and Mali unfolding at the time of writing.

5 The Communauté Financière Africaine (CFA) franc is the name of two currencies used in Africa that are guaranteed by the French treasury: the West African CFA franc (XOF) and

gou, Burkina Faso, in April 1991. This group of experts, led by Justice Keba Mbaye from Senegal,[6] was appointed to conduct a feasibility study on a form of legal collaboration designed to promote economic integration and attract investments.[7]

Integration could be attempted via several methods. It could take the shape of a common frame of reference or a model law, which the states could then use as a point of reference, without any obligation.[8] Another, more constraining, approach would be to establish objectives to be pursued and let the states determine how to implement them.[9] A still deeper form of integration could be attained through unification, that is, by replacing preexisting national laws with uniform laws.[10] Unification would substitute new legislation for current domestic laws in relevant areas of business.

In the end, OHADA framers chose the path of unification,[11] although the treaty expressed this goal by using the all-encompassing—though perhaps more ambiguous—word "harmonization." As part of the process, a new set of unified laws was created that preempted all conflicting domestic provisions. The treaty was opened to all African states, whether or not they were members of the African Union.

A fully fledged international organization, OHADA has an institutional framework that consists of the Council of Ministers (Conseil des Ministres), the Permanent Secretariat (Secrétariat Permanent), the Common Court of Justice and Arbitration (Cour Commune de Justice et d'Arbitrage, or CCJA), and the Regional Training Center for Legal Officers (Ecole Régionale Supérieure de la Magistrature, or ERSUMA). The treaty revisions signed in Québec on October 17, 2008, completed the institutional framework with a fifth

---

the Central African CFA franc (XAF). Although theoretically separate, the currencies are effectively interchangeable.

6 Keba Mbaye died in 2007 after having occupied the offices of chief justice of the Senegalese Supreme Court, chief justice of the Senegalese Constitutional Council, and vice president of the International Court of Justice.

7 Martin Kirsch, *Historique de l'OHADA*, Revue Penant 129 (1998); Barry Walsh, *In Search of Success: Case Studies in Justice Sector Development in Sub-Saharan Africa* 44 (World Bank 2010).

8 For example, US model codes or the Association Capitant and Société de Législation Comparée's Draft Common Frame of Reference on European Contract Law.

9 For example, European Commission (EC) directives.

10 Comp. EU regulations are the most direct form of EU law—as soon as they are passed, they have binding legal force throughout every member state, on a par with national laws. National governments do not have to take action themselves to implement EU regulations; *see* http://ec.europa.eu/eu_law/introduction/what_regulation_en.htm. For more details, *see* J. A. Yakubu, *Community Laws in International Business Transactions*, in *Unified Business Law for Africa: Common Law Perspectives on OHADA* 4 (Claire Moore-Dickerson ed., GMB Publishing 2009). Although harmonization is mentioned in the treaty, OHADA in fact unifies business law, but the (French) word "harmonisation" was used instead of "unification" consciously and for political reasons.

11 See Keba Mbaye, *L'histoire et les objectifs de l'OHADA*, 205 Les Petites Affiches 6 (2004).

component, the Conference of Heads of State and Government. The revised treaty came into force on March 21, 2010.

The main accomplishment of OHADA has been the production of a series of standardized pieces of legislation on business law, known as uniform acts, which are directly applicable in the member states and preempt any relevant domestic legislation. Thus far, nine uniform acts are in force.[12] With most uniform acts in force for more than a decade, it is legitimate to ask whether OHADA has produced the desired effects identified in the Port Louis treaty's preamble, which proclaims the aim of "making progress toward African unity and creating a climate of trust in the economic systems of the contracting States with a view to creating a new center of development in Africa."

Who Are OHADA's Constituents and What Can OHADA Bring Them?

A preliminary matter in assessing OHADA is to identify its constituents. Although this should be an easy task, in fact, the political elites in OHADA countries tend to think of OHADA constituents as judges, lawyers, notaries, and bailiffs, all of whom like to participate in donor-funded seminars on more or less theoretical subjects. But while these are indeed essential actors, OHADA constituents must be more broadly defined.

Geographically, the best place to locate OHADA constituents is in the many marketplaces that characterize Africa. For the purpose of this chapter, the Dantokpa market in Cotonou (Benin), one of the largest marketplaces in West Africa, is the focus. A fascinating place, it is a complex, multilayered, pyramidal structure. The base consists of minor transactions in local goods, usually perishable and cheap. The next level is fabrics, jewelry, and arts and crafts, more expensive and often transported from far away. At the very top of the pyramid is the active money market.

What is most important in places like Dantokpa is not what appears at first sight. It is the credit, rather than the commodities. The Dantokpa market is where accounts are settled, where debts meet and cancel each other out. The complex structure operates almost entirely outside the realm of formal law and ignores OHADA. Therefore, when considering OHADA, one should think about the small merchants at the Dantokpa market as OHADA's constituents.

What precise innovations can OHADA bring its constituents to empower them and promote their welfare? OHADA offers the business community of the OHADA member states some essential "institutions" (in the neo-institutionalist sense of the "humanly devised constraints that structure political,

---

12 The uniform acts cover general commercial law, companies, secured transactions, bankruptcy, arbitration, simplified debt collection and enforcement measures, accounting, carriage of goods by road, and cooperative companies.

economic and social interactions")[13] that can transform uncertainty, which is characterized by imprecise knowledge, into risk, which relates to events that can be assessed with some degree of certainty and can therefore be hedged against.[14] It can provide universal mechanisms that ensure that its constituents are not liable for 100 percent of their losses. It can give its constituents institutions such as pledges without dispossession, which allow them to use their stock as collateral for a loan. It can help the moneylending observed in places like the Dantokpa market ascend to the next level, that of commercial moneylending.

The drafters of OHADA had small merchants in mind when they defined OHADA's ambitious policy goals. But somewhere along the way, OHADA's lofty objectives came into conflict with the entrenched economic logic of autocracy and rentseeking[15] at play in the member states, which typically support contract or property rights enforcement only for regime insiders.

Legal Certainty: The Fundamental Standard

Achievement of the OHADA policy goals should be the ultimate measure of OHADA's success. The Port Louis treaty aims at "making progress toward African unity and creating a climate of trust in the economic systems of the contracting States with a view to creating a new center of development in Africa." The important word here is "trust," which French anthropologist Marcel Mauss describes as "the very foundation of all collective action."

The economies of the OHADA member states are mostly informal and broken into a mosaic of local markets; trust is precisely the engine that could help achieve the aim of OHADA to transform member economies from ones based on a material life focused on survival to an economic life focused on exchange. This goal can be achieved only through larger-scale, more integrated markets, which require two pillars of trust: property protection and contract enforcement.

More fundamentally, trust points to and underlines another central concept articulated in the Port Louis treaty: legal certainty. Because legal certainty connotes more than a simple evaluation of a law's formulation but encompasses the issues of enforcement and observance, this chapter evaluates OHADA against the critically important objective of legal certainty.

The standard of legal certainty must be clearly defined, however, which is not necessarily an easy task. Taking into account that a definition must be

---

13 *See* Douglass North, *Institutions*, 5 J. of Econ. Persp. 97 (1991).

14 *See* H. Root, *Capital and Collusion: The Political Logic of Global Economic Development* 4–6 (Princeton 2006).

15 Rentseeking is a culture in which the principal route to wealth is not creating wealth but taking possession of or benefiting from wealth created by others. Financial Time Lexicon, available at http://lexicon.ft.com/Term?term=rent_seeking.

comprehensive but not too far-reaching, this chapter first uses an operational *a contrario* definition of what legal certainty is not. And there is no better example of what legal certainty is not than the situation found in the member states in pre-OHADA days. At that time, outdated business laws existed on the books, but without implementing regulation and often in contradiction to existing or prior nonabrogated norms. Having no equivalent of specialized commercial courts and with negligible business litigation, business law was largely an abstraction in those countries. What is more, judges had no codes and little if no access to legal reports or periodicals, and they often ignored the issue of which laws applied to which economic activity.[16] Without effective risk management, legal innovations, such as limited liability companies or secured transactions, which are so essential to the successful advance of industrial revolutions, were doomed to remain at the margin of economic development. This situation was among the ills OHADA hoped to redress.

Is it possible to propose a formulation of the legal certainty standard relative to OHADA's ambitions? Keep in mind that OHADA unifies business laws, the main objective of which is the protection of modern property rights[17] and contract enforcement—and here is a useful limit to the definition of legal certainty that also limits the scope of the investigation. The protection of property rights and contract enforcement requires, in the words of Oliver Wendell Holmes, that "people . . . know under what circumstances and how far they will run the risk of coming against what is so much stronger than themselves[,]" which meant "the incidence of the public force through the instrumentality of the courts."[18] That knowledge presupposes "that all law be sufficiently precise to allow the person—if need be, with appropriate advice—to foresee, to a degree that is reasonable in the circumstances, what a given action may entail."

This means that with respect to harmonized business laws:

- laws and decisions must be public and publicly available;
- laws and decisions must be definite and clear in their applicability;
- decisions of courts must be enforced and, to the greatest extent possible, reasoned, so as to provide relevant information on the compliance of conduct with law; and
- persons or officials associated with the application and enforcement of those laws must be easily identifiable and properly trained and equipped to accomplish their duty.

---

16 *See*, e.g., the dismal description made by Xavier Forneris, *Harmonizing Commercial Law in Africa*, 46 Juris Périodique 77, 81 (2001), available at http://www.ohada.com/doctrine/titre/199/Harmonising-commercial-law-in-Africa-the-OHADA.html.

17 Francis Fukuyama's definition of modern property rights is used here, understood as "rights held by individuals, who are free to buy and sell their property without restrictions imposed by kin groups, religious authorities, or the state." Francis Fukuyama, *The Origins of Political Order* 248 (Farrar, Strauss & Giroux 2011).

18 Oliver Wendell Holmes, *The Path of the Law*, 10 Harv. L. Rev. 457 (1897).

Assessment of OHADA in Regard to Legal Certainty

The goal here is to assess OHADA's innovations and claim of empowering member states' populations against the standard of legal certainty, as articulated above. To promote legal certainty, OHADA is based on two pillars: the norms it produces and the institutions designed to produce and apply those norms. OHADA has largely been successful in terms of the production of norms. There are undeniable achievements, mostly concerned with the innovations contained in the formulation of OHADA law and centered on the supranational level, which are detailed here. However, OHADA has encountered serious challenges regarding the application and the reception of the uniform acts. OHADA has an Achilles' heel: the way it is implemented at the state level. Only if the focus is on effective implementation can OHADA deliver results; this, however, does not seem to be the case.

Achievements

In a remarkably short period of time, OHADA has created a new supranational organization—no small feat. The principal achievement of OHADA is that it has largely fulfilled its aim in the production of uniform law. Thus far, OHADA has delivered nine uniform acts that form an innovative, comprehensive, definite, and coherent framework focused primarily on the microlevel, the level of the productive unit. For example:

- The General Commercial Law Act provides the fundamental rules of business activity: merchant status, commercial leases, commercial sale of goods, agency, businesses and movables registry (Registre du Commerce et du Crédit Mobilier, or RCCM), and microbusiness.
- The Companies Act provides for various limited liability structures that protect business operators.
- The Secured Transactions Act provides for various securities protecting creditors against the risk of defaults of their debtors and sets the conditions for the development of commercial lending.
- The Accountancy Act provides for uniform accounting standards based on the true and fair view standard.
- The Simplified Debt Collection Procedures and Enforcement Measures provides operators with modern legal remedies, such as seizures and garnishments, that are available to unpaid judgment creditors to compel judgment debtors to pay up, if need be with the assistance of the police.

The OHADA drafters opted for a uniform law rather than a harmonized one. OHADA is not a model code, which the member states are free to adapt. It is a uniform set of legislation that must be applied with consistency in the member states. On one hand, this uniformity makes implementation less dependent on the governments of the member states, although that is largely theoretical. On the other hand, the policy choice of a uniform law makes it appear more distant from its ultimate constituents and more difficult to reform to respond to local circumstances.

But uniformity means nothing without coherence. In this respect, the coherence of OHADA law rests primarily on Article 10 of the treaty, which provides that the uniform acts preempt all domestic statutes for the subject matter they cover, whether enacted before or after the acts' entry into force. And there cannot be coherence without uniformity of interpretation. Thus, to guarantee uniformity of interpretation, the OHADA framers created the court of justice, the CCJA.

Some examples of innovations that, if properly applied, could have an important impact on OHADA's constituents, include the following:

- The entreprenant status: the General Commercial Law Act, revised in 2010, introduced a status of *entreprenant*, inspired by the *auto-entrepreneur* status in France, which is credited with leading more than 300,000 persons to register an activity in less than a year after its introduction in 2009.
- The Registre du Commerce et du Crédit Mobilier (RCCM): the General Commercial Law Act created a three-tiered registry of businesses and movables, the RCCM. This registry, by recording businesses and movable securities, is an important and essential innovation designed to ensure protection for creditors. As such, it is a key institution to favor the development of moneylending.
- Pledges without dispossession on tangible assets: the Secured Transactions Act, revised in 2010, instituted pledges without dispossession on tangible assets. Provided it becomes a practical reality, this is a welcome innovation designed to use stock or any other means of production as collateral without depriving the grantor of the use of the pledged asset.

A Few Design Flaws

Even though the formal law created by OHADA was well conceived, it is not flawless. For example, why did the drafters consider a bankruptcy act to be a priority in countries with no significant commercial moneylending? As one author put it, "bankruptcy is the unwanted handmaiden of commercial debt."[19] Without significant commercial lending, there is no practical use for a bankruptcy act. This act should have been implemented farther down the road.

The choice of arbitration as the sole alternative dispute resolution method was introduced in OHADA to the detriment of mediation, which would correspond better with the traditional method of conflict resolution known as *palabre*.[20] Arbitration is a hard sell in OHADA countries. Perceived as expensive, the payment of fees up front is often dissuasive, except for very sophisticated businesses. Mediation and conciliation, which, compared with adjudication,

---

19 *See* Wade Channell, *Lessons Not Learned about Legal Reforms*, in *Promoting the Rule of Law Abroad, in Search of Knowledge* 141 (Thomas Carothers ed., Carnegie 2006).

20 *See* J.-G. Bidima, *La palabre, une juridiction de la parole* (Michalon 1997).

are costless alternatives and centered on consensus building, would be easier to sell.

Finally, only two uniform acts (the General Commercial Law Act and the Commonly Owned Businesses Act), and one only very partially, acknowledge the existence of an informal sector, which accounts for 60 to 85 percent of the GDP of the member states.[21]

But these challenges are easy to address in comparison to implementation challenges.

Implementation Challenges

Diligent application of the existing uniform acts should be the priority of OHADA policy makers. Except for employment law—and not everybody agrees on that—the OHADA institutions should stop legislating activity and dedicate attention to the enforcement of the existing uniform acts.

The legislation of risks generates conflicts with norms produced by other regional organizations. Thus, the more legislation there is, the more opportunities there are for conflicts with other regulatory ensembles, because all OHADA member states are also members of monetary unions, such as the Union Economique et Monétaire Ouest Africaine (UEMOA), and trade and customs unions, such as the Economic Community of West African States (ECOWAS). These groups produce regulations, especially in the banking sector. Only once markets become more concentrated should OHADA legislate further.

Regarding proper implementation, OHADA faces various challenges, beginning with the institutional challenges of OHADA itself. OHADA must transform itself into an integrated judicial space in which final judgments on subject matters covered by OHADA are given full faith and credit. Finally, and this is certainly the most difficult challenge, OHADA can succeed only if member states demonstrate the requisite level of political will and dedication to implement OHADA laws.

Institutional Challenges

At the regional level, OHADA institutions are well established. However, they still face budgetary constraints. For example, the total budget of OHADA in 2012 was roughly US$8.3 million, which seems low, especially considering that OHADA must organize an annual conference of heads of states.[22] More important, there seem to be structural problems (not least the use of bud-

21 *See* Prosper Backiny-Yetna, *Secteur informel, Fiscalité et équité, l'exemple du Cameroun,* 104 Statéco (2009); Mireille Razafindrakoto, François Roubaud, & Constance Torelli, *La mesure de l'emploi et du secteur informel: Leçons des enquêtes 1-2-3 en Afrique,* 104 Statéco (2009).

22 *See* Minutes of the Council of Ministers (Dec. 15 & 16, 2011), available at http://www.ohada.org/actualite-cm/en/cmfj/actualite/3610-compte-rendu-de-la-reunion-du-conseil-des-ministres-de-lohada-des-15-et-16-decembre-2011-a-bissau.html.

get) that indicate that simply injecting money won't do the trick. Among all OHADA institutions, the one that seems to be suffering the most is the CCJA, which has backlogs despite a rather modest caseload.[23]

One structural problem can be traced to the treaty itself, which provides that all matters of interpretation of an OHADA provision as a matter of law can be deferred only to the CCJA, which cannot refuse to hear the case if it deems that the matter does not raise any matter of uniform interpretation at the regional level. Although this tenet may appear sound in theory, it has led to difficulties in administrative manageability and has made backlogs unavoidable. Although this provision does remove the final interpretation of OHADA law from the national judiciaries, which are often accused of cooptation by political forces and extractive interests and of solving conflicts of interpretation of OHADA provisions even before states review the matters, it also risks causing jurisdictional conflict with domestic supreme courts and hampers the CCJA's manageability, a critical problem given the scarcity of resources in the member states.

To make matters worse, the Rules of Procedure (Réglement de Procédure) contain no provision for filtering appeals such as those existing before the US Supreme Court, which grants plenary review to an average of only 1 percent of the cases on its docket, or for fast-track proceedings such as those instituted before the French Cour de Cassation in 2001.[24] Such proceedings would give the CCJA the ability to refuse to hear a case by a nonreasoned decision if it deemed that the appeal, which is limited to a matter of legal interpretation, does not raise interpretative issues requiring a CCJA decision. Instead, Article 26 of the Rules of Procedure requires that as soon as an appeal is lodged, the CCJA chief justice must appoint a judge to follow up the case management and report to the court. This is the same procedure used by the French Cour de Cassation before the institution of the fast-track option in 2001, a reform motivated by the buildup of large backlogs.

No Integrated Judicial Space

There is no real judicial space in OHADA, that is to say, a space where final and enforceable decisions of the national judiciary on OHADA matters receive full faith and credit in OHADA member states applying the same law based on a simple recognition and enforcement procedure. Although the treaty provides that CCJA judgments are directly enforceable in the territory of member states under the same conditions as domestic judgments (Article 20 of the Rules of Procedure), it does not contain any jurisdictional provision for transnational matters, nor does it regulate how final domestic judgments that apply uniform law can be applied in other member states.

---

23 It is difficult to understand how a court with nine judges can have backlogs with a docket of a few hundred cases, as compared, for example, with the US Supreme Court, which has the same number of judges and an annual docket of 10,000 cases but little backlog.

24 Known as *procedure de non admission du pourvoi.*

Because of this shortcoming, issues of jurisdiction, recognition, and enforcement within the OHADA judicial space tend to follow national rules, which suffer from the same problems as the laws OHADA replaced: they are frequently outdated, unavailable, unenforced, and/or nonexistent.

Challenges at the State Level

Perhaps the most prominent example of OHADA's enforcement weakness is the Business and Movable Securities Registry (RCCM). The RCCM operates at three levels: local, national, and regional. A creation of the general commercial law that entered into force in 1998, the RCCM is largely a virtual registry. Most discussions have been centered on computerization, viewed as the remedy of all ills. Computerization suffers from its own problems, not least the lack of coordination among actors involved in the process, but the issue has much deeper roots than that. First, the initial filings are made at the local level, then at the national level, and finally at the regional level and little progress can be attained if the focus goes the other way around, that is, from the regional to the local. Second, and this is the more important problem, a registry of collateral cannot be feasible without a proper vital records registry, which none of the member states has managed to create.

Another implementation issue is the articulation of the uniform acts and domestic laws the OHADA acts are intended to replace. In domestic circumstances, new text replacing another indicates that the provisions of older instruments are repealed. That is called *express abrogation*.

Express abrogation is difficult with a supranational law, such as OHADA laws; article 10 of the treaty provides that the uniform acts are "directly applicable and mandatory . . . against any contrary provision in domestic law." Thus, OHADA is an example of tacit abrogation.

To make OHADA work, the member states should have inventoried all texts repealed by OHADA and enacted express abrogation statutes. Yet, not a single country has done that. At best, a proper inventory was made, but no statute has been enacted to repeal preempted instruments. At worst, nothing has been done. In most cases, hefty fees have been paid to consultants to make insufficient inventories. As a result, OHADA provisions coexist with tacitly repealed domestic rules, not a tenable situation regarding legal certainty.

These are just some of the implementation challenges that call for the intervention of the governments of the member states. But these are nothing in comparison to the challenges caused by the necessity to ensure that OHADA becomes a concrete reality for its constituents. In this respect, a reconsideration of the Dantokpa market is in order. The constituents of OHADA are not the judiciary and the various legal professions (attorneys, bailiffs, notaries, and the like) of OHADA member states, but rather the business community, comprising mostly informal actors.

To reach their true constituents and be effective, OHADA's laws must be implemented and applied by a myriad of intermediary players, including accountants, moneylenders, court registries, chambers of commerce, business registration units, microfinance institutions, banks, insurance companies, arbitration and mediation chambers, and all sorts of government officials involved in activities connected with the constitution of capital and the protection of property for business. But OHADA remains largely an abstraction for those actors.

To guarantee the integration of OHADA into domestic legal systems, a first and logical step would have been to carry out an inventory of all agents affected by OHADA and to ensure that these actors are familiar with OHADA and comply with it. To provide one example: the websites of most business registration centers say nothing about the status of *entreprenant* or microbusiness. In the OHADA member states, the status of *entreprenant* exists only virtually.

Similarly, formalization cannot take hold without the cooperation of traditional leaders in rural communities. Nothing was done to familiarize traditional authorities with the advantages of mechanisms such as those promoted by OHADA to transform uncertainty into risk management.

Conclusion

OHADA has come a long way since the 1993 Treaty of Port Louis. Few observers would have expected that a group of states whose track record on coordination was decidedly wanting would be able to achieve the goal of standardizing business laws. The framers of OHADA and international donors assumed that the appropriate social and political institutions required for the experiment to succeed already existed. In retrospect, it was overly optimistic to assume that a set of uniform business laws would be self-enforcing and generate trust toward and among countries in which rent seeking is so entrenched and whose judiciaries are crippled by backlogs, corruption, lack of planning, and limited accountability. Twenty years after the Port Louis treaty, it is time to reintroduce those exogenous parameters into the debate on OHADA.

Legal Innovation for Development

The OHADA Experience

MARC FRILET

In the years following the independence of the French African colonies, international investors and the African business community faced many difficulties in ascertaining the applicable principles of company law in the region.[1] At that time, company law was based on the French Company Act of 1867, which ceased to be in force in France in 1966. Interpretation of the law by local courts was often hazardous, and few reliable precedents existed. This uncertainty was the source of numerous disputes that triggered often unpredictable decisions by local courts, which in turn caused yet more uncertainty and discouraged international investment in these countries.

This volatile situation presented an opportunity for French law firms to develop a practice in Africa providing "authoritative interpretations" of company law. These interpretations were often based on documentation that was not available in Africa. The firms' comparatively easy access to French case law gave them lucrative opportunities in Africa.[2]

It took years to figure out how to overcome this problem. In 1963, Professor René David, a leading scholar in comparative law, organized a conference with the ministries of justice of the former French African colonies to assess the need to harmonize the legal system in the interest of economic development. This meeting set the stage for the emergence of the Economic and Custom Union of West Africa in 1964 and the Economic Community of West African States in 1972. Subsequent enlargement of the scope of these organizations included their extension into the insurance sector during the African conference on insurance markets in 1972.

The African and Mauritius Office for Law Research and Studies (Bureau Africain et Mauritien de Recherches et d'Etudes Législatives, BAMREL) was created in 1975. The purpose of BAMREL was to help signatory states develop their legislation in a harmonized manner. Although BAMREL was not implemented due to a lack of funding,[3] its conception represents the true beginning of the harmonization of business law in the region.

---

1 The OHADA region comprises 17 states: Benin, Burkina Faso, Cameroon, the Central African Republic, Chad, the Comoros, the Democratic Republic of Congo, the Republic of Congo, Equatorial Guinea, Gabon, Guinea, Guinea-Bissau, Ivory Coast, Mali, Niger, Senegal, and Togo.

2 *See* also Georges Meissonnier & Jean-Claude Gautron, *Analyse de la législation africaine en matière de droit des sociétés*, 3 RJPIC 331 (1976).

3 *See* Alhousseini Mouloul, *Comprendre l'organisation pour l'harmonisation en Afrique du Droit des Affaires*, 2nd ed., Working Paper 17 (2008).

The desire of the business community (both in Africa and farther afield) to develop a secure legal system for economic transactions was increasingly expressed, particularly by private operators and the French Council for Investors in Africa (CIAN). In April 1991, during the conference of Ouagadougou (Burkina Faso), which included all the ministries of finance of the franc zone, the decision to progress toward the harmonization of African francophone countries was made. The ministries of finance gave a mandate to a high-level panel of seven members, made up of eminent jurists and specialists in business law, to propose an action plan. The panel was chaired by Keba Mbaye, a Senegalese judge and a former vice-chair of the International Court of Justice.

In October 1992, in a meeting of the heads of state in Libreville (Gabon), the report of the panel was presented and endorsed by President Abdou Diouf.[4] The next step was to appoint a *directoire,* made up of three members, to coordinate and prepare a treaty creating the Organisation pour l'Harmonisation en Afrique du Droit des Affaires (OHADA, also known as the Organization for the Harmonization of Business Law in Africa). The *directoire* was chaired by Mbaye and included Martin Kirsch, honorary counselor of the French Cour de Cassation, and Michel Gentot, chair of the dispute department of the French Conseil d'Etat.

After preparation of the draft treaty and several meetings with experts, judges, and specialists, 14 states[5] signed the treaty in Port Louis (Mauritius) on October 17, 1993;[6] the treaty was revised in Quebec (Canada) on October 17, 2008.[7]

Many of the exchanges were organized under the leadership of Keba Mbaye, especially during the conference in Abidjan in 1993, where techniques for preparing to harmonize business law were presented and tested (inter alia, through the organization of national committees in each country).

A key objective of OHADA, as reported by Seydou Bâ, former chair of the Senegalese Court de Cassation and former president of the OHADA regional supreme court (the Common Court of Justice and Arbitration, or CCJA), is

> to progressively unify the legal framework in the area of business law and to organize a set of legal procedures promoting harmonized and sustainable development in all the Member States. Harmoniza-

---

4 The final communiqué is as follows: The heads of states "approved the project of harmonization of business law elaborated by the Ministries of Finance of the Franc Zone, decided its immediate implementation, and requested to the Ministries of Finance and Justice of all interested States to treat this matter as a priority." Henri Tchantchou, *La supranationalité judiciare dans le cadre de l'OHADA: Etude à la luminère du système des communautés européennes* 22 (L'Harmattan 2009).

5 The 14 signatory states are Benin, Burkina Faso, Cameroon, the Central African Republic, Chad, the Comoros, Equatorial Guinea, Gabon, Ivory Coast, Mali, Niger, the Republic of Congo, Senegal, and Togo.

6 *See* http://www.ohada.com/traite.html.

7 *See* http://www.ohada.com/traite-revise.html.

> tion of business law is a real trigger of growth and should facilitate the implementation of the rule of law.[8]

Legal integration is intended to mirror progress in economic integration at the regional level between Central African and Western African states. To this end, the OHADA member states designed a set of Uniform Acts on business law matters.[9] The nine OHADA Uniform Acts cover three broad areas:

- Commercial relationships and related transactions (general commercial law, security law, transport of goods by roads)
- Establishment and operation of commercial entities (company law and economic interested groups, accounting law)
- Settlement of disputes and regulation of commercial default (arbitration, bankruptcy law, recovery procedures)

Additional acts are in the pipeline for contract law and labor law.

The acts are currently under review on the basis of a reform program organized by the World Bank Group's multidonor Investment Climate Advisory Service (FIAS). The overall project objective is to improve the quality and effectiveness of the legal and institutional framework created by OHADA and therefore help the 17 member countries increase their attractiveness for domestic and foreign private investment.[10]

OHADA is a major legal innovation, unique in the modern world. There is much to be learned by assessing it. This chapter looks at its impact from a private sector perspective.

The Positive Features of OHADA

Several OHADA Uniform Acts replaced old business regulations in participating countries. This move has generally been welcomed by international and local businesses that wish to develop their operations in a secure framework and with good governance. The best features of OHADA include the following:

---

8 Seydou Bâ, speech, in *Fourth International Conference on Law and Economy: La convergence du droit* 48–50 (Ordre des avocats de Paris, Edition Lamy Nov. 2005).

9 The Uniform Acts relate to general commercial law, commercial companies and economic interest groups, securities, recovery procedures and measures of execution, proceedings for wiping out debts, arbitration, undertakings' accounting systems in the signatory states to OHADA, carriage of goods by road, and cooperative credit banks.

10 The reform's program has three components: 1, institutional strengthening of the OHADA Secretariat and project implementation support: to strengthen the institutional capacity of the Permanent Secretariat; 2, institutional strengthening of the Joint Court of Justice and Arbitration (CCJA) and the regional superior magistrate school (ERSUMA); 3, improving corporate financial reporting: to improve and strengthen corporate financial reporting, accounting standards, professional standards and practices, regional professional qualifications, and so on.

- The process of drafting, developing, and promulgating the Uniform Acts is efficient by all modern standards.
- Problems often found in other countries or regions for drafting and adopting new pieces of legislation are minimized in the OHADA countries.
- The problem of striking an appropriate balance between general principles and concepts and specific language is satisfactorily resolved. The Uniform Acts are worded in plain language that is easy to understand, with a minimum of cross-references and definitions. Credit must be given in this respect to the innovative method for the initial drafting of the Uniform Act, which was to invite international law firms to participate.
- The Uniform Acts are limited to key areas of business laws and as such are not particularly politically sensitive. For instance, the Uniform Acts do not cover areas that are often considered sovereign privileges, such as mining, taxation, and criminal penalties.

The Uniform Acts are conducive to good governance and economic development. In this respect, some were designed to educate the users (members of the business community, especially the local business community). This is particularly relevant for the OHADA company law system. As noted by Professor Guyon, the OHADA company law system—as is the case in many civil law countries—is more institutional than contractual in character.[11] He reminded his audience that a role of law is to protect third parties, and the Uniform Act Relating to Commercial Companies and Economic Interest Groups does just that. In his view, OHADA company law could become more contractual in the future as the economy and the capacity of the players develop.

Article 2 of the Uniform Act Relating to Commercial Companies and Economic Interest Groups states: "The provisions of this Uniform Act are mandatory, except in cases where the Act explicitly authorizes a sole partner or the partners of a company to substitute contractual provisions between them for those of this Uniform Act or to supplement the provisions of this Uniform Act with their own provisions."[12]

---

11 IBA Conference on OHADA, Yaoundé (Cameroon), December 1999.

12 Some international experts and scholars who view this act more from a common law perspective may consider it too rigid and not conducive to the facilitation of business activities. If this is true for some sophisticated players, it is not the case for most of the African businesses that need strong guidance and strict boundaries to develop their businesses with legal certainty before reaching the stage of sophisticated techniques. This is an important point to take into account in a "doing business exercise" sponsored by the World Bank. For instance, the obligation to have articles of association drafted or recorded with a public notary has raised debate. For most of the new players in the OHADA region, this obligation is perceived as an element of facilitation of business and governance, and in particular legal certainty for third parties. For some others, it may be considered an unnecessary hurdle limiting the possibility of easily creating a company.

Another debate has been raised concerning the benefits or pitfalls of having a minimum paid-up capital as provided for in the OHADA Uniform Acts. In the OHADA region, this provision is perceived less as a constraint to creating business than as a facilitation of sus-

Some Uniform Acts induce the informal sector of the economy to develop activities in the formal sector by providing for the following:

- Registration of commerce and movable credit (RCCM)
- Disclosure of corporate documentation
- Accounting: The Uniform Act on accounting is generally recognized as a compromise in this respect, taking into account the real situation in the region[13]
- Progressive access to lines of credit through mortgages and pledges
- Simplified forms of company structure, including mandatory provisions for their organization and operation

The response of the business community in Africa to OHADA has generally been positive.[14] The international legal community also has responded positively. An American Bar Association panel made a thorough evaluation of the Uniform Acts and in 1999 proposed useful guidance in various areas.[15]

The Implementation Challenges of OHADA

As with any new legal system, understanding of and compliance with the new regime can be a challenge, especially in Africa because of the overall low level of income, the poor state of the judiciary, the size of the informal sector, and deficiencies in governance. This section discusses some key implementation challenges of OHADA for the business community and for investors.

The interpretation and enforcement of the Uniform Acts by the region's judiciaries is and will remain a significant problem. At the highest level, the CCJA renders authoritative judgments concerning the interpretation of the Uniform Acts[16] and has an impressive track record. However, many decisions concern procedure and jurisdiction, and relatively few concern the substance

---

tainable business activities, because there is no sophisticated banking system and traditional security is difficult to organize and implement.

13 Professor Pérochon, famous for his manual assisting small businesses and owner-managers, was the author of this act. He was a practitioner of both the French system of accounting rules and international accounting standards.

14 The IFEJI/UBIFRANCE survey was conducted in 2003 with the support of the local business community, Conférence Permanente des Chambres Consulaires Africaines et Francophones (CPCCAF), and the Syndicat des Entrepreneurs Français à l'International (SEFI). The answers to the 30 survey questions are a useful reference for appraising issues faced by the business community and proposed actions.

15 A team of US lawyers and judges had reviewed each Uniform Act (four to eight experts for each Uniform Act) . Other reviews were prepared by members of the section of International Law and Practice of the American Bar Association (ABA) and the International Judicial Relations Committee of the United States Judicial Conference under the leadership of William Hannay (OHADA project chair and chairman of the section of International Law and Practice of the ABA), together with two rapporteurs.

16 Paul Gerard Pougoué & Sylvain Sorel Kuate Tameghe, *Les grandes décisions de la cour commune de justice et d'arbitrage de l'OHADA* (L'harmattan 2010).

of the law. The CCJA also provides advice to national governments and judiciaries that is authoritative but limited.

The greatest challenges facing the CCJA are its location, resources, and relationship with national judiciaries. Because of its location in Abidjan and its limited resources, the CCJA cannot perform its functions in an optimum manner. The problem of distance is a major issue for most of the OHADA states, and one that is negatively seen by practitioners in various countries and the international community. The superior courts in member states have resisted acknowledging that the CCJA possesses ultimate jurisdiction. Furthermore, many judges have only limited knowledge of OHADA.

OHADA also includes a comprehensive and unique system of arbitration. Yet, the CCJA also has the authority to conduct arbitration and to rule on administrative issues. However, because this function is not well understood by the private sector and is underused, the number of authoritative awards is limited.

The OHADA arbitration rules are modern and in accord with international standards, but they need to be implemented by administrative services provided by the secretary of the arbitration court. So far, the track record of implementation is limited. Promoting the arbitration system has proved to be a challenge. The system requires improvement in several aspects.[17]

Another challenge relates to the enforcement of the Uniform Acts in terms of criminal sanctions. Without appropriate criminal sanctions, compliance with legislative provisions is haphazard. The OHADA approach to criminal penalties is interesting in this respect. Article 5, paragraph 2, of the treaty provides that "[t]he Uniform Acts may include provisions to give rise to criminal liabilities." Article 10 provides that "Uniform Acts are directly applicable and overriding in the Contracting States notwithstanding any conflict they may give rise to in respect of previous or subsequent enactment of municipal laws."

Because the Uniform Acts are directly enforceable in each member state, criminal offenses should also directly be sanctioned in each member state. However, Article 5, paragraph 3, provides that "Contracting States commit themselves to enforce sentences of offences." Thus, the sanction for criminal offenses is in fact determined by each state. This situation entails enforcement problems and discrimination, because the member states are not harmonizing penalties. This conundrum occurs not only with prison sentences and fines but also with surety provisions and other procedures for enforcement.[18]

---

17 Improvements could include, for instance, the introduction of more prescriptive procedural rules and guidelines governing the appointment and performance of the arbitrators, clarification of foreseeable costs depending on various procedural aspects and organization of the proceedings, and decentralization of the arbitration's administration.

18 Aude-Marie Cartron & Boris Martor, *Eclairage sur la révision du Traité de l'OHADA*, 36 Cahier du Droit de l'Entreprise no. 1 (Jan.–Feb. 2010).

This situation is compounded by the fact that it is not always easy to identify in the Uniform Acts the definition and scope of a criminal offense. Some of the acts, such as the Uniform Act on Recovery Procedures and Measures of Execution, are particularly complex in this regard.[19]

Legal or Regulatory Areas Not Regulated

Many key areas of interest to investors are not covered by the OHADA Uniform Acts, including

- Taxation and issues of tax certainty and conditions of implementation
- Parafiscality[20]
- Customs and related tariffs
- Exchange control and currency fluctuation issues
- Private contract law content and interpretation[21]
- Public contract law content and interpretation
- Permitting risks (risks deriving from governmental or bureaucracy attitude for clearances, nonobjection, approval, and other permits)
- Land availability and land use risks, including the expropriation process and related issues
- Environmental impact studies and related permits
- Administrative or judicial review of adverse bureaucratic decisions
- Public-private partnership issues
- Employment law risks

---

19 Michel Mahouve, *Le système pénal OHADA ou l'uniformisation à mi chemin*, Recueil Penant 87–94 (Jan.–Mar. 2004).

20 Parafiscality is recognized as a major risk for the business community and investors. It is broadly defined as the fees, royalties, local and sundry taxes, and levies not directly listed and not defined in tax code or legislation, mostly payable at the local level or with line ministry organizations, for supporting particular activities or services of such administration and/or public bodies. In most states, parafiscality charges are numerous and in constant development.

21 Several drafts of Uniform Acts are in circulation, but little progress has been made on an *avant-projet* of Uniform Acts since February 2008. One reason is that this *avant-projet* is too close to the UNIDROIT principles. Various meetings have been held on the subject since September 2012, including exchanges between the French Institute of International legal Experts (IFEJI) and the African professors Issah-Saygeh, Pougoué, and Sawadogo on September 2008 (as part of the activities of the international working group set forth by IFEJI with the support of the World Bank and various stakeholders in March 2005: "Legal reform in developing countries—evaluation of the OHADA model"). A comparative analysis has been made on the drafting process and through benchmarking with the European Union effort to assess the benefits of a common European contract law. In Europe, this uniform contract law is progressively taking shape after the publication of a common frame of reference for its harmonization and a tentative draft of an optional legal instrument for international sales published in 2011.

At this point, large international investment projects can realize only limited benefits of OHADA because OHADA does not regulate most major risks.[22] Yet these kinds of projects are essential for development in areas such as infrastructure, public utilities, and mining.

Business Community Expectations

The business community expects that OHADA will contribute to the legal formalization of day-to-day activities, including relationships with states, ministries, public entities, subsovereign entities, and the like. This business community is represented at different levels, particularly with the chambers of commerce.[23]

French investors, who are very active in francophone Africa, have developed a French business community in Africa, represented by the Conseil Français des Investisseurs en Afrique (CIAN) and the Mouvement des Entreprises de France (MEDEF). Members of these organizations are in close contact with African and international lawyers.[24]

In the eyes of the international business community, better and more efficient implementation of the existing Uniform Acts is needed. Three tasks need particular attention:

- Reinforce the program run by the ERSUMA school in Benin (see below) to train the judiciary.
- Design a user-friendly system that encompasses the issues of a particular region and the capacity of the players and then promote arbitration through this system. This means, inter alia, doing the following:
    - Guarantee the appointment of an arbitration tribunal that is independent, professional, and efficient.
    - Guarantee simple and well-understood proceedings in line with local traditions for dispute resolutions.
    - Guarantee a fair and enforceable award within a reasonable time.

---

22 In areas that necessitate major up-front investments and with a very long recovery capacity (often over several decades), it is interesting to analyze the risk matrix developed by the industry leaders and that led to a due diligence ending at limiting the risks at a reasonable level to finance the project. For instance, in large mining projects, the risk matrix identifies 10 to 20 key chapters in which several key issues are generally identified. Some chapters can be well appraised in appropriate regulations, procedures, and reasonable perspectives of good implementation. Examples are expropriation, land use, compensation, resettlement, environmental permits and environmental and social management plans, and sovereign interference.

23 Several chambers have developed an integrated system of exchanges and created entities such as the Conférence Permanente des Chambres Consulaires Africaines et Francophones (CPCCAF).

24 In particular, the French Institute of International Legal Experts (IFEJI), created by the Paris Bar, and the French Ministry of Foreign Affairs select French practitioners (on average, 120 practitioners) with day-to-day expertise in international business law matters.

  - Guarantee an arbitration administration center that is efficient, responsive, fair, and cheap.
  - Allow the possibility of evaluating in advance costs and duration of proceedings.
- Promote the development of uniform "implementing regulations," guidelines, and procedures for the Uniform Acts.

In considering additional Uniform Acts, two actions may do most to help foster international investments in Africa:

- Design an institutional framework that will facilitate long-term public-private relationships in the core public service sector with appropriate guarantees for the stakeholders and a limited impact on state budgets and development aid.
- Design principles of public contract law and procedures that facilitate transactions involving the public sector. These should include improvement in the procurement of public contracts of all kinds and the provision of reasonable guarantees of fair implementation of the various types of contracts between the private and the public sectors, together with efficient procedures in areas such as mining contracts, urban development, forestry, lease of public land, and agriculture projects.

Capacity Building and Empowerment Issues

The international community has been actively building capacity in the OHADA region. For example, the ERSUMA school in Porto-Novo (Benin), which conducts training for the judiciary,[25] provides support to OHADA institutions such as the OHADA national committees. Yet, it is clear that much remains to be done in terms of capacity building and empowerment in regard to OHADA.

The OHADA model has been assessed with a view to further improving the lawmaking process and the legal certainty for the business community. Several international working groups with that focus were established in the mid-2000s, particularly in the wake of two conferences organized by the Paris Bar inviting African experts and practitioners, as well as World Bank specialists, in Washington (2004) and in Paris (2005).[26] These exchanges led to the creation of a joint working group on legal reforms in developing countries, which has as its objectives the evaluation of OHADA and the dissemination of lessons learnt.

The World Bank Group is playing an important role in funding programs to evaluate the content and implementation of the Uniform Acts through the World Bank Group's multidonor Investment Climate Advisory Service

---

25 *See* http://web.ohada.org/ersuma.html.

26 The World Bank was represented by Robert Danino, senior vice president and general counsel of the World Bank, and Michael Klein, chief economist of the IFC (World Bank).

(FIAS). This effort has resulted in a useful revision and improvement of some Uniform Acts (relating to securities and general commercial law), and other acts are in the pipeline (relating to competition law, banking law, intellectual property law, civil societies law, and evidence).[27] The international donor community is also supporting the OHADA institutions.

More work is needed to build capacity in OHADA institutions and to implement provisions on the ground. Specific areas that require attention include

- The efficient implementation of the Trade and Personal Property Credit Register, an instrument for securing transactions and developing the economy
- The organization and selection of the judiciary
- The organization of efficient and user-friendly arbitration centers
- The process of designing and implementing in various states regulations that further develop and adapt the OHADA Uniform Acts at various levels, including the clear abrogation of national regulations that conflict with the Uniform Acts

Josette Nguebou, professor of law at the University of Yaoundé (Cameroon), explored the sensitive relationships between the Uniform Acts and the national laws of the member states. She found that "although national law not conflicting with the Acts remained applicable, nothing prevents the Member States from maintaining and expending regulations which could narrow down its scope or even prevent its effective implementation."[28]

Capacity building and empowerment should also be oriented toward

- Fostering exchanges between scholars and practitioners on the implementation of the Uniform Acts and authoritative case law.
- Training the legal profession in the international business law system.
- Training senior civil servants to engage with the international business community in order to permit them to be on an equal footing with experienced international players when negotiating, implementing, and monitoring their relationships. This would apply, for example, to projects in the oil and gas sector, the mining sector, the infrastructure sector, the utility sector, the agricultural sector, and the forestry sector.
- Enabling more extensive exchanges between the local administrations and the administrations of other countries and regions.
- Implementing more proactive programs in e-learning. Well-prepared programs of e-learning, including appropriate documentation transmitted in

---

27 *See* the harmonization agenda adopted by the Council of Ministers of the OHADA region during the Bangui meeting of March 2001.

28 *See* OHADA Treaty, *Les actes uniformes commentés et annotés*, Juriscope 249 (1999). On this matter, *see* also Marc Frilet, *Implementing the Rule of Law in Sub-Sarahan Africa: Appraisal of the OHADA after a Decade*, 8(3) Bus. L. Intl., 254–67 (Nov. 2007).

advance by electronic means and used as background material for workshops or specialized classes, can be effective at building capacity. The programs should be monitored by teachers or facilitators who have been trained to teach in an e-learning manner, including, when appropriate, direct online contact with authoritative scholars in other countries.[29]

- Fostering new relationships between the public and private sectors to ease the transfer of investment. This was identified as a top priority by multilaterals and by the G20 Business Summit in Cannes (also referred to as the B20 of Cannes) in November 2011. Infrastructure development is seen as essential to achieving the Millennium Development Goals, and to that end the business community has been urged to develop a framework for better projects.[30] Proposals have been made to design a new act on PPP; in June 2011, the council of ministers of OHADA decided to explore that option.

Perfecting a system of equitable public contract law based on concepts and case law should be a priority, especially because some OHADA countries have started to experience the benefits of equitable public contract law for both the private sector and the public sector in landmark and long-term public infrastructure and utility projects.

Conclusions

OHADA has many positive features, and lessons learned from its implementation can be instructional for organizations considering business activities not only in that region but also in other regions of the world.

Improved understanding of the Uniform Acts will help strengthen the investment climate and make it easier to do business in the region. Particular attention should be given to a clearer definition of criminal offenses (including the nature and scope of the criminal penalties). One solution might be to promulgate a Uniform Act on this matter.[31]

---

29 E-learning conducted by faculties of law deserves to be taken into account; *see*, for instance, development of e-learning under the auspices of the International Bar Association (IBA).

30 *See* G20/B20, *Final Report of the Business Summit in Cannes*, 8 (Nov. 2011). In relation to public-private partnerships, the G20 report (p. A-71) says, "without appropriate institutional and legal framework, most of the public-private partnership (PPP) projects proposed for developing countries have a high likelihood of failure." An international working group made of international lawyers with expertise in concession and other PPPs worldwide and representatives of the construction industry has been working on the matter with various agencies for a few years. This group, after reviewing many projects with governments and local authorities, identified 30 issues that need to be addressed in an inclusive manner for the success of long-term concessions and other PPP projects. The publication of a handbook on the conditions of success of concessions and other PPPs, together with an evaluation matrix for concession on other PPP projects, individually or at an institutional, regulatory, or contractual level, is expected in 2012. *See* CICA website, http://www.cicanet.com/.

31 See Achille Ngwanza, *OHADA, Entre adolescence et âge adulte, une crise existentielle, Rapport général de l'université d'été de cercle horizon, club OHADA d'Orléans* (Jul. 1–3 2008).

The greater problem is that regulatory sectors essential for the economic development of Africa, which are not well controlled by national laws or regional organizations, are not yet regulated by Uniform Acts. Looking ahead, it is important to consider new Uniform Acts in key areas where a good regulatory framework already exists. It is also essential to launch an innovative process of capacity building and empowerment in the various directions outlined above, such as developing exchanges between scholars and practitioners, and training members of the legal profession and senior civil servants. Greater participation of legal practitioners experienced in providing advice in Africa may be the key to this process.[32]

Laurent Esso, minister of justice of Cameroon and president of OHADA, reported on the collateral benefit of OHADA in terms of legal innovation. In his view, OHADA is a conduit for convergence between civil law and common law in business law matters. He believes that Cameroon could be a laboratory for facilitating the implementation and interpretation of the OHADA Uniform Acts due to its unique civil law / common law regimes.[33] Professor Barthélemy Mercadal, a specialist in international business law, followed this path by promoting convergence in the interpretation of legal concepts worldwide (inter alia, between the civil law and the common law worlds) based on the same or similar legal provisions and using the OHADA Uniform Acts as a background. Mercadal's extraordinary effort, which led to a publication of *Code IDEF annoté de l'OHADA*,[34] will contribute to encouraging business players at both the national and the international levels to use the Uniform Acts on a regular basis.[35]

OHADA is an advanced and inclusive example of legal innovation for development. As such, the OHADA Uniform Acts are an excellent ground on which to test the benefits of an emerging field focusing on the optimization of legal frameworks and products. Although the contribution of OHADA to this field is already significant, much more can be done to apply lessons for further legal innovation.[36]

---

32 Business community and legal practitioners active in this area include UNIDA, CIAN, MEDEF, IFEJI, and IBA, which have conducted several conferences.

33 *Uniform Commercial Law Infrastructure and Project Finance in Africa*, 215 Intl. Bus. L. (May 2000).

34 http://www.institut-idef.org/-Code-OHADA-annote-.html.

35 *See* also Marc Frilet, *Le raisonnement juridique du monde anglo-saxon: Quelques considérations élémentaires et quelques recettes pour éviter les malentendus contractuels*, in *La revue des entreprises* (MEDEF Jan. 2000).

36 For information on this emerging field, known as *l'art de la légistique*, *see* Carine Gilberg, *L'art de la légistique*, Gazette de Palais 8–10 (Jan. 6–7, 2010); Alexander Flückiger & Christine Guy-Ecabert, *Guider les parlements et les gouvernements pour mieux légiférer—le rôle des guides de légistique* (Schulthess 2008); *Guide pour l'élaboration des textes législatifs et réglementaire*, available at http://www.legifrance.gouv.fr/html/Guide_legistique_2/accueil_guide_leg.htm; Catherine Bergeal, *Savoir rédiger un texte normatif* (Berger-Levrault 2004); Marc Frilet, *Le code civil, une source d'inspiration inégalée pour améliorer la sécurité juridique en matière internationale*, 87 Revue de l'Avocat Conseil d'Entreprise (Dec. 2003).

Index

Page numbers in italics refer to figures and tables.